The Best Bed &

England • Scotland • Wales
26th edition

Jill Darbey

Joanna Mortimer

Sigourney Welles

The finest Bed & Breakfast accommodation in the

British Isles

from the Hebrides to Belgravia

Country Houses, Town Houses, City Apartments, Manor
Houses, Village Cottages, Farmhouses, Castles.

W.W.B.B.A. London. U.K.

1

U.K. ISBN 0-907500-25-0

Typeset by W.W.B.B.A.. London.

Printed and bound in Hong Kong.

© W.W.B.B.A. 2006

Cover photographs; britainonview:J.Henderson/I.Rasmussen/R.Edwards

Contents

Foreword

Bed and Breakfast is a great way to travel and a fantastic way to see the fabulous British countryside. Today thousands of people are discovering for themselves that it is possible to combine high quality accommodation with friendly, personal attention at very reasonable prices. The New York Times said about us that "...after an unannounced inspection of rooms booked through The Worldwide Bed & Breakfast Association it is clear that the standards of comfort and cleanliness are exemplary ...at least as good as in a five star hotel and in most cases, better, reflecting the difference between sensitive hosts taking pride in their homes and itinerant hotel staff doing as little as they can get away with..."

Discerning travellers are turning away from the impersonal hotels with the expensive little refridgerators and microwave breakfasts in each room. How much nicer to have a real English breakfast to begin the day, enough to keep you going until evening. Many of our houses will provide dinner too - often the hostess will be a Cordon Bleu cook and the price will be within your budget. We try to provide the best accommodation possible within a wide range of prices, some as little as £20.00 per person per night, whilst others will be up to £75.00 per person per night. The choice is yours, but you can be certain that each will be the best available in that particular area of the country at that price.

We inspect all the accommodation recommended in this guide. We have our own inspectors who ensure that standards are maintained. And we want to hear from you if you have been dissappointed in any way by your accommodation. We encourage everyone to use the recommendations and complaints page at the back of the book. Let us know your opinion of the accommodation or inform us of any delightful homes you may have come across and would like to recommend for future inclusion.

In order to avoid masses of classification signs and symbols we simply say that each establishment has passed our inspection so you can be sure it is very clean, in good condition and properly run. Then we encourage you to read about each home, what they offer and their respective price range, so that you find the one that best suits your expectations. Our hosts in turn offer hospitality in their own unique style, so each home naturally retains its individuality and interest. We have found this to be a very successful recipe which often leads to lasting friendships.

Bed and Breakfast really is a marvellous way to travel, meeting a delightful cross section of fellow travellers with whom to exchange information and maybe an address or two. This is the fun and real pleasure that is part of Bed and Breakfasting. Once you've tried it you will be a dedicated Best Bed and Breakfaster.

How to use this Guide

To get the full benefits of staying at our Bed & Breakfast homes it is important to appreciate how they differ from hotels, so both hosts & guests know what to expect.

Arrival & Departure

These times are more important to a family than to hotel desk clerks, so your time of arrival (E.T.A.) is vital information when making a reservation either with the home directly or with one of our agencies. This becomes even more important to your reception if you intend travelling overnight & will be arriving in the early morning. So please have this information & your flight number ready when you book your rooms. **At most B & Bs the usual check-in time is 6 P.M. & you will be expected to check out by 10 A.M. on the morning of departure.** These arrangements do vary from home to home. The secret to an enjoyable visit is to let your hosts know as much about your plans as possible & they will do their best to meet your requirements.

Other personal requests

There are a few other details that you should let your hosts know when planning your Bed & Breakfast trip that will make everyone much happier during your visit. Do you smoke? Would you prefer to be in a non-smoking home? Do you suffer from any allergies? Some families have cats, dogs, birds & other pets in the house....Can you make it up a flight of stairs? Would you prefer the ground floor? Do you have any special dietary requirements? Will you be staying for dinner?

Do you prefer a private bathroom or are you prepared to share facilities? Do you prefer a shower instead of a bath? The ages of any children travelling.

In all these cases let your host know what you need & the details can be arranged before you arrive rather than presenting a problem when you are shown to your rooms.

Prices

The prices quoted throughout the guide are per double room per night based on two persons sharing. Single occupancy usually attracts a supplement. Prices will increase during busy seasons. Always confirm the prevailing rate when making a reservation.

Facilities

The bathroom & toilet facilities affect the prices. Sharing is the cheapest, private is a little more costly & en-suite carries a premium.

Descriptions

Rooms are described as follows: Single:1 bed (often quite small). Double:1 large bed (sometimes King or Queensize).
Twin: 2 separate single beds.
Four-poster: a King or Queen size bed with a canopy above supported by four corner posts.
Bathrooms and toilets are described as follows;
Shared: these facilities are shared with some other guests or perhaps the hosts.
Private: for your use only, however they may occasionally be in an adjacent room.
En-suite: private facilities within your bedroom suite.

Making a Reservation

Once you have chosen where you want to stay, have all the following information ready & your reservation will go smoothly without having to run & find more travel documents or ask someone else what they think you should do. Here is a brief check list of what you will probably be asked & examples to illustrate answers:

Dates & number of nights...August 14-19(6 nights).

Estimated time of arrival at the home ...7 P.M.(evening) & flight number.

Type & number of rooms...1 Double & 2 Single.

Toilet & Bathroom facilities...1 Double en-suite) & 2 singles (shared)

Smoking or Non-smoking?

Any allergies?

Special dietary requests?

Children in the party & their ages?

Any other preferences... Is a shower preferred to a bath?

Maximum budget per person per night based on all the above details.

The London Reservation Agency

There is a minimum two night consecutive stay at our London homes.

Reservations for London homes can only be made through one of our Worldwide Bed & Breakfast Agencies. They can be contacted by 'phone, fax, e-mail or on-line from our website at http://www.bestbandb.co.uk.

All reservations must be confirmed with advance payments which are non-refundable in the event of cancellation. You simply pay the balance due after you arrive at the home. The advance payment can be made with major credit & charge cards or by cheque. Cash is the preferred method of paying the balance & always in pounds sterling.

The advance payments confirm each night of your visit, **not just the first one**.

When arriving at a later date or departing at an earlier date than those confirmed, the guest will be liable to pay only the appropriate proportion of the stated balance that is due. For example, staying three nights out of four booked means paying 3/4 of the stated balance due. The advance payment is non-refundable. A minimum of 2 nights will always apply.

Outside London

We encourage you to make use of the information in this guide & contact the homes directly. The hosts may require varying amounts of advance payments & may or may not accept credit & charge cards. Remember, many B&Bs are small, family-run establishments and are unable to accept payment by credit card. The confirmed prices shall be those prevailing on the dates required... as previously mentioned, *the prices shown in this guide are the* **minimum** *& will increase during the busy seasons.*

Alterations

If you wish to alter or change a previously confirmed booking through one of the agencies there will be a further fee of £15 per alteration.

Cancellations

All advance payments for London are non-refundable.

All booking fees outside London are non-refundable.

Notice of cancellation must be given as soon as possible & the following suggested rates shall apply outside London only;

30 - 49 days notice - 80% refund.

10-29 days notice -50% refund.

0 - 9 days notice - No refund.

The Worldwide Bed & Breakfast Agencies reserve the right to alter your accommodation should it be necessary & will inform you of any alteration as soon as possible.

London Reservation Agency

We offer an outstanding selection of accommodation in London. As with all our accommodation each one has been personally inspected so you can be sure of the highest standards. We offer an immensely wide range of accommodation. We have a type, style and location to suit everyone. From city apartments close to shops, museums and galleries to spacious homes in leafy residential suburbs near the river, parks and restaurants. No matter what your reason for visiting London we can accommodate you. Whether on business or vacation the Best Bed & Breakfast provides great accommodation together with a fast, efficient reservation service. Our helpful staff are always happy to advise you on all your accommodation requirements. We are located in London, we know the city and all our hosts. We know how to provide an enjoyable, affordable, hassle free trip. There are plenty of ways to contact us. To make a reservation simply do one of the following;

Website: http://www.bestbandb.co.uk

E-mail: bestbandb@atlas.co.uk

Worldwide call Tel: +44 (0)20 7243 8720 (24Hrs.)

Fax: +44 (0)20 7243 8736

The Discount Offer

This offer is made to people who have bought this book & wish to make reservations for Bed & Breakfast in London through our London Reservation Agency. The offer only applies to a minimum stay of three consecutive nights at one of our London homes between the following dates; January 7. 2006 to April 1. 2006 then from September 15. 2006 to December 1. 2006. Only one discount per booking is allowed. Call the reservation office to make your booking in the normal way & tell the clerk that you have bought the book & wish to have the discount. After a couple of questions the discount will be deducted from the advance payment required to confirm the reservation.

Regions

To assist tourists with information during their travels, counties have been grouped together under Regional Tourist Boards that co-ordinate the various efforts of each county.

The British Tourist Authority has designated these areas in consultation with the English, Scottish & Wales Tourist Boards & we have largely adopted these areas for use in this guide

Counties are listed alphabetically throughout our guide & then have a sub-heading indicating which Tourist Region they belong to.

ENGLAND
Cumbria
County of Cumbria
Northumbria.
Counties of Cleveland, Durham, Northumberland, Tyne & Wear.
North West
Counties of Cheshire, Greater Manchester, Lancashire, Merseyside, High Peaks of Derbyshire.
Yorkshire & Humberside
Counties of North Yorkshire, South Yorkshire, West Yorkshire, Humberside.
Heart of England
Counties of Gloucestershire, Herefordshire & Worcestershire, Shropshire, Staffordshire, Warwickshire, West Midlands.
East Midlands
Counties of Derbyshire, Leicestershire, Nottinghamshire, Rutland, Lincolnshire & Northamptonshire,
East Anglia
Counties of Cambridgeshire, Essex, Norfolk, Suffolk.
West Country
Counties of Cornwall, Devon, Dorset (parts of), Somerset, Wiltshire, Isles of Scilly.
Southern
Counties of Hampshire, Dorset (East & North), Isle of Wight.
South East
Counties of East Sussex, Kent, Surrey, West Sussex.

SCOTLAND
The subdivisions of Scottish Regions in this guide differ slightly from the current Marketing Regions of the Scottish Tourist Board.

The Borders, Dumfries & Galloway
Districts & counties of Scottish Borders, Dumfries & Galloway.
Lothian & Strathclyde
City of Edinburgh, Forth Valley, East Lothian, Kirkaldy, St. Andrews & North-East Fife, Greater Glasgow, Clyde Valley, Ayrshire & Clyde Coast, Burns Country.
Argyll & The Isles
Districts & counties of Oban & Mull, Mid Argyll, Kintyre & Islay, Dunoon, Cowal, Rothesay & Isle of Bute, Isle of Arran.
Perthshire, Loch Lommond & The Trossachs.
Districts & counties of Perthshire, Loch Lomond, Stirling & Trossachs.
The Grampians
Districts & counties of Banff & Buchan, Moray, Gordon, Angus, City of Aberdeen, Kincardine & Deeside, City of Dundee.
The Highlands & Islands
Districts & counties of Shetland, Orkney, Caithness, Sutherland, Ross & Cromarty, Western Isles, South West Ross & Isle of Skye, Inverness, Loch Ness & Nairn, Aviemore & Spey Valley, Fort William & Lochaber.

WALES
The regions are defined as follows:
North Wales
Counties of Anglesey, Conwy, Denbighshire, Flintshire & Gwynedd.
Mid Wales
Counties of Ceredigion & Powys.
South Wales
Counties of Carmarthenshire, Glamorgan, Monmouthshire, Newport, Pembrokeshire & Swansea.
The photographs appearing in the Introductions & Gazeteers are by courtesy of the appropriate Tourist Board for each county or W.W.B.B.A.

Counties map

Each county has been assigned a page number where a more detailed map can be found. These maps include principal towns, major roads & the location of each Bed & Breakfast establishment.

OUTER HEBRIDES

WESTERN ISLES

INNER HEBRIDES

HIGHLANDS

MORAY

ABERDEENSHIRE

ABERDEEN

SCOTLAND
312

PERTHSHIRE & KINROSS

ANGUS

DUNDEE

ARGYLL & BUTE

FIFE

STIRLING

EAST LOTHIAN

NORTH AYRSHIRE

SOUTH LANARKSHIRE

BORDERS

EAST AYRSHIRE

SOUTH AYRSHIRE

DUMFRIES & GALLOWAY

1 INVERCLYDE
2 DUNBARTON & CLYDEBANK
3 RENFREWSHIRE
4 EAST RENFREWSHIRE
5 GLASGOW
6 EAST DUNBARTONSHIRE
7 NORTH LANARKSHIRE
8 FALKIRK
9 CLACKMANNAN
10 WEST LOTHIAN
11 EDINBURGH
12 MID LOTHAIN

North Sea

NORTHUMBERLAND

TYNE AND WEAR
195

CUMBRIA
74

DURHAM

CLEVELAND

YORKSHIRE

HUMBERSIDE
286

Irish Sea

LANCASHIRE
48

MANCHESTER MERSEYSIDE

ENGLAND

FLINTSHIRE
DENBIGHSHIRE

ANGLESEY

CONWY

WREXHAM

CHESHIRE
48

DERBYSHIRE & STAFFORD-SHIRE
90

NOTTINGHAM-SHIRE, LEICESTERSHIRE & RUTLAND
174

LINCOLNSHIRE
182

GWYNEDD

NORFOLK
188

WALES
347

SHROP-SHIRE
212

CEREDIGION

POWYS

HEREFORD & WORCESTER
157

WARWICK-SHIRE
265

CAMBRIDGE-SHIRE & NORTHAMPTON-SHIRE
41

SUFFOLK
239

CARMARTHENSHIRE

MONMOUTH-SHIRE

GLOUCESTER-SHIRE
130

OXFORD-SHIRE
202

BEDFORDSHIRE, BERKSHIRE, BUCKINGHAMSHIRE & HERTFORDSHIRE
31

ESSEX

PEMBROKESHIRE

SWANSEA

NEATH & PORT TALBOT

NEWPORT

CARDIFF

VALE OF GLAMORGAN

LONDON
15

KENT
163

1 BRIDGEND
2 RHONDA CYNON TAFF
3 MERTHYR TYDFIL
4 CAERPHILLY
5 BLAENAU GWENT
6 TORFEN

WILTSHIRE
277

SURREY
245

HAMPSHIRE
147

SUSSEX
251

SOMERSET
220

DORSET
12

DEVON
100

CORNWALL
56

English Channel

9

General Information

To help overseas visitors with planning their trip to Britain, we have compiled the next few pages explaining the basic requirements & customs you will find here.

Before you arrive

Documents you will have to obtain before you arrive;

Valid passports & visas. Citizens of Commonwealth countries or the U.S.A. do not need visas to enter the U.K. Bring your local Driving Licence.

Medical Insurance

This is strongly recommended although visitors will be able to receive free emergency treatment. If you have to stay in hospital in the U.K. you will be asked to pay unless you are a citizen of European Community.

Restrictions on arrival

Immigration procedures can be lengthy & bothersome, be prepared for questions like:

a) where are you staying in the U.K.?
b) do you have a round trip ticket?
c) how long do you intend to stay?
d) how much money are you bringing in?
e) do you have a credit card?

Do not bring any animals with you as they are often subject to 6 months quarantine & there are severe penalties for bringing in pets without appropriate licences. Do not bring any firearms, prohibited drugs or carry these things for anyone else. If you are in doubt about items in your possession, declare them by entering the Red Channel at Customs & seek the advice of an officer.

After you have arrived

You can bring in as much currency as you like. You can change your own currency or travellers cheques at many places at varying rates.

Airports tend to be the most expensive places to change money & the 'Bureau de Change" are often closed at nights. So bring enough Sterling to last you at least 2 or 3 days. Banks often charge commission for changing money. Most Cashcard machines (or A.T.M.'s) will dispense local currency using your charge card, if they are affiliated systems, & don't charge commissions to your account. Major credit cards/charge cards are widely accepted & you may only need to carry small amounts of cash for "pocket money".

Driving

Don't forget to drive on the Left... especially the first time you get into a car... at the airport car hire parking lot... or from the front of a railway station... or straight after breakfast... old habits are hard to shake off. If you need to know the rules, get a copy of the Highway Code. You must wear a seat belt & so must any other front seat passenger. The speed limits are clearly shown in most areas - generally 30 mph. in residential areas (48 kph) & 70 mph on motorways (113 kph.). Traffic lights are usually at the side of the road & not hanging overhead. Car hire is relatively expensive in the U.K. & it is often a good idea to arrange this before you arrive. Mileage charges, V.A.T. (Sales Tax) & insurance are usually charged extra & you will need to be over 21 to hire a car in the U.K. Petrol (gas) is also relatively expensive & you may find petrol stations hard to find or closed at night in rural areas... so fill up often. Driving in London is not a recommended experience for newcomers & parking is also a very complex arrangement which can become a nightmare if the car gets "clamped" (immobilised) or towed away.

General Information

Buses & Coaches

If you are not driving & only want to travel 5-10 miles there are good bus services within most towns & cities, however, rural routes have seriously declined over the last few years. There are regular & fast coach services between the major towns which are very popular - so book ahead to be sure of a seat.

Trains

There is an extensive railway system throughout the U.K. which serves the major towns on a fast & frequent basis. These services are relatively expensive & like most railway systems are subject to delays.

Tubes (Subways)

London is the only city with an extensive subway system although some other towns do have "Metro" trains of linked under & overground systems.

The "tube" is a very popular means of getting around London, but it can get very crowded & unpleasant at "rush hours". It is often the preferred way to get into London from Heathrow Airport in the early morning, when there are long delays on the roads that hold up both buses & taxis with increasingly expensive rides into the city centre, £40 is not unusual for this cab fare, compared with a few pounds on the "tube". The "tube" in London is operated by London Transport which also operates the London bus service ... the famous red buses. They sell tickets which allow you to travel all over London on tubes, buses & trains at very good rates, called Travelcards... a transfer system. Ask your local travel agent about these.

Telephones

When calling the U.K. from abroad always drop the 0 from the area code.

In the U.K. the only free calls are the operator - 100, & emergencies - 999. You may use your calling card to call home which is billed to your account or call collect, ask the operator to "reverse charge" the call. The famous red telephone kiosks are slowly being replaced with glass booths. The internet can now be accessed from some public phone booths. Phonecards are becoming more popular as the number of boxes that only accept these cards increases. Cards can be bought at Post Offices & many newsagents & shops.

Doctors/Chemists

All local police stations have lists of chemists & doctors should you need one, at night, for instance.

Voltage

The standard voltage throughout the country is 240v AC.50Hz. If you bring small electrical appliances with you, a converter will be required.

Tipping

Is not obligatory anywhere but a general guide if you wish to leave a tip for service is between 10%-15%.

Pubs

Most open between 11 a.m. & 11 p.m. and often longer, every day.

You must be over 18 years old to buy & drink alcohol in pubs .

Do not drink and drive. Penalties for being over the legally permitted limit of alcohol are quite severe.

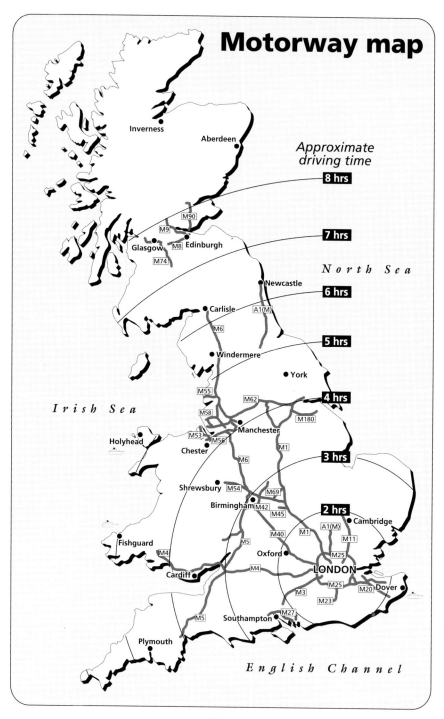

Motorway map

Approximate driving time

8 hrs
7 hrs
6 hrs
5 hrs
4 hrs
3 hrs
2 hrs

North Sea

Irish Sea

English Channel

Inverness
Aberdeen
M90
M9
M8 Edinburgh
Glasgow
M74
Newcastle
Carlisle A1(M)
M6
Windermere
York
M55
M62
M58
M180
M53
Manchester
Holyhead
M56
Chester
M1
M6
Shrewsbury M54
M69
Birmingham M42
M45
M40
M1 A1(M)
Cambridge
M11
Fishguard M4
M5
Oxford
M25
LONDON
Cardiff
M4
M3 M25 M20 Dover
M23
M5 Southampton M27
Plymouth

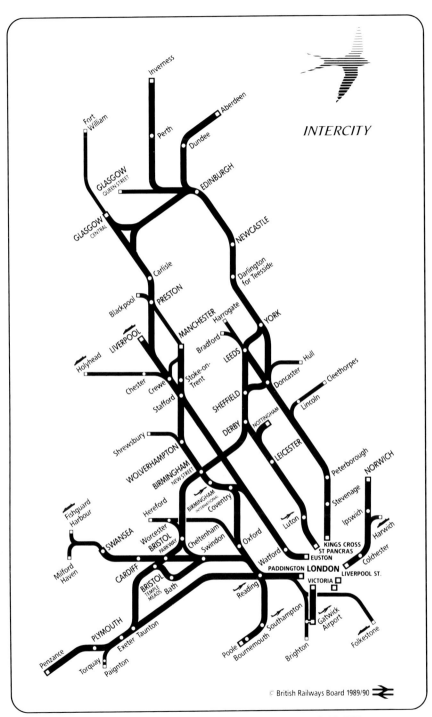

INTERCITY

© British Railways Board 1989/90

13   TLB/90/1008

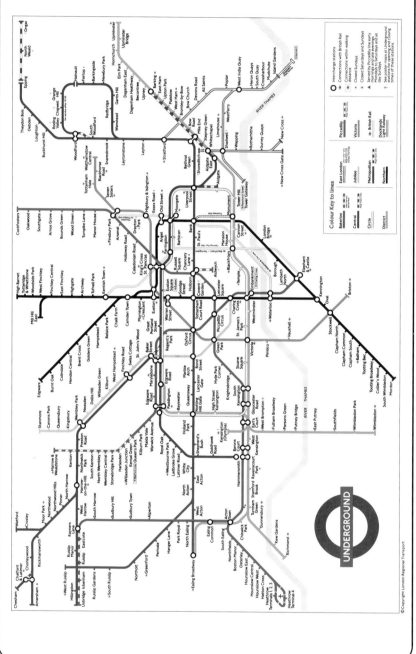

UNDERGROUND

Colour Key to lines

Bakerloo
Central
Circle
District

East London
Jubilee
Metropolitan
Northern

Piccadilly
Victoria
British Rail
Docklands Light Railway

○ Interchange stations
⊕ Connections with British Rail
◆ Connections within walking distance
Closed Sundays
Closed Saturdays and Sundays
▲ Served by Piccadilly line early mornings and late evenings Mondays to Saturdays and all day Sundays
† See poster maps at Underground stations for opening and closing times of these stations

© Copyright London Regional Transport

91/1258

14

LONDON MAP

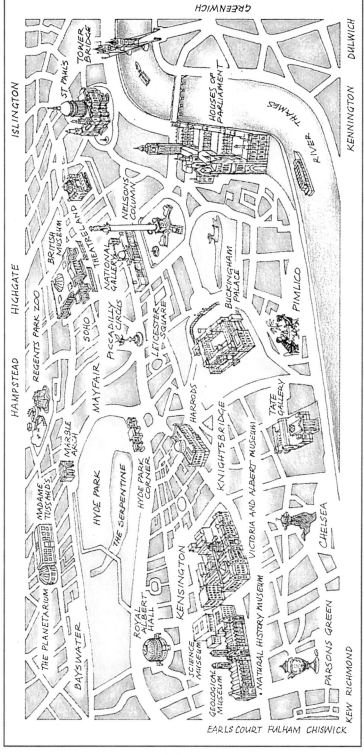

London

Visit our website: www.bestbandb.co.uk

		rate £ from - to per double room	children taken	evening meals	animals taken
Home No. 01 London WWBBA PO Box 31655 London W11 4WR Tel: +44 (0)20-7243-8720 Fax: +44 (0)20-7243-8736 E-mail: bestbandb@atlas.co.uk www.bestbandb.co.uk	Nearest Tube: Putney Bridge An attractive Victorian terraced house, situated in a quiet residential street, yet only 3 mins' walk from the station. 1 spacious double-bedded room with an en-suite bathroom & a twin-bedded room with a private bathroom. Each room is tastefully furnished & has a T.V. & hairdryer. Breakfast is served in the very pleasant dining room. Many good pubs, restaurants & shops locally. An excellent location from which to explore London. Parking by arrangement. Children over 12.	£64.00 to £80.00	Y	N	N
Home No. 06 London WWBBA PO Box 31655 London W11 4WR Tel: +44 (0)20-7243-8720 Fax: +44 (0)20-7243-8736 E-mail: bestbandb@atlas.co.uk www.bestbandb.co.uk	Nearest Tube: East Putney A Victorian terraced house with a traditional family atmosphere & set in a quiet residential street. The friendly hosts offer 1 comfortable twin-bedded room with T.V., overlooking the rear garden, & with an adjacent private bathroom. A large Continental or Full English breakfast is served. Putney is a lovely area with many good shops & restaurants. Transport facilities are excellent & provide easy access to central London.	£58.00 to £76.00	Y	N	N
Home No. 07 London WWBBA PO Box 31655 London W11 4WR Tel: +44 (0)20-7243-8720 Fax +44 (0)20-7243-8736 E-mail: bestbandb@atlas.co.uk www.bestbandb.co.uk	Nearest Tube: Fulham Broadway Set in the heart of Fulham, this is an attractive Victorian maisonette which is elegantly furnished throughout with antiques. The charming host, who is very well-travelled & has an in-depth knowledge of London, offers 2 beautifully furnished double-bedded rooms. Each with tea/coffee-making facilities & an en-suite or private bathroom. In summer, breakfast can be taken in the delightful garden. Only 8 mins' walk from the tube this is an ideal base for exploring London. Many good restaurants & antique shops close by.	£74.00 to £84.00	N	N	N
Home No. 08 London WWBBA PO Box 31655 London W11 4WR Tel: +44 (0)20-7243-8720 Fax: +44 (0)20-7243-8736 E-mail: bestbandb@atlas.co.uk www.bestbandb.co.uk	Nearest Tube: Maida Vale An attractive Victorian maisonette very well situated only 3 mins' walk from the tube. Offering 1 spacious & comfortably furnished twin-bedded room with T.V., tea/coffee-making facilities & an en-suite shower room. Breakfast is served in the pleasant dining area looking out onto the pretty garden. Good local pubs & restaurants. An excellent location providing easy access to many attractions; with a direct tube link to Piccadilly Circus & the Embankment. Also, Paddington Station for the Heathrow Express.	£64.00 to £78.00	N	N	N
Home No. 10 London WWBBA PO Box 31655 London W11 4WR Tel: +44 (0)20-7243-8720 Fax: +44 (0)20-7243-8736 E-mail: bestbandb@atlas.co.uk www.bestbandb.co.uk	Nearest Tube: Lancaster Gate A delightful home set in a quiet garden square, only 5 mins walk from Hyde Park & the station. The apartment has been decorated with great flair & has recently been featured in a style magazine. The beautiful double room has been furnished to a very high standard & there is a contemporary private wet room adjacent. Also, a small library with plasma T.V. in which to relax. Your host is a professional cook & the Continental breakfast is delicious. A perfect location for exploring London.	£84.00 to £98.00	N	N	N

Home No. 17. London.

London
Visit our website: www.bestbandb.co.uk

Home No. 14 London	Nearest Tube: Marble Arch	£74.00 to £90.00	Y	N	N
WWBBA PO Box 31655 London W11 4WR Tel: +44 (0)20-7243-8720 Fax: +44 (0)20-7243-8736 E-mail: bestbandb@atlas.co.uk www.bestbandb.co.uk	Situated in the heart of central London, yet in a surprisingly quiet location, this modern townhouse is the perfect place from which to explore this vibrant city. The charming host offers 3 spacious & attractively furnished double, family or twin-bedded rooms , each has en-suite facilities, T.V. & tea/coffee, etc. Close by are a variety of cafes, bars & restaurants. Hyde Park, the exclusive boutiques of Knightsbridge & Mayfair & a host of attractions are all within easy reach.				
Home No. 17 London WWBBA PO Box 31655 London W11 4WR Tel: +44 (0)20-7243-8720 Fax: +44 (0)20-7243-8736 E-mail: bestbandb@atlas.co.uk www.bestbandb.co.uk	Nearest Tube: Richmond Situated in an excellent 17th-century terrace, this is an outstanding home, elegantly furnished throughout with antiques. 3 guest rooms: 1 double 4-poster, 1 twin-bedded room & a triple with a 4-poster & a single bed. Each has a private bath-room. 2 of the bedrooms have French doors leading onto an Italiante garden, the triple room commands views of the Thames. Historic Richmond with its many shops & riverside restaurants is a short walk. Easy access to central London.	£90.00 to £140.00 *see PHOTO over p. 17*	N	N	N
Home No. 18 London WWBBA Po Box 31655 London W11 4WR Tel: +44 (0)20-7243-8720 Fax: +44 (0)20-7243-8736 E-mail: bestbandb@atlas.co.uk www.bestbandb.co.uk	Nearest Tube: High St. Ken. A beautiful house, furnished with many interesting paintings & situated in the heart of Kensington. The charming host offers 1 light & airy, twin-bedded room with a private bathroom. Also another, equally attractive twin-bedded room, which is ideal for a third or fourth member of the party. Each bedroom is well-furnished & a T.V. is available. Only a short walk from the High Street with its many shops & restaurants & within easy reach of Kensington Palace & gardens, Knightsbridge & the museums. Children over 5.	£70.00 to £86.00	Y	N	N
Home No. 19 London WWBBA PO Box 31655 London W11 4WR Tel: +44 (0)20-7243-8720 Fax: +44 (0)20-7243-8736 E-mail: bestbandb@atlas.co.uk www.bestbandb.co.uk	Nearest Tube: Parsons Green Located in the quiet Parsons Green area of Fulham. This superb house offers accommodation in 1 king-size double-bedded room with private facilities & 2 doubles which share a bathroom. Each room is beautifully decorated & very comfortably furnished. This is a delightful home & the ideal base for visitors to London. Many of the attractions including Buckingham Palace & Knightsbridge are only 15 mins away by tube.	£62.00 to £78.00	N	N	N
Home No. 21 London WWBBA PO Box 31655 London W11 4WR Tel: +44 (0)20-7243-8720 Fax: +44 (0)20-7243-8736 E-mail: bestbandb@atlas.co.uk www.bestbandb.co.uk	Nearest Tube: Hammersmith A charming Victorian terraced house, where the welcoming hosts offer 1 spacious, attractive & comfortably furnished king-size double/twin room with sitting area & a private bathroom & 1 equally attractive twin-bedded room with private shower room. Each with T.V., tea/coffee & hairdryer. Breakfast is served in the dining room. A delightful family home set in a quiet street, yet only 8 mins walk from Hammersmith with its many restaurants etc. Excellent transport facilities provide easy access to Heathrow & central London.	£64.00 to £78.00	Y	N	N

	rate £ from - to per double room	children taken	evening meals	animals taken
Home No. 24 London WWBBA PO Box 31655 London W11 4WR Tel: +44 (0)20-7243-8720 Fax: +44 (0)20-7243-8736 E-mail: bestbandb@atlas.co.uk www.bestbandb.co.uk	Nearest Tube: Parsons Green An elegantly furnished Victorian terraced house, situated in a quiet street yet only 5 mins walk from all transport facilities. Offering 1 delightful double-bedded room which overlooks the rear garden & an equally attractive king-size double/twin-bedded room. Each has a private bathroom, is beautifully decorated & has every comfort. There are 2 small dogs. Parsons Green is an ideal base from which to explore the delights of London & has many excellent restaurants & antique shops.	£70.00 to £80.00	N	N	N
Home No. 31 London WWBBA PO Box 31655 London W11 4WR Tel: +44 (0)20-7243-8720 Fax: +44 (0)20-7243-8736 E-mail: bestbandb@atlas.co.uk www.bestbandb.co.uk	Nearest Tube: Parsons Green A charming Victorian terraced house, situated only minutes from many excellent shops & restaurants in Fulham. The welcoming host has elegantly furnished this property throughout. Accommodation is in 1 attractive double-bedded room. It is very comfortable & has a good private bathroom. There is also a cosy single room for a third member of the party. A large Continental breakfast is served. Situated only a short walk from the station, this is an excellent base from which to explore London. Children over 12.	£60.00 to £76.00	Y	N	N
Home No. 35 London WWBBA PO Box 31655 London W11 4WR Tel: +44 (0)20-7243-8720 Fax: +44 (0)20-7243-8736 E-mail: bestbandb@atlas.co.uk www.bestbandb.co.uk	Nearest Tube: Fulham Broadway Located in the cosmopolitan area of Fulham, this modern townhouse is set in a quiet street & yet is only 5 mins walk from the tube, providing easy access to central London. The friendly host offers 1 twin-bedded room with a private bathroom. Also, 1 double room is available for another member of the party. Each room is tastefully furnished & well-appointed with T.V. & tea/coffee-making facilities. A large Continental breakfast is served. A variety of local restaurants offer a wide choice of international cuisine. Children over 12.	£60.00 to £76.00	Y	N	N
Home No. 38 London WWBBA PO Box 31655 London W11 4WR Tel: +44 (0)20-7243-8720 Fax: +44 (0)20-7243-8736 E-mail: bestbandb@atlas.co.uk www.bestbandb.co.uk	Nearest Tube: Earls Court A lovely apartment situated on the top floor of a Victorian mansion block (with lift access) & only 3 mins walk from Earls Court station. The charming host offers 1 spacious & attractively furnished double bedded room with an en-suite bathroom & T.V. Breakfast is served in the attractive dining area. Easy access to Knightsbridge, South Kensington & the museums & Heathrow. Many good local restaurants.	£70.00 to £78.00	Y	N	N
Home No. 39 London WWBBA PO Box 31655 London W11 4WR Tel: +44 (0)20-7243-8720 Fax: +44 (0)20-7243-8736 E-mail: bestbandb@atlas.co.uk www.bestbandb.co.uk	Nearest Tube: Earls Court A superb home, designer decorated & furnished to the highest standard with antiques throughout. 2 double & 1 twin bedded rooms. Each beautiful bedroom is large & airy with a lovely bathroom en-suite, T.V. & tea/coffee facilities. A large dining room. A delightful garden where breakfast can be served if the weather is good. Guests have their own private entrance. Only 10 mins to Harrods. Children over 12 years. Parking. *see PHOTO over p. 20*	£98.00 to £110.00	Y	N	N

Home No. 39. London.

London

		rate £ from - to per double room	children taken	evening meals	animals taken
Home No. 40 London **WWBBA** **PO Box 31655** **London W11 4WR** **Tel: +44 (0)20-7243-8720** **Fax: +44 (0)20-7243-8736** E-mail: bestbandb@atlas.co.uk **www.bestbandb.co.uk**	Nearest Tube: Gunnersbury A large Victorian residence, with garden, only minutes from the tube station, with easy access to Heathrow, central London, Richmond & beautiful Kew Gardens. The charming host offers 2 spacious guest rooms suitable for doubles or twins & ideal for families. Each room has an en-suite bathroom, T.V., tea/coffee-making facilities & is decorated in natural tones with stripped pine. Children are especially welcome.	£60.00 to £76.00	Y	N	N
Home No. 43 London **WWBBA** **PO Box 31655** **London W11 4WR** **Tel: +44 (0)20-7243-8720** **Fax: +44 (0)20-7243-8736** E-mail: bestbandb@atlas.co.uk **www.bestbandb.co.uk**	Nearest Tube: Earls Court This is a traditional London mews house set in a quiet location, yet only 5 mins walk from the tube. The charming host offers 1 comfortably furnished double-bedded room with T.V., tea/coffee facilities & fridge. The private bathroom is adjacent. A Continental breakfast is served. There is a good selection of restaurants nearby. A great location within easy reach of many attractions. Also, easy access to Heathrow & Gatwick Airports.	£79.00 to £90.00	N	N	N
Home No. 44 London **WWBBA** **PO Box 31655** **London** **W11 4WR** **Tel: +44 (0)20-7243-8720** **Fax: +44 (0)20-7243-8736** E-mail: bestbandb@atlas.co.uk **www.bestbandb.co.uk**	Nearest Tube: Richmond Situated in the heart of delightful Richmond this really is the perfect location for a relaxing break in London. The charming host, who is an interior designer has refurbished this Victorian home & offers 1 gorgeous double-bedded room which has a superb private bathroom adjacent. Delicious Continental breakfasts are served in the lovely kitchen/diner which overlooks a pretty plantsmans garden. Richmond abounds with fashionable shops & restaurants. Within easy reach of several stately homes. Transport facilities are excellent & Waterloo is 15 mins by train.	£74.00 to £84.00	N	N	N
Home No. 48 London **WWBBA** **PO Box 31655** **London W11 4WR** **Tel: +44 (0)20-7243-8720** **Fax: +44 (0)20-7243-8736** E-mail: bestbandb@atlas.co.uk **www.bestbandb.co.uk**	Nearest Tube: Parsons Green A beautifully decorated, very stylish late Victorian house, situated in leafy Parsons Green & only 20 mins. from Harrods by tube. Accommodation is in 2 double/twin-bedded rooms & 1 single room, all are en-suite & have T.V. & tea/coffee-making facilities. Each room is furnished to the highest standards of comfort. A country house breakfast is served. Good local pubs & restaurants.	£85.00 to £100.00	N	N	N
Home No. 49 London **WWBBA** **PO Box 31655** **London W11 4WR** **Tel: +44 (0)20-7243-8720** **Fax: +44 (0)20-7243-8736** **U.S., Canada call:** E-mail: bestbandb@atlas.co.uk **www.bestbandb.co.uk**	Nearest Tube: Parsons Green A lovely Victorian terraced house, which has been tastefully refurbished throughout. The charming & well-travelled hosts offer 1 spacious king-size double/twin-bedded room with an en-suite bathroom & 1 comfortable double-bedded room with a private shower room adjacent. T.V. & tea/coffee-making facilities are available. There are many cafes, restaurants & bars close by & being only 5 mins walk from the tube station; this stylish home is a perfect spot from which to explore London.	£74.00 to £84.00	Y	N	N

London

Visit our website: www.bestbandb.co.uk

		rate £ from - to per double room	children taken	evening meals	animals taken
Home No. 50 London WWBBA PO Box 31655 London W11 4WR Tel: +44 (0)20-7243-8720 Fax: +44 (0)20-7243-8736 E-mail: bestbandb@atlas.co.uk www.bestbandb.co.uk	Nearest Tube: Parsons Green This is a delightful Victorian terraced house which has been beautifully decorated & furnished throughout. The lovely hosts offer 1 very comfortable king-size double-bedded room & 1 attractive single-bedded room. Each room has a T.V. & bottled water etc. & an excellent private bathroom. There are a variety of good bars, bistros & restaurants nearby. Located only 5 mins' walk from the tube station, this is a perfect spot from which to explore London. A charming home.	£80.00 to £100.00	N	N	N
Home No. 51 London WWBBA PO Box 31655 London W11 4WR Tel: +44 (0)20-7243-8720 Fax: +44 (0)20-7243-8736 E-mail: bestbandb@atlas.co.uk www.bestbandb.co.uk	Nearest Tube: Holland Park Set in a quiet, secluded street, this is a modern mews house with an original brick kiln which has been converted into an elegant dining room. Only a few minutes walk from fashionable restaurants, antique shops, Portobello Market & beautiful Holland Park. It has been attractively furnished throughout by the host who is an interior designer. 1 delightful & spacious en-suite double-bedded room & 1 single room with private facilties. Easy access to many of London's attractions.	£79.00 to £90.00	N	N	N
Home No. 52 London WWBBA PO Box 31655 London W11 4WR Tel: +44 (0)20-7243-8720 Fax: +44 (0)20-7243-8736 E-mail: bestbandb@atlas.co.uk www.bestbandb.co.uk	Nearest Tube: South Kensington Located in Chelsea, in a quiet residential street yet, only a short walk from many fashionable shops & restaurants. A charming Victorian terraced house which has been attractively decorated throughout with many interesting prints & artifacts. The friendly hosts offer 1 spacious double-bedded room & an equally comfortable twin-bedded room. Each has an en-suite shower room, T.V. & tea/coffee-making facilities. A delightful home with easy access to the museums at South Kensington, Knightsbridge & Harrods.	£66.00 to £88.00	Y	N	N
Home No. 56 London WWBBA PO Box 31655 London W11 4WR Tel: +44 (0)20-7243-8720 Fax: +44 (0)20-7243-8736 E-mail: bestbandb@atlas.co.uk www.bestbandb.co.uk	Nearest Tube: Hammersmith A lovely house, pleasantly situated in leafy Brook Green mid-way between Hammersmith & Kensington. Offering a spacious & comfortably furnished double bedded room with private bathroom & tea/coffee making facilities which overlooks the rear garden. A pretty lounge with T.V. is often available & in which, guests may choose to relax. An ideal base, with good access to Heathrow & central London.	£66.00 to £76.00	Y	N	N
Home No. 59 London WWBBA Po Box 31655 London W11 4WR Tel: +44 (0)20-7243-8720 Fax: +44 (0)20-7243-8736 E-mail: bestbandb@atlas.co.uk www.bestbandb.co.uk	Nearest Tube: Fulham Broadway Situated in Fulham, with many good restaurants, pubs & antique shops nearby. This is a charming Victorian house, standing in a quiet street. The delightful hosts offer 1 spacious King-size double/twin-bedded room with an exquisite marble en-suite bathroom & another lovely, light & airy twin-bedded room with a beautiful private bathroom adjacent. Each bedroom is well-furnished & has colour T.V., hairdryer & tea/coffee-making facilities. Very good access to central London & the sights by bus or tube.	£64.00 to £78.00	Y	N	N

London

Visit our website: www.bestbandb.co.uk

		rate £ from - to per double room	children taken	evening meals	animals taken
Home No. 60 London **WWBBA** **PO Box 31655** **London W11 4WR** **Tel: +44 (0)20-7243-8720** **Fax: +44 (0)20-7243-8736** E-mail: bestbandb@atlas.co.uk **www.bestbandb.co.uk**	Nearest Tube: High St. Ken. A beautifully appointed home located in a quiet cul-de-sac, close to Kensington Palace. A lift will take you to the 2nd floor accommodation. A delightful, spacious double room with brass bed, T.V., tea/coffee-making facilities & biscuits are also provided. A delicious varied breakfast is also served. Knightsbridge, Kensington & Hyde Park are all just a short walk from here.	£37.00 to £60.00 🚭	N	N	N
Home No. 61 London **WWBBA** **Po Box 31655** **London** **W11 4WR** **Tel: +44 (0)20-7243-8720** **Fax: +44 (0)20-7243-8736** E-mail: bestbandb@atlas.co.uk **www.bestbandb.co.uk**	Nearest Tube: Holland Park A lovely apartment situated on the 7th floor of an Edwardian mansion block with lift access. Offering 1 spacious & attractive double bedded room with a private bathroom, T.V. & a small balcony with rooftop views. A large Continental breakfast is served. The charming host has an extensive knowledge of London & is happy to give advice on what to see & do. Easy access to central London & the sights, beautiful Holland Park, Kensington High Street & many good shops & restaurants. Heathrow Airbus stops nearby.	£33.00 to £50.00	N	N	N
Home No. 63 London **WWBBA** **PO Box 31655** **London** **W11 4WR** **Tel: +44 (0)20-7243-8720** **Fax: +44 (0)20-7243-8736** E-mail: bestbandb@atlas.co.uk **www.bestbandb.co.uk**	Nearest Tube: Sloane Square An attractive 2-storey penthouse apartment with prize-winning roof garden, situated in the heart of fashionable Chelsea & only minutes from the River Thames & the trendy shops & restaurants of the King's Road. The delightful host, who is an artist, is always happy to advise guests on what to see & do. 1 comfortable en-suite double-bedded room. A Continental breakfast is served in the attractive dining room which is adorned with many of the hosts interesting pictures.	£33.00 to £50.00	N	N	N
Home No. 64 London **WWBBA** **PO Box 31655** **London** **W11 4WR** **Tel: +44 (0)20-7243-8720** **Fax: +44 (0)20-7243-8736** E-mail: bestbandb@atlas.co.uk **www.bestbandb.co.uk**	Nearest Tube: Camden Town A unique timber & glass house (designed by the host who is an architect), only a short walk from the station, the market & many excellent shops & restaurants. 1 attractive double-bedded room with T.V. & tea/coffee facilities & an equally attractive single room for a third member of the party. Each room is light & airy, comfortable & modern in design. A private bathroom. A full English or large Breakfast is served in the lovely open-plan kitchen/dining area which overlooks the garden. Easy access to the West End & theatreland.	£40.00 to £58.00 🚭	Y	N	N
Home No. 65 London **WWBBA** **PO Box 31655** **London** **W11 4WR** **Tel: +44 (0)20-7243-8720** **Fax: +44 (0)20-7243-8736** E-mail: bestbandb@atlas.co.uk **www.bestbandb.co.uk**	Nearest Tube: Baker Street An elegant Georgian townhouse, only moments from Baker Street, Regent's Park & Mayfair. It is pleasantly furnished throughout. A selection of charming guest rooms including double, single & triple rooms. Each bedroom is spacious, attractively decorated, & has an en-suite/private bathroom, T.V. & 'phone. An elegant lounge where tea/coffee is available. A large Continental breakfast is served. A delightful home in a marvellous location only minutes from the West End.	£54.00 to £95.00 🚭	N	N	N

London

Visit our website: www.bestbandb.co.uk

		rate £ from - to	children taken	evening meals	animals taken
Home No. 66 London WWBBA Po Box 31655 London W11 4WR Tel: +44 (0)20-7243-8720 Fax: +44 (0)20-7243-8736 E-mail: bestbandb@atlas.co.uk www.bestbandb.co.uk	Nearest Tube: Earls Court A spacious apartment located at garden level offering contemporary accommodation in 1 double bedded room with en-suite facilities, T.V., fridge & 'phone. The friendly host (a fashion designer) has tastefully furnished & pleasantly decorated this apartment with many interesting paintings. Guests may relax in the garden which is accessible from their room. Situated only a few minutes walk from the tube station, this home is within easy reach of museums, galleries & theatres.	£68.00 to £82.00	N	N	N
Home No. 69 London WWBBA Po Box 31655 London W11 4WR Tel: +44 (0)20-7243-8720 Fax: +44 (0)20-7243-8736 E-mail: bestbandb@atlas.co.uk www.bestbandb.co.uk	Nearest Tube: South Kensington A super home from which to explore London, situated only a very short walk from the Natural History & Science Museums & the station. An attractively furnished apartment, located on the 1st floor of an Edwardian conversion, where the friendly host offers 1 light & airy King-size double/twin-bedded room with full en-suite bathroom & T.V. A Continental breakfast is served. A good location with many restaurants etc.	£70.00 to £84.00	N	N	N
Home No. 72 London WWBBA Po Box 31655 London W11 4WR Tel: +44 (0)20-7243-8720 Fax: +44 (0)20-7243-8736 E-mail: bestbandb@atlas.co.uk www.bestbandb.co.uk	Nearest Tube: Baker Street A traditional 4-storey Georgian townhouse in a marvellous location, only a short walk from Madame Tussauds, the Sherlock Holmes museum, Lord's Cricket Ground & Regents Park. The charming hosts, who are artists, offer 2 spacious & comfortably furnished double-bedded rooms (1 with low-beamed ceilings), each with an en-suite bathroom, T.V., tea/coffee-making facilities & views towards Regents Park. An ideal base from which to explore London on foot; the West End, theatreland & Piccadilly are only 10 mins away.	£78.00 to £86.00	Y	N	N
Home No. 76 London WWBBA Po Box 31655 London W11 4WR Tel: +44 (0)20-7243-8720 Fax: +44 (0)20-7243-8736 E-mail: bestbandb@atlas.co.uk www.bestbandb.co.uk	Nearest Tube: Earls Court One king-size double or twin-bedded room with very large en-suite bath & separate shower & 1 king-size double with adjacent private bath & shower. Each room has a colour T.V. & clock/radio & has been beautifully decorated & furnished by this most helpful host. This charming Victorian house is very close to all the best places for shopping, museums, sight-seeing & within walking distance of many excellent restaurants. Easy access to Gatwick & Heathrow Airports.	£64.00 to £80.00	N	N	N
Home No. 77 London WWBBA Po Box 31655 London W11 4WR Tel: +44 (0)20-7243-8720 Fax: +44 (0)20-7243-8736 E-mail: bestbandb@atlas.co.uk www.bestbandb.co.uk	Nearest Tube:Clapham Jt.(B.R.) A large Edwardian house built for Earl Spencer backing onto a private park. Breakfast may be served in the dining room or large conservatory. There is 1 double en-suite room, 1 family room en-suite, 1 twin bedded room with private facilities, also, 1 double room with shared bathroom. Plenty of car parking space. There are two cats & a friendly dog. A charming & most friendly host. Smoking permitted on the ground floor.	£66.00 to £76.00 *see PHOTO over* *p. 25*	N	N	N

Home No. 77 . London.

		rate £ from - to per double room	children taken	evening meals	animals taken
Home No. 78 London **WWBBA** **PO Box 31655** **London W11 4WR** **Tel: +44 (0)20-7243-8720** **Fax: +44 (0)20-7243-8736** E-mail: bestbandb@atlas.co.uk **www.bestbandb.co.uk**	Nearest Tube: Parsons Green An impressive Victorian house with pretty garden in a fashionable area facing a park with a public tennis court. Easy access to central London & excellent shops & restaurants nearby. The charming host is a well-travelled author, with 1 cat. 2 bedrooms, each with a double bed, completely private facilities, T.V. & hairdryer. A full English breakfast is served. Charming guest sitting room (rare in a private home).	£68.00 to £78.00	N	N	N
Home No. 79 London **WWBBA** **PO Box 31655** **London** **W11 4WR** **Tel: +44 (0)20-7243-8720** **Fax: +44 (0)20-7243-8736** E-mail: bestbandb@atlas.co.uk **www.bestbandb.co.uk**	Nearest Tube: East Putney An elegant Victorian house with a pretty garden located in the residential area of Putney. The charming hosts offer 2 stylishly decorated guest rooms, located on the 3rd floor. An attractive & spacious twin room with a lovely private bathroom & one large, sunny double bedroom with shower room en-suite. Each room has colour T.V. & tea/coffee-making facilities. Only 25 minutes to central London by tube or 35 mins' to Windsor by train. There are many excellent local restaurants.	£66.00 to £78.00	Y	N	N
Home No. 83 London **WWBBA** **PO Box 31655** **London** **W11 4WR** **Tel: +44 (0)20-7243-8720** **Fax: +44 (0)20-7243-8736** E-mail: bestbandb@atlas.co.uk **www.bestbandb.co.uk**	Nearest Tube: Stamford Brook A spacious Edwardian house set in a quiet street only 4 mins' walk from the station. The charming hosts offer 1 spacious & beautifully decorated Queen-size double-bedded room with Victorian-style brass bedstead, fridge, T.V./video, trouser press, tea/coffee-making facilities & an excellent bathroom en-suite. Breakfast is served in the conservatory overlooking the garden. Only 7 mins' walk from the River Thames with its variety of riverside pubs. Easy access to central London & Heathrow Airport. Children over 8.	£68.00 to £80.00	Y	N	N
Home No. 85 London **WWBBA** **PO Box 31655** **London** **W11 4WR** **Tel: +44 (0)20-7243-8720** **Fax: +44 (0)20-7243-8736** E-mail: bestbandb@atlas.co.uk **www.bestbandb.co.uk**	Nearest Tube: Fulham Broadway Situated in the heart of Fulham, this is a delightful 3 storey Victorian house conveniently located only 3 mins' walk from the tube. The very friendly hosts offer 1 double-bedded room with an en-suite bathroom & another double-bedded room with a shower room en-suite. Each bedroom is beautifully decorated & very comfortable. T.V. & tea/coffeee facilities are available. There are many famous bars, bistros & restaurants in Fulham Broadway. Heathrow Airport & Londons' many attractions are easily accessible by tube.	£66.00 to £78.00	N	N	N
Home No. 88 London **WWBBA** **PO Box 31655** **London W11 4WR** **Tel: +44 (0)20-7243-8720** **Fax: +44 (0)20-7243-8736** E-mail: bestbandb@atlas.co.uk **www.bestbandb.co.uk**	Nearest Tube: Sloane Square This is an elegantly furnished apartment situated less than 10 mins' walk from the tube. The friendly hosts offer 1 twin-bedded room with an adjacent private bathroom. Breakfast is served in the elegant dining room. Situated in the heart of Chelsea within easy reach of the fashionable shops & restaurants in the King's Road. The museums at South Kensington are a short distance away by bus or tube.	£72.00 to £84.00	N	N	N

Beds:Berks:Bucks:Herts.

Bedfordshire
(Thames & Chilterns)

The county of Bedfordshire is an area of great natural beauty from the Dunstable Downs in the south to the great River Ouse in the north, along with many country parks & historic houses & gardens.

Two famous wildlife parks are to be found, at Woburn &Whipsnade. The Woburn Wild Animal Kingdom is Britain's largest drive-through safari park, with entrance to an exciting leisure park all included in one admission ticket.

Rose gardens. St.Albans. Herts.

Whipsnade Zoo came into existence in the 1930's as a country retreat for the animals of London Zoo, but is now very much a zoo in its own right & renowned for conservation work.

Woburn Abbey, home of the Dukes of Bedford for three centuries, is often described as one of England's finest showplaces. Rebuilt in the 8th century the Abbey houses an important art collection & is surrounded by a magnificent 3,000 acre deer park.

John Bunyan drew on local Bedfordshire features when writing the Pilgrims Progress, & the ruins of Houghton House, his "House Beautiful" still remain.

Buckinghamshire
(Thames & Chilterns)

Buckinghamshire can be divided into two distinct geographical regions: The high Chilterns with their majestic beechwoods & the Vale of Aylesbury chosen by many over the centuries as a beautiful & accessible place to build their historical homes.

The beechwoods of the Chilterns to the south of the county are crisscrossed with quiet lanes & footpaths., Ancient towns & villages like Amersham & Chesham lie tucked away in the folds of the hills & a prehistoric track; the Ichnield Way winds on its 85 mile journey through the countryside.

The Rothschild family chose the Vale of Aylesbury to create several impressive homes, & Waddesdon House & Ascott House are both open to the public. Benjamin Disraeli lived at Hughenden Manor, & Florence Nightingale, "the Lady with the Lamp", at Claydon House. Sir Francis Dashwood, the 18th century eccentric founded the bizarre Hellfire Club, which met in the man-made caves near West Wycombe House.

Berkshire
(Thames & Chilterns)

Berkshire is a compact county but one of great variety & beauty.

In the East is Windsor where the largest inhabited castle in the world stands in its majestic hilltop setting. Nine centuries of English monarchy have lived here, & it is home to the present Queen. The surrounding parkland, enormous yards, vast interior & splendour of the State Apartments make a trip to Windsor Castle an unforgettable experience.

To the West are the gently rolling Berkshire Downs where many a champion racehorse has been trained.

Beds:Berks:Bucks:Herts.

To the north of the county, the River Thames dominates the landscape - an opportunity for a river-bank stroll & a drink at a country pub.

In the south is the Kennet & Avon Canal, a peaceful waterway with horse-drawn barges.

Historically, Berkshire has occupied an important place due to its strategic position commanding roads to & from Oxford & the north, & Bath & the west. Roundheads & Cavaliers clashed twice near Newbury during the 17th century English Civil Wars. Their battles are colourfully recreated by historic societies like the Sealed Knot.

The Tudor period brought great wealth from wool-weaving. Merchants built wonderful houses & some built churches but curiously, there is no cathedral in Berkshire.

Hertfordshire
(Thames & Chilterns)

Old & new exist side by side in Hertfordshire. This attractive county includes historic sites, like the unique Roman theatre in St. Albans, as well as new additions to the landscape such as England's first Garden City at Letchworth.

The countryside varies from the chalk hills & rolling downlands of the Chilterns to rivers, lakes, canals & pretty villages. The county remains largely rural despite many large towns & cities. The Grand Union Canal, built at the end of the 18th century to link the Midlands to London, passes through some glorious scenery, particularly at Cassiobury Park in Watford.

Verulamium was a newly-built town of the Roman Empire. It was the first name of Alban, himself a Roman, who became the first Christian to be martyred for his faith in England. The great Abbey church was built by the Normans around his original church, & it was re-established under the Rule of St. Benedict & named St. Albans some 600 years after his death.

Windsor Castle.

28

Beds:Berks:Bucks:Herts.

Bedfordshire
Gazeteer
Area of outstanding natural beauty.
Dunstable Downs, Ivinghoe Beacon

Historic Houses
Woburn Abbey - house & gardens, extensive art collection, deer park, antiques centre.

Other Things to see & do
Bedford Butterfly Park - set in 10 acres of wild flower hay meadows. A global conservation park.
The Glenn Miller Museum - Bedford
Old Warden - the village houses a collection of working vintage planes. Fying displays each month from April to October.
Shuttleworth Collection - a unique collection of historic aircraft spanning 100 years of flight
Woburn Safari Park
Whipsnade Zoo-Whipsnade

Berkshire Gazeteer
Areas of outstanding natural beauty.
North West Downs.

Historic Houses & Castles
Windsor Castle - Royal Residence at Windsor
State apartments, house, historic treasures. The Cloisters, Windsor Chapel. Mediaeval house.
Basildon Park - Nr. Pangbourne
Overlooking the Thames. 18th century Bath stone building, massive portico & linked pavilions. Painted ceiling in Octagon Room, gilded pier glasses. Garden & wooded walks.
Cliveden - Nr. Taplow
Once the home of Nancy Astor.

Churches
Lambourn (St. Michael & All Saints)
Norman with 15th century chapel. 16th century brasses, glass & tombs.
Padworth (St. John the Baptist)
12th century Norman with plastered exterior, remains of wall paintings, 18th century monuments.

Warfield (St. Michael & All Angels)
14th century decorated style. 15th century wood screen & loft.

Museums
Newbury Museum - Newbury
Natural History & Archaeology -
Paleolithic to Saxon & Mediaeval times.
Household Cavalry Museum - Windsor

Other Things to see & do
Racing - at Newbury, Ascot & Windsor
Highlight of the racing year is the Royal Meeting at Ascot each June, attended by the Queen & other members of the Royal Family.
Antiques - Hungerford is a famous centre for antiques.

Buckinghamshire
Gazeteer
Area of outstanding natural beauty.
Burnham Beeches - 70 acres of unspoilt woodlands, inspiration to poet
Thomas Gray.

Historic Houses
Waddesdon Manor & Ascott House -
homes of the Rothschilds.
Chalfont St. Giles - cottage home of great English poet John Milton.
Old Jordans & the Meeting House - 17th century buildings associated with William Penn, the founder of Pennsylvania & with the Society of Friends, often called the Quakers.

Things to see & do
Buckinghamshire Railway Centre - at Quainton
Vintage steam train rides & largest private railway collection in Britain.
Chalfont Shire Horse Centre -
home of the gentle giants of the horse world.

Beds:Berks:Bucks:Herts.

Hertfordshire
Gazeteer
Areas of outstanding natural beauty.
Parts of the Chilterns.

Historic Houses & Castles
Hatfield House - Hatfield
Home of the Marquess of Salisbury.
Jacobean House & Tudor Palace -
childhood home of Queen Elizabeth I.
Knebworth House - Knebworth
Family home of the Lyttons. 16th century
house transformed into Victorian High
Gothic. Furniture, portraits. Formal
gardens & unique Gertrude Jekyll herb
garden.
Shaw's Corner - Ayot St. Lawrence
Home of George Bernard Shaw.

Cathedrals & Churches
St. Albans Cathedral - St. Albans
9th century foundation, murals, painted
roof over choir, 15th century reredos,
stone rood screen.

Stanstead St. Abbots (St. James)12th
century nave, 13th century chancel, 15th
century tower & porch, 16th century
North chapel, 18th century box pews
& 3-decker pulpit.
Watford (St. Mary)
13 - 15th century. Essex chapel.
Tuscan arcade. Morryson tombs.

Museums
**Rhodes Memorial Museum &
Commonwealth Centre** - at Bishop
Stortford
Zoological Museum - Tring
Gardens
Gardens of the Rose - Chiswell Green
Nr. St Albans
Showgrounds of the Royal National Rose
Society
Capel Manor
Extensive grounds of horticultural college.
Many fine trees, including the largest
copper beech in the country.

Bledlow Village; Bucks.

BEDS/BUCKS
BERKSHIRE
HERTS

Map reference

01 Must	07 Steeds
02 Codd	08 Baron
03 Cook	09 Noy
04 Gaselee	10 Pollock-Hill
05 Digby	

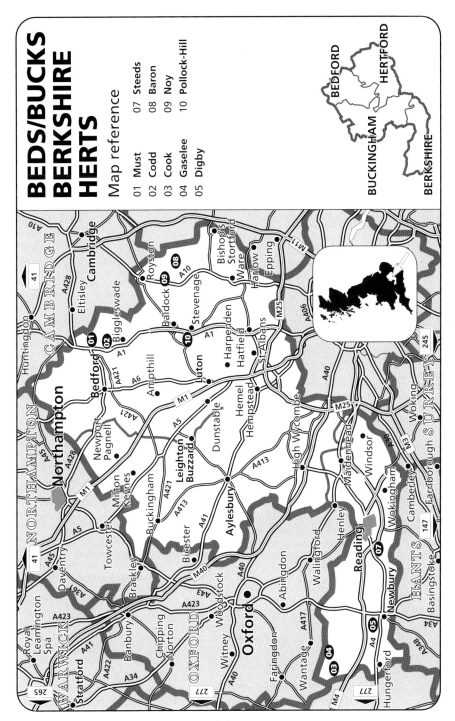

Bedfordshire & Berkshire

Church Farm

Near Rd: A.1, A.421
Church Farm is a Grade II listed, 17th-century part-timber framed house. It is a perfect base for those wanting somewhere a little special & a comfortable place to stay. 3 delightful bedrooms (all en-suite), each with a colour T.V. & a welcome tray. (In the twin room, there is the 'Coat of Arms' of the Stuart Kings.) Breakfast is served in the attractive beamed 17th-century dining room. There are walks around the village & countryside, & inns for evening meals. A haven from a hectic world.
E-mail: churchfarm@amserve.net
www.bestbandb.co.uk

| £55.00 to £65.00 | N | N | N |

Janet Must   Church Farm   41 High Street   Roxton   Bedford MK44 3EB   Bedfordshire
Tel: (01234) 870234   Fax 01234 870234   Open: ALL YEAR   Map Ref No. 01

Highfield Farm

Near Rd: A.1, A.421
A tranquil & very welcoming house with comfort, warmth & a friendly atmosphere in a lovely setting on an arable farm. 9 attractive bedrooms, 8 en-suite, including 4 ground-floor rooms in tastefully converted stables. Highfield Farm is set back off the A.1, giving peaceful seclusion & yet easy access to London, Cambridge, Bedford, the Shuttleworth Collection, the R.S.P.B. & the east-coast ports. Parking. (Animals by arrangement.) Single supplement. Most guests return to this lovely home.
E-mail: margaret@highfield-farm.co.uk
www.highfield-farm.co.uk

| £65.00 to £75.00 | Y | N | Y |

VISA: M'CARD:

Mrs Margaret Codd   Highfield Farm   Tempsford Road   Sandy SG19 2AQ   Bedfordshire
Tel: (01767) 682332   Fax 01767 692503   Open: ALL YEAR   Map Ref No. 02

Lodge Down

Near Rd: A.4, M.4
A warm welcome is assured at Lodge Down, a country house with superb accommodation & en-suite bathrooms, set in lovely grounds. Excellent & varied dining in surrounding villages. Easy access to the M.4 motorway at Jts 14 & 15. 1 hr or less from Heathrow (60 miles), Bath (43 miles) & Oxford (26 miles). This location provides a central base for excursions to Stonehenge, Salisbury & the Cotswolds, etc., or an easy drive to London. Lodge Down is a charming home.
E-mail: lodgedown@hotmail.com
www.lodgedown.co.uk

| £55.00 to £55.00 | N | N | N |

see PHOTO over p. 33

John & Sally Cook   Lodge Down   Ermin Street   Lambourn   Hungerford RG17 7BJ   Berkshire
Tel: (01672) 540304   Fax 01672 540304   Open: ALL YEAR   Map Ref No. 03

Saxon Cottage

Near Rd: B.4000
Saxon Cottage is in the famous racehorse training village of Upper Lambourn & is very close to the gallops. Nick has recently retired from training horses & is happy to take guests to see the gallops in the mornings. 2 comfortable bedrooms (1 double & 1 twin) with private facilities. Also, another twin room, suitable for children. Dinner is by arrangement. A variety of local pubs & restaurants, also serve excellent food. 6 miles from Hungerford & within easy reach of Bath & Oxford.
E-mail: judy.gaselee@virgin.net
www.SmoothHound.co.uk/hotels/saxon-cottage.html

| £60.00 to £60.00 | Y | Y | N |

Judy & Nick Gaselee   Saxon Cottage   Upper Lambourn   Hungerford RG17 8QN   Berkshire
Tel: (01488) 71503   Fax 01488 71585   Open: ALL YEAR (Excl. Xmas & New Year) Map Ref No. 04

Lodge Down. Lambourn.

	rate £ from - to per double room	children taken	evening meals	animals taken

Rookwood Farmhouse

Near Rd: A.4, A.34

This charming & comfortable former farmhouse combines ease of access with rural views & a large garden. The guest bedrooms are in a newly converted coach house which is traditionally furnished & yet affords all modern facilities. In winter, there is a welcoming log fire in the guests' sitting room, while in summer, breakfast is served in the conservatory overlooking the swimming pool. An ideal base for a relaxing break.

E-mail: enquiries@rookwoodfarmhouse.co.uk
www.rookwoodfarmhouse.co.uk

£70.00 to £70.00 — Y — N — N

VISA. M'CARD.

| Mrs Charlotte Digby | Rookwood Farmhouse | Stockcross | Newbury RG20 8JX | Berkshire |
| Tel: (01488) 608676 | FAX 01488 657961 | Open: ALL YEAR | Map Ref No. 05 |

Highwoods

Near Rd: A.4, M.4

A friendly & relaxing atmosphere at this fine Victorian country house set in 4 acres of attractive grounds, with unspoilt, far-reaching views. Offering 3 spacious, comfortable, attractively furnished rooms (1 en-suite) all with colour T.V. etc. Guests are welcome to use the garden & hard tennis court. Also, a gallery specialising in English watercolours & prints. Easy access to London, Heathrow Airport, Windsor, Oxford & Bath.

E-mail: janesteeds@aol.com
www.bestbandb.co.uk

£35.00 to £60.00 — Y — N — N

| Mrs J. Steeds | Highwoods | Hermits Hill | Burghfield Common | Reading RG7 3BG | Berkshire |
| Tel: (0118) 9832320 | Fax 0118 9831070 | Open: ALL YEAR (Excl. Xmas & New Year) | Map Ref No. 07 |

Brick House Farm

Near Rd: B.1038

The farmhouse is situated on the outskirts of the picturesque village of Gt Hormead in an idyllic location and yet within a short drive of the A10. Guests can expect a warm welcome at this peaceful & secluded home. The attractive rooms with their en-suite facilities have delightful views over rolling farmland. All rooms have TV/videos, welcome tray & hairdryers. Tennis court & heated outdoor swimming pool available for guests' use at selected times. Parking. Many guests return.

E-mail: helen@brickhousefarm.net
www.brickhousefarm.net

£55.00 to £65.00 — Y — N — N

| Helen Baron | Brick House Farm | Great Hormead | Buntingford SG9 0PB | Hertfordshire |
| Tel: (01763) 289356 | Open: ALL YEAR | Map Ref No.08 |

Chipping Hall Farm

Near Rd: A. 10

Chipping Hall is an attractive Georgian farmhouse set on a family-run arable farm. Offering 2 attractive guest rooms in the main house, which share a bathroom. Also, in an annexe overlooking the garden, The Old Dairy, offers comfortable accommodation with en-suite facilities. An attractive walled garden with outdoor heated pool for use in the summer. Within easy reach of Duxford Imperial War Museum, Audley End, Cambridge, & Stansted & Luton Airports. Dinner by arrangement.

E-mail: jacquelinenoy@aol.com
www.chippinghall.com

£57.50 to £100.00 — Y — N — N

| Mrs Jacqueline Noy | Chipping Hall Farm | Chipping | Buntingford SG9 0PH | Hertfordshire |
| Tel: (01763) 271514 | Fax 01763 272833 | Open: ALL YEAR (Excl. Xmas) | Map Ref No. 09 |

Homewood. Knebworth.

Hertfordshire

	rate £ from - to per double room	children taken	evening meals	animals taken

Homewood

Near Rd: A.1 M

Homewood is a classic blend of comfort & style: an Edwardian country house which is also a well-equipped family home. It has been used as a location for period drama by the B.B.C., & is often sought out by admirers of its designer, the distinguished architect Edwin Lutyens. You will be treated as a member of the family, or your privacy will be respected. 2 lovely bedrooms, each with en-suite/private bathroom & a family suite. Animals & evening meals (min. 4 persons) by arrangement.
E-mail: bookings@homewood-bb.co.uk
www.homewood-bb.co.uk

£70.00 to £70.00 | Y | Y | N

see PHOTO over
p. 35

Samantha Pollock-Hill   Homewood   Park Lane   Old Knebworth   Stevenage SG3 6PP   Hertfordshire
Tel: (01438) 812105   Fax 01438 812572   Open: ALL YEAR (Excl. Xmas)   Map Ref No. 10

All the establishments mentioned in this guide are members of
The Worldwide Bed & Breakfast Association

When booking your accommodation please mention
The Best Bed & Breakfast

Cambridge & Northants

Cambridgeshire
(East Anglia)

A county very different from any other, this is flat, mysterious, low-lying Fenland crisscrossed by a network of waterways both natural & man-made.

The Fens were once waterlogged, misty marshes but today the rich black peat is drained & grows carrots, sugar beet, celery & the best asparagus in the world.

Drive north across the Fens & slowly you become aware of a great presence dominating the horizon. Ely cathedral, the "ship of the Fens", sails closer. The cathedral is a masterpiece with its graceful form & delicate tracery towers. Begun before the Domesday Book was written, it took the work of a full century before it was ready to have the timbered roof raised up. Norman stonemasons worked with great skill & the majestic nave is glorious in its simplicity. Their work was crowned by the addition of the Octagon in the 14th century. Despite the ravages of the Reformation, the lovely Lady Chapel survives as one of the finest examples of decorated architecture in Britain with its exquisitely fine stone carving.

To the south, the Fens give way to rolling chalk hills & fields of barley, wheat & rye, & Cambridge. Punts gliding through the broad river, between smooth, lawned banks, under willow trees, past college buildings as extravagant as wedding cakes. The names of the colleges resound through the ages - Peterhouse, Corpus Christi, Kings, Queens, Trinity, Emmanuel. A city of learning & progress, & a city of great tradition where cows graze in open spaces, just 500 yards from the market square.

Northamptonshire
(East Midlands)

Northamptonshire has many features to attract & interest the visitor, from the town of Brackley in the south with its charming buildings of mellow stone, to ancient Rockingham Forest in the north. There are lovely churches, splendid historic houses & peaceful waterways.

The Waterways Museum at Stoke Bruerne makes a popular outing, with boat trips available on the Grand Union Canal beside the museum. Horse-racing at Towcester & motor-racing at Silverstone draws the crowds, but there are quieter pleasures in visits to Canons Ashby, or to Sulgrave Manor, home of George Washington's ancestors.

In the pleasantly wooded Rockingham Forest area are delightful villages, one of which is Ashton with its thatched cottages, the scene of the World Conker Championships each October. Mary Queen of Scots was executed at Fotheringay, in the castle of which only the mound remains.

Rockingham Castle has a solid Norman gateway & an Elizabethan hall; Deene Park has family connections with the Earl of Cardigan who led the Charge of the Light Brigade & Kirby Hall is a dramatic Elizabethan ruin.

The county is noted for its parish churches, with fine Saxon examples at Brixworth & at Earl's Barton, as well as the round Church of the Holy Sepulchre in the county town itself.

Northampton has a fine tradition of shoemaking, so it is hardly surprising that boots & shoes & other leather-goods take pride of place in the town';s museums. The town has one of the country's biggest market squares, an historic Royal Theatre & a mighty Wurlitzer Organ to dance to at Turner's Musical Merry-go-round ! !

Cambridge & Northants

Cambridgeshire Gazeteer

Areas of outstanding natural beauty
The Nene Valley

Historic Houses & Castles

Anglesy Abbey - Nr. Cambridge
Origins in the reign of Henry I. Was redesigned into Elizabethan Manor by Fokes family. Houses the Fairhaven collection of Art treasures - stands in 100 acres of Ground.

Hinchingbrooke House - Huntingdon
13th century nunnery converted mid-16th century into Tudor house. Later additions in 17th & 19th centuries.

King's School - Ely
12th & 14th centuries - original stonework & vaulting in the undercroft, original timbering 14th century gateway & monastic barn.

Kimbolton Castle - Kimbolton
Tudor Manor house - has associations with Katherine of Aragon. Remodelled by Vanbrugh 1700's - gatehouse by Robert Adam.

Longthorpe Tower - Nr. Peterborough
13th & 14th century fortification - rare wall paintings.

Peckover House - Wisbech
18th century domestic architecture - charming Victorian garden.

University of Cambridge Colleges
Peterhouse - ---------------- 1284
Clare - ---------------------- 1326
Pembroke -------------------- 1347
Gonville & Caius------------- 1348
Trinity Hall - ----------------- 1350
Corpus Christi - ------------- 1352
King's ----------------------- 1441
Queen's - ------------------- 1448
St. Catherine's ---------------1473
Jesus ------------------------ 1496
Christ's - ---------------------1505
St. John's---------------------1511
Magadalene ----------------1542
Trinity- ---------------------- 1546
Emmanuel-------------------- 1584
Sidney Sussex -------------- 1596
Downing---------------------- 1800

Wimpole Hall - Nr. Cambridge
18th & 19th century - beautiful staterooms - aristocratic house.

Cathedrals & Churches

Alconbury (St. Peter & St. Paul)
13th century chancel & 15th century roof. Broach spire.

Babraham (St. Peter)
13th century tower - 17th century monument.

Ely Cathedral
Rich arcading - west front incomplete. Remarkable interior with Octagon - unique in Gothic architecture.

Great Paxton (Holy Trinity)
12th century.

Harlton (Blessed Virgin Mary)
Perpendicular - decorated transition. 17th century monuments

Hildersham (Holy Trinity)
13th century - effigies, brasses & glass.

Lanwade (St. Nicholas)
15th century - mediaeval fittings

Peterborough Cathedral
Great Norman church fine example - little altered. Painted wooden roof to   nave - remarkable west front - Galilee Porch & spires later additions.

Ramsey (St. Thomas of Canterbury)
12th century arcades - perpendicular nave. Late Norman chancel with Angevin vault.

St. Neots (St. Mary)
15th century

Sutton (St. Andrew)
14th century

Trumpington (St. Mary & St. Nicholas)
14th century. Framed brass of 1289 of Sir Roger de Trumpington.

Westley Waterless (St. Mary the Less)
Decorated. 14th century brass of Sir John & Lady Creke.

Wimpole (St. Andrew)
14th century rebuilt 1749 - splendid heraldic glass.

Yaxley (St. Peter)
15th century chancel screen, wall paintings, fine steeple.

Museums & Galleries

Cromwell Museum - Huntingdon
Exhibiting portraits, documents, etc. of the Cromwellian period.

Fitzwilliam Museum - Cambridge
Gallery of masters, old & modern, ceramics, applied arts, prints & drawing, mediaeval manuscripts, music & art library.

Cambridge & Northants

Scott Polar Research Institute - Cambridge
Relics of expeditions & the equipment used. Current scientific work in Arctic & Antarctic.

University Archives - Cambridge
13th century manuscripts, Charters, Statutes, Royal letters & mandates. Wide variety of records of the University.

University Museum of Archaeology & Anthropology - Cambridge
Collections illustrative of Stone Age in Europe, Africa & Asia.
Britain prehistoric to mediaeval times.
Prehistoric America.

Ethnographic material from South-east Asia, Africa & America.

University Museum of Classical Archaeology - Cambridge
Casts of Greek & Roman Sculpture - representative collection.

Whipple Museum of the History of Science - Cambridge 16th, 17th & 18th century scientific instruments - historic collection.

Other Things to see & do

Nene Valley Railway
Steam railway with locomotives & carriages from many countries.

Caius College; Cambridge.

Cambridge & Northants

Northamptonshire Gazeteer

Historic Houses & Castles

Althorp - Nr. Northampton
Family home of the Princess of Wales, with fine pictures & porcelain.

Boughton House - Nr. Kettering
Furniture, tapestries & pictures in late 17th century building modelled on Versailles, in beautiful parkland.

Canons Ashby House - Nr. Daventry
Small 16th century manor house with gardens & church.

Deene Park - Nr. Corby
Family home for over 4 centuries, surrounded by park, extensive gardens & lake.

Holdenby House - Nr. Northampton
Gardens include part of Elizabethan garden, with original entrance arches, terraces & ponds. Falconry centre. Rare breeds.

Kirby Hall - Nr. Corby
Large Elizabethan mansion with fine gardens.

Lamport Hall - Nr. Northampton
17th & 18th century house with paintings, furniture & china. One of the first garden rockeries in Britain. Programme of concerts & other special events.

Rockingham Castle - Rockingham, Nr. Market Harborough
Norman gateway & walls surrounding mainly Elizabethan house, with pictures & Rockingham china. Extensive gardens with 16th century yew hedge.

Rushton Triangular Lodge - Nr. Kettering
Symbolic of the Trinity, with 3 sides, 3 floors, trefoil windows.

Sulgrave Manor - Nr. Banbury
Early English Manor, home of George Washington's ancestors.

Museums

Abington Museum - Northampton
Domestic & social life collections in former manor house.

Museum of Leathercraft - Northampton
History of leather use, with Queen Victoria's saddle, & Samuel Pepys' wallet.

Waterways Museum - Stoke Bruerne Nr. Towcester
200 years of canal & waterway life, displayed beside the Grand Union Canal.

Cathedrals & Churches

Brixworth Church - Nr. Northampton
One of the finest Anglo-Saxon churches in the country, mostly 7th century.

Earls Barton Church - Nr. Northampton
Fine Anglo-Saxon tower & Norman arch & arcading.

Church of the Holy Sepulchre - Northampton
Largest & best preserved of four remaining round churches in England, dating from 1100.

Other Things to see & do

Billing Aquadrome - Nr. Northampton
Boating, fishing, swimming & amusements.

Wicksteed Park - Kettering
Large playground & variety of amusements for families.

Lilford Park - Nr. Oundle
Birds & farm animals in parkland setting where many special events are held.

Rushton Triangular Lodge.

CAMBRIDGESHIRE & NORTHAMPTONSHIRE

Map reference

01 Hindley
02 Nix
03 Farndale
04 Roper
05 Wood
06 Clarke

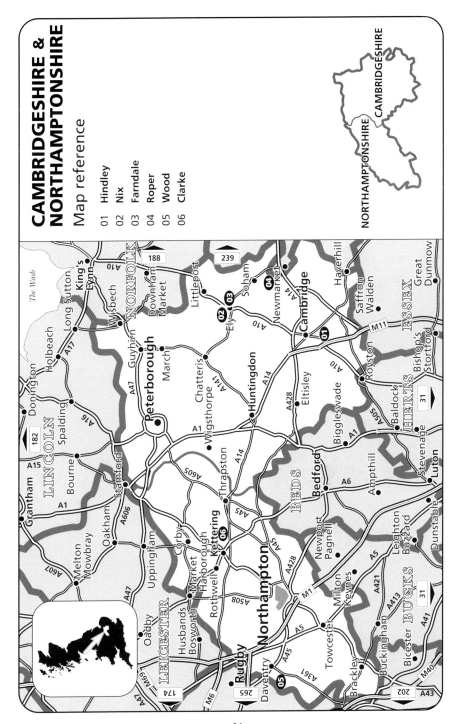

Column headers (diagonal): rate £ from - to per double room | children taken | evening meals | animals taken

Purlins

Near Rd: A.10

Lovely, individually designed family home, with 2 acres of parkland, situated in a quiet, pretty village on the Cam, 4 miles south of Cambridge. An ideal centre for Colleges, Audley End House, the Imperial War Museum & bird watching. There are 3 well-appointed double bedrooms (2 ground-floor), all with en-suite bathrooms, colour T.V. & tea/coffee-making facilities. Varied breakfasts (special diets by arrangement). Restaurants nearby. Children over 8 welcome. Single supplement.

E-mail: dgallh@ndirect.co.uk
www.bestbandb.co.uk

£48.00 to £70.00 — Children taken: Y — Evening meals: N — Animals taken: N (No smoking)

Olga & David Hindley Purlins 12 High Street Little Shelford Cambridge CB2 5ES Cambridgeshire
Tel/Fax: (01223) 842643   Mobile 07785 790204   Open: APR - OCT   Map Ref No. 01

Hill House Farm

Near Rd: A.142, A.10

A warm welcome awaits you at this spacious Victorian farmhouse, situated in the quiet village of Coveney, 3 miles from the cathedral city of Ely. Open views of the surrounding countryside & easy access to Cambridge, Newmarket & Huntingdon. Ideal for touring Cambridgeshire, Norfolk & Suffolk. Wicken Fen & Welney wildfowl refuge nearby. 1 twin & 2 double en-suite rooms, 1 ground floor. All have their own entrance & T.V. etc. A lounge & garden for guests' use. Single supplement.

E-mail: info@hillhousefarm-ely.co.uk
www.hillhousefarm-ely.co.uk

£52.00 to £54.00 — Children taken: N — Evening meals: N — Animals taken: N (No smoking)

VISA: M'CARD:

Mrs Hilary Nix   Hill House Farm   9 Main Street   Coveney   Ely CB6 2DJ   Cambridgeshire
Tel: (01353) 778369   Fax 01353 778369   Open: ALL YEAR (Excl. Xmas)   Map Ref No. 02

Cathedral House

Near Rd: A.10

Although established 10 years ago, Cathedral House remains one of Ely's best kept secrets. Situated within the shadow of Ely's magnificent cathedral, this Grade II listed house, whilst retaining many original features offers well-appointed spacious accommodation in 2 double suites & a twin en-suite. All the rooms overlook the tranquil walled garden. Breakfast is served at the family table where you can meet fellow guests & enjoy convivial conversation. Children over 10 years.

E-mail: farndale@cathedralhouse.co.uk
www.cathedralhouse.co.uk

£70.00 to £90.00 — Children taken: Y — Evening meals: N — Animals taken: N (No smoking)

Jenny Farndale   Cathedral House   17 St Mary's Street   Ely CB7 4ER   Cambridgeshire
Tel: (01353) 662124   Open: ALL YEAR   Map Ref No. 03

Queensberry

Near Rd: A.14, A.142

A delightful Georgian home, featured in many T.V. travel programmes, set in large grounds with croquet lawn & parking. Ideally situated for touring East Anglia, Cambridge, Duxford, Ely Cathedral, Newmarket, Bury St. Edmunds, & many National Trust & English Heritage properties. Equine tours can be arranged. 2 attractive bedrooms, 1 with en-suite facilities & the other with a private bathroom. Fordham is the 1st village off the A.14 on the Newmarket to Ely A.142 road. Good local restaurants. Children & animals by arrangement.

E-mail: queensberry@queensberry196.demon.co.uk

£60.00 to £60.00 — Children taken: Y — Evening meals: N — Animals taken: Y (No smoking)

Jan & Malcolm Roper   Queensberry   196 Carter Street   Fordham CB7 5JU   Cambridgeshire
Tel: (01638) 720916   Fax 01638 720233   Open: ALL YEAR   Map Ref No. 04

rate £ from - to per double room	children taken	evening meals	animals taken		
£80.00 to £100.00	Y	N	N	Near Rd: A.425 — A Victorian former coach house which has been elegantly converted into a large family home with a superb garden. The West Terrace has a commanding view of the open countryside, as seen from the double rooms, whilst the twin room overlooks the lake. The property adjoins the site of a former priory founded in 1175 & is on the Jurassic Way. Silverstone, Stoneleigh, Rugby & Birmingham Airport are within a 45 min. drive. The Old Coach House is a special place to stay. Children over 8. **E-mail: coachhouse@lowercatesby.co.uk www.lowercatesby.co.uk**	**The Old Coach House**
				Clive & Eileen Wood The Old Coach House Lower Catesby Daventry NN11 6LF Northamptonshire *Tel: (01327) 310390 Fax 01327 312220 Open: ALL YEAR (Excl. Xmas & New Year) Map Ref No. 05*	
£64.00 to £76.00	Y	Y	Y	Near Rd: A.14 — Situated in an idyllic Northamptonshire village, Dairy Farm is a charming 17th-century farmhouse, featuring oak beams & inglenook fireplaces. There are comfortable bedrooms, all with en-suite/private bathroom. Families are well catered for. There is a delightful garden, containing an ancient circular dovecote & a charming summer house, for guests to enjoy in a relaxed & friendly atmosphere. Delicious meals, using farmhouse produce (if ordered in advance). Dogs by arrangement. **www.bestbandb.co.uk**	**Dairy Farm**
				Mrs Audrey Clarke Dairy Farm 12 St. Andrews Lane Cranford St. Andrew Kettering NN14 4AQ *Northamptonshire Tel: (01536) 330273 Open: ALL YEAR Map Ref No. 06*	

All the establishments mentioned in this guide are members of
The Worldwide Bed & Breakfast Association

When booking your accommodation please mention
The Best Bed & Breakfast

Cheshire & Lancashire

Cheshire
(North West)

Cheshire is located between the Peak District & the mountains of North Wales & is easily accessible from three major motorways. It has much to attract long visits but is also an ideal stopping-off point for travellers to the Lake District & Scotland, or to North Wales or Ireland. There is good access eastwards to York & the east coast & to the south to Stratford-upon-Avon & to London.

Cheshire can boast seven magnificent stately homes, the most visited zoo outside London, four of Europe's largest garden centres & many popular venues which feature distinctive Cheshire themes such as silk, salt, cheese, antiques & country crafts.

The Cheshire plain with Chester, its fine county town, & its pretty villages, rises up to Alderley Edge in the east from where there are panoramic views, & then climbs dramatically to meet the heights of the Peaks.

To the west is the coastline of the Wirral Peninsula with miles of sandy beaches & dunes &, of course, Liverpool.

The countryside shelters very beautiful houses. Little Moreton Hall near Congleton, is one of the most perfect imaginable. It is a black & white "magpie" house & not one of its walls is perpendicular, yet it has withstood time & weather for nearly four centuries, standing on the waterside gazing at its own reflection.

Tatton Hall is large & imposing & is splendidly furnished with many fine objects on display. The park & gardens are a delight & especially renowned for the azaleas & rhododendrons. In complete contrast is the enormous radio telescope at Jodrell Bank where visitors can be introduced to planetary astronomy in the planetarium.

Chester is a joy; a walk through its streets is like walking through living history. The old city is encircled by city walls enclosing arcaded streets with handsome black & white galleried buildings that blend well with modern life. There are many excellent shops along these "Rows". Chester Cathedral is a fine building of monastic foundation, with a peaceful cloister & outstanding wood carving in the choir stalls. Boat rides can be taken along the River Dee which flows through the city.

Manchester has first rate shopping, restaurants, sporting facilities, theatres & many museums ranging from an excellent costume museum to the fascinating Museum of Science & Industry.

Little Moreton Hall.

Liverpool grew from a tiny fishing village on the northern shores of the Mersey River, receiving its charter from King John in 1207. Commercial & slave trading with the West Indies led to massive expansion in the 17th & 18th centuries. The Liverpool of today owes much to the introduction of the steam ship in the mid 1900s, which enabled thousands of Irish to emigrate when the potatoe famine was at its height in Ireland. This is a city with a reputation for patronage of art, music & sport.

Cheshire & Lancashire

Lancashire
(North West)

Lancashire can prove a surprisingly beautiful county. Despite its industrial history of cotton production, there is magnificent scenery & there are many fine towns & villages. Connections with the Crown & the clashes of the Houses of Lancaster & York have left a rich heritage of buildings with a variety of architecture. There are old stone cottages & farmhouses, as well as manor houses from many centuries.

For lovers of the countryside, Lancashire has the sweeping hills of Bowland, the lovely Ribble Valley, the moors of Rossendale & one mountain, mysterious Pendle Hill.

The Royal Forest of Bowland is a forest without trees, which has provided rich hunting grounds over the centuries. An old windswept pass runs over the heights of Salter Fell & High Cross Fell from Slaidburn, where the Inn, the "Hark to Bounty", was named after the noisiest hound in the squire's pack & used to be the courtroom where strict forest laws were enforced.

Further south, the Trough of Bowland provides an easier route through the hills, & here is the beautiful village of Abbeystead in Wynesdale where monks once farmed the land. The church has stained glass windows portraying shepherds & their flocks & there are pegs in the porch where shepherds hung their crooks.

Below the dramatic hills of Bowland, the green valley of the Ribble climbs from Preston to the Yorkshire Dales. Hangridge Fell, where the tales of witches are almost as numerous as those of Pendle Hill, lies at the beginning of the valley.

Pendle Hill can be reached from the pretty village of Downham which has Tudor, Jacobean & Georgian houses, village stocks & an old inn. Old Pendle rises abruptly to 1831 feet & is a strange land formation. It is shrouded in legend & stories of witchcraft.

Between Pendle Hill & the moors of Rossendale are the textile towns of Nelson, Colne, Burnley, Accrington & Blackburn. The textile industry was well established in Tudor times & the towns grew up as markets for the trading of the cloth woven in the Piece Halls.

The moors which descend to the very edges of the textile towns are wild & beautiful & have many prehistoric tumuli & earthworks. Through the towns & the countryside, winds the Liverpool & Leeds canal, providing an excellent towpath route to see the area.

Lancaster is an historic city boasting the largest castle in England, dating back to Norman times.

Lancashire's coastal resorts are legendary, & Blackpool is Queen of them all with her miles of illuminations & millions of visitors.

Downham Village.

Cheshire & Lancashire

Lancashire Gazeteer

Areas of outstanding natural beauty.
The Forest of Bowland, Parts of Arnside & Silverdale.

Historic Houses & Castles

Rufford Old Hall - Rufford
15th century screen in half-timbered hall of note. Collection of relics of Lancashire life.
Chingle Hall - Nr. Preston
13th century - small manor house with moat. Rose gardens. Haunted!
Astley Hall - Chorley
Elizabethan house reconstructed in 17th century. Houses pictures, tapestries, pottery & furniture.
Gawthorpe Hall - Padiham
17th century manor house with 19th century restoration. Moulded ceilings & some fine panelling. A collection of lace & embroidery.
Bramall Hall - Bramall
Fine example of half-timbered (black & white) manor house built in 14th century & added to in Elizabethan times. .
Lancaster Castle - Lancaster
Largest of English castles - dates back to Norman era.
Astley Hall - Chorley
16th century half-timbered grouped around central court. Rebuilt in the Jacobean manner with long gallery. Unique furniture.
Hoghton Tower - Nr. Preston
16th century - fortified hill-top mansion - magnificent banquet hall. Dramatic building - walled gardens & rose gardens.
Thurnham Hall - Lancaster
13th century origins. 16th century additions & 19th century facade. Beautiful plasterwork of Elizabethan period. Jacobean staircase.

Cathedrals & Churches

Lancaster (St. Mary)
15th century with 18th century tower. Restored chapel - fine stalls.
Whalley (St. Mary)
13th century with 15th century tower, clerestory & aisle windows. Fine wood carving of 15th century canopied stalls.
Halsall (St. Cuthbert)
14th century chancel, 15th century perpendicular spire. 14th century tomb. Original doors, brasses & effigies. 19th century restoration.
Tarleton (St. Mary)
18th century, part 19th century.
Great Mitton (All Hallows)
15th century rood screen, 16th century font cover, 17th century pulpit.

Museums & Galleries

Blackburn Museum - Blackburn
Extensive collections relating to local history archeology, ceramics, geology & natural history. One of the finest collection of coins & fine collection of mediaeval illuminated manuscripts & early printed books.
Bury Museum & Art Gallery - Bury
Houses fine Victorian oil & watercolours. Turner, Constable, Landseer, de Wint.
City Gallery - Manchester
Pre-Raphaelites, Old Masters, Impressionists, modern painters all represented in this fine gallery; also silver & pottery collections.
Higher Mill Museum - Helmshaw
One of the oldest wool textile finishing mills left in Lancashire. Spinning wheels, Hargreave's Spinning Jenny, several of Arkwrights machines, 20 foot water wheel.
Townley Hall Art Gallery & Museum, & Museum of Local Crafts & Industries - Burnley.

Cheshire Gazeteer

Area of outstanding natural beauty
Part of the Peaks National Park
Addington Hall - Macclesfield
15th century Elizabethan Black & White half timbered house.
Bishop Lloyd's House - Chester
17th century half timbered house (restored). Fine carvings. Has associations with Yale University & New Haven, USA.
Chorley Old Hall - Alderley Edge
14th century hall with 16th century Elizabethan wing.
Forfold Hall - Nantwich
17th century Jacobean country house, with fine panelling.

Cheshire & Lancashire

Gawsworth Hall - Macclesfield
Fine Tudor Half timbered Manor House.
Tilting ground. Pictures, furniture,
sculptures, etc.
Lyme Park - Disley
Elizabethan with Palladian exterior by
Leoni. Gibbons carvings. Beautiful park
with herd of red deer.
Peover Hall - Over Peover, Knutsford
16th century- stables of Tudor period;
has the famous magpie ceiling.
Tatton Park - Knutsford
Beautifully decorated & furnished
Georgian House with a fine collection of
glass, china & paintings including Van
Dyke & Canaletto. Landscaping by
Humphrey Repton.
Little Moreton Hall - Nr. Congleton
15th century timbered, moated house
with 16th century wall-paintings.

Cathedrals & Churches

Acton (St. Mary)
13th century with stone seating around
walls. 17th century effigies.
Bunbury (St. Boniface)
14th century collegiate church -
alabaster effigy.
Congleton (St. Peter)
18th century - box pews, brass
candelabrum, 18th century glass.
Chester Cathedral - Chester
Subjected to restoration by Victorians -
14th century choir stalls.
Malpas (St. Oswalds)
15th century - fine screens, some old
stalls, two family chapels.
Mobberley (St. Wilfred)
Mediaeval - 15th century rood screen,
wall paintings, very old glass.
Shotwick (St. Michael)
Twin nave - box pews, 14th century
quatre - foil lights, 3 deck pulpit.
Winwick (St. Oswald)
14th century - splendid roof. Pugin
chancel.
Wrenbury (St. Margaret)
16th century - west gallery, monuments
& hatchments. Box pews.
Liverpool Cathedral - the Anglican
Cathedral was completed in 1980 after
76 years of work. It is of massive
proportions, the largest in the U.K. with
much delicate detailed work.

Museums & Galleries

Grosvenor Museum - Chester
Art, folk history, natural history, Roman
antiquities including a special display of
information about the Roman army.
Chester Heritage Centre - Chester
Interesting exhibition of the architectural
heritage of Chester.
Cheshire Military Museum - Chester
The three local Regiments are
commemorated here.
King Charles Tower - Chester
Chester at the time of the Civil War
illustrated by dioramas.
Museum & Art Gallery - Warrington
Anthropology, geology, ethnology, botany
& natural history. Pottery, porcelain,
glass, collection of early English
watercolours.
West Park Museum & Art Gallery -
Macclesfield
Egyptian collection, oil paintings,
watercolours, sketches by Landseer &
Tunnicliffe.
Norton Priory Museum - Runcorn
Remains of excavated mediaeval priory.
Also wildlife display.
Quarry Bank Mill - Styal
The Mill is a fine example of industrial
building & houses an exhibition of the
cotton industry: the various offices retain
their original furnishing, & the turbine
room has the transmission systems &
two turbines of 1903.
Nether Alderley Mill - Nether Alderley
15th century corn mill which was still
used in 1929. Now restored.
The Albert Dock & Maritime Museum
- Liverpool
Housing the Liverpool Tate Gallery, the
Tate of the North.
Walker Art Gallery - Liverpool
Jodrell Bank - radio telescope &
planetarium.

Historic Monuments

Chester Castle - Chester
Huge square tower remaining.
Roman Amphitheatre - Chester
12th legion site - half excavated.
Beeston Castle - Beeston
Remains of a 13th century fort.
Sandbach Crosses - Sandbach
Carved stone crosses date from the 9th C.

CHESHIRE & LANCASHIRE

Map reference

01 **Hill**   03 **Ahooie**   05 **Rothwell**   07 **J. Smith**

02 **Ikin**   04 **Taylor**   06 **M. Smith**

Column headers (rotated):
- rate £ from - to per double room
- children taken
- evening meals
- animals taken

rate £ from - to per double room	children taken	evening meals	animals taken		

Cotton Farmhouse

£58.00 to £58.00 | Y | N | N | (non-smoking)

Near Rd: A.51

Cotton Farmhouse is surrounded by farmland where Nigel & Clare run a herd of beef cows & their calves & a flock of 300 geese. Wonderfully peaceful but under 4 miles from Chester, it is an ideal base to discover the beautiful city with its Roman origins & unique medieval "rows". All of the bedrooms are large, comfortable & attractively furnished with good attention to detail. Colour T.V., tea/coffee-making facilities, radio & en-suite bathroom for every room. A charming home.
E-mail: info@cottonfarm.co.uk
www.cottonfarm.co.uk

Nigel & Clare Hill   Cotton Farmhouse   Cotton Edmunds   Chester CH3 7PG   Cheshire
Tel: (01244) 336616   Fax 01244 336699   Open: ALL YEAR   Map Ref No. 01

Golborne Manor

£60.00 to £75.00 | Y | Y | N | (non-smoking)

Near Rd: A.41

Golborne Manor is an elegant 19th-century country residence with glorious views, renovated to a high standard & set in 3 1/2 acres of gardens & grounds. Beautifully decorated with spacious en-suite bedrooms. Farmhouse breakfasts. Evening meals (available Mon-Fri) by arrangement. Piano & croquet set available for guests' use. Car park. Easy access for motorways. 10 mins' drive south from Chester on the A.41, turning right a few yards after Van Centre (on the left). Single supplement.
E-mail: annikin@golbornemanor.co.uk
www.golbornemanor.co.uk

Mrs Ann Ikin   Golborne Manor   Platts Lane   Hatton Heath   Chester CH3 9AN   Cheshire
Tel: (01829) 770310   Fax 01829 770370   Open: ALL YEAR   Map Ref No. 02

Longview Hotel & Restaurant

£72.50 to £137.50 | Y | Y | Y | VISA: M'CARD: AMEX:

Near Rd: A.50

Set in this pleasant Cheshire market town overlooking the common is this lovely, friendly hotel, furnished with many antiques that reflect the elegance of this Victorian building. Care has been taken to retain its character, while also providing all comforts for the discerning traveller. All of the 26 en-suite bedrooms are prettily decorated, giving them that cared-for feeling which is echoed throughout the hotel. You are assured of a warm friendly welcome as soon as you step into reception.
E-mail: enquiries@longviewhotel.com
www.longviewhotel.com

Mr & Mrs Ahooie   Longview Hotel   51 & 55 Manchester Road   Knutsford WA16 0LX   Cheshire
Tel: (01565) 632119   Fax 01565 652402   Open: ALL YEAR (Excl. Xmas & New Year)   Map Ref No. 03

Worthenbury Manor

£60.00 to £80.00 | Y | Y | Y | (non-smoking)

see PHOTO over p. 50

Near Rd: A.525, A.41

Surrounded by rolling Cheshire Plains, Welsh Marches & National Trust properties, Worthenbury Manor makes the ideal setting for a relaxing break. In this fully restored Grade II listed building with oak panelling & 4-poster beds, you can indulge yourself with dinner, prepared by a qualified chef using fresh local produce. Guaranteed to be an experience you will want to repeat again & again. An elegant home, situated 2 miles from Bangor on Dee & 4 miles from Malpas. Children over 10.
E-mail: enquiries@worthenburymanor.co.uk
www.worthenburymanor.co.uk

Ian Taylor   Worthenbury Manor   The Manor   Worthenbury   Wrexham LL13 0AW   Cheshire
Tel: (01948) 770342   Open: FEB - NOV   Map Ref No. 04

The Manor.   Worthenbury.

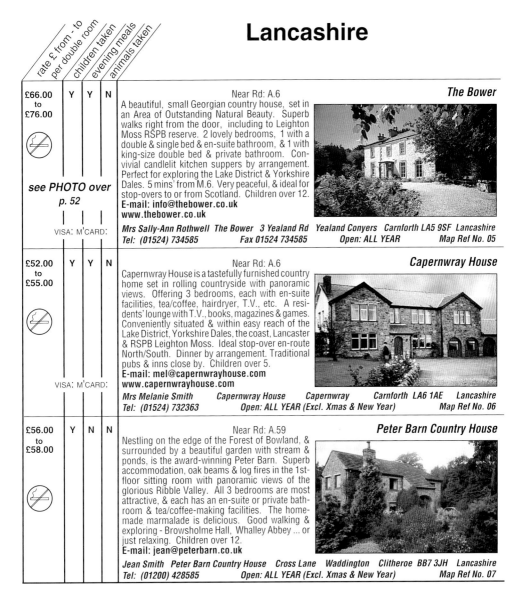

rate £ from - to per double room | children taken | evening meals | animals taken

£66.00 to £76.00 — Y Y N

see PHOTO over p. 52

VISA: M'CARD:

The Bower

Near Rd: A.6

A beautiful, small Georgian country house, set in an Area of Outstanding Natural Beauty. Superb walks right from the door, including to Leighton Moss RSPB reserve. 2 lovely bedrooms, 1 with a double & single bed & en-suite bathroom, & 1 with king-size double bed & private bathroom. Convivial candlelit kitchen suppers by arrangement. Perfect for exploring the Lake District & Yorkshire Dales. 5 mins' from M.6. Very peaceful, & ideal for stop-overs to or from Scotland. Children over 12.
E-mail: info@thebower.co.uk
www.thebower.co.uk

Mrs Sally-Ann Rothwell The Bower 3 Yealand Rd Yealand Conyers Carnforth LA5 9SF Lancashire
Tel: (01524) 734585   Fax 01524 734585   Open: ALL YEAR   Map Ref No. 05

£52.00 to £55.00 — Y Y N

VISA: M'CARD:

Capernwray House

Near Rd: A.6

Capernwray House is a tastefully furnished country home set in rolling countryside with panoramic views. Offering 3 bedrooms, each with en-suite facilities, tea/coffee, hairdryer, T.V., etc. A residents' lounge with T.V., books, magazines & games. Conveniently situated & within easy reach of the Lake District, Yorkshire Dales, the coast, Lancaster & RSPB Leighton Moss. Ideal stop-over en-route North/South. Dinner by arrangement. Traditional pubs & inns close by. Children over 5.
E-mail: mel@capernwrayhouse.com
www.capernwrayhouse.com

Mrs Melanie Smith   Capernwray House   Capernwray   Carnforth LA6 1AE   Lancashire
Tel: (01524) 732363   Open: ALL YEAR (Excl. Xmas & New Year)   Map Ref No. 06

£56.00 to £58.00 — Y N N

Peter Barn Country House

Near Rd: A.59

Nestling on the edge of the Forest of Bowland, & surrounded by a beautiful garden with stream & ponds, is the award-winning Peter Barn. Superb accommodation, oak beams & log fires in the 1st-floor sitting room with panoramic views of the glorious Ribble Valley. All 3 bedrooms are most attractive, & each has an en-suite or private bathroom & tea/coffee-making facilities. The homemade marmalade is delicious. Good walking & exploring - Browsholme Hall, Whalley Abbey ... or just relaxing. Children over 12.
E-mail: jean@peterbarn.co.uk

Jean Smith Peter Barn Country House Cross Lane Waddington Clitheroe BB7 3JH Lancashire
Tel: (01200) 428585   Open: ALL YEAR (Excl. Xmas & New Year)   Map Ref No. 07

Visit our website at:
http://www.bestbandb.co.uk

The Bower. Yealand Conyers.

Cornwall

Cornwall
(West Country)

Cornwall is an ancient Celtic land, a narrow granite peninsula with a magnificent coastline of over 300 miles & wild stretches of moorland.

The north coast, washed by Atlantic breakers, has firm golden sands & soaring cliffs. The magnificent beaches at Bude offer excellent surfing & a few miles to the south you can visit the picturesque harbour at Boscastle & the cliff-top castle at Tintagel with its legends of King Arthur. Newquay, with its beaches stretching for over seven miles, sheltered coves & modern hotels & shops, is the premier resort on Cornwall's Atlantic coast. St. Ives, another surfing resort, has great charm which has attracted artists for so long & is an ideal place from which to explore the Land's End peninsula.

The south coast is a complete contrast - wooded estuaries, sheltered coves, little fishing ports, & popular resorts. Penzance, with its warmth & vivid colours, is an all-the-year-round resort & has wonderful views across the bay to St. Michael's Mount. Here are excellent facilities for sailing & deep-sea fishing, as there are at Falmouth & Fowey with their superb harbours. Mevagissey, Polperro & Looe are fine examples of traditional Cornish fishing villages.

In the far west of Cornwall, you can hear about a fascinating legend: the lost land of Lyonesse - a whole country that was drowned by the sea. The legend goes that the waters cover a rich & fertile country, which had 140 parish churches. The Anglo-Saxon Chronicle records two great storms within a hundred years, which drowned many towns & innumerate people. Submerged forests are known to lie around these coasts - & in Mount's Bay beech trees have been found with the nuts still hanging on the branches, so suddenly were they swamped.

Today, St Michael's Mount & the Isles of Scilly are said to be all that remains of the vanished land. St. Michael's Mount, with its tiny fishing village & dramatic castle, can be visited on foot at low tide or by boat at high water. The Isles of Scilly, 28 miles beyond Land's End, have five inhabited islands, including Tresco with its sub-tropical gardens. Day trips to the numerous uninhabited islands are a special feature of a Scilly holiday.

Inland Cornwall also has its attractions. To the east of Bodmin, the county town, are the open uplands of Bodmin Moor, with the county's highest peaks at Rough Tor & Brown Willy. "Jamaica Inn", immortalised in the novel by Daphne du Maurier, stands on the lonely road across the moor, & "Frenchman's Creek" is on a hidden inlet of the Helford River.

There is a seemingly endless number & variety of Cornish villages in estuaries, wooded, pastoral or moorland settings, & here customs & traditions are maintained. In Helston the famous "Fleury Dance" is still performed, & at the ancient port of Padstow, May Day celebrating involves decorating the houses with green boughs & parading the Hobby Horse through the street to the tune of St. George's Song.

Helford Creek

Cornwall

Cornwall Gazeteer

Areas of outstanding natural beauty.
Almost the entire county.

Historic Houses & Castles

Anthony House - Torpoint
18th century - beautiful & quite unspoiled Queen Anne house, excellent panelling & fine period furnishings.

Cotehele House - Calstock
15th & 16th century house, still contains the original furniture, tapestry, armour, etc.

Ebbingford Manor - Bude
12th century Cornish manor house, with walled garden.

Godolphin House - Helston
Tudor - 17th century colonnaded front.

Lanhydrock - Bodmin
17th century - splendid plaster ceilings, picture gallery with family portraits 17th/20th centuries.

Mount Edgcumbe House - Plymouth
Tudor style mansion - restored after destruction in 1949. Hepplewhite furniture & portrait by Joshua Reynolds.

St. Michael's Mount - Penzance
Mediaeval castle & 17th century with 18th & 19th century additions.

Pencarrow House & Gardens - Bodmin
18th century Georgian Mansion - collection of paintings, china & furniture - mile long drive through fine woodlands & gardens.

Old Post Office - Tintagel
14th century manor house in miniature - large hall used as Post Office for a period, hence the name.

Trewithen - Probus Nr. Truro
Early Georgian house with lovely gardens.

Trerice - St. Newlyn East
16th century Elizabethan house, small with elaborate facade. Excellent fireplaces, plaster ceilings, miniature gallery & minstrels' gallery.

Cathedral & Churches

Altarnun (St. Nonna)
15th century, Norman font, 16th century bench ends, fine rood screen.

Bisland (St. Protus & St. Hyacinth)
15th century granite tower - carved wagon roofs, slate floor. Georgian wine - glass pulpit, fine screen.

Kilkhampton (St. James)
16th century with fine Norman doorway, arcades & wagon roofs.

Laneast (St. Michael or St. Sedwell)
13th century, 15th century enlargement, 16th century pulpit, some painted glass.

Lanteglos-by-Fowley (St. Willow)
14th century, refashioned 15th century, 13th century font, 15th century brasses & altar tomb, 16th century bench ends.

Launcells (St. Andrew)
Interior unrestored - old plaster & ancient roofs remaining, fine Norman font with 17th century cover, box pews, pulpit, reredos, 3 sided alter rails.

Probus (St. Probus & St. Gren)
16th century tower, splendid arcades, three great East windows.

St. Keverne (St. Keverne)
Fine tower & spire. Wall painting in 15th century interior.

St. Neot (St. Neot)
Decorated tower - 16th century exterior, buttressed & double-aisled. Many windows of mediaeval glass renewed in 19th century.

Museums & Galleries

Museum of Witchcraft - Boscastle
Relating to witches, implements & customs.

Military Museum - Bodmin
History of Duke of Cornwall's Light Infantry.

Public Library & Museum - Cambourne
Collections of mineralogy, archaeology, local antiquities & history.

Cornish Museum - East Looe
Collection of relics relating to witchcraft customs & superstitions. Folk life & culture of district.

Helston Borough Museum - Helston
Folk life & culture of area around Lizard.

Museum of Nautical Art - Penzance
Exhibition of salvaged gold & silver treasures from underwater wreck of 1700's.

Museum of Smuggling - Polperro
Activities of smugglers, past & present.

Cornwall

Penlee House Museum - Penlee, Penzance
Archaeology & local history & tin mining exhibits.
Barbara Hepworth Museum - St. Ives
Sculpture, letters, documents, photographs, etc., exhibited in house where Barbara Hepworth lived.
Old Mariners Church - St. Ives
St. Ives Society of Artists hold exhibitions here.
County Museum & Art Gallery - Truro
Ceramics, art local history & antiquities, Cornish mineralogy.

Historic Monuments

Cromwell's Castle - Tresco (Scilly Isles)
17th century castle.
King Charles' Fort - Tresco (Scilly Isles)
16th century fort.
Old Blockhouse - Tresco (Scilly Isles)
16th century coastal battery.
Harry's Wall - St. Mary's (Scilly Isles)
Tudor Coastal battery
Ballowall Barrow - St. Just
Prehistoric barrow.
Pendennis Castle - Falmouth
Fort from time of Henry VII.

Restormel Castle - Lostwithiel
13th century ruins.
St. Mawes Castle - St. Mawes
16th century fortified castle.
Tintagel Castle - Tintagel
Mediaeval ruin on wild coast, King Arthur's legendary castle.

Things to see & do

Camel trail - Padstow to Bodmin
12 miles of recreation path along scenic route, suitable for walkers, cyclists & horse-riders.
Tresco Abbey Gardens - Tresco
Collection of sub-tropical flora
Trethorne Leisure Farm - Launceston
Visitors are encouraged to feed & stroke the farm animals
Seal sanctuary - Gweek Nr. Helston
Seals, exhibition hall, nature walk, aquarium, seal hospital, donkey paddock.
Dobwalls Theme Park - Nr. Liskeard
2 miles of scenically dramatic miniature railway based on the American railroad.
Padstow tropical bird gardens - Padstow
Mynack Theatre - Porthcurno

Lands End.

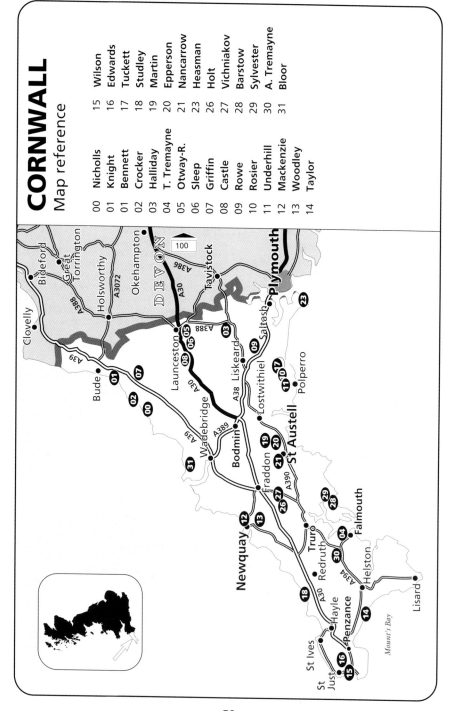

CORNWALL
Map reference

00	Nicholls	15	Wilson
01	Knight	16	Edwards
01	Bennett	17	Tuckett
02	Crocker	18	Studley
03	Halliday	19	Martin
04	T. Tremayne	20	Epperson
05	Otway-R.	21	Nancarrow
06	Sleep	23	Heasman
07	Griffin	26	Holt
08	Castle	27	Vichniakov
09	Rowe	28	Barstow
10	Rosier	29	Sylvester
11	Underhill	30	A. Tremayne
12	Mackenzie	31	Bloor
13	Woodley		
14	Taylor		

rate £ from - to per double room	children taken	evening meals	animals taken	

£59.00 to £79.00 — Y N Y

Trerosewill Farm

Near Rd: A.39

Trerosewill offers luxurious award-winning accommodation overlooking the picturesque fishing village of Boscastle. All rooms are en-suite & equipped to the highest standard. King-size 4-poster bed with en-suite corner bath Jacuzzi. Unsurpassed panoramic sea views of Lundy Island & the North Cornish coast. An extensive breakfast menu including home-made preserves & bread. Kennelling available by arrangement. Farm Trail & badger watching. Children over 7.
E-mail: enquiries@trerosewill.co.uk
www.trerosewill.co.uk

VISA: M'CARD:

Steve & Cheryl Nicholls   Trerosewill Farm   *Paradise   Boscastle PL35 0BL   Cornwall*
Tel: (01840) 250545   Fax 01840 250545   *Open: Mid Feb - Mid Nov   Map Ref No. 00*

£50.00 to £60.00 — N N N

The Lodge

Near Rd: A.39

The Lodge is set in its own extensive gardens with far-reaching rural views. It is approached by a long sweeping drive with ample space for parking. There is a delightful guest lounge with T.V. where tea & coffee are available, & an attractive double room with en-suite facilities. A full English breakfast is served in the dining room, which has stunning views across the valley. The peace & tranquillity of The Lodge offers an excellent base from which to explore beautiful Cornwall.
E-mail: jim.sylvia@ukonline.co.uk
www.bestbandb.co.uk

Mrs Sylvia Bennett   The Lodge   Crackington Haven   Bude EX23 0JW   Cornwall
Tel: (01840) 230347   Fax 01840 230347   Open: ALL YEAR   Map Ref No. 01

£60.00 to £70.00 — Y Y N

Trevigue Farm

Near Rd: A.39

Trevigue is a 16th-century farmhouse, built around a cobbled courtyard, nestled high into the rugged cliffs of north Cornwall. Warm, inviting, exquisitely furnished - a luxurious, peaceful place to stay. Take a short stroll to the top of the cliffs to breath in the staggering views & to work up an appetite for a perfectly cooked breakfast using all local produce. The very popular restaurant is open on Friday & Saturday nights only. A delightful home where you are very welcome. Children over 12.
E-mail: trevigue@talk21.com
www.trevigue.co.uk

VISA: M'CARD:

Janet Crocker   Trevigue Farm   Crackington Haven   Bude EX23 0LR   Cornwall
Tel: (01840) 230492/230418   Fax 01840 230418   Open: FEB - NOV   Map Ref No. 02

£64.00 to £64.00 — Y N N

Browda

Near Rd: A.388

This 250-acre organic farm is sited in a wonderfully quiet & unspoilt river valley & centres around the large, comfortable Grade II listed 17th-century farmhouse. The atmosphere is informal & friendly, the emphasis on quality & simplicity. Bedrooms (1 double en-suite, 1 double with private facilities & 1 single) are traditionally furnished & all overlook the gardens. Eat breakfast outside (weather permitting) & afterwards explore the woods, fields & lakes. No T.V. (2 couples maximum plus 1 if all the same party.) Children over 10.
www.bestbandb.co.uk

Mrs Lavinia Halliday   Browda   Linkinhorne   Callington PL17 7NB   Cornwall
Tel: (01579) 362235   Open: ALL YEAR   Map Ref No. 03

Manor Farm. Crackington Haven.

Cornwall

Column headers (rotated): rate £ from - to / per double room | children taken | evening meals | animals taken

---

£70.00 to £80.00 | N | N | N

(non-smoking symbol)

see PHOTO over p. 58

Near Rd: A.39

Manor Farm

A really super 11th-century manor house, retaining all its former charm & elegance. Mentioned in the 1086 Domesday book, it belonged to the Earl of Mortain, half-brother to William the Conqueror. Delightfully located in a beautiful & secluded position, & surrounded by both attractive gardens & 40 acres of farmland. Guest rooms have private facilities. Staying at Manor Farm is often considered the highlight of the trip. Only 1 mile from the beach. Non-smokers only. West Country winner of the Best Bed & Breakfast award.
www.bestbandb.co.uk

Mrs Muriel Knight   *Manor Farm*   Crackington Haven EX23 0JW   *Cornwall*
Tel: (01840) 230304   Open: ALL YEAR (Excl. Xmas Day)   Map Ref No. 01

£70.00 to £80.00 | Y | Y | N

(non-smoking symbol)

VISA: M'CARD:

Near Rd: A.39

'The Home' Country House Hotel

A quiet & charming country house, with views over Maenporth & Falmouth Bay. Accommodation is in 18 comfortable rooms, 16 with a private/en-suite bath/shower. All have tea/coffee-making facilities. A colour-T.V. lounge & bar are available, & guests may relax in the beautiful sheltered garden. A golf course & boating facilities nearby. A friendly host, who prepares delicious meals using local produce. Special diets provided for by arrangement. Children over 10. Animals by arrangement.
www.bestbandb.co.uk

T. P. Tremayne   *'The Home' Country House Hotel*   Penjerrick Budock Water Falmouth TR11 5EE
Tel: (01326) 250427   Fax 01326 250143   Open: APR - OCT   Map Ref No. 04

£70.00 to £70.00 | Y | Y | Y

(non-smoking symbol)

Near Rd: B.3254

Hornacott

Hornacott nestles in the River Inny Valley with sloping gardens & a stream surrounded by fields. Offering a spacious suite of rooms in a wing of the house, with a private sitting room, bedroom & en-suite bathroom & an additional single room for an accompanying family member/friend. Guests really enjoy the space, comfort & privacy amidst peaceful surroundings & the visitors book is a testament to happy guests, many of whom return again. Evening meals & animals by arrangement.
E-mail: otwayruthven@btinternet.com
www.hornacott.co.uk

Jos & Mary-Anne Otway-Ruthven   *Hornacott*   South Petherwin Launceston PL15 7LH Cornwall
Tel: (01566) 782461   Fax 01566 782461   Open: ALL YEAR (Excl. Xmas)   Map Ref No. 05

£50.00 to £60.00 | Y | N | N

(non-smoking symbol)

VISA: M'CARD:

Near Rd: A.30

Trevadlock Farm

Superb accommodation on a working farm in the heart of the countryside. Delicious breakfasts, using local produce, just perfect for a relaxing holiday. Ideally placed for touring Cornwall & Devon north & south coasts, Eden, Heligan & National Trust properties. A.30 - 1 1/2 miles. Well-appointed rooms with hospitality trays, T.V. & hairdryers & central heating; so enjoy a special break at any time of year. London 4 hrs. Children over 5. See web site for more.
E-mail: trevadlock@farming.co.uk
www.trevadlock.co.uk

Mrs Barbara Sleep   *Trevadlock Farm*   *Trevadlock*   Launceston PL15 7PW   *Cornwall*
Tel: (01566) 782239   Fax 01566 782239   Open: ALL YEAR   Map Ref No. 06

---

	rate £ from - to per double room	children taken	evening meals	animals taken

Wheatley Farm

Near Rd: A.39, A.30

Superb accommodation in a lovely character Victorian farmhouse awaits you at Wheatley Farm. Peaceful location, perfect for a relaxing holiday, which brings guests back time & time again. Excellent base for exploring Cornwall & Devon, within easy reach of the Eden Project & near the coast. Luxury indoor heated swimming pool, plus sauna & spa. Home-made food, using local produce - superb dinners. A lovely welcoming place to stay at any time of year. Children over 12.
E-mail: valerie@wheatley-farm.co.uk
www.wheatley-farm.co.uk

£58.00 to £63.00 — Y / Y / N

VISA: M'CARD:

Mrs Valerie Griffin Wheatley Farm Maxworthy Launceston PL15 8LY Cornwall
Tel: (01566) 781232 Open: FEB - OCT Map Ref No. 07

Trekenner Court

Near Rd: A.395

Trekenner Court is in a tranquil spot with glorious views over Bodmin Moor. Set in 4 acres, it's built around a Mediterranean-style courtyard with Oleanders & geraniums. In good weather breakfast outside by the fountain with fresh orange juice, local bacon, sausages & eggs from the family's hens. Dinner by arrangement. En-suite bedrooms & guest sitting-room. Many pubs & restaurants nearby. The glorious surfing beaches of North Cornwall are 20 mins, golf 5 mins, Eden 45 mins, gardens & National Trust properties. Stabling.
E-mail: trekennercourt@hotmail.co.uk

£60.00 to £60.00 — Y / Y / N

Mr & Mrs J. Castle Trekenner Court Pipers Pool Launceston PL15 8QG Cornwall
Tel: (01566) 880118 Open: ALL YEAR Map Ref No.08

Tregondale Farm

Near Rd: A.390, A.38

The Rowe family make your stay special. There is a wealth of charm & period features in this manor house with original walled garden. Peaceful, lovely countryside. 3 pretty en-suite bedrooms with T.V. & tea/coffee. Log fires. Home local produce a speciality. Tennis court. Woodland Farm Trail. 200 acre mixed farm, an abundance of wildlife & flowers, award-winning pedigree south Devon cattle & lambs in spring. Near many National Trust properties, Heligan Garden & Eden Project. Looe 6 miles.
E-mail: tregondale@connectfree.co.uk
www.tregondalefarm.co.uk

£50.00 to £60.00 — Y / Y / N

VISA: M'CARD:

Stephanie Rowe Tregondale Farm Menheniot Liskeard PL14 3RG Cornwall
Tel: (01579) 342407 Fax 01579 342407 Open: ALL YEAR Map Ref No. 09

Allhays Country Bed & Breakfast

Near Rd: A.387

Allhays is a spacious family house built in the late 1930s, set in its own peaceful gardens with breathtaking views over the wild & romantic remoteness of Talland Bay. Ideal for walking the coastal path. Many National Trust properties are nearby, as well as the Lost Gardens of Heligan & the Eden Project. Very comfortable accommodation. Ample car parking. Extensive breakfasts with home-baked breads, free range & organic produce. Peace & quiet. Children over 9 years.
E-mail: info@allhays.co.uk
www.allhays.co.uk

£70.00 to £90.00 — Y / N / N

VISA: M'CARD: AMEX:

Mr & Mrs Barry Rosier Allhays Country Bed & Breakfast Porthallow Talland Bay Looe PL13 2JB
Tel: (01503) 273188 Open: ALL YEAR (Excl. Dec) Map Ref No. 10

Trenance Lodge.   Newquay.

	rate £ from - to per double room	children taken	evening meals	animals taken

Higher Polgassic

Near Rd: A.387

Higher Polgassic is a modern bungalow with 3 very comfortable en-suite guest rooms. Situated in peaceful countryside with far-reaching views. A large parking area & 2 1/2 acres of grounds. Superb breakfasts & evening meals (by arrangement). 1 1/2 miles from the beach & the spectacular coastal path. Polperro, Fowey & Looe are nearby. Higher Polgassic is also within easy reach of Cornwall's many gardens & the Eden Project.

E-mail: info@higherpolgassic.co.uk
www.higherpolgassic.co.uk

£50.00 to £60.00 — Y Y Y

(non-smoking)

June & David Underhill   Higher Polgassic   Lansallos   Looe PL13 2PY   Cornwall
Tel: (01503) 272454   Fax 01503 272454   Open: ALL YEAR   Map Ref No. 11

Trenance Lodge Hotel

Near Rd: A.392

An attractive house standing in its own grounds, overlooking the lakes & gardens of Trenance Valley, leading to the Gannel Estuary. The restaurant has a reputation for serving the finest fresh local food in elegant surroundings. Adjoining the restaurant is a spacious, relaxing bar lounge. Accommodation is in 5 comfortable bedrooms, en-suite, with T.V., radio & tea/coffee facilities. An excellent base for touring, with a warm welcome assured.

E-mail: info@trenance-lodge.co.uk
www.trenance-lodge.co.uk

£60.00 to £70.00 — N Y N

see PHOTO over p. 61

VISA: M'CARD:

Mac & Jennie Mackenzie   Trenance Lodge Hotel   83 Trenance Road   Newquay TR7 2HW   Cornwall
Tel: (01637) 876702   Fax 01637 878772   Open: ALL YEAR   Map Ref No. 12

Degembris Farmhouse

Near Rd: A.3058

The original manor house of Degembris was built in the 16th century & is now used as a barn. The present-day house, surrounded by attractive gardens, was built a mere 200 years ago, & its slate-hung exterior blends well with the rolling countryside. 5 bedrooms, 3 en-suite, each prettily decorated, with dried flowers & stripped pine enhancing the country atmosphere. Hearty breakfasts are served. Centrally situated in superb countryside, yet close to the sea, this is the perfect holiday base.

E-mail: kathy@degembris.co.uk
www.degembris.co.uk

£56.00 to £60.00 — Y N N

(non-smoking)

VISA: M'CARD:

Kathy Woodley   Degembris Farmhouse   St. Newlyn East   Newquay TR8 5HY   Cornwall
Tel: (01872) 510555   Fax 01872 510230   Open: ALL YEAR (Excl. Xmas)   Map Ref No. 13

Ednovean Farm

Near Rd: A.394

A small farm nestling above the peaceful village of Perranuthnoe, with glorious views towards St. Michael's Mount & Mounts Bay. A stunning 17th-century barn, lovingly renovated, with elegant, country-style en-suite bedrooms, some with private terraces or 4-poster beds. All with little luxuries to spoil you. Stroll to the village, cliff-top walks, secluded coves or just enjoy the view. The perfect spot for a relaxing break.

E-mail: info@ednoveanfarm.co.uk
www.ednoveanfarm.co.uk

£75.00 to £95.00 — N N N

(non-smoking)

see PHOTO over p. 63

VISA: M'CARD:

Mr & Mrs C. Taylor   Ednovean Farm   Perranuthnoe   Nr. Penzance TR20 9LZ   Cornwall
Tel: (01736) 711883   Fax 01736 710480   Open: ALL YEAR (Excl. Xmas)   Map Ref No. 14

Ednovean Farm   Perranuthnoe.

Trenderway Farm. Pelynt.

Cornwall

Column headers (rotated):
- rate £ from - to per double room
- children taken
- evening meals taken
- animals taken

Boscean Country Hotel

£50.00 to £56.00	Y	Y	N

🚭 (no smoking symbol)

VISA: M'CARD:

Near Rd: A.3071

Set in 3 acres of private walled gardens in an Area of Outstanding Natural Beauty on the heritage coast. The Boscean Country Hotel is an ideal base from which to explore west Cornwall. Built in 1912, this Edwardian country house has a magnificent oak panelled entrance hall, lounge, dining room & staircase from which there are stunning sea views. 12 en-suite bedrooms. Log fires. Licensed bar & evening meals. Children over 7.
E-mail: boscean@aol.com
www.bosceancountryhotel.co.uk

Dennis & Linda Wilson   Boscean Country Hotel   Bosweddon Road   St. Just   Penzance TR19 7QP
Tel: (01736) 788748   Fax 01736 788748   Open: ALL YEAR   Map Ref No. 15

The Mews B & B

£60.00 to £65.00	Y	N	N

🚭 (no smoking symbol)

VISA: M'CARD: AMEX:

Near Rd: A.30

An attractive granite 18th-century home, overlooking a cobbled courtyard within 2 acres of lush, tropical grounds amidst a private medieval estate. The spacious family room, with en-suite bathroom, is elegantly appointed & traditional Cornish or local fish breakfasts are your hosts' specialities. Perfectly located to explore St. Michael's Mount, Land's End, St. Ives, Truro, the Minack, Eden, National Trust Gardens & abundant coves & beaches together with services for the magical Isles of Scilly. Self-catering cottage available.
E-mail: michael.edwards49@btinternet.com

Janet & Michael Edwards   The Mews B & B   Rosehill   Penzance TR20 8TE   Cornwall
Tel: (01736) 350411   Fax 01736 350411   Open: ALL YEAR   Map Ref No. 16

Trenderway Farm

£70.00 to £90.00	N	N	N

🚭 (no smoking symbol)

see PHOTO over p. 64

VISA: M'CARD:

Near Rd: A.387

Built in the late 16th century, this attractive award-winning farmhouse is set in peaceful, beautiful countryside at the head of the Polperro valley, 5 mins' from the fishing ports of Looe & Polperro. Bedrooms here are superb, individually decorated with the flair of a professional interior designer. All bedrooms have large en-suite facilities with bath & shower. Excellent restaurants & inns are nearby. Perfectly located to visit historic houses, The Lost Gardens of Heligan & the Eden Project.
E-mail: enquiries@trenderwayfarmholidays.co.uk
www.trenderwayfarmholidays.co.uk

Lynne & Anthony Tuckett   Trenderway Farm   Pelynt   Polperro PL13 2LY   Cornwall
Tel: (01503) 272214   Fax 01503 272991   Open: ALL YEAR (Excl. Xmas)   Map Ref No. 17

Aviary Court

£72.00 to £75.00	Y	Y	N

VISA: M'CARD:

Near Rd: A.30

Couples return each year to this charming 300-year-old country house set in 2 acres of secluded, well-kept gardens with tennis court. An ideal touring location - coast 5 mins' away & St. Ives Tate, Heligan, Eden Project, St. Michael's Mount & Maritime Museum all within easy reach. 6 bedrooms with en-suite, tea/coffee facilities, biscuits, phone & view of the gardens. The restaurant serves delicious food (prior arrangement advisable) with a selection of wine. Children over 3 yrs.
E-mail: info@aviarycourthotel.co.uk
www.aviarycourthotel.co.uk

The Studley Family   Aviary Court   Mary's Well   Illogan   Redruth TR16 4QZ   Cornwall
Tel: (01209) 842256   Fax 01209 843744   Open: ALL YEAR   Map Ref No. 18

Nanscawen House. St. Blazey.

Cornwall

rate £ from - to per double room	children taken	evening meals	animals taken

---

£92.00 to £110.00

🚭 (no smoking)

see PHOTO over p. 66

VISA: M'CARD:

Y	N	N

Nanscawen Manor House

Near Rd: A.390

A beautiful 15th-century manor house with an elegant, stately Georgian wing, set in 5 acres of grounds with stunning views across a romantic valley. Keith & Fiona offer you a relaxed welcome & friendly hospitality. Enjoy the heated outdoor swimming pool. The luxurious bedrooms are all en-suite, & beautifully decorated to the highest standards, with spa baths. Breakfasts are a real treat. Ideal for visiting Heligan, Fowey, Lanhydrock & the Eden Project (2 miles.) Children over 12.
E-mail: keith@nanscawen.com
www.nanscawen.com

Keith Martin   Nanscawen Manor House   Prideaux Rd Luxulyan Nr. St. Blazey St. Austell PL24 2SR
Tel: (01726) 814488   Open: ALL YEAR   Map Ref No. 19

£100.00 to £120.00

🚭 (no smoking)

see PHOTO over p. 68

VISA: M'CARD: AMEX:

N	Y	N

Anchorage House

Near Rd: A.390

Anchorage House is a national award-winning, luxury guest lodge that has the feel of a small, private hotel offering candlelit suppers, Spa treatments, pool & gym. Located in the centre of Cornwall & only 5 mins from the Eden Project & Carlyon Bay beach & golf, guests are treated to large, comfy beds, sparkling clean bedrooms, luxurious bathrooms with huge tubs & separate power showers. Breakfast is divine & suppers in the Glass Room magical. Everything is immaculate.
E-mail: stay@anchoragehouse.co.uk
www.anchoragehouse.co.uk

Jane & Steve Epperson   Anchorage House   Nettles Corner   Boscundle   St. Austell PL25 3RH
Tel: (01726) 814071   Open: MAR - NOV   Map Ref No. 20

£65.00 to £70.00

🚭 (no smoking)

VISA: M'CARD:

Y	N	N

Poltarrow Farm

Near Rd: A.390

The charming farmhouse is set in 45 acres with commanding views across rolling countryside. The individually decorated & attractively furnished en-suite bedrooms include T.V. & tea/coffee tray. Breakfast is served in the conservatory & is made using fresh local & organic produce. Enjoy a swim in the indoor heated swimming pool or just relax in front of a log fire in the quiet & comfortable sitting room. Ideally situated for visiting both the Eden Project & Heligan Gardens. Children over 5.
E-mail: enquire@poltarrow.co.uk
www.poltarrow.co.uk

Judith Nancarrow   Poltarrow Farm   St. Mewan   St. Austell PL26 7DR   Cornwall
Tel: (01726) 67111   Fax 01726 67111   Open: ALL YEAR (Excl. Xmas & New Year)   Map Ref No. 21

£50.00 to £70.00

🚭 (no smoking)

Y	Y	N

Cliff House

Near Rd: A.374

This Grade II listed, 17th-century building, converted from 2 cottages into 1 house around 150 years ago. Although modernised to include en-suite facilities, it still retains many original features. A drawing room, with wonderful views, log fires, T.V. etc. is available for guests' use. It has a large balcony overlooking Plymouth Sound, Cawsand Bay & the village. Ann is an enthusiastic wholefood cook, & meals (by arrangement) include home-made soups, mousses & freshly baked bread.
E-mail: chkingsand@aol.com
www.cliffhouse-kingsand.co.uk

Ann Heasman   Cliff House   Devonport Hill   Kingsand   Torpoint PL10 1NJ   Cornwall
Tel: (01752) 823110   Fax 01752 822595   Open: ALL YEAR   Map Ref No. 23

Anchorage House Guest Lodge. Tregrehan.

Column headers (rotated):
- rate £ from - to per double room
- children taken
- evening meals taken
- animals taken

Sheviock Barton

£60.00 to £60.00	Y	N	Y

VISA:

Near Rd: A.374

Situated in the centre of the small unspoilt village of Sheviock, directly opposite the 13th-century church. The 300-year-old house has been sympathetically restored & offers 3 bedrooms (1 family & 2 doubles), each with T.V. & en-suite facilities. Also, a guest sitting room plus a games room. Enjoy breakfast in the farmhouse kitchen with Aga. Set on the Rame Peninsula, there are many beaches within easy reach & lovely fishing villages & country houses to visit. Eden Project - 35 mins' by car.
E-mail: thebarton@sheviock.freeserve.co.uk
www.sheviockbarton.co.uk

Carol & Tony Johnson   Sheviock Barton   Sheviock   Torpoint PL11 3EH   Cornwall
Tel: (01503) 230793 Mobile 07775 688403 Open: ALL YEAR (Ex. Xmas & New Year) Map Ref No. 25

Oxturn House

£52.00 to £60.00	Y	N	N

Near Rd: A.30

Barbara & Ian's main priority is your comfort & care at Oxturn House. The bedrooms are spacious & prettily decorated with lovely rural views & include 2 super king-size doubles/twins with all amenities. Guests are welcome to relax in the elegant drawing room, the garden or on the terrace. A local pub serves good food & other restaurants are a short drive. Truro is 10 mins' by car & there is easy access to the Eden Project, Heligan Gardens & both coasts. Children over 12.
E-mail: oxturnhouse@hotmail.com
www.oxturnhouse.co.uk

Mrs Barabara Holt   Oxturn House   Ladock   Truro TR2 4NQ   Cornwall
Tel: (01726) 884348   Fax 01726 884248   Open: FEB - NOV   Map Ref No. 26

Bissick Old Mill

£69.00 to £75.00	Y	N	N

VISA: M'CARD:

Near Rd: A.30, A.390

Bissick Old Mill, formerly a working corn mill, is conveniently situated in the village of Ladock (10 mins' drive from Truro), & provides exceptional standards of comfort, cuisine & hospitality. Its central position makes it an ideal base from which to visit all areas of Cornwall, whether it be on business or purely for pleasure. A residential licence. Children over 10 years welcome. A perfect spot for a relaxing holiday.
E-mail: sonia.v@bissickoldmill.ndo.co.uk
www.bestbandb.co.uk

Mikhail & Sonia Vichniakov   Bissick Old Mill   Ladock   Truro TR2 4PG   Cornwall
Tel: (01726) 882557   Fax 01726 884057   Open: FEB - NOV   Map Ref No. 27

Crugsillick Manor

£86.00 to £114.00	Y	Y	Y

VISA: M'CARD:

Near Rd: A.3078

A hidden treasure of the Roseland Peninsula, one of Cornwall's loveliest areas - meandering lanes, unspoilt fishing villages & sheltered coves. This beautiful Grade II listed Queen Anne manor house, offers peace & comfort. Stroll down the smugglers' path below the house to glorious beaches & spectacular coastline, visit historic houses, the Eden Project & Falmouth's Maritime Museum. Dine on freshly caught seafood & home-grown vegetables. Children 12+. Dogs by arrangement.
E-mail: barstow@adtel.co.uk
www.adtel.co.uk

Oliver & Rosemary Barstow   Crugsillick Manor   Ruan High Lanes   Truro TR2 5LJ   Cornwall
Tel: (01872) 501214   Fax 01872 501874   Open: ALL YEAR   Map Ref No. 28

Cornwall

Polsue Manor

Near Rd: A.3078

Graham & Annabelle Sylvester moved to Polsue Manor 7 years ago. It is very much a family-run B & B. While staying here you are well-placed for the Eden Project, Lost Gardens of Heligan, Trewithen & many of the outstanding National Trust gardens. A footpath leads to a wide, safe, sandy beach. En-suite bathrooms, attractively decorated bedrooms, a well-proportioned sitting room & dining room and a warm welcome await you at Polsue Manor.
E-mail: annabellesylvester@tiscali.co.uk
www.polsuemanor.co.uk

| | £80.00 to £80.00 | Y | N | Y |

VISA: M'CARD:

Graham & Annabelle Sylvester   **Polsue Manor**   **Ruanhighlanes**   **Truro TR2 5LU**   **Cornwall**
Tel: (01872) 501270   Fax 01872 501177   Open: ALL YEAR   Map Ref No. 29

Apple Tree Cottage

Near Rd: A.39

Apple Tree Cottage, set amid rolling countryside with delightful gardens & river, is furnished with country antiques & has a warm, welcoming atmos-phere. The large lounge has a log fire, & traditional farmhouse breakfasts, cooked on the Aga, are taken in the sunlit dining room. The attractive bedrooms have pine double beds, tea/coffee facili-ties, washbasins & lovely views. Several National Trust gardens & the famous Trebah Gardens on the Helford River are close by. Children over 10.
E-mail: appletreecottage@talk21.com
www.cornwall-online.co.uk

| | £56.00 to £60.00 | Y | N | Y |

Ann Tremayne   **Apple Tree Cottage**   **Laity Moor**   **Ponsanooth**   **Truro TR3 7HR**   **Cornwall**
Tel: (01872) 865047   Open: ALL YEAR (Excl. Xmas)   Map Ref No. 30

Porteath Barn

Near Rd: B.3314

A beautifully converted 'H' shaped barn offering guest accommodation in 1 wing on the ground floor. Situated in a secluded valley of 8 acres with a track leading down to the coast path & beach at low tide. An easy drive to the Eden Project & many famous Cornish gardens. Many good eating houses from pubs to Michelin-starred restaurants within a few miles. Rock is a 10-min. drive for watersports & a ferry to Padstow. Children over 12.
E-mail: mbloor@ukonline.co.uk
www.bestbandb.co.uk

| | £60.00 to £70.00 | Y | N | Y |

Michael & Jo Bloor   **Porteath Barn**   **St. Minver**   **Wadebridge PL27 6RA**   **Cornwall**
Tel: (01208) 863605   Fax 01208 863954   Mobile 0771 2591725   Open: ALL YEAR   Map Ref No. 31

Visit our website at:
http://www.bestbandb.co.uk

Cumbria

Cumbria

The Lake District National Park is deservedly famous for its magnificent scenery. Here, England's highest mountains & rugged fells surround shimmering lakes & green valleys. But there is more to Cumbria than the beauty of the Lake District. It also has a splendid coastline, easily accessible from the main lakeland centres, as well as a border region where the Pennines, the backbone of England, reach their highest point, towering over the Eden valley.

Formation of the dramatic Lakeland scenery began in the Caledonian period when earth movements raised & folded the already ancient rocks, submerging the whole mass underseas & covering it with limestone. During the ice age great glaciers ground out the lake beds & dales of todays landscape. There is tremendous variety, from the craggy outcrops of the Borrowdale Volcanics with Skiddaw at 3054 feet, to the gentle dales, the open moorlands & the lakes themselves. Each lake is distinctive, some with steep mountain sides sliding straight to the water's edge, others more open with sloping wooded hillsides. Ellerwater, the enchanting "lake of swans" is surrounded by reed & willows at the foot of Langdale. The charm of Ullswater inspired Wordsworth's famous poem "Daffodils". Whilst many lakes are deliberately left undisturbed for those seeking peace, there are others - notably Windermere - where a variety of water sports can be enjoyed. The changeable weather of the mountainous region can produce a sudden transformation in the character of a tranquil lake, raising choppy waves across the darkened surface to break along the shoreline. It is all part of the fascination of Lakeland.

Fell walking is the best way to appreciate the full beauty of the area. There are gentle walks along the dales, & the tops of the ridges are accessible to walkers with suitable footwear & an eye to the weather.

Ponytrekking is another popular way to explore the countryside & there are many centres catering even for inexperienced riders.

There are steamboats on lakes such as Coniston & Ullswater, where you can appreciate the scenery. On Windermere there are a variety of boats for hire, & facilities for water-skiing.

Traditional crafts & skills are on display widely. Craft centres at Keswick, Ambleside & Grasmere, & the annual exhibition of the Guild of Lakeland Craftsmen held in Windermere from mid-July to early September represent the widest variety of craft artistry.

Fairs & festivals flourish in Lakeland. The famous Appleby Horse Fair, held in June is the largest fair of its kind in the world & attracts a huge gypsy gathering. Traditional agriculture shows, sheep dog trials & local sporting events abound. The Grasmere Sports, held each August include gruelling fell races, Cumberland & Westmoreland wrestling, hound trails & pole-leaping.

The traditional custom of "Rush-bearing" when the earth floors of the churches were strewn with rushes still survives as a procession in Ambleside & Grasmere & many other villages in the summer months

The coast of Cumbria stretches from the estuaries of Grange-over-Sands & Burrow-in-Furness by way of the beautiful beaches between Bootle & Cardurnock, to the mouth of the Solway Firth. The coastal areas, especially the estuaries, are excellent for bird-watching. The sand dunes north of the Esk are famous for the colony of black-headed gulls which can be visited by arrangement, & the colony of seabirds at St. Bees Head is the largest in Britain.

Cumbria

Cumbria
Gazeteer
Area of outstanding natural beauty.
The Lake District National Park.

House & Castles
Carlisle Castle - Carlisle
12th century. Massive Norman keep - half-moon battery - ramparts, portcullis & gatehouse.
Brough Castle - Kirby Stephen
13th century - on site of Roman Station between York & Carlisle.
Dacre Castle - Penrith
14th century - massive pele tower.
Sizergh Castle - Kendal
14th century - pele tower - 15th century great hall. English & French furniture, silver & china - Jacobean relics. 18th century gardens.
Belle Island - Boweness-on-Windermere
18th century - interior by Adams Brothers, portraits by Romney.
Swarthmoor Hall - Ulverston
Elizabethan house, mullioned windows, oak staircase, panelled rooms. Home of George Fox - birthplace of Quakerism - belongs to Society of Friends.
Lorton Hall - Cockermouth
15th century pele tower, priest holes, oak panelling, Jacobean furniture.
Muncaster Castle - Ravenglass
14th century with 15th & 19th century additions - site of Roman tower.
Rusland Hall - Ulveston
Georgian mansion with period panelling, sculpture, furniture, paintings.
Levens Hall - Kendal
Elizabethan - very fine panelling & plasterwork - famous topiary garden.
Hill Top - Sawrey
17th century farmhouse home of Beatrix Potter - contains her furniture, china & some of original drawings for her children's books.
Dove Cottage - Town End, Grasmere
William Wordsworth's cottage - still contains his furnishing & his personal effects as in his lifetime.
Brantwood
The Coniston home of John Ruskin, said to be the most beautifully situated house in the Lake District. Exhibition, gardens, bookshops & tearooms.

Cathedrals & Churches
Carlisle Cathedral - Carlisle
1130. 15th century choir stalls with painted backs - carved misericords, 16th century screen, painted roof.
Cartmel Priory (St. Mary Virgin)
15th century stalls, 17th century screen, large east window, curious central tower.
Lanercost Priory (St. Mary Magdalene)
12th century - Augustinian - north aisle now forms Parish church.
Greystoke (St. Andrew)
14th/15th century. 19th century misericords. Lovely glass in chancel.
Brougham (St. Wilfred)
15th century carved altarpiece.
Furness Abbey
12th century monastery beautiful setting. Shap Abbey
12th century with 16th century tower.

Museums & Galleries
Abbot Hall - Kendal
18th century, Georgian house with period furniture, porcelain, silver, pictures, etc. Also contains modern galleries with contemporary paintings, sculptures & ceramics. Changing exhibitions on show.
Carlisle Museum & Art Gallery - Carlisle
Archaeological & natural history collections. National centre of studies of Roman Britain. Art gallery principally exhibiting paintings & porcelain.
Hawkshead Courthouse - Kendal
Exhibition of domestic & working life housed in mediaeval building.
Helena Thompson Museum - Workington
displays Victorian family life & objects of the period.
Lakeland Motor Museum - Holker Hall - Grange-over-Sands
Exhibits cars, bicycles, tricycles, motor cycles, etc., & model cars.
Millom Folk Museum - St. George's Road, Millom
Reconstructions of drift in iron ore mine, miner's cottage kitchen, blacksmith's forge & agricultural relics.
Ravenglass Railway Museum - Ravenglass
History of railways relics, models, etc.

Cumbria

Wordsworth Museum - Town End, Grasmere
Personal effects, first editions, manuscripts, & general exhibits from the time of William Wordsworth.
Border Regiment Museum - The Castle, Carlisle.
Collection of uniforms, weapons, trophies, documents, medals from 1702, to the present time.
Whitehaven Museum - Whitehaven
History & development of area show in geology, paleontology, archaeology, natural history, etc. Interesting maritime past.
Fitz Park Museum & Art Gallery - Keswick.

Collection of manuscripts - Wordsworth, Walpole, Coleridge, Southey.
The Beatrix Potter Gallery - Hawkshead

Things to see & do

Fell Walking - there is good walking throughout Cumbria, but check weather reports, clothing & footwear before tackling the heights.
Pony-trekking - opportunities for novice & experienced riders.
Watersports - Windermere is the ideal centre for sailing, waterskiing, windsurfing, scuba-diving.
Golf - championship course to the north at Silloth.

Grasmere.

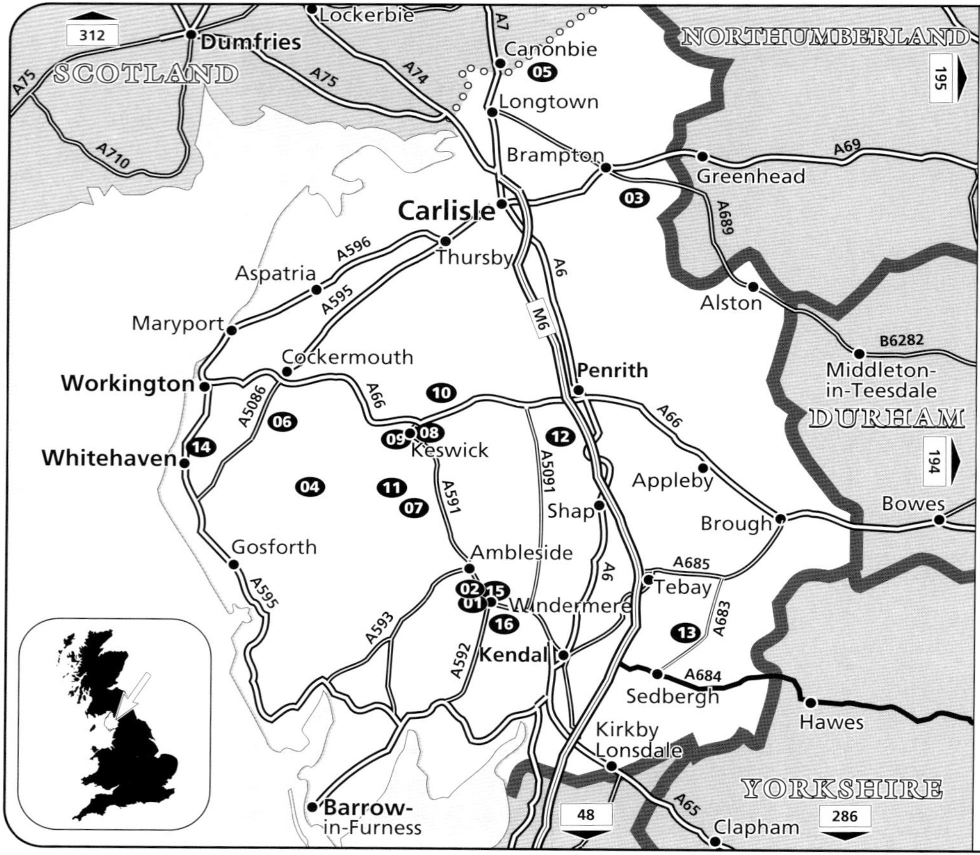

CUMBRIA

Map reference

01	Kirby	09	Coy
02	Ewing	10	Jameison
03	Stobbart	11	Lowe
04	McKenzie	12	White
05	Sisson	13	Clowes
06	Thompson	14	Saxon
07	Clark	15	Holcroft
08	Miller	15	Duncan
09	Jones	16	Blaney

NORTHUMBERLAND

195

DURHAM

194

YORKSHIRE

286

Middleton-in-Teesdale

B6282

Bowes

Hawes

Greenhead

A69

Alston

A689

Brough

Clapham

A65

03

Penrith

A66

Appleby

A685

A683

Tebay

13

A684

Sedbergh

Kirkby Lonsdale

48

Canonbie

05

Longtown

Brampton

A7

Lockerbie

A74

A6

M6

12

A5091

Shap

A6

Windermere

16

Kendal

Carlisle

Thursby

10

Keswick

08

A591

11

07

02 15

01

Ambleside

A592

A593

Dumfries

SCOTLAND

312

A710

A75

Aspatria

A596

A595

Cockermouth

A66

06

A5086

04

Gosforth

A595

Barrow-in-Furness

Maryport

Workington

14

Whitehaven

74

Wood House.   Buttermere .

	rate £ from - to per double room	children taken	evening meals	animals taken

Buckle Yeat

Near Rd: A.591

Buckle Yeat is famous for its connections with Beatrix Potter. Although over 200 years old, it has been sympathetically & tastefully refurbished. There is a large lounge with log fire & an attractive dining room which also serves morning coffee & afternoon teas. There are 6 comfortable en-suite bedrooms. Many good local pubs & restaurants offer excellent meals. Buckle Yeat is in an ideal position for touring Lakeland, with walks, fishing & birdwatching all nearby. Animals by arrangement.
E-mail: info@buckle-yeat.co.uk
www.buckle-yeat.co.uk

£60.00 to £65.00 — Y N Y

VISA: M'CARD: AMEX:

Robert & Helen Kirby   Buckle Yeat   Nr. Sawrey   Hawkshead   Ambleside LA22 0LF   Cumbria
Tel: (015394) 36446   Open: ALL YEAR   Map Ref No. 01

Beechwood

Near Rd: A.591

Beechwood is superbly situated in Bowness-on-Windermere, set back from the road overlooking the quiet Rose Gardens. Bedrooms are individually decorated to a very high standard & many have king-size beds & a small sofa. All rooms have T.V./video & cd player. A complimentary video library is available & there is also an elegantly refurbished lounge in which to relax. Beechwood is a 5 min. stroll to the Lake & Esplanade, with many shops & restaurants close by.
E-mail: enquiries@beechwoodlakes.co.uk
www.beechwoodlakes.co.uk

£55.00 to £100.00 — N N N

VISA: M'CARD:

Mr & Mrs C A Ewing   Beechwood   Beresford Road   Bowness-on-Windermere LA23 2JG   Cumbria
Tel: (015394) 43403   Open: ALL YEAR   Map Ref No. 02

Hullerbank

Near Rd: A.69

Attractive pink-washed Georgian style farmhouse dated 1635-1751 standing in its own grounds, near the picturesque village of Talkin, 2 1/2 miles from Brampton. Superb walking country & central for Hadrian's Wall, the Lake District & the Borders. A friendly, relaxed atmosphere awaits. 3 bedrooms with private facilities, tea/coffee & T.V. & a sitting room with inglenook fireplace & separate dining room where excellent breakfasts are served. 2 inns with restaurant facilities nearby. Children over 12.
E-mail: info@hullerbank.freeserve.co.uk
www.hullerbank.co.uk

£54.00 to £56.00 — Y N N

VISA: M'CARD:

Sheila Stobbart   Hullerbank   Talkin   Brampton CA8 1LB   Cumbria
Tel: (016977) 46668   Fax 016977 46668   Open: FEB - DEC   Map Ref No. 03

Wood House

Near Rd: A.66

The view overlooking Wood House was chosen by J.M.W. Turner RA for his famous painting of Buttermere in 1798. A visitor describing the interior has written, "The furnishings & decor are serene & beautiful though completely unpretentious." En-suite bedrooms have spellbinding views over the lake. BBC Good Food Magazine - "Excellent dinners & breakfasts are served in the elegant dining room." Good walks. Boats & fishing. Red Squirrels live in the grounds.
E-mail: woodhouse.guest@virgin.net
www.wdhse.co.uk

£78.00 to £90.00 — N Y N

see PHOTO over
p. 75

Michael & Judy McKenzie   Wood House   Buttermere CA13 9XA   Cumbria
Tel: (017687) 70208   Fax 017687 70241   Open: FEB - NOV   Map Ref No. 04

Bessiestown Farm. Catlowdy.

New House Farm. Lorton.

Cumbria

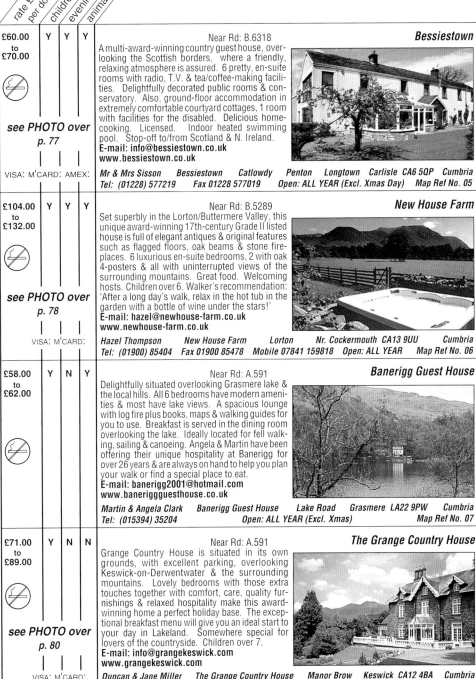

rate £ from - to per double room	children taken	evening meals	animals taken

Bessiestown

£60.00 to £70.00

Y | Y | Y

see PHOTO over p. 77

Near Rd: B.6318

A multi-award-winning country guest house, overlooking the Scottish borders, where a friendly, relaxing atmosphere is assured. 6 pretty, en-suite rooms with radio, T.V. & tea/coffee-making facilities. Delightfully decorated public rooms & conservatory. Also, ground-floor accommodation in extremely comfortable courtyard cottages, 1 room with facilities for the disabled. Delicious home-cooking. Licensed. Indoor heated swimming pool. Stop-off to/from Scotland & N. Ireland.
E-mail: info@bessiestown.co.uk
www.bessiestown.co.uk

VISA: M'CARD: AMEX:

Mr & Mrs Sisson   Bessiestown   Catlowdy   Penton   Longtown   Carlisle CA6 5QP   Cumbria
Tel: (01228) 577219   Fax 01228 577019   Open: ALL YEAR (Excl. Xmas Day)   Map Ref No. 05

New House Farm

£104.00 to £132.00

Y | Y | Y

see PHOTO over p. 78

Near Rd: B.5289

Set superbly in the Lorton/Buttermere Valley, this unique award-winning 17th-century Grade II listed house is full of elegant antiques & original features such as flagged floors, oak beams & stone fireplaces. 6 luxurious en-suite bedrooms, 2 with oak 4-posters & all with uninterrupted views of the surrounding mountains. Great food. Welcoming hosts. Children over 6. Walker's recommendation: 'After a long day's walk, relax in the hot tub in the garden with a bottle of wine under the stars!'
E-mail: hazel@newhouse-farm.co.uk
www.newhouse-farm.co.uk

VISA: M'CARD:

Hazel Thompson   New House Farm   Lorton   Nr. Cockermouth CA13 9UU   Cumbria
Tel: (01900) 85404   Fax 01900 85478   Mobile 07841 159818   Open: ALL YEAR   Map Ref No. 06

Banerigg Guest House

£58.00 to £62.00

Y | N | Y

Near Rd: A.591

Delightfully situated overlooking Grasmere lake & the local hills. All 6 bedrooms have modern amenities & most have lake views. A spacious lounge with log fire plus books, maps & walking guides for you to use. Breakfast is served in the dining room overlooking the lake. Ideally located for fell walking, sailing & canoeing. Angela & Martin have been offering their unique hospitality at Banerigg for over 26 years & are always on hand to help you plan your walk or find a special place to eat.
E-mail: banerigg2001@hotmail.com
www.baneriggguesthouse.co.uk

Martin & Angela Clark   Banerigg Guest House   Lake Road   Grasmere LA22 9PW   Cumbria
Tel: (015394) 35204   Open: ALL YEAR (Excl. Xmas)   Map Ref No. 07

The Grange Country House

£71.00 to £89.00

Y | N | N

see PHOTO over p. 80

Near Rd: A.591

Grange Country House is situated in its own grounds, with excellent parking, overlooking Keswick-on-Derwentwater & the surrounding mountains. Lovely bedrooms with those extra touches together with comfort, care, quality furnishings & relaxed hospitality make this award-winning home a perfect holiday base. The exceptional breakfast menu will give you an ideal start to your day in Lakeland. Somewhere special for lovers of the countryside. Children over 7.
E-mail: info@grangekeswick.com
www.grangekeswick.com

VISA: M'CARD:

Duncan & Jane Miller   The Grange Country House   Manor Brow   Keswick CA12 4BA   Cumbria
Tel: 017687 72500   Open: MAR - NOV   Map Ref No. 08

The Grange Country House Hotel. Keswick

Greystones. Keswick.

Cumbria

Greystones Hotel

Near Rd: A.591

Greystones enjoys an enviable position overlooking the grounds of St. John's Church, & has excellent fell views. It is just a short walk to the market square & Lake Derwentwater. There are 8 delightful en-suite rooms, each with T.V., hot drinks tray & a folder of suggested walks & tours. Private parking. An excellent base for a relaxing break. Children over 9 welcome. A charming base from which to explore the Lakes & the surrounding area.
E-mail: greystones@keslakes.freeserve.co.uk
www.greystones.tv

£50.00 to £62.00	Y	N	N

see PHOTO over
p. 81

VISA: M'CARD:

Robert & Janet Jones   Greystones Hotel   Ambleside Road   Keswick CA12 4DP   Cumbria
Tel: (017687) 73108   Open: JAN - NOV   Map Ref No. 09

Scales Farm Country Guest House

Near Rd: A.66

Stunning open views & a warm friendly welcome await you at Scales Farm, a traditional 17th-century fells farmhouse sensitively modernised to provide accommodation of the highest standard. All bedrooms are en-suite, centrally heated, with tea/coffee-making facilities, colour T.V. & fridges. Separate entrance from private car park allows guests access to rooms & traditional lounge. Lakeland Inn/Restaurant next door. A lovely base for touring or walking.
E-mail: scales@scalesfarm.com
www.scalesfarm.com

£56.00 to £62.00	Y	N	Y

VISA: M'CARD:

Alan & Angela Jameison   Scales Farm Country Guest House   Scales   Threlkeld   Keswick CA12 4SY
Tel: (017687) 79660   Fax 017687 79510   Open: ALL YEAR (Excl. Xmas)   Map Ref No. 10

Dale Head Hall Lakeside Hotel

Near Rd: A.591

Lose yourself in the ancient woodlands & mature gardens of an Elizabethan country manor, set serenely on the shores of Lake Thirlmere. Delicious dinners prepared by mother & daughter, using fresh produce from the Victorian kitchen garden, served with fine wines in the oak-beamed dining room. 12 individually decorated bedrooms, some with 4-posters, each with bath/shower rooms. Together with the lounge & bar, there are unspoilt views across lawns, lakes & fells.
E-mail: onthelakeside@daleheadhall.co.uk
www.daleheadhall.co.uk

£100.00 to £120.00	Y	Y	N

see PHOTO over
p. 83

VISA: M'CARD: AMEX:

Alan & Shirley Lowe   Dale Head Hall Lakeside Hotel   Lake Thirlmere   Keswick CA12 4TN   Cumbria
Tel: (017687) 72478   Fax 017687 71070   Open: FEB - DEC   Map Ref No. 11

Lairbeck Hotel

Near Rd: A.66

Featured on television's 'Wish You Were Here?' holiday programme, Lairbeck Hotel is only 10 mins walk from Keswick town centre, in a secluded location with superb mountain views. Here you can treat yourself to traditional, award-winning dining & hospitality in a friendly informal atmosphere & relax in front of cosy log fires. All 14 bedrooms are en-suite & individually decorated. Single & ground-floor rooms available. Spacious parking. Children over 5 years welcome.
E-mail: bbb@lairbeckhotel-keswick.co.uk
www.lairbeckhotel-keswick.co.uk

£82.00 to £94.00	Y	Y	N

VISA: M'CARD:

Roger & Irene Coy   Lairbeck Hotel   Vicarage Hill   Keswick CA12 5QB   Cumbria
Tel: (017687) 73373   Fax 017687 73144   Open: Mid MAR - DEC   Map Ref No. 09

Dale Head Hall.   Lake Thirlmere.

	rate £ from - to per double room	children taken	evening meals	animals taken

Beckfoot Country House

Near Rd: A.66, A.6

A fine old residence featuring a half-panelled hall, staircase & attractive panelled dining room. Set in 3 acres of grounds in the delightful Lake District, it is a quiet, peaceful retreat for a holiday base, & is within easy reach of the many pleasure spots in the area. Offering 7 rooms, all with private shower/bathroom & tea/coffee-making facilities. A dining room, drawing & reading room. This is a delightful base for a touring holiday. Dogs by arrangement.

E-mail: info@beckfoot.co.uk
www.beckfoot.co.uk

£76.00 to £96.00 — Y N Y

VISA: M'CARD: AMEX:

Mrs Lesley White   Beckfoot Country House   Helton   Nr. Penrith CA10 2QB   Cumbria
Tel: (01931) 713241   Fax 01931 713391   Open: MAR - NOV   Map Ref No. 12

The Cross Keys Temperance Inn

Near Rd: A.683

For those looking for an inn full of character situated in one of the most magnificent of Dales settings, the Cross Keys offers excellent food & accommodation. The restaurant provides wonderful home-produced food with a wide choice to suit all tastes and, although a Temperance Inn, guests are invited to bring along the drink of their choice. The delightful bedrooms offer full en-suite facilities. The Cross Keys is a charming home.

E-mail: clowes@freeuk.com
www.cautleyspout.co.uk

£70.00 to £70.00 — Y Y N

(non-smoking)

VISA: M'CARD:

Alan & Chris Clowes   The Cross Keys Temperance Inn   Cautley   Sedbergh LA10 5NE   Cumbria
Tel: (015396) 20284   Fax 015396 21966   Open: ALL YEAR   Map Ref No. 13

Moresby Hall

Near Rd: A.595

Grade I listed Moresby Hall dates from around 1250, although the front facade dates from approx. 1620. Enjoy genuine hospitality in this charming country house, which offers 4 beautifully appointed bedrooms, including the De Ashby Suite with 4-poster bed & power shower/steam room en-suite. Evening meals are freshly prepared by Jane & served in the elegant dining room. Situated close to Whitehaven, it is also convenient for visiting the Lakes, Cockermouth & Keswick. Children over 8.

E-mail: bestbandb@moresbyhall.co.uk
www.moresbyhall.co.uk

£90.00 to £130.00 — Y Y N

(non-smoking)

VISA: M'CARD: AMEX:

Jane & David Saxon   Moresby Hall   Moresby   Whitehaven CA28 6PJ   Cumbria
Tel: (01946) 696317   Fax 01946 694385   Open: ALL YEAR   Map Ref No. 14

The Fairfield

Near Rd: A.591

Fairfield is a small friendly, family-run B & B in a 200-year-old house, set in its own grounds with a large beautiful garden & terrace. Close to the waterfront & with its own car park, 200 metres from the shops, pubs/restaurants & waterfront of Bowness. Fairfield is an ideal base for exploring the area. 10 en-suite bedrooms with modern facilities. Bar & free internet access are available. Generous breakfasts are a speciality. Dinner available during the low season only. Animals by arrangement.

E-mail: info@the-fairfield.co.uk
www.the-fairfield.co.uk

£58.00 to £94.00 — Y Y Y

(non-smoking)

see PHOTO over p. 85

VISA: M'CARD: AMEX:

Tony & Liz Blaney   The Fairfield   Brantfell Road   Bowness-on-Windermere   Windermere LA23 3AE
Tel: (015394) 46565   Open: ALL YEAR (Excl. Xmas)   Map Ref No. 16

The Fairfield. Bowness-on-Windermere.

Cumbria

		rate £ from - to per double room	evening meals	children taken	animals taken

Lynwood Guest House

Near Rd: A.591

A Victorian Lakeland stone house built in 1865, offering 5 centrally heated bedrooms, each with en-suite bathrooms, all with modern amenities including colour T.V. & tea/coffee-making facilities. Guests may relax in the T.V. lounge available throughout the day. Centrally located, only 150 yards from village shops & restaurants, & only 5 mins' from the bus & railway station. The host is a Lakeland tour guide, & is happy to assist in planning your stay. Children over 5 years.
E-mail: enquires@lynwood-guest-house.co.uk
www.lynwood-guest-house.co.uk

£40.00 to £55.00 — Y | N | N

Brian & Frances Holcroft Lynwood Guest House *Broad Street* *Windermere LA23 2AB Cumbria*
Tel: (015394) 42550 Fax 015394 42550 *Open: ALL YEAR* *Map Ref No. 15*

Blenheim Lodge

Near Rd: A.5074

Peaceful, friendly guest house, ideally situated in an elevated position, nestled against woodlands & boasting panoramic views of Lake Windermere. Next to the Dalesway - 1/2 min walk to a welcome drink & hot bath! Single, double, family & twin bedrooms with en-suite/private facilities & a lounge with fireplace. Breakfast options include fresh local produce & home-baked croissants. Bowness centre & Lake Windermere are 5 mins' walk. Free country club membership & fishing permits.
E-mail: enquiries@blenheim-lodge.com
www.blenheim-lodge.com

£70.00 to £110.00 — Y | N | N

VISA: M'CARD:

Mr & Mrs Duncan Blenheim Lodge Brantfell Road Bowness-on-Windermere Windermere LA23 3AE
Tel: (015394) 43440 *Open: ALL YEAR* *Map Ref No. 15*

All the establishments mentioned in this guide are members of
The Worldwide Bed & Breakfast Association

WORLDWIDE BED & BREAKFAST ASSOCIATION

When booking your accommodation please mention
The Best Bed & Breakfast

Derbyshire & Staffordshire

Derbyshire
(East Midlands)

A county with everything but the sea, this was Lord Byron's opinion of Derbyshire, & the special beauty of the Peak District was recognised by its designation as Britain's first National Park.

Purple heather moors surround craggy limestone outcrops & green hills drop to sheltered meadows or to deep gorges & tumbling rivers.

Derbyshire's lovely dales have delightful names too - Dove Dale, Monk's Dale, Raven's Dale, Water-cum-Jolly-Dale, & they are perfect for walking. The more adventurous can take up the challenge of the Pennine Way, a 270 mile pathway from Edale to the Scottish border.

The grit rock faces offer good climbing, particularly at High Tor above the River Derwent, & underground there are extensive & spectacular caverns. There are show caves at the Heights of Abraham, which you reach by cable-car, & at Castleton, source of the rare Blue John mineral, & at Pole's Cavern in Buxton where there are remarkable stalactites & stalagmites.

Buxton's splendid Crescent reflects the town's spa heritage, & the Opera House is host to an International Festival each summer.

The waters at Matlock too were prized for their curative properties & a great Hydro was built there in the last century, to give treatment to the hundreds of people who came to "take the waters".

Bakewell is a lovely small town with a fascinating market, some fine buildings & the genuine Bakewell Pudding, (known elsewhere as Bakewell tart).

Well-dressing is a custom carried on throughout the summer in the villages & towns. It is a thanksgiving for the water, that predates the arrival of Christianity in Britain. Flower-petals, leaves, moss & bark are pressed in

Haddon Hall; Derby.

Derbyshire & Staffordshire

intricate designs into frames of wet clay & erected over the wells, where they stay damp & fresh for days.

The mining of lead & the prosperity of the farms brought great wealth to the landowning families who were able to employ the finest of architects & craftsmen to design & build their great houses. Haddon Hall is a perfectly preserved 12th century manor house with with terraced gardens of roses & old-fashioned flowers. 17th century Chatsworth, the "Palace of the Peak", houses a splendid collection of paintings, drawings, furniture & books, & stands in gardens with elaborate fountains.

Staffordshire
(Heart of England)

Staffordshire is a contrast of town & county. Miles of moorland & dramatic landscapes lie to the north of the country, & to the south is the Vale of Trent & the greenery of Cannock Chase. But the name of Staffordshire invokes that of the Potteries, the area around Stoke-on-Trent where the world-renowned ceramics are made.

The factories that produce the Royal Doulton, Minton, Spode & Coalport china will arrange tours for visitors, & there is a purpose-built visitor centre at Barlaston displaying the famous Wedgwood tradition.

The Gladstone Pottery Museum is set in a huge Victorian potbank, & the award-winning City museum in Stoke-on-Trent has a remarkable ceramics collection.

There is lovely scenery to be found where the moorlands of Staffordshire meet the crags & valleys of the Peak District National Park. From the wild & windy valleys of The Roaches (from the French 'roche') you can look across the county to Cheshire & Wales. Drivers can take high moorland roads that are marked out as scenic routes.

The valleys of the Dove & Manifold are beautiful limestone dales & ideal for walking or for cycling. Sir Izzak Walton, author of 'The Compleat Angler', drew his inspiration, & his trout, from the waters here.

The valley of the River Churnet is both pretty & peaceful, being largely inaccessible to cars. The Caldon Canal, with its colourful narrowboats, follows the course of the river & there are canalside pubs, picnic areas, boat rides & woodland trails to enjoy. The river runs through the grounds of mock-Gothic Alton Towers, now a leisure park.

The Vale of Trent is largely rural with small market towns, villages, river & canals.

Cannock Chase covers 20 square miles of heath & woodland & is the home of the largest herd of fallow deer in England. Shugborough Hall stands in the Chase. The ancestral home of Lord Lichfeld, it also houses the Staffordshire County Museum & a farm for rare breeds including the famous Tamworth Pig.

Burton-on-Trent is known as the home of the British brewery industry & there are two museums in the town devoted to the history of beer.

Lichfield is a small & picturesque city with a cathedral which dates from the 12th century & has three graceful spires known as the 'Ladies of the Vale'. Dr. Samuel Johnson was born in the city & his house is now a museum dedicated to his life & work.

One of the Vale's villages retains its mediaeval tradition by performing the Abbot's Bromley Horn Dance every September.

Derbyshire & Staffordshire

Derbyshire

Gazeteer

Areas of outstanding natural beauty.
Peak National Park. The Dales.

Houses & Castles

Chatsworth - Bakewell
17th century, built for 1st. Duke of Devonshire. Furniture, paintings & drawings, books, etc. Fine gardens & parklands.
Haddon Hall - Bakewell
Mediaeval manor house - complete. Terraced rose gardens.
Hardwick Hall - Nr. Chesterfield
16th century - said to be more glass than wall. Fine furniture, tapestries & furnishings. Herb garden.
Kedlestone Hall - Derby
18th century - built on site of 12th century Manor house. Work of Robert Adam - has world famous marble hall. Old Master paintings. 11th century church nearby.
Melbourne Hall - Nr. Derby
12th century origins - restored by Sir John Coke. Fine collection of pictures & works of art. Magnificent gardens & famous wrought iron pagoda
Sudbury Hall - Sudbury
Has examples of work of the greatest craftsmen of the period-Grinling Gibbons,Pierce and Laguerre.
Winster Market House Nr. Matlock
17th century stone built market house.

Cathedrals & Churches

Chesterfield (St. Mary & All Saints)
13th & 14th centuries.
4 chapels, polygonal apse, mediaeval screens, Jacobean pulpit.
Derby (All Saints)
Perpendicular tower - classical style - 17th century plate, 18th century screen.
Melbourne (St. Michael & St. Mary)
Norman with two west towers & crossing tower.
Splendid plate, 18th century screen.
Normbury (St. Mary & St. Barloke)
14th century - perpendicular tower. Wood carving & brasses.
Wirksworth (St. Mary)
13th century, restored & enlarged.

Staffordshire

Gazeteer

Houses & Castles

Ancient High House - Stafford
16th century - largest timber-framed town house in England.
Shugborough - Nr. Stafford
Ancestral home of the Earl of Lichfield. Mansion house, paintings, silver, ceramics, furniture. County Museum. Rare Breeds Farm.
Moseley Old Hall - Nr. Wolverhampton
Elizabethan house formerly half-timbered.
Stafford Castle
Large & well-preserved Norman castle in grounds with castle trail.
Tamworth Castle
Norman motte & bailey castle with later additions. Museum.

Cathedrals & Churches

Croxden Abbey
12th century foundation Cistercian abbey. Ruins of 13th century church.
Ingestre (St. Mary the Virgin)
A rare Wren church built in1676.
Lichfield Cathedral
Unique triple-spired 12th century cathedral.
Tamworth (St. Editha's)
Founded 963, rebuilt 14th century. Unusual double spiral staircase.
Tutbury (St. Mary's)
Norman church with impressive West front.

Museums & Galleries

City Museum & Art Gallery - Stoke-on-Trent
Modern award-winning museum. Ceramics, decorative arts, etc.
Dr. Johnson Birthplace Museum - Lichfield
Gladstone Pottery Museum - Longton
Izaak Walton Cottage & Museum - Shallowfield, Nr. Stafford
National Brewery Museum & the Bass Museum of Brewing-both in Stoke-on-Trent
Stafford Art Gallery & Craft Shop - Stafford
Major gallery for the visual arts & centre for quality craftsmanship.

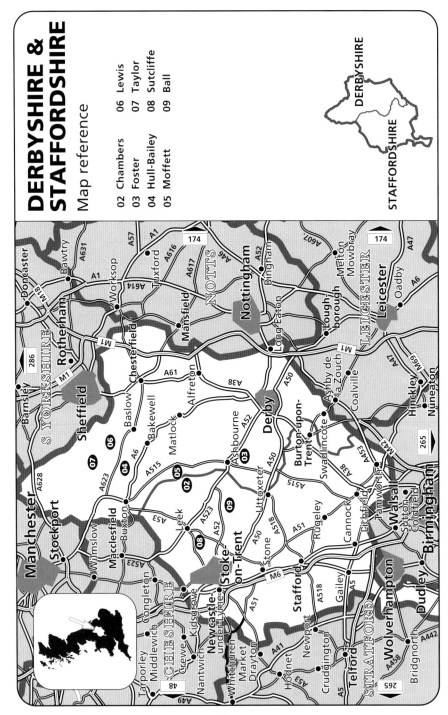

DERBYSHIRE & STAFFORDSHIRE

Map reference

02 Chambers	06 Lewis
03 Foster	07 Taylor
04 Hull-Bailey	08 Sutcliffe
05 Moffett	09 Ball

Cressbrook Hall. Cressbrook.

Derbyshire

Stanshope Hall

Near Rd: A.515

Stanshope Hall, with its informal feel but with every comfort, stands in splendid isolation among the dry stone walls of the southern Peak District. Walks from the door lead to verdant Dovedale or the undiscovered seclusion of the Manifold Valley. The attractive en-suite rooms have hand-painted walls & frescos in the bathrooms. Candle-lit dinners (by arrangement) prepared using uncomplicated but imaginative recipes with local & garden produce.
E-mail: naomi@stanshope.demon.co.uk
www.stanshope.net

| £80.00 to £90.00 | Y | Y | N |

VISA: M'CARD:

Naomi Chambers & Nicholas Lourie   Stanshope Hall   Stanshope   Ashbourne DE6 2AD Derbyshire
Tel: (01335) 310278   Fax 01335 310470   Open: ALL YEAR (Excl. Xmas)   Map Ref No. 02

Shirley Hall

Near Rd: A.52

Shirley Hall is a lovely, peaceful old farmhouse, just to the south of Ashbourne, close to the village of Shirley. In the centre of rolling pastureland enjoy the tranquillity of this part-moated, timbered farmhouse, surrounded by a large lawned garden. 3 attractive bedrooms with en-suite bathrooms, T.V. & tea/coffee-making facilities. The full English breakfast with home-made bread & preserves is renowned. The village pub is excellent for evening meals. Coarse-fishing available. Woodland walks.
E-mail: sylviafoster@shirleyhallfarm.com
www.shirleyhallfarm.com

| £56.00 to £64.00 | Y | N | N |

Mrs Sylvia Foster   Shirley Hall   Hall Lane   Shirley   Ashbourne DE6 3AS   Derbyshire
Tel: (01335) 360346   Fax 01335 360346   Open: ALL YEAR   Map Ref No. 03

Cressbrook Hall

Near Rd: A.6

Cressbrook Hall, built 170 years ago, is an imposing country residence stunningly situated on the edge of the steep limestone gorge carved by the River Wye close to Monsal Dale. Surrounded by beautiful gardens & private rural grounds, Cressbrook Hall is memorable for its fine architecture & lovely interiors. Elegant en-suite rooms are complemented by an exquisite period dining room. (Evening meals are available for groups of 10+.)
E-mail: stay@cressbrookhall.co.uk
www.cressbrookhall.co.uk

| £85.00 to £105.00 | Y | N | N |

see PHOTO over
p. 91

VISA: M'CARD:

Mrs B Hull-Bailey   Cressbrook Hall   Cressbrook   Nr. Buxton SK17 8SY   Derbyshire
Tel: (01298)871289   Fax 01298 871845   Open: ALL YEAR   Map Ref No. 04

Biggin Hall

Near Rd: A.515

A delightful 17th-century old hall, Grade II* listed, completely restored & keeping all the character of its origins, with massive oak beams. 19 comfortable rooms, all charmingly furnished, 1 with a 4-poster bed, all with en-suite facilities & modern amenities. Guests have the choice of 2 sitting rooms, 1 with a log fire, 1 with colour T.V. & library, & there is a lovely garden. The house is beautifully furnished, with many antiques. Non-smoking areas. Children 12 & over. Dogs by arrangement.
E-mail: enquiries@bigginhall.co.uk
www.bigginhall.co.uk

| £70.00 to £126.00 | Y | Y | Y |

see PHOTO over
p. 93

VISA: M'CARD: AMEX:

James Moffett   Biggin Hall   Biggin-by-Hartington   Buxton SK17 0DH   Derbyshire
Tel: (01298) 84451   Fax 01298 84681   Open: ALL YEAR   Map Ref No. 05

Biggin Hall.   Biggin by Hartington.

Delf View House. Eyam.

Derbyshire & Staffordshire

rate £ from - to per double room	children taken	evening meals	animals taken		

| £70.00 to £90.00 | Y | N | N | Near Rd: A.623 | **Delf View House** |

Beautiful & tranquil accommodation in an elegant listed Georgian country house in historic Eyam village in the magnificent Peak National Park. Guests are warmly welcomed in the drawing room, delightfully furnished with antiques, pictures & books. 3 bedrooms, 1 en-suite, include a Sheraton 4-poster & 18th-century French twin beds. Sumptuous breakfasts served in the oak-beamed dining room. Restaurants nearby. Ideal for visiting Chatsworth, Haddon & Eyam Hall. Children 12+.
E-mail: lewis@delfview.co.uk
www.delfview.co.uk

see PHOTO over p. 94

David & Meirlys Lewis	Delf View House	Church Street	Eyam S32 5QH	Derbyshire
Tel: (01433) 631533	Fax 01433 631972	Open: ALL YEAR		Map Ref No. 06

| £70.00 to £85.00 | Y | N | Y | Near Rd: A.6187 | **Underleigh House** |

Set in an idyllic & peaceful location amidst glorious scenery, this extended cottage & barn conversion (dating from 1873) is the perfect base for exploring the Peak District. Underleigh is in the heart of magnificent walking country & offers 6 en-suite rooms, furnished to a high standard with many thoughtful extras included. Delicious breakfasts in the flagstoned dining hall feature local & home-made specialities. The beamed lounge with a log fire is the perfect place to relax. Children over 12.
E-mail: underleigh.house@btconnect.com
www.underleighhouse.co.uk

see PHOTO over p. 96

VISA: M'CARD:

Philip & Vivienne Taylor	Underleigh House	Off Edale Road	Hope	Hope Valley S33 6RF	Derbys.
Tel: (01433) 621372	Fax 01433 621324	Open: ALL YEAR (Excl. Xmas & New Year)			Map Ref No. 07

| £60.00 to £70.00 | Y | N | N | Near Rd: A.520 | **Choir Cottage & Choir House** |

This 17th-century stone cottage, once a resting place for ostlers, now provides beautifully appointed, comfortable bedrooms, with full en-suite facilities, central heating, colour T.V., tea/coffee tray & 'phone. The Pine Room & Rose Room have 4-poster beds, & 1 is suitable as a family suite. Quiet location convenient for the Peak District, potteries & Alton Towers. Excellent food & careful attention to detail assured.
E-mail: enquiries@choircottage.co.uk
www.choircottage.co.uk

Mrs Elaine Sutcliffe	Choir Cottage & Choir House	Ostlers Lane	Cheddleton	Leek ST13 7HS	Staffs.
Tel: (01538) 360561	Mobile 07719 617078	Open: ALL YEAR			Map Ref No. 08

| £52.00 to £58.00 | Y | N | N | Near Rd: A.50 | **Manor House Farm** |

A beautiful Grade II listed farmhouse, set amid rolling hills & rivers. Accommodation is in 3 attractive bedrooms, all with 4-poster beds & an en-suite bathroom. (1 can be used as a twin.) Tastefully furnished with antiques & retaining traditional features including an oak-panelled breakfast room. Guests may relax in the extensive gardens with grass tennis court & Victorian summer house. Ideal for visiting Alton Towers, the Peak District or the potteries.
E-mail: cm_ball@yahoo.co.uk
www.4posteraccom.com

VISA: M'CARD: AMEX:

C. M. Ball	Manor House Farm	Prestwood	Denstone	Uttoxeter ST14 5DD	Staffordshire
Tel: (01889) 590415	Fax 01335 342198	Open: ALL YEAR			Map Ref No. 09

Underleigh House. Hope.

Devon

Devon
(West Country)

Here is a county of tremendous variety. Two glorious & contrasting coastlines with miles of sandy beaches, sheltered coves & rugged cliffs. There are friendly resorts & quiet villages of cob & thatch, two historic cities, & a host of country towns & tiny hamlets as well as the wild open spaces of two national parks.

From the grandeur of Hartland Point east to Foreland Point where Exmoor reaches the sea, the north Devon coast is incomparable. At Westward Ho!, Croyde & Woolacombe the rolling surf washes the golden beaches & out to sea stands beautiful Lundy Island, ideal for bird watching, climbing & walking. The tiny village of Clovelly with its cobbled street tumbles down the cliffside to the sea. Ilfracombe is a friendly resort town & the twin towns of Lynton & Lynmouth are joined by a cliff railway.

The south coast is a colourful mixture of soaring red sandstone cliffs dropping to sheltered sandy coves & the palm trees of the English Riviera. This is one of England's great holiday coasts with a string of popular resorts; Seaton, Sidmouth, Budleigh Salterton, Exmouth, Dawlish, Teignmouth & the trio of Torquay, Paignton & Brixham that make up Torbay. To the south, beyond Berry Head are Dartmouth, rich in navy tradition, & Salcombe, a premiere sailing centre in the deep inlet of the Kingsbridge estuary. Plymouth is a happy blend of holiday resort, tourist centre, historic & modern city, & the meeting-point for the wonderful old sailing vessels for the Tall Ships Race.

Inland the magnificent wilderness of Dartmoor National Park offers miles of sweeping moorland, granite tors, clear streams & wooded valleys, ancient stone circles & clapper bridges. The tors, as the Dartmoor peaks, are called are easily climbed & the views from the tops are superb. Widecombe-in-the-Moor, with its imposing church tower, & much photographed Buckland-in-the-Moor are only two of Dartmoor's lovely villages.

The Exmoor National Park straddles the Devon/Somerset border. It is a land of wild heather moorland above deep wooded valleys & sparkling streams, the home of red deer, soaring buzzards & of legendary Lorna Doone from R.D. Blackmore's novel. The south west peninsula coastal path follows the whole of the Exmoor coastline affording dramatic scenery & spectacular views, notably from Countisbury Hill.

The seafaring traditions of Devon are well-known. Sir Walter Raleigh set sail from Plymouth to Carolina in 1584; Sir Francis Drake began his circumnavigation of the world at Plymouth in the "Golden Hind" & fought the Spanish Armada off Plymouth Sound. The Pilgrim Fathers sailed from here & it was to here that Sir Francis Chichester returned having sailed around the world in 1967.

Exeter's maritime tradition is commemorated in an excellent museum located in converted riverside warehouses but the city's chief glory is the magnificent 13th century cathedral of St. Mary & St. Peter, built in an unusual decorated Gothic style, with its west front covered in statues.

The River Dart near Dittisham.

Devon

Devon

Gazeteer

Areas of outstanding natural beauty.
North, South, East Devon.

Houses & Castles

Arlington Court - Barnstaple
Regency house, collection of shell, pewter & model ships.

Bickleigh Castle - Nr. Tiverton
Thatched Jacobean wing. Great Hall & armoury. Early Norman chapel, gardens & moat.

Buckland Abbey - Nr. Plymouth
13th century Cistercian monastery - 16th century alterations. Home of Drake - contains his relics & folk gallery.

Bradley Manor - Newton Abbot
15th century Manor house with perpendicular chapel.

Cadhay - Ottery St. Mary
16th century Elizabethan Manor house.

Castle Drogo - Nr.Chagford
Designed by Lutyens - built of granite, standing over 900 feet above the gorge of the Teign river.

Chambercombe Manor - Illfracombe
14th-15th century Manor house.

Castle Hill - Nr. Barnstaple
18th century Palladian mansion - fine furniture of period, pictures, porcelain & tapestries.

Hayes Barton - Nr. Otterton
16th century plaster & thatch house. Birthplace of Walter Raleigh.

Oldway - Paignton
19th century house having rooms designed to be replicas of rooms at the Palace of Versailles.

Powederham Castle - Nr. Exeter
14th century mediaeval castle much damaged in Civil War. Altered in 18th & 19th centuries. Fine music room by Wyatt.

Saltram House - Plymouth
Some remnants of Tudor house built into George II house, with two rooms by Robert Adam. Excellent plasterwork & woodwork.

Shute Barton - Nr. Axminster
14th century battlemented Manor house with Tudor & Elizabethan additions.

Tiverton Castle - Nr. Tiverton
Fortress of Henry I. Chapel of St. Francis. Gallery of Joan of Arc.

Torre Abbey Mansion - Torquay
Abbey ruins, tithe barn. Mansion house with paintings & furniture.

Cathedrals & Churches

Atherington (St. Mary)
Perpendicular style - mediaeval effigies & glass, original rood loft. Fine screens, 15th century bench ends.

Ashton (St. John the Baptist)
15th century - mediaeval screens, glass & wall paintings. Elizabethan pulpit with canopy, 17th century altar railing.

Bere Ferrers (St. Andrew)
14th century rebuilding - 14th century glass, 16th century benches, Norman font.

Bridford (St. Thomas a Becket)
Perpendicular style - mediaeval glass & woodwork. Excellent rood screen c.1530.

Cullompton (St. Andrew)
15th century perpendicular - Jacobean west gallery - fan tracery in roof, exterior carvings.

Exeter Cathedral
13th century decorated - Norman towers. Interior tierceron ribbed vault (Gothic) carved corbels & bosses, moulded piers & arches. Original pulpitum c.1320. Choir stalls with earliest misericords in England c.1260.

Haccombe (St. Blaize)
13th century effigies, 14th century glass, 17th century brasses, 19th century screen, pulpit & reredos.

Kentisbeare (St. Mary)
Perpendicular style - checkered tower. 16th century rood screen.

Ottery St. Mary (St. Mary)
13th century, 14th century clock, fan vaulted roof, tomb with canopy, minstrel's gallery, gilded wooden eagle. 18th century pulpit.

Parracombe (St. Petrock)
Unrestored Georgian - 16th century benches, mostly perpendicular, early English chancel.

Sutcombe (St. Andrew)
15th century - some part Norman. 16th century bench ends, restored rood screen, mediaeval glass & floor tiles.

Swimbrige (St. James)
14th century tower & spire - mediaeval stone pulpit, 15th century rood screen, font cover of Renaissance period.

Devon

Tawstock (St. Peter)
14th century, Italian plasterwork ceiling, mediaeval glass, Renaissance memorial pew, Bath monument.
Buckfast Abbey
Living Benedictine monastery, built on mediaeval foundation. Famous for works of art in church, modern stained glass, tonic wine & bee-keeping.

Museums & Galleries

Bideford Museum - Bideford
Geology, maps, prints, shipwright's tools, North Devon pottery.
Burton Art Gallery - Bideford
Hubert Coop collection of paintings etc.
Butterwalk Museum - Dartmouth
17th century row of half timbered buildings, nautical museum. 140 model ships.
Newcomen Engine House - Nr. Butterwalk Museum
Original Newcomen atmospheric/pressure steam engine c.1725.
Royal Albert Memorial Museum Art Gallery - Exeter
Collections of English watercolours, paintings, glass & ceramics, local silver, natural history & anthropology.
Rougemont House Museum - Exeter
Collections of archaeology & local history. Costume & lace collection
Guildhall - Exeter
Mediaeval structure with Tudor frontage - City regalia & silver.
Exeter Maritime Museum - Exeter
Largest collection in the world of working boats, afloat, ashore & under cover.
The Steam & Countryside Museum - Exmouth
Very large working layout - hundreds of exhibits.
Including Victorian farmhouse - farmyard pets for children.
Shebbear - North Devon
Alcott Farm Museum with unique collections of agricultural implements & photographs, etc.
The Elizabethan House - Totnes
Period costumes & furnishings, tools, toys, domestic articles, etc.
The Elizabethan House - Plymouth
16th century house with period furnishings.

City Museum & Art Gallery - Plymouth
Collections of pictures & porcelain, English & Italian drawing. Reynolds' family portraits, early printed books, ship models.
Cookworthy Museum - Kingsbridge
Story of china clay. Local history, shipbuilding tools, rural life.
Honiton & Allhallows Public Museum - Honiton
Collection of Honiton lace, implements etc. Complete Devon Kitchen.
Lyn & Exmoor Museum - Lynton
Life & history of Exmoor.
Torquay & Natural History Society Museum - Torquay
Collection illustrating Kent's Cavern & other caves - natural history & folkculture.

Historic Monuments

Okehampton Castle - Okehampton
11th -14th century chapel, keep & hall.
Totnes Castle - Totnes
13th - 14th century ruins of Castle.
Blackbury Castle - Southleigh
Hill fort - well preserved.
Dartmouth Castle - Dartmouth
15th century castle - coastal defence.
Lydford Castle - Lydford
12th century stone keep built upon site of Saxon fortress town.
Hound Tor - Manaton
Ruins of mediaeval hamlet.

Other things to see & do

The Big Sheep - Abbotsham
Sheep-milking parlour, with gallery, dairy & production rooms. Exhibition & play area.
Dartington Crystal - Torrington
Watch skilled craftworkers make lead crystalware. Glass centre & exhibition.
Dartmoor Wildlife Park - Sparkwell Nr. Plymouth
Over 100 species, including tigers, lions, bears, deer, birds of prey & waterfowl.
The Devon Guild of Craftsmen - Riverside Mill, Bovey Tracey
Series of quality exhibitions throughout the year.
Paignton Zoological & Botanical Gardens - Paignton
Third largest zoo in England. Botanical gardens, tropical house, "The Ark" family activity centre.

DEVON
Map reference

01 Payne	19 Cuming
02 Laugharne	20 Pardoe
03 Pirrie	21 Turner
04 Leedom	22 Napier-Bell
05 Daniel	23 Scharenguivel
06 Todd	24 Sampson
07 Whitby	25 Rowlatt
08 Renshaw	26 Cunningham
09 Witting	27 D. Wright
10 Gardner	28 Tucker
10 M. Wright	29 Brown
11 Hyde	30 Pugsley
12 Jennings	31 Strong
13 Orchard	32 French
14 Pile	33 Grimley
15 Merchant	34 Worth
16 Oakey	35 Bidwell
17 Bell	36 Gozzard
18 Gregson	

Column headers (rotated):
- rate £ from - to per double room
- children taken
- evening meals
- animals taken

£64.00 to £68.00 | Y | Y | N

(No smoking symbol)

VISA: M'CARD:

Huxtable Farm

Near Rd: A.361

Enjoy a memorable candlelit dinner of farm/local produce with complimentary home-made wine in this wonderful medieval longhouse with original oak panelling, beams & bread ovens. This secluded sheep farm with abundant wildlife & panoramic views is ideally situated on the Tarka Trail for exploring Exmoor & N. Devon's coastline. Tennis court, sauna, fitness & games room. Log fires. 5 en-suite bedrooms & 1 with a private bathroom, each with T.V. etc. Dinner by prior arrangement.
E-mail: bandb@huxtablefarm.co.uk
www.huxtablefarm.co.uk

Jackie & Antony Payne   *Huxtable Farm*   *West Buckland*   *Barnstaple*   *EX32 0SR*   *Devon*
Tel: (01598) 760254   *Fax 01598 760254*   *Open: JAN - NOV*   *Map Ref No. 01*

£60.00 to £65.00 | Y | N | N

(No smoking symbol)

VISA: M'CARD: AMEX:

The Mount

Near Rd: A.39

The Mount is a small, interesting Georgian house which is full of character & charm. It is set in a pretty garden with large handsome trees. A peaceful haven yet only 5 mins' walk from the town centre with its quay, narrow streets & medieval bridge. The 8 bedrooms are tastefully furnished & have en-suite facilities & T.V.. (1 ground-floor room.) Conveniently situated for Exmoor, Dartmoor, Clovelly, Lundy & the beautiful North Devon coastline with its sandy beaches & rugged cliffs.
E-mail: andrew@themountbideford.fsnet.co.uk
www.themount1.cjb.net

Andrew & Heather Laugharne   *The Mount*   *Northdown Road*   *Bideford*   *EX39 3LP*   *Devon*
Tel: (01237) 473748   *Open: ALL YEAR (Excl. Xmas)*   *Map Ref No. 02*

£35.00 to £90.00 | Y | N | Y

(No smoking symbol)

VISA: M'CARD:

The Pines at Eastleigh

Near Rd: A.39

A Georgian country house set in 7 acres with magnificent views over the Torridge estuary to Lundy Island. Selected by the AA as "one of Britain's Best in 2005". Log fires, king-size beds, garden room bar with library. Breakfasts use home-produced ingredients: fruit from the garden, home-made yoghurt & prize-winning local meats. Ground-floor rooms are available. All rooms are en-suite, some with feature bathrooms. All have T.V., tea/coffee facilities etc. Children over 9.
E-mail: pirrie@thepinesateastleigh.co.uk
www.thepinesateastleigh.co.uk

Lynn Pirrie   *The Pines at Eastleigh*   *Eastleigh*   *Bideford*   *EX39 4PA*   *Devon*
Tel: (01271) 860561   *Open: ALL YEAR*   *Map Ref No. 03*

£70.00 to £70.00 | N | Y | N

(No smoking symbol)

Cherryford House

Near Rd: A.30

'Far from the madding crowd' Cherryford House is situated in idyllic surroundings with 'the prettiest of walks' & 'food to die for' according to discerning guests, which is cooked by Graham. If you live to eat & enjoy a dinner party atmosphere (maximum 6 guests) it's a must to stay with the Leedoms in Gidleigh. Accommodation is in 3 delightful double rooms - all en-suite. Experience Bed & breakfast with style at Cherryford House.
E-mail: stay@cherryfordhouse.co.uk
www.cherryfordhouse.co.uk

Mrs Pauline Leedom   *Cherryford House*   *Gidleigh*   *Chagford*   *TQ13 8HS*   *Devon*
Tel: (01647) 433260   *Fax 01647 433637*   *Open: ALL YEAR*   *Map Ref No. 04*

Column headers (rotated): rate £ from - to per double room | children taken | evening meals | animals taken

Parford Well

Near Rd: A.382

This attractive house is a restful & friendly home. Good quality & style are combined in the comfortable bedrooms, which together with the guests' sitting room overlook the well-tended walled garden & surrounding meadows. There are wonderful walks on the doorstep both in the wooded valley of the River Teign & on the open moor. There is also a charming thatched Inn, just around the corner. Children over 8 years.
Email: tim@parfordwell.co.uk
www.parfordwell.co.uk

£60.00 to £75.00 — Y | N | N

Tim Daniel Parford Well Sandy Park Chagford TQ13 8JW Devon
Tel: (01647) 433353 Open: ALL YEAR Map Ref No. 05

Smallicombe Farm

Near Rd: A.35, A.30

Relax & enjoy an idyllic rural setting yet be close to the coast. Smallicombe nestles in 70 acres of ancient pasture & woodland. The ground-floor 'Garden Suite' (wheelchair accessible) of sitting room, bedroom & bathroom together with the 2 upstairs en-suite bedrooms overlook an unspoilt valley landscape. The sitting room is inviting with its huge inglenook. Treat yourself to a scrumptious farmhouse breakfast including award-winning sausages from your hosts Rare Breed Berkshire pigs.
E-mail: maggie_todd@yahoo.com
www.smallicombe.com

£54.00 to £64.00 — Y | N | N

VISA: M'CARD:

Maggie Todd Smallicombe Farm Northleigh Colyton EX24 6BU Devon
Tel: (01404) 831310 Fax 01404 831431 Open: ALL YEAR Map Ref No. 06

2 Taw Vale Terrace

Near Rd: A.377

A spacious Grade II listed Georgian style residence & grounds on the edge of Crediton. A family home with a warm welcome for up to 6 guests. The High Street is but a 10-minute stroll for a variety of eating establishments, friendly local shops & leisure facilities. This comfortable home is within easy reach of Exeter, Dartmoor, Exmoor & both coasts. It is also ideally positioned for touring the West Country by car or public transport.
www.bestbandb.co.uk

£50.00 to £50.00 — Y | N | N

VISA: M'CARD:

Sylvia & Peter Whitby 2 Taw Vale Terrace Station Road Crediton EX17 3BU Devon
Tel: (01363) 777879 Fax 01363 777879 Open: ALL YEAR Map Ref No. 07

The New Inn

Near Rd: A.377

The New Inn is a 13th-century thatched inn nestling in a quiet valley by the side of a brook. Accommodation in this attractive property includes 5 (non-smoking) en-suite bedrooms with 'phone, T.V. & tea/coffee-making facilities. There is also an extensive menu, using fresh local produce whenever possible. Local amenities include several golf courses, fishing, horse riding & sport & leisure facilities. Easy access to Dartmoor, Exmoor & the north & south Devon coasts.
E-mail: enquiries@thenewinncoleford.co.uk
www.thenewinncoleford.co.uk

£55.00 to £85.00 — Y | Y | N

VISA: M'CARD: AMEX:

Simon & Meliisa Renshaw The New Inn Coleford Crediton EX17 5BZ Devon
Tel: 01363 84242 Fax 01363 85044 Open: ALL YEAR Map Ref No. 08

Devon

Column headers (rotated): rate £ from - to per double room | children taken | evening meals | animals taken

---

Easton Court

£64.00 to £72.00	Y	N	Y

(No Smoking)

VISA: M'CARD:

Near Rd: A.382

Home of 'Brideshead Revisited', Easton Court is a charming Tudor country house, set in 4 acres of grounds within the Dartmoor National Park. The Edwardian wing houses 5 lovely en-suite guest rooms, all with stunning views towards the Teign Valley Gorge. The light & airy guest lounge/ breakfast room & access to the delightful gardens completes this luxury accommodation. An ideal base for touring Dartmoor & the West Country. Children over 10. Animals by arrangement.
E-mail: stay@easton.co.uk
www.easton.co.uk

Debra & Paul Witting	Easton Court	Easton Cross	Chagford	Dartmoor TQ13 8JL	Devon
Tel: (01647) 433469	Fax 01647 433654		Open: ALL YEAR		Map Ref No. 09

Reka Dom

£72.00 to £80.00	Y	Y	Y

(No Smoking)

Near Rd: M.5, A.38

Reka Dom is a 17th-century Heritage Merchant's House in the historic town of Topsham, with panoramic estuary, sea & countryside views. Offering 3 suites with private facilities. Each room is tastefully furnished with T.V./video/DVD, etc. Reka Dom is renowned for its hospitality & offers a wide choice at breakfast, with organic produce where possible. Evening meals by arrangement. Reiki Healing, massage & beauty therapies are available in the calm of this unique setting.
E-mail: beautifulhouse@hotmail.com
www.rekadom.co.uk

Marlene & Richard Gardner	Reka Dom	43 The Strand	Topsham	Exeter EX3 0AY	Devon
Tel: (01392) 873385		Open: ALL YEAR			Map Ref No. 10

The Galley 'Fish & Seafood' Restaurant

£75.00 to £250.00	Y	Y	N

(No Smoking)

VISA: M'CARD:

Near Rd: M.5 Jt.30

Discovering the secret is just the beginning with celebrity & Masterchef Paul Da-Costa-Greaves, who also happens to be an aromatherapist & spiritual healer & runs his kitchen under the guidance of Zen. Luxury nautical themed accommodation, with award-winning prime fish & seafood restaurant & panoramic river views. Children over 12. What dreams are made of...
E-mail: fish@galleyrestaurant.co.uk
www.galleyrestaurant.co.uk

The Galley 'Fish & Seafood' Restaurant & Spa with Cabins	41 Fore Street	Topsham	Exeter	EX3 0HU
Tel: 0845 6026862	Mobile 07956 396765	Open: ALL YEAR		Map Ref No. 10

Raffles

£62.00 to £64.00	Y	N	Y

VISA: M'CARD:

Near Rd: A.30

Raffles is a large Victorian house, very central & close to the University, retaining many original architectural features. The owners have applied their experience in the antique trade to enhance decorations & furnishings. It is a friendly house with personal service. Organic food is our preference. Off-street parking available. For further information & photographs, visit our web site or telephone for a brochure.
E-mail: raffleshtl@btinternet.com
www.raffles-exeter.co.uk

Rick & Sue Hyde	Raffles	11 Blackall Road	Exeter EX4 4HD	Devon
Tel: (01392) 270200	Fax 01392 270200	Open: ALL YEAR		Map Ref No. 11

	rate £ from - to per double room	children taken	evening meals	animals taken

Leworthy Farmhouse

Near Rd: A.388

A charming Georgian farmhouse nestling in an unspoilt backwater with lawns, meadow & a fishing lake. The inviting guest rooms are beautifully furnished with antiques or pine & have en-suite/private facilities, T.V., & hospitality tray. A peaceful lounge in which to relax with chiming clocks & sparkling Victoriana china. A farmhouse breakfast with free-range eggs is served or kippers, prunes, porridge etc. Good walking, cycling & fishing nearby & 20 mins' from the north Cornish coast.
E-mail: leworthyfarmhouse@yahoo.co.uk
www.leworthyfarmhouse.co.uk

£55.00 to £65.00 — Y — N — N

see PHOTO over p. 105

Mrs Pat Jennings   Leworthy Farmhouse   Lower Leworthy   Nr. Pyworthy   Holsworthy EX22 6SJ
Tel: (01409) 259469   Fax 01409 259469   Open: ALL YEAR   Map Ref No. 12

Highcliffe House

Near Rd: A.39

Highcliffe House, originally built c.1860 as a gentleman's summer residence, stands in its own grounds above Lynton with magnificent views of the Exmoor coastline & hills across the Bristol Channel to Wales. With exceptionally appointed bedrooms, some with super king-size feature wooden beds, Karen & Michael offer a high degree of comfort coupled with the very best of English hospitality. A touch of luxury, in a very special place to stay. Evening meals by arrangement. Children over 12.
E-mail: info@highcliffehouse.co.uk
www.highcliffehouse.co.uk

£72.00 to £96.00 — Y — Y — N

VISA: M'CARD: AMEX:

Karen & Mike Orchard   Highcliffe House   Sinai Hill   Lynton EX35 6AR   Devon
Tel: (01598) 752235   Fax 01598 753815   Open: FEB - NOV   Map Ref No. 13

Coombe Farm

Near Rd: A.39

Coombe Farm is a 365-acre, hill-sheep farm, with an early-17th-century farmhouse set betwixt Lynmouth & the legendary Doone Valley. The coast path runs through the farm at Desolate. All within the spectacular Exmoor National Park. The en-suite bedrooms include 1 double, 1 twin & 2 family rooms. All have hot-drink facilities, shaver points, & bath & hand towels. Central heating. A lounge with woodburner fire & colour T.V..
E-mail: coombefarm@freeuk.com
www.brendonvalley.co.uk/coombe_farm.htm.

£49.00 to £56.00 — Y — N — N

VISA: M'CARD:

Susan Pile   Coombe Farm   Countisbury   Lynton EX35 6NF   Devon
Tel: (01598) 741236   Open: MAR - NOV   Map Ref No. 14

Great Sloncombe Farm

Near Rd: A.382

Great Sloncombe Farm is a listed, granite-&-cob-built, 13th-century farmhouse. Set in a peaceful Dartmoor valley, the rambling house has a magical atmosphere, & is furnished with oak & pine, antique china & interesting old photographs. The 3 warm & pleasant bedrooms are all en-suite & have every facility included. Delicious breakfasts, with home-made bread are served. Children over 8 years by arrangement.
E-mail: hmerchant@sloncombe.freeserve.co.uk
www.greatsloncombefarm.co.uk

£56.00 to £62.00 — Y — N — Y

Trudie Merchant   Great Sloncombe Farm   Moretonhampstead TQ13 8QF   Devon
Tel: (01647) 440595   Fax 01647 440595   Open: ALL YEAR   Map Ref No. 15

Leworthy Farmhouse B & B.   Lower Loworthy.

	rate £ from - to per double room	children taken	evening meals	animals taken

Great Doccombe Farm

Near Rd: A.30

Great Doccombe Farm is situated in the pretty hamlet of Doccombe, within the Dartmoor National Park, on the B.3212 from Exeter. An ideal base for walking in the Teign Valley & nearby moors, with golf, riding & fishing nearby. This lovely 16th-century granite farmhouse is surrounded by gardens & fields. The bedrooms (1 ground-floor) are all en-suite, & have shower, T.V. & tea/coffee facilities. A traditional English breakfast is served. Great Doccombe Farm is a perfect place to relax.

E-mail: david.oakey3@btopenworld.com
www.greatdoccombefarm.co.uk

£48.00 to £48.00 — Y N N

Gill & David Oakey   Great Doccombe Farm   Doccombe   Moretonhampstead TQ13 8SS   Devon
Tel: (01647) 440694   Open: ALL YEAR   Map Ref No. 16

Sampsons Farm Hotel Restaurant

Near Rd: A.38, A.380

Sampsons is a welcoming thatched farmhouse, set in its own grounds in a sleepy village & yet it is only 5 mins from the A.38 & A.380. There are a wealth of oak beams, log fires, history & tranquillity & a renowned (award-winning) restaurant serving delicious country produce. Pretty en-suite rooms in the barn conversions around the courtyard., some with private patios & a luxurious spacious suite. Also, charming en-suite rooms in the farmhouse. Lovely river & meadow walks. Children over 10.

E-mail: nigel@sampsonsfarm.com
www.sampsonsfarm.com

£50.00 to £85.00 — Y Y Y

VISA: M'CARD:

Nigel Bell   Sampsons Farm Hotel Restaurant   Preston   Newton Abbot TQ12 3PP   Devon
Tel: (01626) 354913   Fax 01626 332673   Open: ALL YEAR   Map Ref No. 17

Penpark

Near Rd: A.38

Situated within the Dartmoor National Park with magnificent hilltop views, Penpark is an elegant country house designed by Clough Williams Ellis of Portmeirion fame. There are 5 acres of formal & informal gardens & a tennis court. 3 charming rooms with private facilities. 1 double/twin with balcony, 1 double room & the garden room, which is a double/family room with 3 double-glazed doors opening onto the garden. Breakfasts a speciality. A wide choice of very good pubs & restaurants.

E-mail: maddy@penpark.co.uk
www.penpark.co.uk

£64.00 to £70.00 — Y N N

see PHOTO over
p. 107

Mrs Madeleine Gregson   Penpark   Bickington   Newton Abbot TQ12 6LH   Devon
Tel: (01626) 821314   Fax 01626 821101   Open: ALL YEAR   Map Ref No. 18

Great Wooston Farm

Near Rd: A.30

Great Wooston Farm was once part of the Manor House Estate owned by Lord Hambledon. Situated high above the Teign Valley in the Dartmoor National Park, with views across the moors. Plenty of walks, golf, fishing & riding nearby. The farmhouse is surrounded by a delightful garden of 1/2 an acre, also barbeque & picnic area. 3 bedrooms, 2 en-suite, 1 with 4-poster bed, 1 with private bathroom. Excellent breakfasts. Also, a guests' lounge for your relaxation. Children over 8.

E-mail: info@greatwoostonfarm.com
www.greatwoostonfarm.com

£55.00 to £62.00 — Y N N

VISA: M'CARD:

Mrs Mary Cuming   Great Wooston Farm   Moretonhampstead   Newton Abbot TQ13 8QA   Devon
Tel/Fax: (01647) 440367   Mobile 07798 670590   Open: ALL YEAR   Map Ref No. 19

Penpark. Bickington.

	rate £ from - to per double room	children taken	evening meals	animals taken

Stowford House

Near Rd: A.30

A warm welcome & fabulous breakfasts await you at this delightful Georgian country house. Perfectly located for exploring Devon & Cornwall, including the lovely Tamar Valley, Dartmoor & the coast. The world renowned Eden Project & several National Trust properties are nearby. The 3 large bedrooms, the elegant drawing room & garden ensure a relaxing stay. The area offers walking, cycling, golf, riding & sailing. There is an excellent pub & restaurants nearby. Children over 12.
E-mail: alison@stowfordhouse.com
www.stowfordhouse.com

£55.00 to £65.00 — Y — N — N

VISA: M'CARD:

Alison Pardoe   Stowford House   Lewdown   Okehampton EX20 4BZ   Devon
Tel: (01566) 783415   Fax 01566 783489   Open: ALL YEAR (Excl. Xmas)   Map Ref No. 20

Westways

Near Rd: A.38, A.386

Situated approx. 3 1/2 miles from Plymouth city centre, this attractive detached house offers pleasant accommodation in 3 well-furnished (non-smoking) rooms, with tea/coffee-making facilities. Excellent breakfasts are served in the elegant dining room. Guests may choose to relax & plan their excursions in the comfortable sitting room or make use of the small T.V. room. A homely & friendly base both for visitors wishing to make the most of the many attractions in the area, & for touring Devon. Children over 12.
E-mail: turner.jd@btopenworld.com

£25.00 to £60.00 — Y — N — N

VISA: M'CARD:

John & Daphne Turner   Westways   706 Budshead Road   Crownhill   Plymouth PL6 5DY   Devon
Tel: (01752) 776617   Mobile 0777 8479696   Open: ALL YEAR   Map Ref No. 21

Brookdale House

Near Rd: A.38

Brookdale House is a Grade II listed Tudor style house, situated in a peaceful secluded valley with delightful grounds. Offering 3 individually designed bedrooms, with T.V. & tea/coffee-making facilities. Each room is elegantly furnished with antiques in period style. A delicious Aga-cooked breakfast is served using only the finest local ingredients. A charming home, perfect for a relaxing break & an ideal base for exploring Dartmoor or the coastal attractions. Animals by arrangement.
E-mail: christa_naips@yahoo.co.uk
www.brookdalehouse.com

£50.00 to £55.00 — Y — N — Y

Mrs Christa Napier-Bell   Brookdale House   North Huish   South Brent TQ10 9NF   Devon
Tel: (01548) 821661   Open: ALL YEAR   Map Ref No. 22

Coombe House

Near Rd: A.38

Gracious Georgian residence set in 33 acres in a designated Area of Outstanding Natural Beauty. 4 en-suite bedrooms, some with 4-posters, with T.V., radio, hairdryer & tea/coffee tray. Elegant dining room & guest lounge with log fire. Delicious home-cooked food prepared using fresh local produce (by arrangement). The coast, Dartmoor, Totnes, Salcombe, Plymouth & Exeter are all within easy reach. Children over 12 years. Also, 4 barn conversions for self-catering.
E-mail: coombehouse@hotmail.com
www.coombehouse.uk.com

£60.00 to £90.00 — Y — Y — N

see PHOTO over p. 109

Faith & John Scharenguivel   Coombe House   North Huish   South Brent TQ10 9NJ   Devon
Tel: (01548) 821277   Fax 01548 821277   Open: ALL YEAR   Map Ref No. 23

Coombe House.   North Huish.

Devon

Kerscott Farm

Near Rd: A.361

Kerscott Farm offers quality accommodation at a sensible price. This peaceful Exmoor working farm & olde worlde farmhouse is mentioned in the Domesday Book (1086). It has an absolutely fascinating interior with many antiques, pictures & china - a rare find. There are beautiful, extensive views. There are 3 pretty & tastefully furnished en-suite bedrooms with T.V. & tea/coffee-making facilities. Wholesome country cooking, pure spring water. An elegant home.
E-mail: kerscott.farm@virgin.net
www.devon-bandb.co.uk

	rate £	children	evening	animals
	£52.00 to £56.00	N	Y	N

Theresa Sampson   Kerscott Farm   Ash Mill   South Molton EX36 4QG   Devon
Tel: (01769) 550262   Fax 01769 550910   Open: ALL YEAR (Excl. Xmas & New Year) Map Ref No. 24

Tor Cottage

Near Rd: A.30

Award-winning Tor Cottage has a warm & relaxed atmosphere & nestles in its own private valley. 18 acres of wildlife hillsides. Lovely gardens & a streamside setting. Beautifully appointed en-suite bed/sitting rooms with log fires & a private terrace. Sumptuous breakfasts. Dinner booking service at local restaurants. Heated outdoor pool (summer). Tranquil base adjacent Dartmoor Valley. Central for touring Devon/Cornwall. 45 min. drive to the Eden Project. Special rate autumn/spring breaks.
E-mail: info@torcottage.co.uk
www.torcottage.co.uk

	rate £	children	evening	animals
	£140.00 to £150.00	N	Y	N

see PHOTO over
p. 111

VISA: M'CARD:

Mrs Maureen Rowlatt   Tor Cottage   Chillaton   Nr. Tavistock PL16 0JE   Devon
Tel: (01822) 860248   Fax 01822 860126   Open: ALL YEAR (Excl. Xmas & New Year) Map Ref No. 25

Burnville House

Near Rd: A.386

This substantial Georgian house stands in informal gardens amidst beech woods & rhododendrons in the heart of a 250 acre livestock farm within Dartmoor National Park. Large comfortable bedrooms furnished with antiques have stunning moorland views & luxurious bathrooms. Delicious food made with local produce, log fires, the perfect place to relax, unwind & absorb the beauty & tranquillity of Dartmoor. Heated pool, tennis court & clay pigeon shooting available.
E-mail: burnvillef@aol.com
www.burnville.co.uk

	rate £	children	evening	animals
	£60.00 to £70.00	Y	Y	Y

Victoria Cunningham   Burnville House   Brentor   Tavistock PL19 0NE   Devon
Tel: (01822) 820443   Open: ALL YEAR   Map Ref No.26

Quither Mill

Near Rd: A.30

Quither Mill is situated in a sleepy hamlet & is Grade II listed, being of architectural & historical interest. Dating from the 18th century, the mill wheel & workings are intact. Guests enjoy the comfort of beautiful beamed en-suite bedrooms & full English breakfast. The hosts are proud of their reputation for fine cooking drawn from 20 years in the hotel world, which makes dinner a memorable experience. A delightful home.
E-mail: quither.mill@virgin.net
www.quithermill.co.uk

	rate £	children	evening	animals
	£76.00 to £76.00	N	Y	N

VISA: M'CARD:

David & Jill Wright   Quither Mill   Chillaton   Tavistock PL19 0PZ   Devon
Tel: Tel: (01822) 860160   Fax 01822 860160   Open: ALL YEAR   Map Ref No. 27

Tor Cottage. Chillaton.

Devon

Beera Farmhouse

Near Rd: A.30

Beera is a large, traditional stone built Victorian farmhouse set in an Area of Outstanding Natural Beauty. The farm is a 160-acre beef & sheep farm on the bank of the river Tamar. Guests may walk on the farm & take in the beautiful scenery. 3 attractive en-suite bedrooms (1 with 4-poster), each with T.V. & tea/coffee facilities. Evening meals by arrangement. Ideal for touring the West Country & within easy reach of the coast, Dartmoor National Park, National Trust properties & the Eden Project.

E-mail: hilary.tucker@farming.co.uk
www.beera-farm.co.uk

£60.00 to £80.00	Y Y N	

VISA: M'CARD:

Hilary Tucker   Beera Farmhouse   Milton Abbot   Tavistock PL19 8PL   Devon
Tel: (01822) 870216   Fax 01822 870216   Open: ALL YEAR (Excl. Xmas & New Year) Map Ref No. 28

Wytchwood

Near Rd: A.381

Award-winning Wytchwood has an outstanding reputation for lavish hospitality & traditional home-cooking. To stay here is to be truly pampered! Panoramic views, beautiful garden, stylish interior design & pretty bedrooms with en-suite/private bathrooms fulfil every expectation. Home-made bread & rolls, jams, preserves, orchard honey & garden produce. Delicious Devonshire cream teas, sponges & cakes. Many culinary awards. A warm welcome is always assured at Wytchwood.

E-mail: Wytchwood@onetel.com
www.richardsonbrown.com

£60.00 to £80.00   Y N N

see PHOTO over p. 113

VISA: M'CARD:

Jennifer Richardson Brown   Wytchwood   West Buckeridge   Teignmouth TQ14 8NF   Devon
Tel: (01626) 773482   Mobile 07971 783454   Open: ALL YEAR   Map Ref No. 29

Hornhill Farmhouse

Near Rd: A.361

Hornhill, originally a coaching inn, has panoramic views over the beautiful Exe valley. Set in a large garden & surrounded by farmland. The charming hosts offer guests comfort, warmth, delicious home-cooking & a happy atmosphere. The house, furnished with antiques, has 3 attractive bedrooms (1 with a Victorian 4-poster), each with private bathroom, T.V. & tea/coffee facilities. 1 is suitable for the partially disabled. Guests may relax in the drawing room, with plenty of books & a log fire.

E-mail: hornhill@tinyworld.co.uk
www.hornhill-farmhouse.co.uk

£55.00 to £55.00   N N N

Barbara Pugsley   Hornhill Farmhouse   Exeter Hill   Tiverton EX16 4PL   Devon
Tel/Fax: (01884) 253352   Open: ALL YEAR (Excl. Xmas & New Year)   Map Ref No. 30

West Bradley

Near Rd: B.3137

West Bradley offers total immersion amidst beauty with fields on either side of a long drive, Dartmoor views, bluebells in spring, a sparkling stream & a pretty garden. Privacy too, in the 18th-century upside down barn on the side of a 17th-century Devon long house. A handmade oak staircase, oak floors, rugs, a large bed & a good sofabed. Excellent riding & stabling available for your own horse. Perfect for a relaxing break. Single supplement.

E-mail: martin.strong@btinternet.com
www.bestbandb.co.uk

£58.00 to £70.00   Y N N

Phillida & Martin Strong   West Bradley   Templeton   Tiverton EX16 8BJ   Devon
Tel: (01884) 253220   Fax 01884 259504   Open: ALL YEAR   Map Ref No. 31

Wytchwood. West Buckeridge.

Devon

Fairmount House Hotel

Near Rd: A.380

Experience somewhere special & feel completely at home in the tranquillity, warmth & informal atmosphere of this small hotel. Offering 8 comfortable en-suite bedrooms, unhurried breakfasts & undisturbed evenings. (2 lower-ground-floor rooms have private doors opening onto the garden.) Renowned for its mild climate, Torquay boasts a profusion of sub-tropical plants & miles of beaches & sheltered coves. Fairmount offers quality, comfort & genuine friendly service.

E-mail: stay@fairmounthousehotel.co.uk
www.fairmounthousehotel.co.uk

| £50.00 to £66.00 | Y | Y | Y |

VISA: M'CARD:

Mike & Wendy French   Fairmount House Hotel   Herbert Road   Chelston   Torquay TQ2 6RW
Tel: (01803) 605446   Fax 01803 605446   Open: ALL YEAR   Map Ref No. 32

Parliament House

Near Rd: A.385

An ancient rambling thatched house where in 1688 William of Orange is said to have held his first parliament. The simple interior has many interesting details. One of the bedrooms has a double Victorian brass bed with a sunny en-suite shower/bathroom & the other is a super king/twin with a blue 'toile de Jouy' private bathroom. Delicious breakfasts made from locally sourced produce are served in the panelled dining room. The garden is a delight to relax in.

E-mail: parliamenthouse@btopenworld.com
www.bestbandb.co.uk

| £65.00 to £75.00 | N | N | N |

Harry & Carole Grimley   Parliament House   Longcombe   Nr. Totnes TQ9 6PR   Devon
Tel: (01803) 840288   Open: ALL YEAR   Map Ref No. 33

Orchard House

Near Rd: A.381

Surrounded by quiet countryside in a beautiful valley between Totnes & Kingsbridge, Orchard House is ideally placed for the nearby South Devon coastline & Dartmoor. It offers 3 wonderfully furnished en-suite bedrooms, each with T.V., clock/radio & tea/coffee facilities etc. Also, guests' sitting room with antiques & log fire. In the spacious dining room breakfasts are served on a large platter using local produce & home-made preserves. Large garden. Parking. Children over 3 years.

E-mail: helen@orchard-house-halwell.co.uk
www.orchard-house-halwell.co.uk

| £50.00 to £55.00 | Y | N | N |

see PHOTO over
p. 115

Mrs Helen Worth   Orchard House   Horner   Halwell   Totnes TQ9 7LB   Devon
Tel: (01548) 821448   Open: MAR - OCT   Map Ref No. 34

Lower Norton Farmhouse

Near Rd: A.381

Only 10 mins' from the sea, perfectly situated for exploring the ancient south Devon towns of Dartmouth, Totnes & Kingsbridge. The lovely Georgian farm house nestles in an outstandingly beautiful valley. You will be treated as family in a relaxed atmosphere. Stay all day, sit in the lounge, on the terrace with a cream tea or visit the National Trust houses close by. Superb en-suite rooms, great breakfasts & candlelit dinners in a 400-year-old dining hall - wonderful. Children over 9.

E-mail: lowernorton@tiscali.co.uk
www.smoothhound.co.uk/hotels/lowernorton

| £55.00 to £65.00 | Y | Y | N |

Glynis & Peter Bidwell   Lower Norton Farmhouse   Coles Cross   Nr. East Allington   Totnes TQ9 7RL
Tel: (01548) 521246   Open: ALL YEAR   Map Ref No. 35

Orchard House.   Horner.

		rate £ from - to per double room	children taken	evening meals	animals taken
Stokehill Farmhouse	Near Rd: A.386 Stokehill is a beautiful Victorian country house, set in lovely grounds on the edge of the Dartmoor National Park. The house is richly furnished with large, attractive, well-equipped bedrooms, which command stunning views. An elegant drawing room, conservatory & the lovely gardens are available for use by the residents. Parking. Guests can dine at a nearby award-winning pub. The house is ideally situated for enjoying the many & varied delights of Devon & Cornwall. Children over 9. **E-mail: enquiries@stokehillfarmhouse.co.uk** **www.stokehillfarmhouse.co.uk**	£55.00 to £60.00	Y	N	N
Mrs Ruth Gozzard Stokehill Farmhouse Tel: (01822) 853791 Fax 01822 853791	Stokehill Lane Crapstone Yelverton PL20 7PP Open: ALL YEAR (Excl. Xmas) Map Ref No. 36				

Dorset

Dorset
(West Country)

The unspoilt nature of this gem of a county is emphasised by the designation of virtually all of the coast & much of the inland country as an Area of Outstanding Natural Beauty. Along the coast from Christchurch to Lyme Regis there are a fascinating variety of sandy beaches, towering cliffs & single banks, whilst inland is a rich mixture of downland, lonely heaths, fertile valleys, historic houses & lovely villages of thatch & mellow stone buildings.

Thomas Hardy was born here & took the Dorset countryside as a background for many of his novels. Few writers can have stamped their identity on a county more than Hardy on Dorset, forever to be known as the "Hardy Country". Fortunately most of the area that he so lovingly described remains unchanged, including Egdon Heath & the county town of Dorchester, famous as Casterbridge.

In the midst of the rolling chalk hills which stretch along the Storr Valley lies picturesque Cerne Abbas, with its late mediaeval houses & cottages & the ruins of a Benedictine Abbey. At Godmanstone is the tiny thatched "Smiths Arms" claiming to be the smallest pub in England.

The north of the county is pastoral with lovely views over broad Blackmoor Vale. Here is the ancient hilltop town of Shaftesbury, with cobbled Gold Hill, one of the most photographed streets in the country.

Coastal Dorset is spectacular. Poole harbour is an enormous, almost circular bay, an exciting mixture of 20th century activity, ships of many nations & beautiful building of the 15th, 18th & early 19th centuries.

Westwards lies the popular resort of Swanage, where the sandy beach & sheltered bay are excellent for swimming. From here to Weymouth is a marvellous stretch of coast with scenic wonders like Lulworth Cove & the arch of Durdle Door.

Chesil Beach is an extraordinary bank of graded pebbles, as perilous to shipping today as it was 1,000 years ago. It is separated from the mainland by a sheltered lagoon known as the Fleet. From here a range of giant cliffs rises to 617 feet at Golden Gap & stretches westwards to Lyme Regis, beloved by Jane Austen who wrote "Persuasion" whilst living here.

Dorset has many interesting archaeological features. Near Dorchester is Maiden Castle, huge earthwork fortifications on a site first inhabited 6,000 years ago. The Badbury rings wind round a wooded hilltop near Wimborne Minster; legend has it that King Arthur's soul, in the form of a raven, inhabited this "dread" wood. The giant of Cerne Abbas is a figure of a man 180 feet high carved into the chalk hillside. Long associated with fertility there is still speculation about the figures' origins, one theory suggesting it is a Romano-British depiction of Hercules. A Roman amphitheatre can be seen at Dorchester, & today's road still follows the Roman route to Weymouth.

Corfe Castle.

Dorset

Dorset
Gazeteer

Areas of outstanding natural beauty.
The Entire County.

Houses & Castles

Athelthampton
Mediaeval house - one of the finest in all
England. Formal gardens.

Barneston Manor - Nr. Church Knowle
13th - 16th century stone built manor
house.

Forde Abbey - Nr. Chard
12th century Cistercian monastery -
noted Mortlake tapestries.

Manor House - Sandford Orcas
Mansion of Tudor period, furnished with
period furniture, antiques, silver, china,
glass, paintings.

Hardy's Cottage - Higher Bockampton
Birthplace of Thomas Hardy, author
(1840-1928).

Milton Abbey - Nr. Blandford
18th century Georgian house built on
original site of 15th century abbey.

Purse Caundle Manor - Purse Caundle
Mediaeval Manor - furnished in style of
period.

Parnham House - Beaminster
Tudor Manor - some later work by Nash.
Leaded windows & heraldic plasterwork.
Home of John Makepeace & the
International School for Craftsmen in
Wood. House, gardens & workshops.

Sherborne Castle - Sherborne
16th century mansion - continuously
occupied by Digby family.

No. 3 Trinity Street - Weymouth
Tudor cottages now converted into one
house, furnished 17th century.

Smedmore - Kimmeridge
18th century manor.

Wolfeton House - Dorchester
Mediaeval & Elizabethan Manor. Fine
stone work, great stair. 17th century
furniture - Jacobean ceilings &
fireplaces.

Cathedrals & Churches

Bere Regis (St. John the Baptist)
12th century foundation - enlarged in
13th & 15th centuries.
Timber roof & nave, fine arcades.
16th century seating.

Blandford (St. Peter & St. Paul)
18th century - ashlar - Georgian design.
Galleries, pulpit, box pews, font & mayoral
seat.

Bradford Abbas (St. Mary)
14th century - parapets & pinnacled
tower, panelled roof. 15th century bench
ends, stone rood screen. 17th century
pulpit.

Cerne Abbas (St. Mary)
13th century - rebuilt 15th & 16th
centuries, 14th century wall paintings, 15th
century tower, stone screen, pulpit
possibly 11th century.

Chalbury (dedication unknown)
13th century origin - 14th century east
windows, timber bellcote. Plastered walls,
box pews, 3-decker pulpit, west gallery.

Christchurch (Christ Church)
Norman nave - ribbed plaster vaulting -
perpendicular spire. Tudor renaissance
Salisbury chantry - screen with Tree of
Jesse: notable misericord seats.

Milton Abbey (Sts. Mary, Michael,
Sampson & Branwaleder)
14th century pulpitum & sedilla, 15th
century reredos & canopy, 16th century
monument, Milton effigies 1775.

Sherborne (St. Mary)
Largely Norman but some Saxon remains
- excellent fan vaulting, of nave & choir.
12th & 13th century effigies - 15th century
painted glass.

Studland (St. Nicholas)
12th century - best Norman church in the
country. 12th century font, 13th century
east windows.

Whitchurch Canonicorum (St. Candida
& Holy Cross)
12th & 13th century. 12th century font,
relics of patroness in 13th century shrine,
15th century painted glass, 15th century
tower.

Wimbourne Minster (St. Cuthberga)
12th century central tower & arcade,
otherwise 13th-15th century. Former
collegiate church. Georgian glass, some
Jacobean stalls & screen. Monuments &
famed clock of 14th century.

Yetminster (St. Andrew)
13th century chancel - 15th century rebuilt
with embattled parapets. 16th century
brasses & seating.

Dorset

Museums & Galleries

Abbey Ruins - Shaftesbury
Relics excavated from Benedictine Nunnery founded by Alfred the Great.

Russell-Cotes Art Gallery & Museum - Bournemouth
17th-20th century oil paintings, watercolours, sculptures, ceramics, miniatures, etc.

Rothesay Museum - Bournemouth
English porcelain, 17th century furniture, collection of early Italian paintings, arms & armour, ethnography, etc.

Bournemouth Natural Science Society's Museum
Archaeology & local natural history.

Brewery Farm Museum - Milton Abbas
Brewing & village bygones from Dorset.

Dorset County Museum - Dorchester
Geology, natural history, pre-history. Thomas Hardy memorabilia

Philpot Museum - Lyme Regis
Old documents & prints, fossils, lace & old fire engine.

Guildhall Museum - Poole
Social & civic life of Poole during 18th & 19th centuries displayed in two-storey Georgian market house.

Scapolen's Court - Poole
14th century house of local merchant

exhibiting local & archaeological history of town, also industrial archaeology.

Sherborne Museum - Sherborne
Local history & geology - abbey of AD 705, Sherborne missal AD 1400, 18th century local silk industry.

Gallery 24 - Shaftesbury
Art exhibitions - paintings, pottery, etc.

Red House Museum & Art Gallery - Christchurch
Natural history & antiques of the region. Georgian house with herb garden.

Priest's House Museum - Wimbourne Minster
Tudor building in garden exhibiting local archaeology & history.

Other things to see & do

Abbotsbury Swannery - Abbotsbury
Unique colony of Swans established by monks in the 14th century. 16th century duck decoy, reed walk, information centre.

Dorset Rare Breeds Centre - Park Farm, Gillingham

Poole Potteries - the Quay, Poole

Sea Life Centre - Weymouth
Variety of displays, including Ocean Tunnel, sharks, living "touch" pools.

West Bay.

DORSET

Map reference

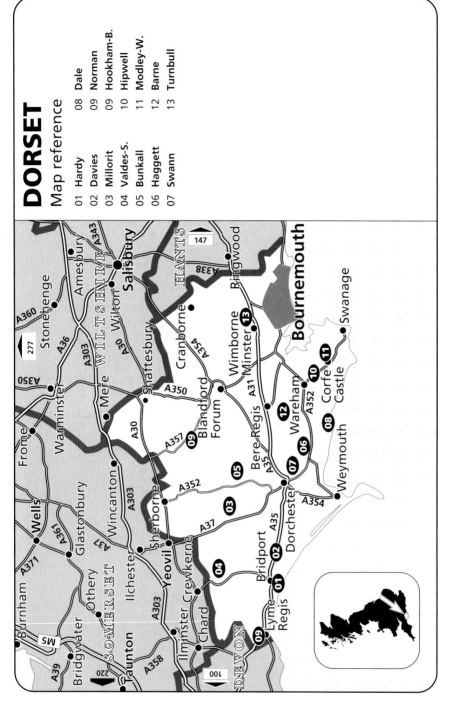

Dorset

rate £ from - to / per double room / children taken / evening meals / animals taken

£56.00 to £68.00	Y	N	Y

VISA: M'CARD:

Britmead House

Near Rd: A.35

A friendly welcome in a relaxed & comfortable atmosphere. Renowned for good food, a high standard of facilities, personal service & attention to detail. Situated between Bridport, the fishing harbour of West Bay, Chesil Beach & the Dorset Coastal Path. 8 individually decorated en-suite bedrooms, 3 on the ground floor, all with T.V., tea/coffee-making facilities & hairdryer. South-facing lounge & dining room overlook the garden & open countryside beyond. Parking.
E-mail: britmead@talk21.com
www.britmeadhouse.co.uk

Louisa & Alan Hardy   Britmead House   154 West Bay Road   Bridport DT6 4EG   Dorset
Tel: (01308) 422941   Fax 01308 422516   Open: ALL YEAR   Map Ref No. 01

£75.00 to £85.00	Y	Y	Y

VISA: M'CARD:

Innsacre Farmhouse

Near Rd: A.35

17th-century farmhouse & barn in a magical & peaceful setting. Hidden midway between Lyme Regis & Dorchester, 3 miles from the sea & National Trust coastal path. South-facing, 10 acres of spinneys, steep hillsides, orchard & lawns in a beautiful setting. A mix of French rustic style, English comfort & a genuine, warm welcome. All rooms en-suite (with T.V. etc). Cosy sitting-room, log fires, beams & delicious breakfasts. Parking. Licensed. Children over 9. Single supplement.
E-mail: innsacre.farmhouse@btinternet.com
www.innsacre.com

Sydney & Jayne Davies   Innsacre Farmhouse   Shipton Gorge   Bridport DT6 4LJ   Dorset
Tel: (01308) 456137 Fax 01308 421187 Open: ALL YEAR (Excl. Xmas & New Year) Map Ref No. 02

£70.00 to £70.00	N	N	N

Woodwalls House

Near Rd: A.356, A.37

Woodwalls is a pretty country house set in 12 acres of its own grounds, surrounded by wild flower meadows, woods & fields, creating a haven of peace & tranquillity. 2 light, airy bedrooms, 1 double en-suite & 1 twin with private bathroom, each with colour T.V. & tea/coffee-making facilities are available for guests. A pretty award-winning pub serving excellent food is within easy reach. Your hosts pride themselves on their breakfasts, which include honey from their own bees & home-made marmalade. A delightful home.
www.bestbandb.co.uk

Mrs Sally Valdes-Scott   Woodwalls House   Corscombe   Dorchester DT2 0NT   Dorset
Tel: (01935) 891477   Fax 01935 891477   Open: ALL YEAR (Excl. Xmas)   Map Ref No. 04

£70.00 to £70.00	Y	N	Y

Holyleas House

Near Rd: B.3143

The family labrador will welcome you to this elegant country house set in 1/2 acre of pretty walled gardens. A peaceful village surrounded by rolling hills & good walks yet only 10 miles from Sherborne & Dorchester & 30 mins' from the World Heritage coast. Superb gardens & many historic houses close by. Double & twin en-suite rooms with many extra touches & guests' own sitting-room. Sumptuous breakfasts with locally sourced & organic produce. Village pub within walking distance.
E-mail: tiabunkall@holyleas.fsnet.co.uk
www.holyleashouse.co.uk

Mrs Tia Bunkall   Holyleas House   Buckland Newton   Dorchester DT2 7DP   Dorset
Tel: (01300) 345214   Fax 01305 264488   Open: ALL YEAR (Excl. Xmas)   Map Ref No. 05

	rate £ from - to per double room	children taken	evening meals	animals taken

Brambles

Near Rd: A.37

Set in beautiful, tranquil countryside, Brambles is a pretty thatched cottage offering every comfort, superb views & a friendly welcome. There is a choice of en-suite twin, double or single rooms, all very comfortable & with colour T.V. & tea/coffee-making facilities. Pretty garden available for relaxing in. Full English or Continental breakfast served. Evening meals available by prior arrangement. There are many interesting places to visit & wonderful walks for enthusiasts.
www.bestbandb.co.uk

£60.00 to £60.00 — Y Y N

see PHOTO over p. 123

Anita & Andre Millorit   Brambles   Woolcombe   Melbury Bubb   Dorchester DT2 0NJ   Dorset
Tel: (01935) 83672   Open: ALL YEAR (Excl. Xmas)   Map Ref No. 03

Long Acre

Near Rd: A.352

Peaceful & secluded country home set in an acre of garden surrounded by fields in the pretty village of Owermoigne. Near the World Heritage Jurassic coast & Dorchester (7 miles). 2 bedrooms, 1 en-suite, with T.V. etc. An excellent base to explore unspoilt Hardy countryside. Moreton Church (world renowned for unique engraved Whistler windows & burial place of Lawrence of Arabia), Bovington Tank Museum, Monkey World & more. Excellent local pubs. Mainline rail station 2 miles.
E-mail: tessa.tripp@homecall.co.uk
www.longacre-dorset.co.uk

£50.00 to £75.00 — Y N N

Mrs T. Tripp & Mrs D. Haggett   Long Acre   25 Moreton Road   Owermoigne   Dorchester DT2 8HY
Tel: (01305) 853806   Open: ALL YEAR (Excl. Xmas & New Year)   Map Ref No. 06

Yoah Cottage

Near Rd: A.352

Yoah Cottage is a most characterful Grade II listed 17th-century cottage - old beams, inglenook fireplaces, antiques, old rugs, modern paintings etc. Its owners are also ceramic sculptors so the house is full of their own work. There are 2 twin-bedded guest bedrooms with guest bathroom & sitting room with log fire when cold. Lovely garden. Delicious food. In the heart of Thomas Hardy country & 10 mins' drive from World Heritage Jurassic Coast. Evening meals & animals by arrangement. Children over 7.
www.bestbandb.co.uk

£40.00 to £60.00 — Y Y Y

Mrs R N Swann   Yoah Cottage   West Knighton   Dorchester DT2 8PE   Dorset
Tel: (01305) 852087   Open: ALL YEAR   Map Ref No. 07

Gatton House

Near Rd: A.352

Spectacularly positioned, quiet & comfortable, this small hotel is set amongst the Purbeck Hills, yet only a strolling distance from famous Lulworth Cove. The house has a spacious breakfast room, 8 attractive bedrooms (all en-suite) & a lounge with T.V.. Outside, the terrace provides a perfect venue for morning coffee or afternoon tea. Gatton House is an ideal location for walking or touring Dorset's beauty spots, & it is within easy reach of Bournemouth, Poole, Swanage, Dorchester & Weymouth.
E-mail: mike@gattonhouse.co.uk
www.gattonhouse.co.uk

£64.00 to £84.00 — N N N

VISA: M'CARD:

Avril & Mike Dale   Gatton House   Main Road   West Lulworth   Lulworth Cove BH20 5RL
Tel: (01929) 400252   Fax 01929 400252   Open: MAR - OCT   Map Ref No. 08

Brambles. Woolcombe.

	rate £ from – to per double room	children taken	evening meals	animals taken

The Red House

Near Rd: A.3052

This distinguished house, set in mature grounds, enjoys spectacular coastal views, & yet is only a short walk to the centre of Lyme Regis. The 3 en-suite bedrooms (1 for family use; 2 are especially spacious) are furnished with every comfort, in-cluding tea/coffee makers, T.V., clock-radio, desk, armchairs & a drink refrigerator. Fresh flowers & magazines are among the little extras. Breakfast can be taken on the garden balcony. Evening meals by arrangement. Parking. Children over 8.
E-mail: red.house@virgin.net
www.SmoothHound.co.uk/hotels/redhous2.html

£46.00 to £64.00 — Y — Y — N

VISA: M'CARD:

Tony & Vicky Norman   The Red House   Sidmouth Road   Lyme Regis DT7 3ES   Dorset
Tel: (01297) 442055   Fax 01297 442055   Open: Easter - Early NOV   Map Ref No. 09

Stourcastle Lodge

Near Rd: A.357

Stourcastle Lodge was rebuilt in the 18th century. Jill & Ken run the lodge in a friendly & relaxed manner, but offer a professional service with a high standard of cuisine & accommodation. All rooms are en-suite & overlook the south-facing garden. Guests may unwind in the secluded garden during the warmer months or toast their toes in front of the log fire on wintery evenings. An ideal base for exploring Dorset & its many attractions.
E-mail: enquiries@stourcastle-lodge.co.uk
www.stourcastle-lodge.co.uk

£78.00 to £92.00 — N — Y — N

see PHOTO over p. 125

VISA: M'CARD:

Jilly & Kenny Hookham-Bassett   Stourcastle Lodge   Gough's Close   Sturminster Newton DT10 1BU
Tel: (01258) 472320   Fax 01258 473381   Open: ALL YEAR   Map Ref No. 09

Gold Court House

Near Rd: A.351

Gold Court House is a charming Georgian house with walled garden on a small square on the south-side of Wareham. It offers 3 light & airy double or twin rooms with private bathrooms & all facilities at hand, at your request. Wareham is ideally situated for exploring the magnificent coastline of South Dorset & the Isle of Purbeck. Your hosts are always pleased to help & advise on the numerous places of interest, sporting activities & where to dine. (Evening meals are available Nov - Feb.) Children over 10.
E-mail: info@goldcourthouse.co.uk
www.goldcourthouse.co.uk

£60.00 to £60.00 — Y — Y — N

Anthea & Michael Hipwell   Gold Court House   St. John's Hill   Wareham BH20 4LZ   Dorset
Tel: (01929) 553320 Fax 01929 553320   Open: ALL YEAR (Excl. Xmas & New Year)   Map Ref No. 10

Springbrook Cottage

Near Rd: A.351

Springbrook Cottage is a beautiful house which is set in an acre of garden, lawn & shrubs including mature trees. There is an attractive conservatory in which guests may choose to relax, which boasts lovely views down to the valley beyond. Tradition-ally furnished with antiques, the property offers attractive accommodation in 2 charming bedrooms. The light & airy rooms are very comfortable. A delicious breakfast is served. Evening meals by prior arrangement. A large games room. A lovely base from which to explore the Dorset countryside.
www.bestbandb.co.uk

£70.00 to £70.00 — Y — Y — N

Mrs G. Modley-Wingfield   Springbrook Cottage   Springbrook Close   Corfe Castle Wareham BH20 5HS
Tel: (01929) 480509   Open: ALL YEAR   Map Ref No. 11

Stourcastle Lodge. Sturminster Newton.

Dorset

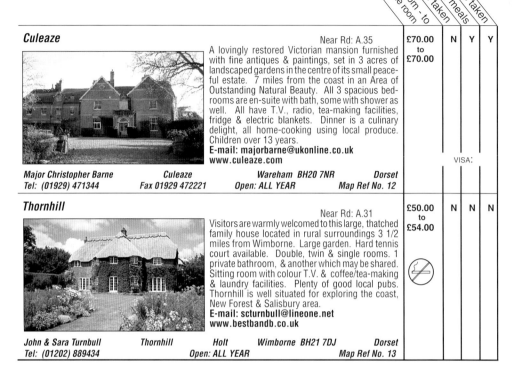

Culeaze	Near Rd: A.35	£70.00 to £70.00	N	Y	Y

A lovingly restored Victorian mansion furnished with fine antiques & paintings, set in 3 acres of landscaped gardens in the centre of its small peaceful estate. 7 miles from the coast in an Area of Outstanding Natural Beauty. All 3 spacious bedrooms are en-suite with bath, some with shower as well. All have T.V., radio, tea-making facilities, fridge & electric blankets. Dinner is a culinary delight, all home-cooking using local produce. Children over 13 years.
E-mail: majorbarne@ukonline.co.uk
www.culeaze.com

VISA:

Major Christopher Barne *Culeaze* *Wareham BH20 7NR* *Dorset*
Tel: (01929) 471344   Fax 01929 472221   Open: ALL YEAR   Map Ref No. 12

Thornhill — Near Rd: A.31 — £50.00 to £54.00 — N N N

Visitors are warmly welcomed to this large, thatched family house located in rural surroundings 3 1/2 miles from Wimborne. Large garden. Hard tennis court available. Double, twin & single rooms. 1 private bathroom, & another which may be shared. Sitting room with colour T.V. & coffee/tea-making & laundry facilities. Plenty of good local pubs. Thornhill is well situated for exploring the coast, New Forest & Salisbury area.
E-mail: scturnbull@lineone.net
www.bestbandb.co.uk

John & Sara Turnbull *Thornhill* *Holt* *Wimborne BH21 7DJ* *Dorset*
Tel: (01202) 889434   Open: ALL YEAR   Map Ref No. 13

All the establishments mentioned in this guide are members of
The Worldwide Bed & Breakfast Association

When booking your accommodation please mention
The Best Bed & Breakfast

Gloucestershire

Gloucestershire
(Heart of England)

The landscape is so varied the people speak not of one Gloucestershire but of three - Cotswold, Vale & Forest. The rounded hills of the Cotswolds sweep & fold in graceful compositions to form a soft & beautiful landscape in which nestle many pretty villages. To the east there are wonderful views of the Vale of Berkeley & Severn, & across to the dark wooded slopes of the Forest of Dean on the Welsh borders.

Hill Forts, ancient trackways & long barrows of neolithic peoples can be explored, & remains of many villas from late Roman times can be seen. A local saying "Scratch Gloucester & find Rome" reveals the lasting influence of the Roman presence. Three major roads mark the path of invasion & settlement. Akeman street leads to London, Ermine street & the Fosse Way to the north east. A stretch of Roman road with its original surface can be seen at Blackpool Bridge in the Forest of Dean, & Cirencester's museum reflects its status as the second most important Roman city in the country.

Offa's Dyke, 80 miles of bank & ditch on the Welsh border was the work of the Anglo-Saxons of Mercia who invaded in the wake of the Romans. Cotswold means "hills of the sheepcotes" in the Anglo-Saxon tongue, & much of the heritage of the area has its roots in the wealth created by the wool industry here.

Fine Norman churches such as those at Tewkesbury & Bishops Cleeve were overshadowed by the development of the perpendicular style of building made possible by the growing prosperity. Handsome 15th century church towers crown many wool towns & villages as at Northleach, Chipping Camden & Cirencester, & Gloucester has a splendid 14th century cathedral. Detailing on church buildings gives recognition to the source of the wealth-cloth-workers shears are depicted on the north west buttresses of Grantham church tower & couchant rams decorate church buttresses at Compton Bedale.

Wool & cloth weaving dominated life here in the 14th & 15th centuries with most families dependent on the industry. The cottage craft of weaving was gradually overtaken by larger looms & water power. A water mill can be seen in the beautiful village of Lower Slaughter & the cottages of Arlington Row in Bibury were a weaving factory.

The Cotswold weaving industry gave way to the growing force of the Lancashire mills but a few centres survive. At Witney you can still buy the locally made blankets for which the town is famous.

From the 16th century the wealthy gentry built parks & mansions. Amongst the most notable are the Jacobean Manor house at Stanway & the contrasting Palladian style mansion at Barnsley Park. Elizabethan timber frame buildings can be seen at Didbrook, Dymock & Deerhurst but houses in the local mellow golden limestone are more common, with Chipping Camden providing excellent examples.

Cheltenham was only a village when, in 1716 a local farmer noticed a flock of pigeons pecking at grains of salt around a saline spring in his fields. He began to bottle & sell the water & in 1784 his son-in-law, Henry Skillicorne, built a pump room & the place received the name of Cheltenham Spa. Physicians published treatises on the healing qualities of the waters, visitors began to flock there & Cheltenham grew in style & elegance.

Gloucestershire

Gloucestershire Gazeteer

Areas of outstanding natural beauty
The Cotswolds, Malvern Hills & the Wye Valley.

Houses & Castles

Ashleworth Court - Ashleworth
15th century limestone Manor house.
Badminton House - Badminton
Built in the reign of Charles II.
Stone newel staircase.
Berkeley Castle - Berkeley
12th century castle - still occupied by the Berkeley family. Magnificent collections of furniture, paintings, tapestries & carved timber work. Lovely terraced gardens & deer park.
Chavenage - Tetbury
Elizabethan Cotswold Manor house, Cromwellian associations.
Clearwell Castle - Nr. Coleford
A Georgian neo-Gothic house said to be oldest in Britain, recently restored.
Court House - Painswick
Cotswold Manor house - has original court room & bedchamber of Charles I.
Splendid panelling & antique furniture.
Dodington House - Chipping Sodbury
Perfect 18th century house with superb staircase. Landscape by Capability Brown.
Horton Court - Horton
Cotswold manor house altered & restored in 19th century.
Kelmscott Manor - Nr. Lechlade
16th century country house - 17th century additions. Examples of work of William Morris, Rosetti & Burne-Jones.
Owlpen Manor - Nr. Dursley
Historic group of traditional Cotswold stone buildings. Tudor Manor house with church, barn, court house & a grist mill. Holds a rare set of 17th century painted cloth wall hangings.
Snowshill Manor - Broadway
Tudor house with 17th century facade. Unique collection of musical instruments & clocks, toys, etc. Formal garden.
Sudeley Castle - Winchcombe
12th century - home of Katherine Parr, is rich in historical associations, contains art treasures & relics of bygone days.

Cathedrals & Churches

Bishops Cleeve (St. Michael & All Saints)
12th century with 17th century gallery. Magnificent Norman west front & south porch. Decorated chancel. Fine window.
Bledington (St.Leonards)
15th century glass in this perpendicular church, Norman bellcote. Early English east window.
Buckland (St. Michael)
13th century nave arcades. 17th century oak panelling, 15th century glass.
Cirencester (St. John the Baptist)
A magnificent church - remarkable exterior, 3 storey porch, 2 storey oriel windows, traceries & pinnacles. Wine-glass pulpit c.1450. 15th century glass in east window, monuments in Lady chapel.
Gloucester Cathedral
Birthplace of Perpendicular style in 14th century. Fan vaulting, east windows commemorate Battle of Crecy - Norman Chapter House.
Hailes Abbey - Winchcombe
14th century wall paintings, 15th century tiles, glass & screen, 17th century pulpit. Elizabethan benches.
Iron Acton (St. James the Less)
Perpendicular - 15th century memorial cross. 19th century mosaic floors, Laudian alter rails, Jacobean pulpit, effigies.
Newland (All Saints)
13th century, restored 18th century. Pinnacled west tower, effigies.
Prinknash Abbey - Gloucester
14th & 16th century - Benedictine Abbey.
Tewkesbury Abbey - Tewkesbury
Dates back to Norman times, contains Romanesque & Gothic styles. 14th century monuments.
Yate (St. Mary)
Splendid perpendicular tower.

Museums & Galleries

Bishop Hooper's Lodgings - Gloucester
3 Tudor timber frame buildings - museum of domestic life & agriculture in Gloucester since 1500.
Bourton Motor Museum - Bourton-on-the-Water
Collection of cars & motor cycles.
Cheltenham Art Gallery - Cheltenham.

Gloucestershire

Lower Slaughter.

Gallery of Dutch paintings, collection of oils, watercolours, pottery, porcelain, English & Chinese; furniture.
City Wall & Bastion - Gloucester
Roman & mediaeval city defences in an underground exhibition room.
Stroud Museum - Cirencester
Depicts earlier settlements in the area & has a very fine collection of Roman antiquities.

Historic Monuments

Chedworth Roman Villa - Yanworth
Remains of Romano-British villa.
Belas Knap Long Barrow - Charlton Abbots
Neolithic burial ground - three burial chambers with external entrances.
Hailes Abbey - Stanway
Ruins of beautiful mediaeval abbey built by son of King John, 1246.
Witcombe Roman Villa - Nr. Birdlip

Large Roman villa - Hypocaust & mosaic pavements preserved.
Ashleworth Tithe Barn - Ashleworth
15th century tithe barn - 120 feet long - stone built, interesting roof timbering.
Odda's Chapel - Deerhurst
Rare Saxon chapel dating back to 1056.
Hetty Pegler's Tump - UleLong Barrow- fairly complete, chamber is 120 feet long.

Other things to see & do

Cheltenham International Festival of Music & Literature - Annual event.
Cotswolds Farm Park - dozens of rare breeds of farm animals.
The Three Choirs Festival - music festival staged in alternating years at Gloucester, Hereford & Worcester Cathedrals.
Slimbridge - Peter Scott's Wildfowl Trust.

GLOUCESTERSHIRE

Map reference

01	Bolton	13	Hodges
01	Wright	14	Rodger
02	Thornely	15	Whitton
03	Moodie	16	Lucas
04	Gamez	17	Dean
05	Gisby	18	McGrigor
06	Wilson	19	Mason
07	Yardley	20	Atkinson
08	Keyser	21	Thurston
09	Parsons	22	Peacock
10	Baxter	23	Solomon
11	Paton	24	Helm
12	Annis		

130

Clapton Manor. Clapton on the Hill.

Column headers (angled): rate £ from .. to per double room | children taken | evening meals taken | animals taken

Clapton Manor

Near Rd: A.40, A.429

Clapton Manor dates from 1550 & sits at the top of a very quiet village with stunning views. It is an informal yet elegant family home with children & dogs. Guests have their own sitting room with log fire, lots of books & magazines. There are 2 bedrooms (1 can be a twin or a double). Each bedroom is beautifully furnished & has en-suite facilities. Lovely gardens where chickens waddle preparing to lay eggs for your breakfast. Fantastic walking (or even running!) straight from the house.
E-mail: bandb@claptonmanor.co.uk
www.claptonmanor.co.uk

James & Karin Bolton   Clapton Manor   Clapton-on-the-Hill   Bourton-on-the-Water GL54 2LG
Tel: (01451) 810202   Fax 01451 821804   Open: ALL YEAR (Excl. Xmas)   Map Ref No. 01

£80.00 to £90.00 | Y | N | N

see PHOTO over p. 131

VISA: M'CARD:

Farncombe

Near Rd: A.429

Come & share the peace, tranquillity & superb views of Farncombe, & eat, drink & sleep - smoke-free - 700ft above sea level & only 2 miles from Bourton-on-the-Water. 2 attractive doubles with showers, & 1 twin en-suite. A spacious dining room, with tea/coffee facilities, & a comfortable T.V. lounge. Tourist information, maps & books, & current menus for your choice when eating out. Numerous walks & drives, with easy access to all attractions & places of interest. Children over 12.
E-mail: julia@farncombecotswolds.com
www.farncombecotswolds.com

Julia Wright   Farncombe   Clapton-on-the-Hill   Bourton-on-the-Water GL54 2LG
Tel/Fax: (01451) 820120   Mobile 07714 703142   Open: Mid Jan - Mid Dec   Map Ref No. 01

£47.00 to £49.00 | Y | N | N

Eastcote Cottage

Near Rd: A.38

Eastcote is a charming 200-year-old stone house located in a lovely rural setting, with splendid views across open countryside. Guests have a choice of 2 very comfortable bedrooms with modern amenities. A colour-T.V. lounge is also available for guests' use. Conveniently situated for the M.4/M.5 interchange for the Cotswolds, with Bristol, Bath, Cheltenham & the Wye Valley easily accessible. Private parking available.
E-mail: ann@nickthornely.co.uk
www.bestbandb.co.uk

Mrs Ann Thornely   Eastcote Cottage   Crossways Lane   Thornbury   Bristol BS35 3UE   Glos.
Tel: (01454) 413106   Fax 01454 281812   Open: ALL YEAR (Excl. Xmas)   Map Ref No. 02

£56.00 to £60.00 | Y | N | N

The Elms

Near Rd: A.38

An elegant Grade II listed village house set in attractive 2-acre gardens with comfortable suite & a self-contained cottage. Convenient for Bristol, M.4/M.5 interchange. Great emphasis is placed on immaculate, luxurious standards & green issues. Breakfasts are organic when possible. Allergy sufferers are welcome & the environment is kept as pollutant free as possible. Guests are requested not to use scented products. The owners are great animal & garden lovers. Hard tennis court.
E-mail: b&b@theelmsmoodie.co.uk
www.theelmsmoodie.co.uk

David & Suzanne Moodie   The Elms   Olveston   Bristol BS35 4DR   Gloucestershire
Tel: (01454) 614559   Fax 01454 618607   Open: ALL YEAR   Map Ref No. 03

£70.00 to £80.00 | N | N | Y

Rectory Farmhouse. Lower Swell.

	rate £ from - to per double room	children taken	evening meals	animals taken

Georgian House

Near Rd: A.40

Take 3 beautiful bedrooms in an elegant Georgian home, set them among the charming terraces of Montpellier, only 5 mins' from the Promenade, add a warm welcome from your hosts, Penny & Alex, & there you have Georgian House. Each en-suite room has T.V. with satellite, 'phone with modem socket, ironing facilities, trouser press & fridge. The delicious English breakfasts include fresh fruit - the perfect combination! Parking available.

E-mail: penny@georgianhouse.net
www.georgianhouse.net

£75.00 to £85.00 — N N N

VISA: M'CARD: AMEX:

Penny & Alex Gamez   Georgian House   77 Montpellier Terrace   Cheltenham GL50 1XA
Tel: (01242) 515577 Fax 01242 545929 Open: ALL YEAR (Excl. Xmas & New Year) Map Ref No. 04

Rectory Farmhouse

Near Rd: A.429

Rectory Farmhouse is an historic 17th-century traditional Cotswold farmhouse located in the quiet hamlet of Lower Swell, which lies about 1 mile to the west of the well-known market town of Stow-on-the-Wold. It is elegantly furnished throughout & boasts superb double bedrooms, enjoying stunning views over open countryside. All bedrooms have luxurious en-suite bathrooms. Chipping Campden & Bourton-on-the-Water are just a short drive away. Cheltenham, Oxford & Stratford-upon-Avon are all easily accessible. Children over 16.

E-mail: rectory.farmhouse@cw-warwick.co.uk

£80.00 to £86.00 — Y N N

see PHOTO over
p. 133

Sybil Gisby   Rectory Farmhouse   Lower Swell Nr. Stow-on-the-Wold Cheltenham GL54 1LH
Tel: (01451) 832351   Open: ALL YEAR   Map Ref No. 05

Westward

Near Rd: A.40

The Wilson families share this beautiful Grade II listed Georgian house on the scarp of the Cotswolds above Sudeley Castle, sitting within its own 600-acre estate with spectacular views to the Malverns. The heart of the Cotswolds is very close, with Broadway, Oxford & Stratford within easy reach. The Wilsons combine good food - Susie trained at Prue Leith's - with elegance & comfort in their delightful English family home. 3 elegant en-suite rooms available. Children over 12.

E-mail: jimw@haldon.co.uk
www.westward-sudeley.co.uk

£80.00 to £100.00 — Y N N

see PHOTO over
p. 135

VISA: M'CARD:

Susie & Jim Wilson   Westward   Sudeley   Winchcombe   Cheltenham GL54 5JB
Tel: (01242) 604372   Fax 01242 604640   Open: ALL YEAR (Excl. Xmas)   Map Ref No. 06

Nineveh Farm

Near Rd: A.44

Multi-award-winning Nineveh is a 200 year old farmhouse, which is ideally situated for visiting the Cotswolds, Stratford-upon-Avon, Warwick Castle & Blenheim Palace. With antique furnishings, log fires in winter, flagstone floors & beams, all rooms enjoy superb views over open countryside. Complementary tea & cakes on arrival & free use of cycles (subject to availability.) Nearby pubs/restaurants in Mickleton village. Children over 12.

E-mail: stay@ninevehfarm.co.uk
www.ninevehfarm.co.uk

£65.00 to £70.00 — Y N N

VISA: M'CARD:

Alison & Michael Yardley Nineveh Farm   Campden Road Mickleton Chipping Campden GL55 6PS
Tel: (01386) 438923   Open: ALL YEAR   Map Ref No. 07

Westward. Sudeley.

Gloucestershire

Lady Lamb Farm

Near Rd: A.417

Lady Lamb Farm is a Cotswold-stone farmhouse, surrounded by countryside & situated less than a mile from the small market town of Fairford. 2 attractively furnished guest rooms, each with T.V. & tea/coffee facilities. (1 is en-suite.) A swimming pool & tennis court are available. Set on the edge of the Cotswolds, Bath, Oxford & many Cotswold towns, & wonderful gardens are within easy reach. Cotswold Water Park offers a wide range of watersports. Golf, riding & fishing are available nearby. Single supplement. Dogs by arrangement.
E-mail: jekeyser1@aol.com

| £65.00 to £65.00 | Y | N | Y |

Mrs J. Keyser   Lady Lamb Farm   Meysey Hampton   Cirencester GL7 5LH   Gloucestershire
Tel: (01285) 712206   Fax 01285 712206   Open: ALL YEAR   Map Ref No. 08

Winstone Glebe

Near Rd: A.417

A small Georgian rectory overlooking a Saxon church in a Domesday-listed village, & enjoying spectacular rural views. Ideal for exploring Cotswold market towns, with their medieval churches, antique shops & rich local history. 3 bedrooms, with private/en-suite bathrooms. Being an Area of Outstanding Natural Beauty, there are signposted walks. The more energetic can borrow a bicycle & explore, or just enjoy warm hospitality & good food cooked by Susanna. Single supplement.
E-mail: sparsons@winstoneglebe.com
www.winstoneglebe.com

| £74.00 to £84.00 | Y | Y | Y |

see PHOTO over p. 137

VISA: M'CARD:

Shaun & Susanna Parsons   Winstone Glebe   Winstone   Cirencester GL7 7LN   Gloucestershire
Tel: (01285) 821451   Fax 01285 821094   Open: ALL YEAR (Excl. Xmas)   Map Ref No. 09

The Old House

Near Rd: A.429

The 17th-century Old House is situated in a peaceful rural hamlet, with lovely views & a pretty garden. The 3 charming bedrooms are light, sunny & restful with all amenities. Food is delicious, organic & free range where possible & is served in the panelled dining room. Bread is baked daily. Fresh flowers abound. Excellent pub 1 1/2 miles away & plenty more to choose from within 15 minutes drive. Animals by arrangement.
E-mail: baxter@calmsden.freeserve.co.uk
www.theoldhouse-calmsden.co.uk

| £65.00 to £80.00 | Y | N | Y |

Mrs Bridget Baxter   The Old House   Calmsden   Nr. Cirencester GL7 5ET   Gloucestershire
Tel: (01285) 831240   Open: MAR - NOV   Map Ref No. 10

Milton Farm

Near Rd: A.417

Milton Farm is a working farm set in spectacular Cotswold countryside, on the edge of this most attractive market town. The impressive Georgian farmhouse has luxuriously spacious & distinctive en-suite bedrooms. Warm hospitality & real farmhouse Aga-cooked breakfasts, from locally sourced produce. Superb restaurants & pubs locally. Exceptionally welcoming for business guests, walkers, cyclists, fishermen & visitors to the Cotswold Water Park. Wireless Internet access available.
E-mail: stay@milton-farm.co.uk
www.milton-farm.co.uk

| £50.00 to £60.00 | Y | N | Y |

VISA: M'CARD:

Suzie Paton   Milton Farm   Fairford GL7 4HZ   Gloucestershire
Tel: (01285) 712205   Fax 01285 711349   Open: ALL YEAR (Excl. Xmas & New Year)   Map Ref No. 11

Winstone Glebe. Winstone.

Gloucestershire

	rate £ from - to per double room	children taken	evening meals	animals taken

Evington Hill Farm

Near Rd: A.38

Crown your Gloucestershire visit at this lovely 16th-century house. Take tea & home-made cake in the sunny conservatory, stay in the antique pine furnished bedrooms with their beautiful new spacious bathrooms. 1 has a 4-poster bed, all have T.V. & hostess tray. The old beamed sitting room with log burning fire is perfect for a relaxing drink. Set in 4 acres with ample parking. A games room & hard tennis court available. 2 holiday cottages available for extended stays.

E-mail: evingtonfarm@gmail.com
www.evingtonhillfarm.co.uk

£72.00 to £90.00 — Y N N

Keith & Joyce Annis   Evington Hill Farm   Tewkesbury Road   The Leigh   Gloucester GL19 4AQ
Tel: (01242) 680255   Open: ALL YEAR   Map Ref No. 12

The Old Vicarage

Near Rd: A.38

A Victorian vicarage in 1 3/4 acres of gardens with views towards the Cotswold escarpment & Malvern Hills, & a footpath from a garden gate leading to a riverside pub & the Severn Way. There are 3 delightful rooms (2 en-suite) have T.V., hairdryer, hospitality tray & fridge. An English country house breakfast is served with a log fire burning in the hearth when chilly. A secluded retreat with a relaxed ambience, a short drive from Cheltenham, Gloucester & Tewkesbury.

E-mail: bandb.nov@btconnect.com
www.bestbandb.co.uk

£56.00 to £60.00 — Y N Y

Mrs Shirley Hodges   The Old Vicarage   Norton   Gloucester GL2 9LR   Gloucestershire
Tel: (01452) 739295/731214   Fax 01452 739091   Open: ALL YEAR   Map Ref No. 13

The Old Farm

Near Rd: A.40

Nestling in an idyllic valley, this 16th-century farmhouse offers tranquillity surrounded by oak beams, fireplaces & character yet it is within easy reach of the Royal Forest of Dean, Cheltenham & Cotswolds. Relax with afternoon tea, in front of the fire or in the sunny garden. Pretty en-suite bedrooms, including 4-poster. Breakfasts made from local produce, free-range eggs from your host's hens & home-made preserves. Good local pub with restaurant. Dogs by arrangement. Children over 12.

E-mail: BBB@the-old-farm.co.uk
www.the-old-farm.co.uk

£54.00 to £65.00 — Y N Y

see PHOTO over p. 139

VISA: M'CARD:

Lucy Rodger   The Old Farm   Barrel Lane   Longhope GL17 0LR   Gloucestershire
Tel: (01452) 830252   Mobile 0790 5683029   Open: ALL YEAR (Excl. Xmas & N. Y.)   Map Ref No. 14

Edale House

Near Rd: A.48

Edale House is a fine Georgian residence facing the cricket green in the village of Parkend at the heart of the Royal Forest of Dean. Once the home of local G.P. Bill Tandy, author of 'A Doctor in the Forest', the house has been tastefully restored to provide comfortable en-suite accommodation with every facility for guests. Enjoy delicious & imaginative cuisine prepared by your hosts. (Evening meals are available Thurs-Mon.) Fully licensed. Children over 12. Animals by arrangement.

E-mail: enquiry@edalehouse.co.uk
www.edalehouse.co.uk

£51.00 to £62.00 — Y Y Y

VISA: M'CARD:

Pat & Brian Whitton   Edale House   Folly Road   Parkend   Nr. Lydney GL15 4JF   Gloucestershire
Tel: (01594) 562835   Fax 01594 564488   Open: ALL YEAR   Map Ref No. 15

The Old Farm.   Longhope .

Column headings (rotated): rate £ from - to per double room | children taken | evening meals | animals taken

Gunn Mill House

Near Rd: A.40

Bounded by its mill stream & the Forest of Dean, the Lucas' Georgian home stands in 5 acres of gardens & meadows. Refurbished to a high standard, the galleried sitting room & attractive large en-suite bedrooms (all doubles, twins, family suites) are filled with antiques & collectables. Fresh local produce used where possible for delicious breakfasts & evening meals, which are available on request. Home-made jams, chutneys & marmalade. Vegetarians catered for. Liquor licence.

E-mail: info@gunnmillhouse.co.uk
www.gunnmillhouse.co.uk

£55.00 to £80.00 | Y | Y | Y

see PHOTO over p. 141

Mr & Mrs Lucas   Gunn Mill House   Lower Spout Lane   Mitcheldean GL17 0EA   Gloucestershire
Tel: (01594) 827577   Fax 01594 827577   Open: ALL YEAR   Map Ref No. 16

VISA: M'CARD: AMEX:

Treetops Guest House

Near Rd: A.44

A beautiful family home offering traditional bed & breakfast. There are 6 attractive bedrooms, all with en-suite facilities & 2 of which are on the ground floor and thus suitable for disabled persons or wheelchair users. All rooms have T.V., radio and tea/coffee-making facilities. Cots and high chairs available. Delightful secluded gardens to relax in. Ideally situated for exploring the Cotswolds. A warm and homely atmosphere awaits you here.

E-mail: treetops1@talk21.com
www.treetopscotswolds.co.uk

£52.00 to £55.00 | Y | N | N

VISA: M'CARD: AMEX:

Mrs E. M. Dean   Treetops Guest House   London Road   Moreton-in-Marsh GL56 0HE   Glos.
Tel: (01608) 651036   Fax 01608 651036   Open: ALL YEAR (Excl. Xmas)   Map Ref No. 17

Wren House

Near Rd: A.429, A.44

Wren House is an attractive, peacefully situated Cotswold stone house on the edge of Donnington, 2 miles north of Stow-on-the-Wold. Dating from the 15th-century, it has been recently renovated & combines original charm with modern comfort. The bedrooms are simply yet elegantly decorated & can be double or twin. The bathrooms are new & all rooms have a sunny, southern aspect overlooking the garden. A stylish drawing room with log fire in winter. Children over 7. Dinner by arrangement.

E-mail: enquiries@wrenhouse.net
www.wrenhouse.net

£90.00 to £90.00 | Y | Y | N

Kiloran McGrigor   Wren House   Donnington   Moreton-in-Marsh GL56 0XZ   Gloucestershire
Tel: (01451) 831787   Mobile 07802 676673   Open: Easter - Nov   Map Ref No.18

Lower Farm House

Near Rd: A.436

3 miles from Stow-on-the-Wold, this listed Grade II Georgian farmhouse, in the peaceful village of Adlestrop, is set in the heart of the beautiful Cotswold countryside. Stratford, Oxford & Broadway are within easy reach. Guests have the use of a private sitting room with open fire & dining room. 2 delightful bedrooms with en-suite/private bathrooms & glorious views. The house is fully centrally heated. You will receive a warm welcome & good food in this elegant yet comfortable family home. Children & animals by prior arrangement.

E-mail: zelie.mason@talk21.com

£84.00 to £90.00 | Y | Y | Y

Nicholas & Zelie Mason   Lower Farm House   Adlestrop   Moreton-in-Marsh GL56 0YR   Glos.
Tel: (01608) 658756   Fax 01608 659458   Open: ALL YEAR (Excl. Xmas)   Map Ref No. 19

Gunn Mill House. Mitcheldean.

Gloucestershire

Cotteswold House

Near Rd: A.40, A.429

Conveniently situated in Northleach Market Place, a Grade II listed building, 400 years old. Featuring beamed ceilings, original wood panelling, Tudor archway & carved fireplace. Stay in the old Hayloft double, Mullions twin-bedded room or the Tudor suite with 4-poster bed, canopied corner bath & shower & private lounge. Take a stroll around the town, visit local pubs & restaurants, or return to the comfort of Cotteswold House for a meal, by arrangement. Holiday cottage. Children by over 12.
E-mail: cotteswoldhouse@aol.com
www.cotteswoldhouse.com

£65.00 to £80.00 | Y | Y | N

VISA: M'CARD:

Margaret & David Atkinson   Cotteswold House   Market Place   Northleach GL54 3EG   Glos.
Tel: (01451) 860493   Fax 01451 860493   Open: ALL YEAR   Map Ref No. 20

Danby Lodge

Near Rd: A.48

Danby Lodge (Grade II listed) was built in the 17th century & commissioned by King Charles II in 1668, on the recommendation of Samuel Pepys. Sitting in 2 acres of woodland gardens, the Lodge has magnificent views across the Dean Forest & Severn Vale. Many original features, from oak beams to a wishing well. Bedrooms are en-suite & well-appointed throughout. Outdoor heated pool (summer only). Ideal for exploring the Royal Forest of Dean & the Cotswolds. Children over 12.
E-mail: raine@danbylodge.co.uk
www.danbylodge.co.uk

£75.00 to £95.00 | Y | Y | N

Raine Thurston   Danby Lodge   Yorkley   Royal Forest of Dean GL15 4YH   Gloucestershire
Tel: (01594) 562840   Fax 01594 564510   Open: ALL YEAR   Map Ref No. 21

Cinderhill House

Near Rd: A.466

A pretty, 14th-century house tucked into the hill below the castle in St. Briavels, with magnificent views across the Wye Valley to the Brecon Beacons & Black Mountains. A lovingly restored & tastefully furnished house with 3 beautiful bedrooms, all with king or queen-size beds & an en-suite bathroom. Gillie is a professional cook, & takes delight in ensuring that all meals are well cooked using local produce. Also, a romantic cottage hideaway with a king-size bed. Licensed. Children over 8.
E-mail: cinderhill.house@virgin.net
www.cinderhillhouse.co.uk

£80.00 to £96.00 | Y | Y | N

Gillie Peacock   Cinderhill House   St. Briavels GL15 6RH   Gloucestershire
Tel: (01594) 530393   Fax 01594 530098   Open: ALL YEAR   Map Ref No. 22

Hunters Lodge

Near Rd: A.46, A.419

A friendly and helpful welcome is assured for guests at this beautifully furnished Cotswold stone country house situated adjoining 600 acres of National Trust common land and a golf course. All bedrooms have T.V., tea/coffee-making facilities & en-suite/private bathrooms. A visitors' lounge, with colour T.V., adjoins a delightful conservatory over-looking a large garden. An ideal centre for Bath, Cheltenham, Cirencester & the Cotswolds. Peter is a registered tourist guide. Children over 12.
E-mail: hunterslodge@hotmail.com
www.cotswoldsbandb.co.uk

£55.00 to £60.00 | Y | N | N

see PHOTO over
p. 143

Margaret & Peter Helm   Hunters Lodge   31, Dr. Browns Road   Minchinhampton   Stroud GL6 9BT
Tel: (01453) 883588   Fax 01453 731449   Open: ALL YEAR (Excl. Xmas)   Map Ref No. 24

Hunters Lodge. Minchinhampton.

	rate £ from - to per double room	children taken	evening meals	animals taken

Pretoria Villa

Near Rd: A.419
Enjoy luxurious bed & breakfast in a relaxed family country house set in peaceful secluded gardens. Spacious bedrooms, with en-suite/private facilities. Hospitality trays, hairdryers & bathrobes in all rooms. Guests have their own comfortable lounge & delicious breakfasts are served in the dining room. Evening meals by prior arrangement, although many good eating places nearby. An excellent base from which to explore the Cotswolds. Personal service & your comfort are guaranteed.
E-mail: glynis@gsolomon.freeserve.co.uk
www.bedandbreakfast-cotswold.co.uk

£56.00 to £56.00	Y	Y	N

Mrs Glynis Solomon   Pretoria Villa   Wells Road   Eastcombe   Stroud GL6 7EE   Gloucestershire
Tel/Fax: (01452) 770435   Mobile 07816 323615   Open: ALL YEAR (Excl. Xmas)   Map Ref No. 23

All the establishments mentioned in this guide are members of
The Worldwide Bed & Breakfast Association

When booking your accommodation please mention
The Best Bed & Breakfast

Hampshire & Isle of Wight

Hampshire
(Southern)

Hampshire is located in the centre of the south coast of England & is blessed with much beautiful & unspoilt countryside. Wide open vistas of rich downland contrast with deep woodlands. Rivers & sparkling streams run through tranquil valleys passing nestling villages. There is a splendid coastline with seaside resorts & harbours, the cathedral city of Winchester & the "jewel" of Hampshire, the Isle of Wight.

The north of the county is known as the Hampshire Borders. Part of this countryside was immortalised by Richard Adams & the rabbits of 'Watership Down'. Beacon Hill is a notable hill-top landmark. From its slopes some of the earliest aeroplane flights were made by De Haviland in 1909. Pleasure trips & tow-path walks can be taken along the restored Basingstoke Canal.

The New Forest is probably the area most frequented by visitors. It is a landscape of great character with thatched cottages, glades & streams & a romantic beauty. There are herds of deer & the New Forest ponies wander at will. To the N.W. of Beaulieu are some of the most idyllic parts of the old forest, with fewer villages & many little streams that flow into the Avon. Lyndhurst, the "capital" of the New Forest offers a range of shops & has a contentious 19th century church constructed in scarlet brickwork banded with yellow, unusual ornamental decoration, & stained glass windows by William Morris.

The Roman city of Winchester became the capital city of Saxon Wessex & is today the capital of Hampshire. It is famous for its beautiful mediaeval cathedral, built during the reign of William the Conquerer & his notorious son Rufus. It contains the great Winchester Bible.

William completed the famous Domesday Book in the city, & Richard Coeur de Lion was crowned in the cathedral in 1194.

Portsmouth & Southampton are major ports & historic maritime cities with a wealth of castles, forts & Naval attractions from battleships to museums.

The channel of the Solent guarded by Martello towers, holds not only Southampton but numerous yachting centres, such as Hamble, Lymington & Bucklers Hard where the ships for Admiral Lord Nelson's fleet were built.

The River Test.

The Isle of Wight

The Isle of Wight lies across the sheltered waters of the Solent, & is easily reached by car or passenger ferry. The chalk stacks of the Needles & the multi-coloured sand at Alum Bay are among the best known of the island's natural attractions & there are many excellent beaches & other bays to enjoy. Cowes is a famous international sailing centre with a large number of yachting events throughout the summer. Ventnor, the most southerly resort is known as the "Madeira of England" & has an exotic botanic garden. Inland is an excellent network of footpaths & trails & many castles, manors & stately homes.

Hampshire & Isle of Wight

Hampshire

Gazeteer

Areas of outstanding natural beauty.
East & South Hampshire, North Wessex Downs & Chichester Harbour.

Houses & Castles

Avington Park - Winchester
16th century red brick house, enlarged in 17th century by the addition of two wings & a classical portico. Stateroom, ballroom with wonderful ceiling. Red drawing room, library, etc.

Beaulieu Abbey & Palace House - Beaulieu
12th century Cistercian abbey - the original gatehouse of abbey converted to palace house 1538. Houses historic car museum.

Breamore House - Breamore
16th century Elizabethan Manor House, tapestries, furniture, paintings. Also museum.

Jane Austen's Home - Chawston
Personal effects of the famous writer.

Broadlands - Romsey
16th century - park & garden created by Capability Brown. Home of the Earl Mountbatten of Burma.

Mottisfont Abbey - Nr. Romsey
12th century Augustinian Priory until Dissolution. Painting by Rex Whistler trompe l'oeil in Gothic manner.

Stratfield Saye House - Reading
17th century house presented to the Duke of Wellington 1817. Now contains his possessions - also wild fowl sanctuary.

Sandham Memorial Chapel - Sandham, Nr. Newbury
Paintings by Stanley Spencer cover the walls.

The Vyne - Sherbourne St. John
16th century red brick chapel with Renaissance glass & rare linenfold panelling. Alterations made in 1654 - classical portico. Palladian staircase dates form 1760.

West Green House - Hartley Wintney
18th century red brick house set in a walled garden.

Appuldurcombe House - Wroxall, Isle of Wight
The only house in the 'Grand Manner' on the island. Beautiful English baroque east facade. House now an empty shell standing in fine park.

Osbourne House - East Cowes, Isle of Wight
Queen Victoria's seaside residence.

Carisbrooke Castle - Isle of Wight
Oldest parts 12th century, but there was a wooden castle on the mound before that. Museum in castle.

Cathedrals & Churches

Winchester Cathedral
Largest Gothic church in Europe. Norman & perpendicular styles, three sets of mediaeval paintings, marble font c.1180. Stalls c.1320 with 60 misericords. Extensive mediaeval tiled floor.

Breamore (St. Mary) - Breamore
10th century Saxon. Double splayed windows, stone rood.

East Meon (All Saints)
15th century rebuilding of Norman fabric. Tournai marble front.

Idsworth (St. Hubert)
16th century chapel - 18th century bell turret. 14th century paintings in chancel.

Pamber (dedication unknown)
Early English - Norman central tower, 15th central pews, wooden effigy of knight c.1270.

Romsey (St. Mary & St. Ethelfleda)
Norman - 13th century effigy of a lady - Saxon rood & carving of crucifixion, 16th century painted reredos.

Silchester (St. Mary)
Norman, perpendicular, 14th century effigy of a lady, 15th century screen, Early English chancel with painted patterns on south window splays, Jacobean pulpit with domed canopy.

Winchester (St. Cross)
12th century. Original chapel to Hospital. Style changing from Norman at east to decorated at west. Tiles, glass, wall painting.

HAMPSHIRE
Map reference

01	Mallam	08	Barnfield
02	Biddolph	09	Ames
03	Chetwynd-T.	10	Baigent
04	Buckley	11	Ford
05	Cadman	12	Lightfoot
06	Pritchett	13	Hughes
07	Iles	14	Talbot

Wokingham • Woking • Guildford
Farnborough
SURREY
Wokingham
245
251
A272
Milford
Farnham Haslemere Petworth Pulborough Arundel
Camberley Aldershot A31 Hindhead Midhurst Bognor
BERKS Alton Petersfield A286 Chichester Regis
Newbury Basingstoke M3 New A272 A3 SUSSEX A27
A339 A30 Alresford Havant Portsmouth
Andover A34 A33 A32 Fareham Selsey
A343 Winchester Eastleigh M27 Gosport Ryde Sandown
Hungerford A30 A272 Romsey Southampton Cowes Shanklin
WILTSHIRE A36 A326 Lyndhurst Newport Niton
Upavon Salisbury A31 Lymington The Solent Isle of Wight
277 Stonehenge A343 Ringwood A337 Freshwater
Amesbury A338 Cranborne Bournemouth
Wilton A354 A360 DORSET
120
31
English Channel

Hampshire

Broadwater

Near Rd: A.303

Broadwater is a 17th-century, listed, thatched cottage situated in a peaceful unspoilt village just off the A.303. It is an ideal base for sightseeing in Hampshire, with easy access to the West Country & London. The cottage offers 2 delightful, double/ twin-bedded rooms, both with en-suite facilities. Guests have a private & comfortable sitting/dining room with an open log fire & a very pretty garden to enjoy. Home-made bread. Colour T.V.. Children over 8. Self-catering in a thatched barn is available.
E-mail: broadwater@dmac.co.uk
www.broadwaterbandb.co.uk

£60.00 to £70.00 | Y | N | N

VISA: M'CARD:

Mrs Carolyn Mallam   Broadwater   Amport   Nr. Andover SP11 8AY   Hampshire
Tel/Fax: (01264) 772240   Open: ALL YEAR (Excl. Xmas & New Year)   Map Ref No. 01

May Cottage

Near Rd: A.303

May Cottage dates back to 1740 & is situated in the heart of this picturesque tranquil village with Post Office & old inn. A most comfortable home with 2 doubles & 1 twin room with en-suite/private bathrooms. All with T.V. & tea trays. Guests' own sitting/dining room with T.V.. An ideal base for visiting ancient cities, stately homes & gardens, yet within easy reach of ports & airports. 2 good local inns which offer food. Parking. Children over 5. (Hosts can be contacted on mobile 07768 242166).
E-mail: info@maycottage-thruxton.co.uk
www.maycottage-thruxton.co.uk

£70.00 to £80.00 | Y | N | N

see PHOTO over
p. 149

Tom & Fiona Biddolph   May Cottage   Thruxton   Nr. Andover SP11 8LZ   Hampshire
Tel: (01264) 771241   Fax 01264 771770   Open: ALL YEAR   Map Ref No. 02

Gunville House

Near Rd: A.303

Gunville House is a charming thatched, beamed family house, dating from the 18th century in a secluded, rural situation, 5 mins' from the A.303. Offering 1 twin bedroom & 1 single, both with en-suite bath & shower & T.V. etc. Ideally situated for Salisbury, Winchester, Stonehenge, Marlborough & many famous Hampshire/Wiltshire attractions. Fly fishing, golf, clay pigeon shooting can all be arranged locally. Good pub within easy walking distance. Single room from £35. Children over 5.
E-mail: pct@onetel.com
www.gunvillehouse.co.uk

£70.00 to £70.00 | Y | Y | Y

Mrs Sarah Chetwynd-Talbot   Gunville House   Grateley   Andover SP11 8JQ   Hampshire
Tel: (01264) 889206   Fax 01264 889060   Open: ALL YEAR   Map Ref No. 03

Tothill House

Near Rd: A.35

An Edwardian country house set in 12 acres of woodland. An Area of Outstanding Natural Beauty noted for its flora & fauna. 5 mins' from Burley village, a popular New Forest tourist attraction. Offering good food & 3 attractive rooms, 2 with en-suite facilities & 1 with a private bathroom. Each individually decorated, with T.V. & tea-making facilities. Very secluded, with peace & tranquillity. Local sporting & recreational activities, & a variety of places to visit. The perfect spot for a relaxing break. Children over 16 years.
www.newforest.demon.co.uk/tothillhouse.htm

£70.00 to £70.00 | Y | N | N

Mrs Wendy Buckley   Tothill House   Black Lane   Thorney Hill   Bransgore   Christchurch BH23 8DZ
Tel: (01425) 674414   Fax 01425 672235   Open: FEB - NOV   Map Ref No. 04

May Cottage.   Thruxton.

Hampshire

	rate £ from - to per double room	evening meals	children taken	animals taken

Cottage Crest

Near Rd: A.338

Woodgreen is a typical New Forest village, with cottages surrounded by thick hedges to keep out the cattle & ponies. Cottage Crest is a Victorian drover's cottage set high in its own 4 acres, & enjoying superb views of the River Avon & valley below. Bedrooms are spacious & decorated to a very high standard. All have an en-suite bathroom/ shower & W.C.. Children over 8 yrs. Cottage Crest is an ideal base from which to explore Hampshire.
E-mail: lupita_cadman@yahoo.co.uk
www.cottage-crest.co.uk

£56.00 to £60.00 — Y — N — N

Mrs G. Cadman   Cottage Crest   Castle Hill   Woodgreen   Nr. Fordingbridge SP6 2AX   Hampshire
Tel: (01725) 512009   Open: ALL YEAR   Map Ref No. 05

Under Rock

Near Rd: A.3055

Historical Georgian house set in large secluded gardens near Horseshoe Bay & southern coastal paths, with isolated coves, narrow ravines or chines, soaring cliffs, high chalk downland, & country walks. 3 rooms - single/double, double & twin. T.V., tea/coffee trays. All have their own bath/ shower & W.C.. Guest lounge & terrace, a peaceful, relaxed setting. Picturesque Bonchurch village has literary associations including Thackeray, Dickens & Swinburne. Between Shanklin & Ventnor.
www.under-rock.co.uk

£54.00 to £60.00 — N — N — N

James Pritchett   Under Rock   Shore Road   Bonchurch   Ventnor   Isle of Wight PO38 1RF
Tel: (01983) 855274   Open: ALL YEAR (Excl. Xmas & New Year)   Map Ref No. 06

Briantcroft

Near Rd: A.337

Enjoy the grace & elegance of this Edwardian house with its spacious & luxurious rooms. Set in peaceful surroundings, at the edge of the New Forest, Briantcroft is 10 mins' walk to the beach. The 3 large bedroom suites are individually themed, with en-suite/private facilities, T.V., 3-seater sofas & a refreshment tray. Breakfast is a gourmet experience with traditional & other tempting choices using fresh & local produce. Full colour brochure/ menu on request. Children over 8.
E-mail: florence.iles@lineone.net
www.briantcroft.co.uk

£60.00 to £90.00 — Y — N — N

VISA: M'CARD:

Florence Iles   Briantcroft   George Road   Milford-on-Sea   Lymington SO41 0RS   Hampshire
Tel: (01590) 644355   Fax 01590 644185   Open: ALL YEAR   Map Ref No. 07

The Nurse's Cottage

Near Rd: B.3055

One of the New Forest's premier accommodations, the former home of Sway's District Nurses has won many awards for hospitality, service, good food & wine, & consideration for disabled guests. Recipient of several Best Breakfast awards, the overnight rates include Afternoon Tea on arrival & a 3-Course Dinner featuring a seasonally-changing menu complemented by the 68-bin wine list. Situated on the ground floor, the 4 bedrooms offer every comfort. Reduced rates for 2+ nights. Children over 9.
E-mail: nurses.cottage@lineone.net
www.nursescottage.co.uk

£150.00 to £160.00 — Y — Y — Y

VISA: M'CARD: AMEX:

Mr R. A. Barnfield   The Nurse's Cottage   Station Road   Sway   Lymington SO41 6BA   Hampshire
Tel: (01590) 683402   Fax 01590 683402   Open: ALL YEAR   Map Ref No. 08

Ormonde House Hotel. Lyndhurst.

Hampshire

Ormonde House Hotel

Near Rd: A.35

Ormonde House is set back from the main road opposite the open forest; ideal for an early morning walk. Lyndhurst village is just 5 mins' walk & Exbury Gardens, the National Motor Museum & Beaulieu 20 mins' drive. The popular licensed restaurant offers freshly prepared dishes. There are 19 pretty en-suite bedrooms & 4 luxury self-contained suites, all with T.V., 'phone etc., suites have full kitchens. Superior Plus rooms & suites with zip & link king-size beds & whirlpool baths.
E-mail: enquiries@ormondehouse.co.uk
www.ormondehouse.co.uk

£70.00 to £120.00 | Y | Y | Y

see PHOTO over p. 151

VISA: M'CARD: AMEX:

Mr. Paul Ames   Ormonde House Hotel   Southampton Road   Lyndhurst SO43 7BT   Hampshire
Tel: (02380) 282806   Fax 02380 282004   Open: ALL YEAR (Excl. Xmas)   Map Ref No. 09

Trotton Farm

Near Rd: A.272

This charming home, set in 200 acres of farmland, offers comfortable accommodation in 2 twin-bedded rooms & 1 double-bedded room, each with en-suite shower & modern amenities, including tea/coffee-making facilities. Residents' lounge is available throughout the day. Games room & pretty garden for guests' relaxation. Ideally situated for visiting many local, historical & sporting attractions, & 1 hour from Gatwick & Heathrow Airports. Single supplement.
E-mail: baigentfarms@farmersweekly.net
www.bestbandb.co.uk

£50.00 to £60.00 | Y | N | Y

Mrs J. E. Baigent   Trotton Farm   Trotton   Petersfield GU31 5EN   Hampshire
Tel: (01730) 813618   Fax 01730 816093   Open: ALL YEAR   Map Ref No. 10

Holmans

Near Rd: A.35, A.31

Holmans is a charming country house in the heart of the New Forest, set in 4 acres with stabling available for guests' own horses. Superb walking, horse riding & carriage driving, with a golf course nearby. A warm, friendly welcome is assured at this elegant home, which is ideal for a relaxing break. All bedrooms are tastefully furnished & en-suite with tea/coffee-making facilities, radio & hairdryers. Colour T.V. in guests' lounge with adjoining orangery & log fires in winter.
www.bestbandb.co.uk

£68.00 to £68.00 | Y | N | Y

Robin & Mary Ford   Holmans   Bisterne Close   Burley   Ringwood BH24 4AZ   Hampshire
Tel: (01425) 402307   Fax 01425 402307   Open: ALL YEAR (Excl. Xmas)   Map Ref No. 11

Crofton Country B & B

Near Rd: A.27

Nestling in 2 acres of garden, Crofton offers quality accommodation within the tranquil setting of a small hamlet in the beautiful Test Valley. A large family room, a twin room & a single room, all tastefully decorated & each with tea/coffee, T.V. & DVD, etc. Delicious breakfasts are served in the conservatory. A guest lounge & kitchen with fridge & microwave. Located just 4 miles north of Romsey, making Salisbury, Winchester, New Forest & south coast resorts accessible. Children over 12.
E-mail: pauline@croftonbandb.com
www.croftonbandb.com

£30.00 to £60.00 | Y | N | N

VISA: M'CARD:

Mrs Pauline Lightfoot   Crofton Country B & B   Kent's Oak   Awbridge   Romsey SO51 0HH
Tel: (01794) 340333   Fax 01794 340333   Open: ALL YEAR   Map Ref No. 12

Hampshire

rate £ from - to per double room	children taken	evening meals	animals taken		
£50.00 to £65.00	Y	N	Y		

Ranvilles Farm House

Near Rd: A.3090

Ranvilles Farm House dates from the 13th century when Richard De Ranville came from Normandy & settled with his family. Now this Grade II listed house provides a peaceful setting surrounded by 5 acres of gardens & paddock. All rooms, with extra large beds, are attractively furnished with antiques, & have an en-suite bathroom/shower room. Only 3 miles from the New Forest & just over a mile from Romsey - equidistant from the 2 cathedral cities of Winchester & Salisbury. Single supplement.
E-mail: info@ranvilles.com
www.ranvilles.com

Anthea Hughes	*Ranvilles Farm House*	*Romsey SO51 6AA*	*Hampshire*
Tel: (02380) 814481	*Fax 02380 814481*	*Open: ALL YEAR*	*Map Ref No. 13*

£90.00 to £90.00	Y	Y	Y

VISA: M'CARD:

Church Farm

Near Rd: A.303, A.30

Church Farm is a 15th-century tithe barn with Georgian & modern additions. It features an adjacent coach house & converted groom's cottage, where guests may be totally self-contained, or be welcomed to the log-fired family drawing room & dine on locally produced fresh food. Accommodation is in 6 beautiful bedrooms for guests, all with a private bathroom, T.V. & tea/coffee-making facilities. The swimming pool & croquet are available to guests. Tennis court adjacent.
www.bestbandb.co.uk

James & Jean Talbot	*Church Farm*	*Barton Stacey*	*Winchester SO21 3RR*	*Hampshire*
Tel: (01962) 760268	*Fax 01962 761825*		*Open: ALL YEAR*	*Map Ref No. 14*

All the establishments mentioned in this guide are members of
The Worldwide Bed & Breakfast Association

When booking your accommodation please mention
The Best Bed & Breakfast

Hereford & Worcester

Hereford & Worcester
(Heart of England)

Hereford is a beautiful ancient city standing on the banks of the River Wye, almost a crossing point between England & Wales. It is a market centre for the Marches, the border area which has a very particular history of its own.

Hereford Cathedral has a massive sandstone tower & is a fitting venue for the Three Choirs festival which dates from 1727, taking place yearly in one or the other of the three great cathedrals of Hereford, Worcester & Gloucester.

The county is fortunate in having many well preserved historic buildings. Charming "black & white" villages abound here, romantically set in a soft green landscape.

The Royal Forest of Dean spreads its oak & beech trees over 22,000 acres. When people first made their homes in the woodlands it was vaster still. There are rich deposits of coal & iron mined for centuries by the foresters, & the trees have always been felled for charcoal. Ancient courts still exist where forest dwellers can & do claim their rights to use the forest's resources.

The landscape alters dramatically as the land rises to merge with the great Black Mountain range at heights of over 2,600 feet. It is not possible to take cars everywhere but a narrow mountain road, Gospel Pass, takes traffic from Hay-on-Wye to Llanthony with superb views of the upper Wye Valley.

The Pre-Cambrian Malvern Hills form a natural boundary between Herefordshire & Worcestershire & from the highest view points you can see over 14 counties. At their feet nestle pretty little villages such as Eastonor with its 19th century castle in revived Norman style that looks quite mediaeval amongst the parklands & gardens.

There are, in fact, five Malverns. The largest predictably known as Great

Malvern was a fashionable 19th century spa & is noted for the purity of the water which is bottled & sold countrywide.

The Priory at Malvern is rich in 15th century stained glass & has a fine collection of mediaeval tiles made locally. William Langland, the 14th century author of "Piers Ploughman", was educated at the Priory & is said to have been sleeping on the Malvern Hills when he had the visionary experience which led to the creation of the poem. Sir Edward Elgar was born, lived & worked here & his "Dream of Gerontius" had its first performance in Hereford Cathedral in 1902.

In Worcestershire another glorious cathedral, with what remains of its monastic buildings, founded in the 11th century, stands beside the River Severn. College Close in Worcester is a lovely group of buildings carefully preserved & very English in character.

The Severn appears to be a very lazy waterway but flood waters can reach astonshing heights, & the "Severn Bore" is a famous phenomenon.

A cruise along the river is a pleasant way to spend a day seeing villages & churches from a different perspective, possibly visiting a riverside inn. To the south of the county lie the undulating Vales of Evesham & Broadway - described as the show village of England.

The Malvern Hills.

Hereford & Worcester

Hereford & Worcester Gazeteer

Areas of outstanding natural beauty.
The Malvern Hills, The Cotswolds, The Wye Valley.

Historic Houses & Castles

Berrington Hall - Leominster
18th century - painted & plastered ceilings. Landscape by Capability Brown.

Brilley - Cwmmau Farmhouse - Whitney-on-Wye
17th century timber-framed & stone tiled farmhouse.

Burton Court - Eardisland
14th century great hall. Exhibition of European & Oriental costume & curios. Model fairground.

Croft Castle - Nr. Leominster
Castle on the Welsh border - inhabited by Croft family for 900 years.

Dinmore Manor - Nr. Hereford
14th century chapel & cloister.

Eastnor Castle - Nr. Ledbury
19th century - Castellated, containing pictures & armour. Arboretum.

Eye Manor - Leominster
17th century Carolean Manor house - excellent plasterwork, paintings, costumes, books, secret passage. Collection of dolls.

Hanbury Hall - Nr. Droitwich
18th century red brick house - only two rooms & painted ceilings on exhibition.

Harvington Hall - Kidderminster
Tudor Manor house with moat, priest's hiding places.

The Greyfriars - Worcester
15th century timber-framed building adjoins Franciscan Priory.

Hellen's - Much Marcle
13th century manorial house of brick & stone. Contains the Great hall with stone table - bedroom of Queen Mary. Much of the original furnishings remain.

Kentchurch Court - Hereford
14th century fortified border Manor house. Paintings & Carvings by Grinling Gibbons.

Moccas Court - Moccas
18th century - designed by Adam - Parklands by Capability Brown - under restoration.

Pembridge Castle - Welsh Newton
17th century moated castle.

Sutton Court - Mordiford
Palladian mansion by Wyatt, watercolours, embroideries, china.

Cathedrals & Churches

Amestry (St. John the Baptist & St.Alkmund)
16th century rood screen.

Abbey Dore (St. Mary & Holy Trinity)
17th century glass & great oak screen - early English architecture.

Brinsop (St. George)
14th century, screen & glass, alabaster reredos, windows in memory of Wordsworth, carved Norman tympanum.

Bredon (St. Giles)
12th century - central tower & spire. Mediaeval heraldic tiles, tombs & early glass.

Brockhampton (St. Eadburgh)
1902. Central tower & thatched roof.

Castle Frome (St. Michael & All Angles)
12th century carved font, 17th century effigies in alabaster.

Chaddesley Corbett (St. Cassian)
14th century monuments, 12th century font.

Elmley (St. Mary)
12th century & 15th century font, tower, gargoyles, mediaeval.

Great Witley (St. Michael)
Baroque - Plasterwork, painted ceiling, painted glass, very fine example.

Hereford (All Saints)
13th-14th centuries, spire, splendid choir stalls, chained library.

Hereford Cathedral
Small cathedral.
Fine central tower c.1325, splendid porch, brasses, early English Lady Chapel with lancet windows. Red sandstone.

Kilpeck (St. Mary & St. David)
Romanesque style - mediaeval windows - fine carvings.

Leominster (St. Peter & St. Paul)
12th century doorway, fine Norman arches, decorated windows.

Much Marcle (St. Bartholomew)
13th century. 14th & 17th century monuments.

Hereford & Worcester

Worcester Cathedral
11th -16th centry. Fine cloisters & crypt.
Tomb of King John
 Worcester (St. Swithun)
18th century - furnishings untouched.
Ceiling vaulted in plaster.

Museums& Galleries

 Hereford City Museum & Art Gallery
Collections of natural history & archeology,
costumes, textiles embroideries, toys,
agricultural I bygones.
Paintings by local artists, examples of
applied art, silver, pottery & porcelain.
The Old House - Hereford
Jacobean period museum with furnishings
of time.
Churchill Gardens Museum -   Hereford
Extensive costume collection, fine
furniture, work by local artists.
Almonry Museum - Evesham
Anglo-British. Roman-British, mediaeval -
monastic remains.

Avoncroft Museum of Buildings -
Stoke Heath.
Open air museum showing buildings of
reconstructed iron-age dwellings to 15th
century merchants homes.
City Museum & Art Gallery
Local History, archaeology, natural history,
environmental studies.
Dyson Perins Museums of Worcester
Porcelain - Worcester
Most comprehensive collection of old
Worcester in the world.
The Commandery   - Sidbury
15th century timber-framed building, was
originally a hospital. Royalist H.Q. during
battle of Worcester 1651.

Other things to see & do

Three choirs Festival - an annual event,
held in the cathedrals of Hereford,
Worcester & Gloucestershire, alternately.

The River Severn at Bewdley.

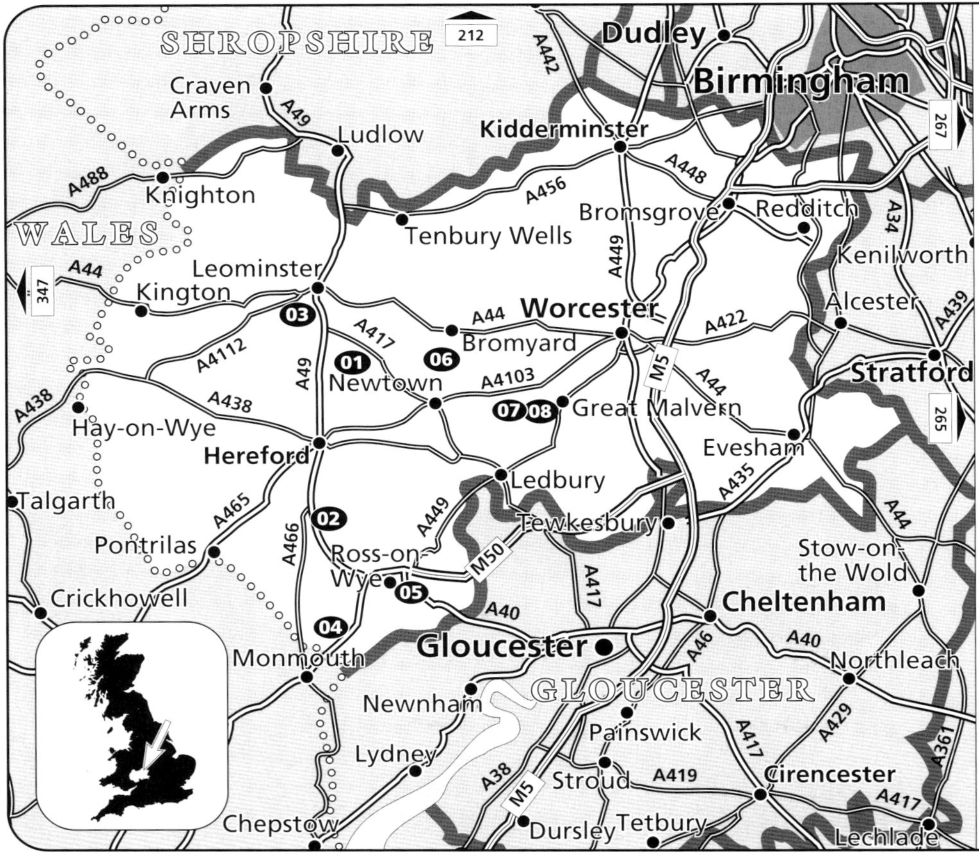

HEREFORD & WORCESTER

Map reference

01 Bengry
02 Lee
03 Fothergill
04 Jarvis
05 Anderson
06 Young
07 Quincy
08 Williams

	rate £ from - to per double room	children taken	evening meals	animals taken

The Vauld Farm

Near Rd: A.49

The Vauld Farm is a delightful 16th-century black-&-white former farmhouse, set in a beautiful garden. It retains many period features throughout & affords attractive accommodation. There are 4 charming & elegantly furnished bedrooms, each with an en-suite bathroom, T.V. & tea/coffee-making facilities. (1 with 4-poster.) Hearty breakfasts & delicious evening meals are served in the tastefully decorated dining room. A beautiful home & the perfect location for a relaxing break.
www.bestbandb.co.uk

£50.00 to £70.00 — N — Y — N

Mr & Mrs J. Bengry   The Vauld Farm   The Vauld   Marden   Hereford HR1 3HA   Herefordshire
Tel: (01568) 797898   Open: ALL YEAR   Map Ref No. 01

Cwm Craig Farm

Near Rd: A.49

Spacious Georgian farmhouse, surrounded by superb unspoilt countryside. Situated between the cathedral city of Hereford & Ross-on-Wye, & just a few mins' drive from the Wye Valley. Ideal base for touring the Forest of Dean. All 3 bedrooms are comfortably furnished & have modern amenities, shaver points, tea/coffee-making facilities & an en-suite bathroom. There is a lounge & separated dining room, both with colour T.V.. A delicious full English breakfast is served.
www.bestbandb.co.uk

£44.00 to £48.00 — Y — N — N

Mrs G. Lee   Cwm Craig Farm   Little Dewchurch   Hereford HR2 6PS   Herefordshire
Tel: (01432) 840250   Fax 01432 840250   Open: ALL YEAR   Map Ref No. 02

Highfield

Near Rd: A.44, A.49

Catherine & Marguerite hope you will feel welcome & at home in their elegant Edwardian house & its pleasant rural surroundings. The 3 (1 double & 2 twin) attractive bedrooms are very comfortable & all have a bathroom (1 twin is en-suite.) There is an interesting large garden & a restful T.V. lounge in which you are invited to relax. The homemade food is lovingly prepared & delicious. Reduced rates are available for longer stays.
E-mail: info@stay-at-highfield.co.uk
www.stay-at-highfield.co.uk

£52.00 to £56.00 — N — Y — N

Catherine & Marguerite Fothergill   Highfield   Ivington Road   Leominster HR6 8QD   Herefordshire
Tel: (01568) 613216   Open: ALL YEAR   Map Ref No. 03

Portland House

Near Rd: A.40

Portland House is uniquely placed to experience & enjoy an area of outstanding natural beauty in the Wye Valley. The house, which is Grade 11 listed, was built in 1676 & is elegant but cosy, & full of character & charm. In its history it has been a lunatic asylum - around the Georgian period- (you don't have to be mad to stay with us but it helps!) And, a young gentlemens' academy in the Victorian era. All rooms ensuite & tastefully furnished. M2 accessibility disabled suite. Children over 8.
E-mail: j.jarvis@virgin.net
www.portlandguesthouse.co.uk

£55.00 to £80.00 — Y — Y — N

VISA: M'CARD: AMEX:

Jenny Jarvis   Portland House   Whitchurch   Ross-on-Wye HR9 6DB   Herefordshire
Tel: (01600) 890757   Open: FEB - DEC   Map Ref No. 04

rate £ from - to per double room	children taken	evening meals	animals taken		

£54.00 to £62.00

Y Y Y

🚭

VISA⦂ M'CARD⦂ AMEX⦂

Lea House

Near Rd: A.40

In a small village betwixt the Royal Forest of Dean & the spectacular Wye Valley this 16th-century coaching inn has been prettily refurbished with exposed beams, an inglenook fireplace & imaginative décor - the perfect place to relax. Home-made breads, preserves & freshly squeezed orange juice complement the award-winning breakfasts. There are 3 individually styled bedrooms (king-size/twin/family) with en-suite/private bathrooms. Dinner is available on request.

E-mail: enquiries@leahousebandb.com
www.leahousebandb.com

| Mrs Caroline Anderson | Lea House | Lea | Ross-on-Wye HR9 7JZ | Herefordshire |
| Tel/Fax: (01989) 750652 | | Mobile 07810 200594 | Open: ALL YEAR | Map Ref No. 05 |

£55.00 to £60.00

Y Y N

🚭

Dovecote Barn

Near Rd: A.465

You will be warmly welcomed at this charming Grade II listed 17th-century converted barn set in 2 acres of garden, overlooking peaceful countryside & ideally situated for exploring historic Herefordshire. 2 well-appointed double bedrooms (T.V., radio, electric blankets, tea/coffee-making facilities etc.) with private/en-suite bathrooms. Lavish breakfasts, locally sourced, & dinners by arrangement or Roger & Judy will taxi you for free to one of the superb local pubs or restaurants.

E-mail: dovecotebarn@mail.com
www.dovecotebarn.co.uk

| Roger & Judy Young | Dovecote Barn | Stoke Lacy HR7 4HJ | Herefordshire |
| Tel: (01432) 820968 | Fax 01432 820969 | Open: ALL YEAR | Map Ref No. 06 |

£60.00 to £90.00

Y N N

🚭

Old Country House

Near Rd: A.4103

A warm welcome awaits you at our 600-year-old family home, in a large & beautiful garden, & 220 acres of traditional farmland close to the Malvern Hills. 3 very comfortable double rooms with private/ensuite bathrooms & large reception & sitting rooms. The extensive breakfasts encompass local & organic food when possible & we hold a Green Business Award. A haven for cyclists, walkers & nature lovers. Good eating places nearby. Single rates vary between £35-£55.

E-mail: ella@oldcountryhouse.co.uk
www.oldcountryhouse.co.uk

| Ella Grace Quincy | Old Country House | Old Country Farm | Mathon | Malvern WR13 5PS |
| Worcestershire | | Tel: (01886) 880867 | Open: ALL YEAR | Map Ref No. 07 |

£70.00 to £80.00

N Y N

🚭

Wyche Keep

Near Rd: B.4218

Wyche Keep is a unique arts-&-crafts castle-style house, perched high on the Malvern Hills, built by the family of Sir Stanley Baldwin, Prime Minister, to enjoy spectacular 60-mile views, with a long history of elegant entertaining. 3 large double suites, including a 4-poster. Traditional English cooking is a speciality, & guests can savour memorable 4-course candlelit dinners, selected from fresh local vegetables & game, served in a 'house party' atmosphere. Private parking.

E-mail: wychekeep@aol.com
www.wychekeep.co.uk

| Jon & Judith Williams | Wyche Keep | 22 Wyche Road | Malvern WR14 4EG | Worcestershire |
| Tel: (01684) 567018 | Fax 01684 892304 | | Open: ALL YEAR | Map Ref No. 08 |

Kent

Kent
(South East)

Kent is best known as "the garden of England". At its heart is a tranquil landscape of apple & cherry orchards, hop-fields & oast-houses, but there are also empty downs, chalk sea-cliffs, rich marshlands, sea ports, castles & the glory of Canterbury Cathedral.

The dramatic chalk ridgeway of the North Downs links the White Cliffs of Dover with the north of the county which extends into the edge of London. It was a trade route in ancient times following the high downs above the Weald, dense forest in those days. It can be followed today & it offers broad views of the now agricultural Weald.

The pilgrims who flocked to Canterbury in the 12th-15th centuries, (colourfully portrayed in Chaucer's Canterbury Tales), probably used the path of the Roman Watling Street rather than the high ridgeway.

Canterbury was the cradle of Christianity in southern England & is by tradition the seat of the Primate of All England. This site, on the River Stour, has been settled since the earliest times & became a Saxon stonghold under King Ethelbert of Kent. He established a church here, but it was in Norman times that the first great building work was carried out, to be continued in stages until the 15th century. The result is a blending of styles with early Norman work, a later Norman choir, a vaulted nave in Gothic style & a great tower of Tudor design. Thomas Becket was murdered on the steps of the Cathedral in 1170. The town retains much of its mediaeval character with half-timbered weavers' cottages, old churches & the twin towers of the west gate.

Two main styles of building give the villages of Kent their special character. The Kentish yeoman's house was the home of the wealthier farmers & is found throughout the county. It is a timber-frame building with white lath & plaster walls & a hipped roof of red tiles. Rather more modest in style is a small weatherboard house, usually painted white or cream. Rolvenden & Groombridge have the typical charm of a Kentish village whilst Tunbridge Wells is an attractive town, with a paved parade known as the Pantiles & excellent antique shops.

There are grand houses & castles throughout the county. Leeds Castle stands in a lake & dates back to the 9th century. It has beautifully landscaped parkland. Knowle House is an impressive Jacobean & Tudor Manor House with rough ragstone walls, & acres of deer-park & woodland.

Kent is easily accessible from the Channel Ports, Gatwick Airport & London.

Leeds Castle.

Kent

Kent Gazeteer

Areas of outstanding natural beauty.
Kent Downs.

Historic Houses & Castles

Aylesford, The Friars - Nr. Maidstone
13th century Friary & shrine of Our Lady, (much restored), 14th century cloisters - original.

Allington Castle -Nr. Maidstone
13th century. One time home of Tudor poet Thomas Wyatt. Restored early 20th century. Icons & Renaissance paintings.

Black Charles - Nr. Sevenoaks
14th century Hall house - Tudor fireplaces, beautiful panelling.

Boughton Monchelsea Place - Nr. Maidstone
Elizabethan Manor House - grey stone battlements - 18th century landscaped park, wonderful views of Weald of Kent.

Chartwell - Westerham
Home of Sir Winston Churchill.
Chiddingstone Castle - Nr. Edenbridge
18th century Gothic revival building encasing old remains of original Manor House - Royal Stuart & Jacobite collection.
Ancient Egyptian collection - Japanese netsuke, etc.

Eyehorne Manor - Hollingbourne
15th century Manor house with 17th century additions.

Cobham Hall - Cobham
16th century house - Gothic & Renaissance - Wyatt interior. Now school for girls.

Fairfield - Eastry, Sandwich
13th-14th centuries - moated castle. Was home of Anne Boleyn. Beautiful gardens with unique collection of classical statuary.

Knole - Sevenoaks
15th century - splendid Jacobean interior - 17th & 18th century furniture. One of the largest private houses in England.

Leeds Castle- Nr. Maidstone
Built in middle of the lake, it was the home of the mediaeval Queens of England.

Lullingstone Castle - Eynsford
14th century mansion house - frequented by Henry VIII & Queen Anne.
Still occupied by descendants of the original owners

Long Barn - Sevenoaks
14th century house - said to be home of William Caxton. Restored by Edwin Lutyens; 16th century barn added to enlarge house. Galleried hall - fine beaming & fireplaces. Lovely gardens created by Sir Harold Nicholson & his wife Vita Sackville-West.

Owletts - Cobham
Carolean house of red brick with plasterwork ceiling & fine staircase.

Owl House - Lamberhurst
16th century cottage, tile hung; said to be home of wool smuggler. Charming gardens.

Penshurst Place - Tonbridge
14th century house with mediaeval Great Hall perfectly preserved.English Gothic. Birthplace of Elizabethan poet, Sir Philip Sidney
Fine staterooms, splendid picture gallery, famous toy museum. Tudor gardens & orchards.

Saltwood Castle - Nr. Hythe
Mediaeval - very fine castle & is privately occupied. Was lived in by Sir Ralph de Broc, murderer of Thomas a Becket.

Squerreys Court - Westerham
Manor house of William & Mary period, with furniture, paintings & tapestries of time. Connections with General Wolfe.

Stoneacre - Otham
15th century yeoman's half-timbered house.

Cathedrals & Churches

Brook (St. Mary)
11th century paintings in this unaltered early Norman church.

Brookland (St. Augustine)
13th century & some later part. Crown-post roofs, detached wooden belfry with conical cap. 12th century lead font.

Canterbury Cathedral
12th century wall paintings, 12th & 13th century stained glass. Very fine Norman crypt. Early perpendicular nave & cloisters which have heraldic bosses. Wonderful central tower.

Charing (St. Peter & St. Paul)
13th & 15th century interior with 15th century tower. 17th century restoration.

Kent

Cobham (St. Mary)
16th century carved & painted tombs - unequalled collection of brasses in county.
Elham (St. Mary the Virgin)
Norman wall with 13th century arcades, perpendicular clerestory. Restored by Eden.
Lullingstone (St. Botolph)
14th century mainly - 16th century wood screen. Painted glass monuments.
Newington-on-the-Street (St. Mary the Virgin)
13th & 14th century - fine tower. 13th century tomb. Wall paintings.
Rochester Cathedral
Norman facade & nave, otherwise early English.
12th century west door. 14th century doorway to Chapter room.
Stone (St. Mary)
13th century - decorated - paintings, 15th century brass, 16th century tomb.
Woodchurch (All Saints)
13th century, having late Norman font & priest's brass of 1320. Arcades alternating octagonal & rounded columns. Triple lancets with banded marble shafting at east end.

Museums & Galleries

Royal Museums - Canterbury
Archaeological, geological, mineralogical exhibits, natural history, pottery & porcelain. Engravings, prints & pictures.
Westgate - Canterbury
Museum of armour, etc. in 14th century gatehouse of city.
Dartford District Museum - Dartford
Roman, Saxon & natural history.
Deal Museum - Deal
Prehistoric & historic antiquities.
Dicken's House Museum - Broadstairs
Personalia of Dickens; prints, costume & Victoriana.
Down House - Downe
The home of Charles Darwin for 40 years, now his memorial & museum.
Dover Museum - Dover
Roman pottery, ceramics, coins, zoology, geology, local history, etc.
Faversham Heritage Society - Faversham
1000 years of history & heritage.
Folkestone Museum & Art Gallery - Folkestone
Archeology, local history & sciences.

Herne Bay Museum - Herne Bay
Stone, Bronze & Early Iron Age specimens. Roman material from Reculver excavations. Items of local & Kentish interest.
Museum & Art Gallery - Maidstone
16th century manor house exhibiting natural history & archaeolgical collections. Costume Gallery, bygones, ceramics, 17th century works by Dutch & Italian painters. Regimental museum

Historic Monuments

Eynsford Castle - Eynsford
12th century castle remains.
Rochester Castle - Rochester
Storied keep - 1126-39
Roman Fort & Anglo-Saxon Church - Reculver
Excavated remains of 3rd century fort & Saxon church.
Little Kit's Coty House - Aylesford
Ruins of burial chambers from 2 long barrows.
Lullingstone Roman Villa - Lullingstone
Roman farmstead excavations.
Roman Fort & Town - Richborough
Roman 'Rutupiae' & fort
Tonbridge Castle - Tonbridge
12th century curtain walls, shell of keep & 14th century gatehouse.
Dover Castle - Dover
Keep built by Henry II in 1180. Outer curtain built 13th century.

Gardens

Chilham Castle Gardens - Nr. Canterbury
25 acre gardens of Jacobean house, laid out by Tradescant.
Lake garden, fine trees & birds of prey. Jousting & mediaeval banquets.
Great Comp Gardens - Nr. Borough Green
Outstanding 7 acre garden with old brick walls.
Owl House Gardens - Lamberhurst
16th century smugglers cottage with beautiful gardens of roses, daffodils & rhododendrons.
Sissinghurst Castle Gardens - Sissinghurst
Famous gardens created by Vita Sackville-West around the remains of an Elizabethan mansion.

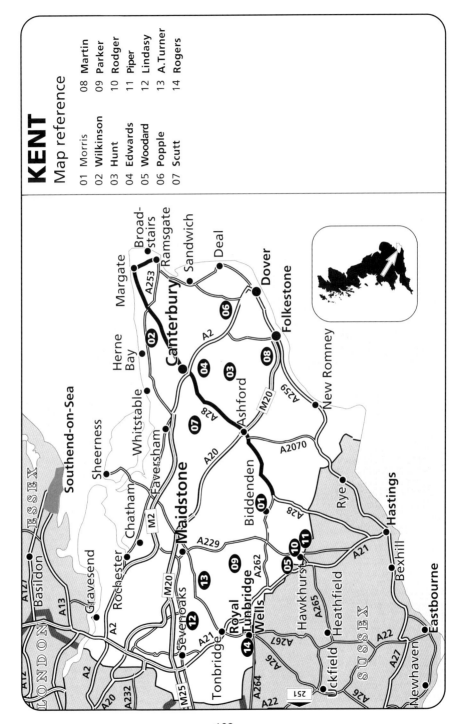

KENT
Map reference

01 Morris	08 Martin
02 Wilkinson	09 Parker
03 Hunt	10 Rodger
04 Edwards	11 Piper
05 Woodard	12 Lindasy
06 Popple	13 A.Turner
07 Scutt	14 Rogers

Kent

	rate £ from - to per double room	children taken	evening meals	animals taken

Tudor Cottage

Near Rd: A.262

Tudor Cottage is a beautiful 15th century house in the centre of the charming and historic village of Biddenden with 2 good restaurants nearby. Accommodation is in 3 delightful double bedrooms 2 en-suite, 1 with private facilities, each well-equipped with colour TV and tea/coffee making facilities. Tudor Cottage is an ideal location from which to explore beautiful Kent and East Sussex. Children over 5 years.

E-mail: suemorris.biddenden@virgin.net
www.tudorcottagebiddenden.co.uk

£40.00 to £60.00 — Y — N — N

Susan Morris   Tudor Cottage   25 High Street   Biddenden   Ashford TN27 8AL   Kent
Tel: (01580) 291913   Open: ALL YEAR   Map Ref No. 01

Chislet Court Farm

Near Rd: A.28, A.299

A listed Queen Anne farmhouse, set in mature gardens with views overlooking the surrounding countryside & the ancient village church. The 2 large comfortable bedrooms are en-suite with T.V. etc. & overlook the garden & church. Guests are welcome to wander round the garden or relax in the conservatory - where breakfast is served. Chislet Court Farm is an ideal base for exploring Canterbury & the Kent countryside.

E-mail: kathy@chisletcourtfarm.com
www.chisletcourtfarm.com

£70.00 to £70.00 — N — N — N

Kathy Wilkinson   Chislet Court Farm   Chislet   Canterbury CT3 4DU   Kent
Tel: (01227) 860309   Fax 01227 860444   Open: ALL YEAR (Excl. Xmas)   Map Ref No. 02

Bower Farm House

Near Rd: B.2068

The house is a 17th Century Kentish Farmhouse with exposed beams and inglenook fireplaces. The 2 bedrooms are charmingly appointed with tea/coffee, radios & private facilities. The large dinning area adjoins a guest lounge with TV. Home-laid eggs, home-baked bread are part of a full English Breakfast. The front gate opens onto the largest common in the SE & there are plenty of footpaths & nature reserves in the area. Canterbury with its cathedral is only a 10 minute drive away.

E-mail: nick@bowerbb.freeserve.co.uk
www.bowerfarmhouse.co.uk

£50.00 to £60.00 — Y — N — Y

Nick Hunt   Bower Farm House   Bossingham Road   Stelling Minnis   Canterbury CT4 6BB   Kent
Tel: (01227) 709430   Open: ALL YEAR (Excl. Xmas)   Map Ref No.03

Elmstone Court

Near Rd: A.2

The dream of losing yourself down a country lane & happening upon an unexpected treasure...fulfil the dream. Grade II listed Elmstone Court is charming. Madeleine & Philip undertake to provide the best accommodation & cuisine, all set in the beautiful Elham Valley, an Area of Outstanding Natural Beauty, yet only 20 mins' from Eurotunnel, Dover ferry port & Ashford International station. Canterbury, Whitstable Harbour & beaches also closeby. Bedrooms offer en-suite shower rooms etc.

E-mail: info@elmstonecourt.com
www.elmstonecourt.com

£90.00 to £110.00 — Y — Y — N

Madeleine Edwards   Elmstone Court   Out Elmstead Lane   Barham   Canterbury CT4 6PH   Kent
Tel: (01227) 830433   Fax 01227 832405   Open: ALL YEAR   Map Ref No. 04

Kent

rate £ from - to per double room	children taken	evening meals taken	animals taken		

£65.00 to £75.00 — Y N N — 🚭

(non-smoking)

Southgate-Little Fowlers

Near Rd: A.268

17th-century historical country house with antique furnishings & a warm, welcoming atmosphere. Beautiful bedrooms, 1 king-size 4-poster, 1 king-size brass bed or a twin, all en-suite with wonderful views & many thoughtful extras. Superb breakfast served in the magnificent Victorian room or original Victorian conservatory housing impressive Muscat vine & collection of plants. 15th-century inns nearby. Near to Bodiam, Scotney, Rye, Sissinghurst, Battle & Dixter. Children over 9.
E-mail: Susan.Woodard@southgate.uk.net
www.southgate.uk.net

Susan Woodard   Southgate-Little Fowlers   Rye Road   Hawkhurst   Cranbrook TN18 5DA   Kent
Tel: (01580) 752526   Fax 01580 752526   Open: ALL YEAR (Excl. Xmas)   Map Ref No. 05

£58.00 to £60.00 — Y N N — 🚭

VISA: M'CARD:

Sunshine Cottage

Near Rd: A.2

A 17th-century, Grade II listed cottage, overlooking Shepherdswell village green, with a wealth of beams, an inglenook fireplace & 2 lounges. Tastefully furnished, & with a homely atmosphere. 6 attractive bedrooms. A pretty garden & courtyard are available to guests. Good home-cooking & home-made preserves. Good food also available at a nearby pub. Shepherdswell is situated halfway between Canterbury & Dover, 25 mins' from the Channel Tunnel. BR station 5 mins' walk away.
www.sunshine-cottage.co.uk

BN & L Popple   Sunshine Cottage   The Green   Shepherdswell   Dover CT15 7LQ   Kent
Tel: (01304) 831359   Mobile 0788 9572676   Open: ALL YEAR   Map Ref No. 06

£60.00 to £70.00 — Y N N — 🚭

VISA: M'CARD:

Leaveland Court

Near Rd: A.251

Guests are guaranteed a warm welcome on arrival at this enchanting 15th-century timbered farmhouse set in delightful gardens. Situated in a quiet rural setting, between Leaveland church & woodlands, & surrounded by a 500-acre downland farm. Ideally placed with the M2 & Faversham 5 mins, Canterbury 20 mins & 30 mins to channel ports. Bedrooms have en-suite facilities. Heated outdoor swimming pool. Caring hosts & generous breakfasts ensure an enjoyable stay.
E-mail: email@leavelandcourt.co.uk
www.leavelandcourt.co.uk

Mrs Corrine Scutt   Leaveland Court   Leaveland   Faversham ME13 0NP   Kent
Tel: (01233) 740596   Fax 01233 740015   Open: FEB - NOV   Map Ref No. 07

£35.00 to £75.00 — Y N N — 🚭

Pigeonwood House

Near Rd: A.260

Pigeonwood House is the original, 19th-century farmhouse of the surrounding area, positioned in rural tranquillity in chalk downland. The 2 guest bedrooms have beautiful panoramic views over the surrounding countryside & many guests return for the homely, relaxing atmosphere. Pigeonwood House is ideally situated for touring historic Kent as well as having the Channel tunnel & ports close by. Children over 6 are welcome.
E-mail: samandmary@aol.com
www.pigeonwood.com

Mrs Mary Martin   Pigeonwood House   Arpinge   Folkestone CT18 8AQ   Kent
Tel: (01303) 891111   Mobile 07967 925867   Open: APR-OCT   Map Ref No. 08

Conghurst Farm. Hawkhurst.

Kent

West Winchet

rate £ from - to per double room	children taken	evening meals taken	animals taken
£45.00 to £65.00	Y	N	Y

(non-smoking)

Near Rd: A.262

West Winchet is an elegant Victorian house surrounded by parkland in a secluded & peaceful setting. 2 beautifully decorated rooms, 1 double with en-suite bathroom & 1 twin with en-suite shower room. Each with T.V., radio & tea/coffee facilities. Both rooms are on the ground floor, & the twin-bedded room has French windows onto the terrace & into the garden. A magnificent drawing room for guests' use. An ideal touring centre for Kent & East Sussex. 2 1/2 miles mainline station (London 55 mins). Children over 5.
E-mail: annieparker@jpa-ltd.co.uk

Mrs Annie Parker   West Winchet   Winchet Hill   Goudhurst TN17 1JX   Kent
Tel: (01580) 212024 Fax 01580 212250 Open: ALL YEAR (Excl. Xmas & New Year) Map Ref No. 09

The Wren's Nest

rate £ from - to per double room	children taken	evening meals taken	animals taken
£62.00 to £62.00	Y	N	N

(non-smoking)

Near Rd: A.21

Built in traditional Kentish style, with oak beams & vaulted ceilings, The Wren's Nest suites have been designed specifically for the comfort & pleasure of guests. The suites are spacious & beautifully furnished & are well-equipped with colour T.V., tea/coffee-making facilities, tourist information literature, etc. & excellent en-suite bathrooms. The suites are entered via their own front door allowing absolute privacy. Hearty English breakfasts are served in the main house. An idyllic rural setting, well-placed for touring, walking & birdwatching. Children over 10.

Lynne Rodger   The Wren's Nest   Hastings Road   Hawkhurst TN18 4RT   Kent
Tel: (01580) 754919   Fax 01580 754919   Open: MAR - DEC   Map Ref No. 10

Conghurst Farm

rate £ from - to per double room	children taken	evening meals taken	animals taken
£60.00 to £70.00	Y	Y	N

(non-smoking)

see PHOTO over p. 166

Near Rd: A.268

Set in peaceful, totally unspoilt countryside, Conghurst Farm offers a perfect spot for a restful holiday. Within easy reach of all the marvellous houses & gardens that this part of the country has to offer. 3 very comfortable bedrooms, all with en-suite/private bathrooms. There is a drawing room, a separate T.V. room &, in the summer, a delightful garden for guests to enjoy. Evening meals are available Thursday-Monday inclusive. An ideal base from which to explore Kent. Children over 12.
E-mail: rosa@conghurst.co.uk
www.SmoothHound.co.uk/hotels/conghurst.html

Mrs Rosemary Piper   Conghurst Farm   Conghurst Lane   Hawkhurst TN18 4RW   Kent
Tel: (01580) 753331   Fax 01580 754579   Open: FEB - NOV   Map Ref No. 11

Jordans

rate £ from - to per double room	children taken	evening meals taken	animals taken
£72.00 to £76.00	Y	N	N

(non-smoking)

see PHOTO over p. 168

Near Rd: A.227

Beautiful, picture-postcard, 15th-century Tudor house (awarded a 'Historic Building of Kent' plaque) in the picturesque village of Plaxtol, among orchards & parkland. The house has been featured on T.V. & is beautifully furnished, with leaded windows, inglenook fireplaces, massive oak beams & an enchanting old English garden with rambler roses & espalier trees. Within easy reach are Ightham Mote, Leeds & Hever Castles, Penshurst, Chartwell & Knole. 3 lovely rooms, 2 with en-suite/private facilities. London 35 mins' by train, & easy access to airports. Children over 12.

Mrs Jo Lindsay N.D.D., A.T.D.   Jordans   Sheet Hill   Plaxtol   Sevenoaks TN15 0PU   Kent
Tel: (01732) 810379   Open: Mid JAN - Mid DEC   Map Ref No. 12

Jordans. Plaxtol.

rate £ from - to per double room	children taken	evening meals	animals taken		
£60.00 to £68.00 🚭	Y	N	N	Near Rd: A.26 A warm, friendly welcome & imaginative cooking is to be found in this beautiful 19th-century oast. An en-suite bedroom in the barn & 2 roundel bedrooms provide comfortable accommodation. The house is furnished with interesting antiques, & the lovely garden overlooks open country. Excellent communications make it an ideal base for visiting many historic houses & gardens. London 40 mins' by rail. Children over 12 years. E-mail: leavers_oast@hotmail.com www.leaversoast.co.uk	*Leavers Oast*

Anne Turner   Leavers Oast   Stanford Lane   Hadlow   Tonbridge TN11 0JN   Kent
Tel: (01732) 850924   Mobile 07771 663250   Fax 01732 850924   Open: ALL YEAR   Map Ref No. 13

£58.00 to £70.00 🚭	N	N	Y	Near Rd: A.21 Ash Tree Cottage is situated in a quiet private road just above the famous Pantiles, & within a few mins' walk of the high street & railway station. There are 2 charming & attractively furnished bedrooms with en-suite bathrooms, radio, T.V., tea/coffee-making facilities & plenty of tourist information. There is an excellent choice of restaurants & country pubs nearby, & many places of interest are within easy reach. E-mail: rogersashtree@excite.com www.bestbandb.co.uk	*Ash Tree Cottage*

Richard & Sue Rogers   Ash Tree Cottage   7 Eden Road   Tunbridge Wells TN1 1TS   Kent
Tel: (01892) 541317   Fax 01892 616770   Open: ALL YEAR (Excl. Xmas & New Year) Map Ref No. 14

All the establishments mentioned in this guide are members of
The Worldwide Bed & Breakfast Association

When booking your accommodation please mention
The Best Bed & Breakfast

Leicestershire, Nottinghamshire & Rutland

Leicestershire
(East Midlands)

Rural Leicestershire is rich in grazing land, a peaceful, undramatic landscape broken up by the waterways that flow through in the south of the county.

The River Avon passes on its way to Stratford, running by 17th century Stanford Hall & its motorcycle museum. The Leicester section of the Grand Union Canal was once very important for the transportation of goods from the factories of the Midlands to London Docks. It passes through a fascinating series of multiple locks at Foxton. The decorative barges, the 'narrow boats' are pleasure craft these days rather than the life-blood of the closed community of boat people who lived & worked out their lives on the canals.

Rutland was formerly England's smallest county, but was absorbed into East Leicestershire in the 1970's. Recently, once again, it has become a county in its' own right. Rutland Water, is one of Europe's largest reservoirs & an attractive setting for sailing, fishing or enjoying a trip on the pleasure cruiser. There is also the Rutland Theatre at Tolethorpe Hall, where a summer season of Shakespeare's plays is presented in the open air.

Melton Mowbray is famous for its pork pies & it is also the centre of Stilton cheese country. The "King of Cheeses" is made mainly in the Vale of Belvoir where Leicestershire meets Nottinghamshire, & the battlements & turrets of Belvoir Castle overlook the scene from its hill-top.

To the north-west the Charnwood Forest area is pleasantly wooded & the deer park at Bradgate surrounding the ruined home of Lady Jane Grey, England's nine-day queen, is a popular attraction.

Nottinghamshire
(East Midlands)

Nottinghamshire has a diversity of landscape from forest to farmland, from coal mines to industrial areas.

The north of the county is dominated by the expanse of Sherwood Forest, smaller now than in the time of legendary Robin Hood & his Merry Men, but still a lovely old woodland of Oak & Birch.

The Dukeries are so called because of the numerous ducal houses built in the area & there is beautiful parkland on these great estates that can be visited. Clumber Park, for instance has a huge lake & a double avenue of Limes.

Newstead Abbey was a mediaeval priory converted into the Byron family home in the 16th century. It houses the poet Byron's manuscripts & possessions & is set in wonderful gardens.

More modest is the terraced house in Eastwood, where D.H. Lawrence was born into the mining community on which his novels are based.

Nottingham was recorded in the Domesday Book as a thriving community & that tradition continues. It was here that Arkwright perfected his cotton-spinning machinery & went on to develop steam as a power source for industry.

Textiles, shoes, bicycles & tobacco are all famous Nottingham products, & the story of Nottingham Lace can be discovered at the Lace Hall, housed in a former church.

Nottingham Castle, high on Castle Rock, was built & destroyed & rebuilt many times during its history. It now houses the city's Art Gallery & Museum. The Castle towers over the ancient 'Trip to Jerusalem' Inn, said to be so named because crusaders stopped there for a drink on their way to fight in the Holy Land.

Leicestershire, Nottinghamshire & Rutland

Leicestershire Gazeteer

Areas of outstanding natural beauty.
Charnwood Forest, Rutland Water.

Historic Houses & Castles

Belvoir Castle - Nr. Grantham
Overlooking the Vale of Belvoir, castle rebuilt in 1816, with many special events including jousting tournaments. Home of the Duke of Rutland since Henry VIII. Paintings, furniture, historic armoury, military museums, magnificent stateroom.

Belvoir Castle

Belgrave Hall - Leicester
18th century Queen Anne house - furnishing of 18th & 19th centuries.
Langton Hall - Nr. Market Harborough
Privately occupied - perfect English country house from mediaeval times - drawing rooms have 18th century Venetian lace.

Oakham Castle - Oakham
Norman banqueting hall of late 12th C.
Stanford Hall - Nr Lutterworth
17th century William & Mary house - collection of Stuart relics & pictures, antiques & costumes of family from Elizabeth I onward. Motor cycle museum.
Stapleford Park - Nr. Melton Mowbray
Old wing dated 1500, restored 1663. Extended to mansion in 1670. Collection of pictures, tapestries, furniture & Balston's Staffordshire portrait figures of Victorian age.

Cathedrals & Churches

Breedon-on-the-Hill (St. Mary & St. Hardulph)
Norman & 13th century. Jacobean canopied pew, 18th century carvings.
Empingham (St. Peter)
14th century west tower, front & crocketed spire. Early English interior - double piscina, triple sedilla.
Lyddington (St. Andrew)
Perpendicular in the main - mediaeval wall paintings & brasses.
Staunton Harol (Holy Trinity)
17th century - quite unique Cromwellian church - painted ceilings.

Museums & Galleries

Bosworth Battlefield Visitor Centre - Nr Market Bosworth
Exhibitions, models, battlefield trails at site of 1485 Battle of Bosworth where Richard III lost his life & crown to Henry.
Leicestershire Museum of Technology - Leicester
Beam engines, steam shovel, knitting machinery & other aspects of the county's industrial past.
Leicester Museum & Art Gallery - Leicester
Painting collection.
18th & 19th century, watercolours & drawings, 20th century French paintings, Old Master & modern prints. English silver & ceramics, special exhibitions.
Jewry Wall Museum & Site - Leicester
Roman wall & baths site adjoining museum of archaeology.

Leicestershire, Nottinghamshire & Rutland

Melton Carnegie Museum-Melton Mowbray
Displays of Stilton cheese, pork pies & other aspects of the past & present life of the area.

Rutland County Museum - Oakham
Domestic & agricultural life of Rutland, England's smallest county.

Donnington Collection of Single-Seater Racing Cars - Castle Donington
Large collection of grand prix racing cars & racing motorcycles, adjoining Donington Park racing circuit..

Wygson's House Museum of Costume - Leicestershire
Costume, accessories & shop settings in late mediaeval buildings.

The Bellfoundry Museum - Loughborough
Moulding, casting, tuning & fitting of bells, with conducted tours of bellfoundry.

Historic Monuments

The Castle - Ashby-de-la-Zouch
14th century with tower added in 15th century.

Kirby Muxloe Castle - Kirby Muxloe
15th century fortified manor house with moat ruins.

Other things to see & do

Twin lakes at Melton Bowbray. Theme park.

Belton House. Nr grantham

Twycross Zoo - Nr. Atherstone
Gorillas, orang-utans, chimpanzees, gibbons, elephants, giraffes, lions & many other animals.

The Battlefield Line Nr. Market Bosworth
Steam railway & collection of railway relics, adjoining Bosworth Battlefield.

Great Central Railway - Loughborough
Steam railway over 5-mile route in Charnwood Forest area, with steam & diesel museum.

Rutland Railway Museum - Nr. Oakham
Industrial steam & diesel locomotives. wagons from quarries, mines & factories.

Nottinghamshire Gazeteer
Historic Houses & Castles

Holme Pierrepont Hall - Nr. Nottingham
Outstanding red brick Tudor manor, in continuous family ownership, with 19th century courtyard garden.

Newark Castle - Newark
Dramatic castle ruins on riverside site, once one of the most important castles of the north.

Newstead Abbey - Nr. Mansfield
Priory converted to country mansion, home of poet Lord Byron with many of his possessions & manuscripts on display. Beautiful parkland, lakes & gardens.

Nottingham Castle - Nottingham
17th century residence on site of mediaeval castle.
Fine collections of ceramics, silver, Nottingham alabaster carvings, local historical displays. Art gallery. Special exhibitions & events.

Wollaton Hall - Nottingham
Elizabethan mansion now housing natural history exhibits. Stands in deer park, with Industrial Museum in former stables, illustrating the city's bicycle, hosiery, lace, pharmaceutical & other industries.

Cathedrals & Churches

Egmanton (St. Mary)
Magnificent interior by Comper. Norman doorway & font. Canopied rood screen, 17th century altar.

Newark (St. Mary Magdalene)
15th century. 2 painted panels of "Dance of Death". Reredos by Comper.

Southwell Cathedral
Norman nave, unvaulted, fine early English choir. Decorated pulpitum, 6 canopied stalls, fine misericords. Octagonal chapter house..

Terseval (St. Catherine)
12th century - interior 17th century unrestored.

Museums & Galleries

Castlegate Museum - Nottingham
Row of Georgian terraced houses showing costume & textile collection.
Lace making equipment & lace collection.

Leicestershire, Nottinghamshire & Rutland

Nottingham Castle Museum - Nottingham
Collections of ceramics, glass & silver. Alabaster carvings.

D.H. Lawrence Birthplace - Eastwood
Home of the novelist & poet, as it would have been at time of his birth, 1885.

Millgate Museum of Social & Folk Life - Newark
Local social & folk life, with craft workshops.

Brewhouse Yard Museum - Nottingham
Daily life in Nottingham, displayed in 17th century cottages & rock-cut cellars.

The Lace Hall - Nottingham
The story of Nottingham Lace audio-visual display & exhibition with lace shops, in fine converted church.

Museum of Costume & Textiles - Nottingham
Costumes, lace & textiles on display in fine Georgian buildings.

Bassetlaw Museum - Retford
Local history of north Nottinghamshire.

Canal Museum - Nottinghamshire
History of the River Trent & canal history, in former canal warehouse.

Ruddington Framework Knitters' Museum - Ruddington
Unique complex of early 19th-century framework knitters' buildings with over 20 hand frames in restored workshop.

Other things to see & do

The Tales of Robin Hood - Nottingham
A 'flight to adventure' from mediaeval Nottingham to Sherwood Forest through the tales of the world's most famous outlaw.

Clumber Park - Nr. Worksop
Landscaped parkland, with double avenue of limes, lake, chapel. One of the Dukeries' estates, though the house no longer remains.

Rufford - Nr. Ollerton
Parkland, lake & gallery with fine crafts, around ruin of Cistercian abbey.

Sherwood Forest Visitor Centre - Nr. Edwinstowe
Robin Hood exhibition.
450 acres of ancient oak woodland associated with the outlaw & his merry men.

Sherwood Forest Farm Park - Nr. Edwinstowe
Rare breeds of cattle, sheep, pigs & goats. Lake with wildfowl.

White Post Farm Centre - Farnsfield, Nr Newark
Working modern farm with crops & many animals, including cows, sheep, pigs, hens, geese, ducks, llamas, horses. Indoor displays & exhibits.

Newark Castle.

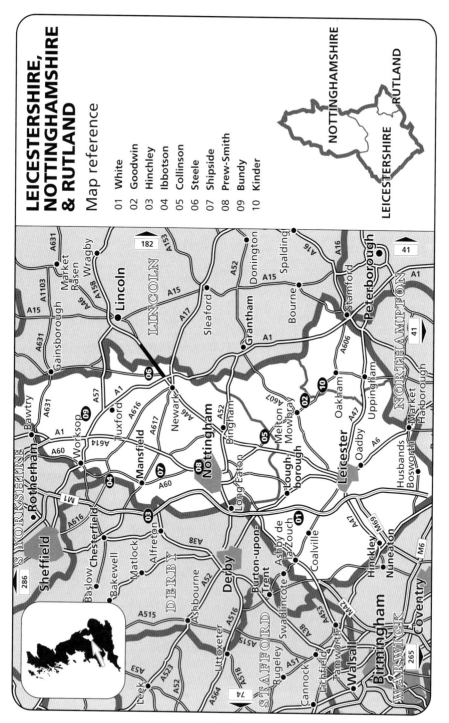

LEICESTERSHIRE, NOTTINGHAMSHIRE & RUTLAND

Map reference

01 White
02 Goodwin
03 Hinchley
04 Ibbotson
05 Collinson
06 Steele
07 Shipside
08 Prew-Smith
09 Bundy
10 Kinder

NOTTINGHAMSHIRE

RUTLAND

LEICESTERSHIRE

Column headers (rotated):
- rate £ from - to per double room
- children taken
- evening meals
- animals taken

Abbots Oak Country House

rate £ from-to per double room	children taken	evening meals	animals taken
£65.00 to £100.00	Y	Y	Y

Near Rd: A.50, A.511

A Grade II listed building with a wealth of oak panelling, & including the staircase reputedly from Nell Gwynn's town house. Set in mature gardens & woodland, with natural granite outcrops. There are 3 delightful rooms, all with en-suite bathrooms. Open fires create a warm & welcoming atmosphere, & Carolyn's superb dinners are served in the candlelit dining room. Stratford, Belvoir Castle & Rutland Water can all be reached within the hour. Tennis court, billiard room. Children over 6.

E-mail: admin@abbotsoak.com
www.abbotsoak.com

Carolyn Voce & Audrey White Abbots Oak Country House Warren Hills Rd Coalville LE67 4UY Leics.
Tel: (01530) 832328   Fax 01530 832328   Open: ALL YEAR   Map Ref No. 01

Hillside House

rate £ from-to per double room	children taken	evening meals	animals taken
£44.00 to £50.00	Y	N	N

Near Rd: A.606

Charmingly converted farm buildings with superb views over open countryside, in the small village of Burton Lazars. Comfortable accommodation is offered in 1 double & 2 twin-bedded rooms, each with an en-suite/private bathroom. All have tea/coffee facilities & T.V.. A pleasant garden to relax in. Close to Melton Mowbray, famous for its pork pies & Stilton cheese, & with Burghley House, Belvoir Castle & Rutland Water within easy reach. Children over 9. Single supplement.

E-mail: hillhs27@aol.com
www.hillside-house.co.uk

Mrs Sue Goodwin Hillside House 27 Melton Road Burton Lazars Melton Mowbray LE14 2UR Leics.
Tel: (01664) 566312   Fax 01664 501819 Open: ALL YEAR (Excl. Xmas & New Year) Map Ref No. 02

Titchfield House

rate £ from-to per double room	children taken	evening meals	animals taken
£40.00 to £40.00	Y	N	Y

Near Rd: A.617

This is 2 houses converted into 1 family-run guest house, offering 6 comfortable rooms, a lounge with T.V., a kitchen for guests' use, a bathroom & showers. It also has an adjoining garage. Near to Mansfield, which is a busy market town. Sherwood Forest & the Peak District are both easily accessible. Titchfield Guest House is a very handy location for touring this lovely area, & for onward travel. A warm & friendly welcome is assured at this charming home. Animals by arrangement.

www.bestbandb.co.uk

VISA: M'CARD:

Mrs Betty Hinchley Titchfield House 300/302 Chesterfield Road North Mansfield NG19 7QU Notts.
Tel: (01623) 810356/810921   Fax 01623 810356   Open: ALL YEAR   Map Ref No. 03

Blue Barn Farm

rate £ from-to per double room	children taken	evening meals	animals taken
£48.00 to £52.00	Y	N	N

Near Rd: A.616

An enjoyable visit is guaranteed at this family-run, 250-acre farm, set in tranquil countryside on the edge of Sherwood Forest (Robin Hood country). 3 guest bedrooms, each with modern amenities including h&c, tea/coffee-making facilities & a guest bathroom with shower. 1 bedroom is en-suite. A colour-T.V. lounge & garden are also available. Guests are very welcome to walk around the farm. Many interesting places, catering for all tastes, only a short journey away.

E-mail: bluebarnfarm@supanet.com
www.bluebarnfarm-notts.co.uk

June M. Ibbotson   Blue Barn Farm   Langwith   Mansfield NG20 9JD   Nottinghamshire
Tel: (01623) 742248 Fax 01623 742248 Open: ALL YEAR (Excl. Xmas & New Year) Map Ref No. 04

Nottinghamshire

Sulney Fields

Near Rd: A.606

Sulney Fields is situated in a quiet position on the edge of a small village & offers spacious accommodation with spectacular views over the Vale of Belvoir. Each of the 3 attractive bedrooms has private facilities & a T.V. & tea/coffee-making facilities. (2 of the rooms have access via a stair lift.) A delicious full English breakfast is served from 07.30 until 09.30 each day. An ideal base, within easy reach of Nottingham, Loughborough, Leicester & Melton Mowbray. A choice of pubs within 1 mile.
www.bestbandb.co.uk

| £50.00 to £55.00 | Y | N | Y |

Hilary Collinson Sulney Fields Colonel's Lane Upper Broughton Melton Mowbray LE14 3BD Notts.
Tel: (01664) 822204   Fax 01664 823976   Open: ALL YEAR (Excl. Xmas)   Map Ref No. 05

The Old Vicarage

Near Rd: A.1133

A mile from Newark showground & 2 miles from the A.1, this fine Victorian vicarage stands in secluded grounds next to one of the oldest churches in Nottinghamshire. It is reputed that Mary Queen of Scots stayed at Langford as a guest of the Earl of Shrewsbury. Southwell's beautiful minster & the cathedral city of Lincoln are nearby, Newark is 3 miles. Jerry bakes the bread & vegetables come from the enchanting garden. Rooms are spacious with Victorian baths. Single supplement. Dinner & animals by prior arrangement. Children over 12.
E-mail: jillie.steele@virgin.net

| £70.00 to £80.00 | Y | Y | Y |

VISA: M'CARD:

Jerry & Jillie Steele The Old Vicarage Holme Road Langford Newark NG23 7RT Nottinghamshire
Tel: (01636) 705031   Fax 01636 708728   Open: ALL YEAR   Map Ref No. 06

Holly Lodge

Near Rd: A.60

Holly Lodge is situated just off the A.60, 10 miles north of Nottingham. This attractive former hunting lodge stands in 15 acres of grounds. The 4 comfortable & attractive, en-suite guest rooms are housed within the converted stables. There are panoramic countryside views on all sides, with woodland walks, tennis, golf & riding nearby. Ideally situated for a peaceful, rural holiday base with a relaxed & friendly atmosphere.
E-mail: ann.hollylodge@ukonline.co.uk
www.hollylodgenotts.co.uk

| £59.00 to £64.00 | Y | N | N |

see PHOTO over
p. 177

VISA: M'CARD: AMEX:

Ann Shipside Holly Lodge Ricket Lane Blidworth Nottingham NG21 0NQ Nottinghamshire
Tel: (01623) 793853   Fax 01623 490977   Open: ALL YEAR   Map Ref No. 07

The Yellow House

Near Rd: A.60

The Yellow House is a 1930's semi-detached house, which is set in a very quiet road. The house is very comfortable & the bedroom is elegantly decorated in cream & green, has T.V. & tea/coffee-making facilities & its own en-suite shower room. Breakfast may be taken on the terrace in fine weather. The city centre is a couple of miles away & Sherwood Forest is 20 mins' to the north. Suzanne, an ex-model & much travelled, is happy to collect you from the station & extends a friendly welcome on arrival. Single supplement.
E-mail: suzanne.prewsmith1@btinternet.com

| £35.00 to £55.00 | N | N | N |

Mrs S Prew-Smith The Yellow House 7 Littlegreen Road Woodthorpe Nottingham NG5 4LE Notts.
Tel: (0115) 9262280   Open: ALL YEAR   Map Ref No. 08

Holly Lodge. Blidworth.

Nottinghamshire & Rutland

The Barns Country Guest House

Near Rd: A.1

The Barns Country Guest House is an ideal location for couples. This beautifully converted 18th-century barn boasts oak beams & pretty bedrooms, all en-suite with full facilities, with a 4-poster room for special occasions. Enjoy a delicious Aga-cooked breakfast including those suitable for vegetarians, served in a spacious yet comfortable dining room. This is an interesting base for touring, located at Babworth, home of the Pilgrim Fathers, Robin Hood country & Clumber Park. Children over 8.
E-mail: enquiries@thebarns.co.uk
www.thebarns.co.uk

£56.00 to £76.00 — Y — N — N

VISA: M'CARD:

Nigel & Sue Bundy   The Barns Country Guest House   Morton Farm   Babworth   Retford DN22 8HA
Nottinghamshire   Tel: (01777) 706336   Fax - on request   Open: ALL YEAR   Map Ref No. 09

Torr Lodge

Near Rd: A.1

A warm welcome awaits you at Torr Lodge, Barrow, in the heart of scenic Rutland, England's smallest county. Belvoir Castle, Burghley House & Geoff Hamilton's famous gardens are all within easy reach, as is Rutland Water. Georgiana has been in the hospitality business for many years & offers tastefully furnished en-suite accommodation, home-cooking on an Aga & hearty breakfasts. Dinner available by arrangement. Children over 12.
E-mail: reservations@torrlodge.co.uk
www.torrlodge.co.uk

£55.00 to £55.00 — Y — Y — Y

Mrs Georgiana Kinder   Torr Lodge   Main Street   Barrow   Nr. Oakham LE15 7PE   Rutland
Tel: (01572) 813396   Open: ALL YEAR   Map Ref No. 10

All the establishments mentioned in this guide are members of
The Worldwide Bed & Breakfast Association

When booking your accommodation please mention
The Best Bed & Breakfast

Lincolnshire

Lincolnshire
(East Midlands)

Lincolnshire is an intriguing mixture of coast & country, of flat fens & gently rising wolds.

There are the popular resorts of Skegness & Mablethorpe as well as quieter coastal regions where flocks of wild birds take food & shelter in the dunes. Gibraltar Point & Saltfleetby are large nature reserves.

Fresh vegetables for much of Britain are produced in the rich soil of the Lincolnshire fens, & windmills punctuate the skyline. There is a unique 8-sailed windmill at Heckington. In spring the fields are ablaze with the red & yellow of tulips. The bulb industry flourishes around Spalding & Holbeach, & in early May tulip flowers in abundance decorate the huge floats of the Spalding Flower Parade.

The city of Lincoln has cobbled streets & ancient buildings & a very beautiful triple-towered Cathedral which shares its hill-top site with the Castle, both dating from the 11th century. There is a 17th century library by Wren in the Cathedral, which has amongst its treasures one of the four original copies of Magna Carta.

Boston has a huge parish church with a distincive octagonal tower which can be seen for miles across the surrounding fenland, & is commonly known as the 'Boston Stump'. The Guildhall Museum displays many aspects of the town's history, including the cells where the early Pilgrim Fathers were imprisioned after their attempt to flee to the Netherlands to find religious freedom. They eventually made the journey & hence to America.

One of England's most outstanding towns is Stamford. It has lovely churches, ancient inns & other fine buildings in a mellow stone.

Sir Isaac Newton was born at Woolsthorpe Manor & educated at nearby Grantham where there is a museum which illustrates his life & work.

The poet Tennyson was born in the village of Somersby, where his father was Rector.

Lincoln Cathedral.

Lincolnshire

Lincolnshire Gazeteer

Areas of outstanding natural beauty.
Lincolnshire Wolds.

Historic Houses & Castles

Auborn House - Nr. Lincoln
16th century house with imposing carved staircase & panelled rooms.
Belton House - Grantham
House built 1684-88 - said to be by Christopher Wren - work by Grinling Gibbons & Wyatt also. Paintings, furniture, porcelain, tapestries, Duke of Windsor mementoes. A great English house with formal gardens & extensive grounds with orangery.
Doddington Hall - Doddington, Nr. Lincoln
16th century Elizabethan mansion with elegant Georgian rooms & gabled Tudor gatehouse. Fine furniture, paintings, porcelain, etc. Formal walled knot gardens, roses & wild gardens.
Burghley House - Stamford
Elizabethan - England's largest & grandest house of the era. Famous for its beautiful painted ceilings, silver fireplaces & art treasures.
Gumby Hall - Burgh-le-Marsh
17th century manor house. Ancient gardens.
Harrington Hall - Spilsby
Mentioned in the Domesday Book - has mediaeval stone base - Carolinean manor house in red brick. Some alterations in 1678 to mullioned windows. Panelling, furnishings of 17th & 18th century.
Marston Hall - Grantham
16th century manor house. Ancient gardens.
The Old Hall - Gainsborough
Fine mediaeval manor house built in 1480's with original kitchen, rebuilt after original hall destroyed during Wars of the Roses. Tower & wings, Great Hall. It was the first meeting place of the "Dissenters", later known as the Pilgrim Fathers.
Woolsthorpe Manor - Grantham
17th century house. Birthplace of Sir Isaac Newton.
Fydell House - Boston
18th century house, now Pilgrim College.

Lincoln Castle - Lincoln
William the Conqueror castle, with complete curtain wall & Norman shell keep. Towers & wall walk. Unique prisoners' chapel.
Tattershall Castle - Tattershall
100 foot high brick keep of 15th century moated castle, with fine views over surrounding country.

Cathedrals & Churches

Addlethorpe (St. Nicholas)
15th century - mediaeval stained glass - original woodwork.
Boston (St. Botolph)
14th century decorated - very large parish church. Beautiful south porch, carved stalls.
Brant Broughton (St. Helens)
13th century arcades - decorated tower & spire - perpendicular clerestory. Exterior decoration.
Ewerby (St. Andrew)
Decorated - splendid example of period - very fine spire. 14th century effigy.
Fleet (St. Mary Magdalene)
14th century - early English arcades - perpendicular windows - detached tower & spire.
Folkingham (St. Andrew)
14th century arcades - 15th century windows - perpendicular tower - early English chancel.
Gedney (St. Mary Magdalene)
Perpendicular spire (unfinished). Early English tower. 13th-14th century monuments, 14th-15th century stained glass.
Grantham (St. Wulfram)
14th century tower & spire - Norman pillars - perpendicular chantry - 14th century vaulted crypt.
Lincoln Cathedral - Lincoln
Magnificent triple-towered Gothic building on fine hill-top site.
Norman west front,
13th century - some 14th century additions. Norman work from 1072. Angel choir - carved & decorated pulpitum - 13th century chapter house - 17th century library by Wren (containing one of the four original copies of Magna Carta).

Lincolnshire

St. Botolph's Church - Boston
Fine parish church, one of the largest in the country, with 272 foot octagonal tower dominating the surrounding fens.
Long Sutton (St. Mary)
15th century south porch, mediaeval brass lectern, very fine early English spire.
Louth (St. James)
Early 16th century - mediaeval Gothic - wonderful spire.
Scotter (St. Peter)
Saxon to perpendicular - early English nave - 15th century rood screen.
Stow (St. Mary)
Norman - very fine example, particularly west door. Wall painting.
Silk Willoughby (St. Denis)
14th century - tower with spire & flying buttresses. 15th-17th century pulpit.
Stainfield (St. Andrew)
Queen Anne - mediaeval armour & early needlework.
Theddlethorpe (All Saints)
14th century - 15th century & reredos of 15th century, 16th century parcloses, 15th century brasses - some mediaeval glass.
Wrangle (St. Mary the Virgin & St. Nicholas)
Early English - decorated - perpendicular - Elizabethan pulpit. 14th century east window & glass.

Museums & Galleries

Alford Manor House - Alford
Tudor manor house - thatched - folk museum. Nearby windmill.
Boston Guildhall Museum - Boston
15th century building with mayor's parlour, court room & cells where Pilgrim Fathers were imprisoned in 1607. Local exhibits.
Lincoln Cathedral Library - Lincoln
Built by Wren housing early printed books & mediaeval manuscripts.
Lincoln Cathedral Treasury - Lincoln
Diocesan gold & silver plate.
Lincoln City & Country Museum - Lincoln
Prehistoric, Roman & mediaeval antiquities with local associations. Armour & local history.
Museum of Lincolnshire Life - Lincoln
Domestic, agricultural, industrial & social history of the county. Edwardian room settings, shop settings, agricultural machinery.

Usher Gallery - Lincoln
Paintings, watches, miniatures, porcelain, silver, coins & medals. Temporary exhibitions. Tennyson collection. Works of English watercolourist Peter de Wint.
Grantham Museum - Grantham
Archeology, prehistoric, Saxon & Roman. Local history with special display about Sir Isaac Newton, born nearby & educated in Grantham.
Church Farm Museum - Skegness
Farmhouse & buildings with local agricultural collections & temporary exhibitions & special events.
Stamford Museum - Stamford
Local history museum, with temporary special exhibitions.
Battle of Britain Memorial Flight - Coningsby
Lancaster bomber, five Spitfires & two Hurricanes with other Battle of Britain memorabilia.
National Cycle Museum - Lincoln
Development of the cycle.
Stamford Steam Brewery Museum - Stamford
Complete Victorian steam brewery with 19th century equipment.

Other things to see & do

Springfield - Spalding
Show gardens of the British bulb industry, & home of the Spalding Flower Parade each May. Summer bedding plants & roses.
Butlins Funcoast World - Skegness
Funsplash Water World with amusements & entertainments
Castle Leisure Park - Tattershall
Windsurfing, water-skiing, sailing, fishing & other sports & leisure facilities.
Long Sutton Butterfly Park - Long Sutton
Walk-through tropical butterfly house with outdoor wildflower meadows & pets corner.
Skegness Natureland Marine Zoo - Skegness
Seal sanctuary with aquaria, tropical house, pets corner & butterfly house.
Windmills - at Lincoln (Ellis Mill - 4 sails), Boston (Maud Foster - 5 sails), Burgh-le-Marsh (5 sails), Alford (5 sails), Sibsey (6 sails), Heckington (8 sails).

LINCOLNSHIRE
Map reference

01 Brotherton
02 Armstrong
03 Sharman
04 Clarke
05 Needham
06 Woods

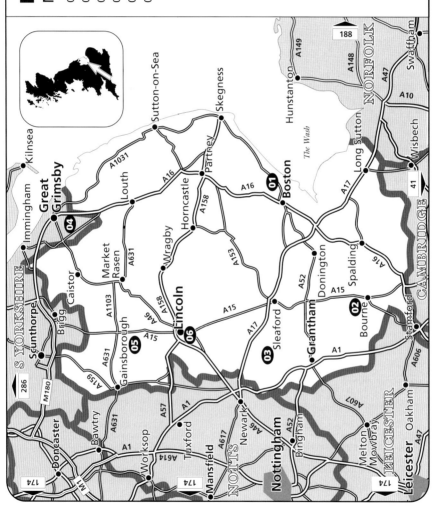

Lincolnshire

The Old Vicarage

£45.00 to £55.00 | Y | Y | Y

Near Rd: A.52

The Old Vicarage is a beautiful Queen Anne house in tranquil Wrangle, 9 miles north of historic Boston. Boston Church - the Stump - is the largest parish church in England & is well known the world over. Boston has historic links with the Pilgrim Fathers. Wrangle lies at the edge of the Fens, on the corner of the Wash. The Brothertons love entertaining & offer great comfort & top-class home-cooking, based on local & home-grown produce. Animals by arrangement.
E-mail: jb141@aol.com

Mr & Mrs Michael Brotherton   The Old Vicarage   Wrangle   Boston PE22 9EP   Lincolnshire
Tel: (01205) 870688   Fax 01205 871857   Open: ALL YEAR (Excl. Xmas)   Map Ref No. 01

Cawthorpe Hall

£70.00 to £80.00 | Y | Y | Y

Near Rd: A.15

This fine, old, listed house is surrounded by a large pretty garden & fields of roses supplying the rose distillery with fragrant blooms. The rooms are bright, spacious, comfortably furnished & have bathrooms en-suite. A full English breakfast will be served in a family country kitchen. Evening meals are available by arrangement. Country lovers can enjoy beautiful woodland walks. Horse riding or golf, Grimsthorpe Castle & Park are all within easy reach. A charming home.
E-mail: armstrong@cawthorpebandb.co.uk
www.cawthorpebandb.co.uk

Mrs Chantal Armstrong   Cawthorpe Hall   Cawthorpe   Bourne PE10 0AB   Lincolnshire
Tel: (01778) 423830 Fax 01778 426620   Open: ALL YEAR (Excl. Xmas & New Year) Map Ref No. 02

Gelston Grange Farm

£50.00 to £55.00 | Y | N | N

Near Rd: A.1, A.17

A warm welcome awaits you at Gelston Grange, a period farmhouse dated 1840, with many original features. Set in a large garden, it overlooks open countryside & has parking. All bedrooms are en-suite, designed with comfort in mind & are pleasing to the eye, with many thoughtful extras. Delicious breakfasts are served in the dining room, with a log fire on chilly mornings. Approx. 3 miles from A.1 or A.17. Central for Lincoln, Grantham, Stamford & Newark. Children over 10.
E-mail: janet@gelstongrange.fsnet.co.uk
www.gelstongrange.co.uk

J. Sharman   Gelston Grange Farm   Nr. Marston   Grantham NG32 2AQ   Lincolnshire
Tel: (01400) 250281   Open: Mid JAN - Mid DEC   Map Ref No. 03

The Old Farmhouse

£40.00 to £60.00 | Y | N | N

Near Rd: A.18

Situated in the Wolds, The Old Farmhouse is an 18th-century treasure recently renovated to a very high standard. Stunning inside & out, & set in a truly peaceful location overlooking a gentle valley. A large comfortable lounge with inglenook fireplace & old beams is provided for you to relax in. 2 beautifully furnished bedrooms with all amenities. An excellent choice of local pubs. Well-placed for golf, country walks, the coast & horse racing. Covered parking & horse livery available. Children over 7 years. A charming home.
E-mail: nicola@hatcliffe.freeserve.co.uk

Nicola Clarke   The Old Farmhouse   Low Road   Hatcliffe   Nr. Grimsby DN37 0SH   Lincolnshire
Tel: (01472) 824455   Mobile 07818 272523   Open: ALL YEAR (Excl. Xmas & N.Y.)   Map Ref No. 04

Lincolnshire

	rate £ from - to per double room	children taken	evening meals	animals taken

Church Farm

Near Rd: A.15

A large, traditional 19th-century farm house set in an acre of mature secluded gardens. Completely refurbished in 2004 to a very high standard. Offering 1 twin room with en-suite facilities, 1 double & 1 single with shared bathroom. All with tea/coffee-making facilities. Residents lounge with open fire & T.V. Full English breakfast offered with alternatives of fruit, muesli etc. according to dietary requirements. The historic city of Lincoln is only 10 mins' away. Children over 5.
E-mail: info@churchfarm-fillingham.co.uk
www.churchfarm-fillingham.co.uk

£49.00 to £54.00	Y	N	N

Kathleen Needham   Church Farm   High Street   Fillingham   Lincoln DN21 5BS   Lincolnshire
Tel: (01427) 668279   Open: ALL YEAR (Excl. Xmas & New Year)   Map Ref No. 05

Carline Guest House

Near Rd: A.57, A.46

Barrie & Jackie Woods extend a warm welcome. Excellent accommodation, in 6 attractively furnished bedrooms, each with en-suite facilities, T.V., radio, beverage facilities, hairdryers & trouser press. The Carline is a short, pleasant stroll from the Lawns Tourism & Conference Centre, & from the historic Uphill area of Lincoln. There are several restaurants & public houses nearby for your lunch or evening meal. Ask for recommendations.
E-mail: sales@carlineguesthouse.co.uk
www.carlineguesthouse.co.uk

£48.00 to £50.00	Y	N	N

Barrie & Jackie Woods   Carline Guest House   1-3 Carline Road   Lincoln LN1 1HL   Lincolnshire
Tel: (01522) 530422   Fax 01522 530422   Open: ALL YEAR (Excl. Xmas & New Year)   Map Ref No. 06

All the establishments mentioned in this guide are members of
The Worldwide Bed & Breakfast Association

When booking your accommodation please mention
The Best Bed & Breakfast

Norfolk

Norfolk
(East Anglia)

One of the largest of the old counties, Norfolk is divided by rivers from neighbouring counties & pushes out into the sea on the north & east sides. This is old East Anglia.

Inland there is great concentration on agriculture where fields are hedged with hawthorn which blossoms like snow in summer. A great deal of land drainage is required & the area is crisscrossed by dykes & ditches - some of them dating back to Roman times.

Holkham Hall.

The Norfolk Broads were formed by the flooding of mediaeval peat diggings to form miles & miles of inland waterways, navigable & safe. On a bright summer's day, on a peaceful backwater bounded by reed & sedge, the Broads seem like paradise. Here are hidden treasures like the Bittern, that shyest of birds, the Swallowtail butterfly & the rare Marsh orchid.

Contrasting with the still inland waters is a lively coastline which takes in a host of towns & villages as it arcs around The Wash. Here are the joys of the seaside at its best, miles of safe & sandy golden beaches to delight children, dunes & salt marshes where bird-life flourishes, & busy ports & fishing villages with pink-washed cottages.

Cromer is a little seaside town with a pier & a prom, cream teas & candy floss, where red, white & blue fishing boats are drawn up on the beach.

Hunstanton is more decorous, with a broad green sweeping down to the cliffs. Great Yarmouth is a boisterous resort. It has a beach that runs for miles, with pony rides & almost every amusement imaginable.

It is possible to take a boat into the heart of Norwich, past warehouses, factories & new penthouses, & under stone & iron bridges. Walking along the riverbank you reach Pulls Ferry where a perfectly proportioned grey flint gateway arcs over what was once a canal dug to transport stone to the cathedral site. Norwich Cathedral is magnificent, with a sharply soaring spire, beautiful cloisters & fine 15th century carving preserved in the choir stalls. Cathedral Close is perfectly preserved, as is Elm Hill, a cobbled street from mediaeval times. There are many little shops & narrow alleys going down to the river.

Norfolk is a county much loved by the Royal family & the Queen has a home at Sandringham. It is no castle, but a solid, comfortable family home with red brick turrets & French windows opening onto the terrace.

Norfolk

Norfolk Gazeteer

Areas of outstanding beauty.

Norfolk coast (part)

Historic Houses & Castles

Anna Sewell House - Great Yarmouth
17th century Tudor frontage. Birthplace of writer Anna Sewell.

Blicking Hall - Aylsham
Great Jacobean house. Fine Russian tapestry, long gallery with exceptional ceiling. Formal garden.

Felbrigg Hall - Nr. Cromer
17th century, good Georgian interior. Set in wooded parklands.

Holkham Hall - Wells
Fine Palladian mansion of 1734.
Paintings, statuary, tapestries, furnishings & formal garden by Berry.

Houghton Hall - Wells
18th century mansion. Pictures, china & staterooms.

Oxburgh Hall - Swafftham
Late 15th century moated house. Fine gatehouse tower. Needlework by Mary Queen of Scots.

Wolterton Hall - Nr. Norwich
Built in 1741 contains tapestries, porcelain, furniture.

Trinity Hospital - Castle Rising
17th century, nine brick & tile almshouses, court chapel & treasury.

Cathedrals & Churches

Attleborough (St. Mary)
Norman with late 14th century. Fine rood screen & frescoes.

Barton Turf (St. Michael & All Angles)
Magnificent screen with painting of the Nine Orders of Angles.

Beeston-next-Mileham (St. Mary)
14th century. Perpendicular clerestory tower & spire. Hammer Beam roof, parclose screens, benches, front cover. Tracery in nave & chancel windows.

Cawston (St. Agnes)
Tower faced with freestone. Painted screens, wall paintings, tower, screen & gallery. 15th century angel roof.

East Harding (St. Peter & St. Paul)
14th century, some 15th century alterations. Monuments of 15th-17th century. Splendid mediaeval glass.

Erpingham (St. Mary)
14th century military brass to John de Erpingham, 16th century   Rhenish glass. Fine tower.

Gunton (St. Andrew)
18th century. Robert Adam - classical interior in dark wood - gilded.

King's Lynn (St. Margaret)
Norman foundation. Two fine 14th century Flemish brasses, 14th century screens, reredos by Bodley, interesting Georgian pulpit with sounding board.

Norwich Cathedral
Romanesque & late Gothic with 15th century spire. Perpendicular lierne vaults in nave, transeptsand presbytery.

Ranworth (St. Helens)
15th century screen, very fine example. Sarum Antiphoner, 14th century illuminated manuscript - East Anglian work.

Salle (St. Peter & St. Paul)
15th century. Highly decorated west tower & porches. Mediaeval glass, pulpit with 15th century panels & Jacobean tester. Stalls, misericords, brasses & monuments, sacrament font.

Terrington (St. Clement)
Detached perpendicular tower. Western front has fire-light window & canopied niches. Georgian panelling west of nave. 17th century painted font cover. Jacobean commandment boards.

Trunch (St. Botolph)
15th century screen with painted panels, mediaeval glass, famous font canopy with fine carving & painting, ringer's gallery, Elizabethan monument.

Wiggenhall (St. Germans)
17th century pulpit, table, clerk's desk & chair, bench ends 15th century.

Wymondham (St. Mary & St. Thomas of Canterbury)
Norman origins including arcades & triforium windows, 13th century font fragments, complete 15th century font. 15th century clerestory & roof. Comper reredos, famous Corporas Case, rare example of 13th century Opus Anglicanum.

Museums & Galleries

Norwich Castle Museum
Art collection, local & natural history,

Norfolk

Strangers Hall - Norwich
Mediaeval mansion furnished as museum of urban domestic life in 16th-19th centuries.

St. Peter Hungate Church Museum - Norwich
15th century church for the exhibition of ecclesiastical art & East Anglican antiquities.

Sainsbury Centre for Visual Arts - University, Norwich
Collection of modern art, ancient, classical & mediaeval art, Art Nouveau, 20th century constructivist art.

Bridewell Museum of Local Industries - Norwich
Crafts, industries & aspects of city life.

Museum of Social History - King's Lynn
Exhibition of domestic life & dress, etc., noted glass collection.

Bishop Bonner's Cottages
Restored cottages with coloured East Anglia pargetting, c. 1502, museum of archaeological discoveries, exhibition of rural crafts.

The Guildhall - Thetford
Duleep Singh Collection of Norfolk & Suffolk portraits.

Shirehall Museum - Walsingham
18th century court room having original fittings, illustrating Walsingham life.

Historic Monuments

Binham Priory & Cross - Binham
12th century ruins of Benedictine foundation.

Caister Castle - Great Yarmouth
15th century moated castle - ruins. Now motor museum.

The Castle - Burgh Castle
3rd century Saxon fort - walls - ruin.

Mannington Hall - Saxthorpe
Saxon church ruin in gardens of 15th century moated house.

Castle Rising - Castle Rising
Splendid Norman keep & earthworks.

Castle Acre Priory & Castle Gate - Swaffham

Other things to see & do

African Violet Centre - Terrington St. Clements.
60 varieties of African Violets. Talks & Tours.

Norfolk Lavender Centre - Heacham
Open to the public in July & August. Demonstrations of harvesting & distilling the oil.

Thetford Forest
Forest walks, rides & picnic places amongst conifers, oak, beech & birch.

The Broads.

NORFOLK
Map reference

02 Morrish
03 Birkbeck
04 Ellis
05 Pugh
06 Douglas
07 Meynell

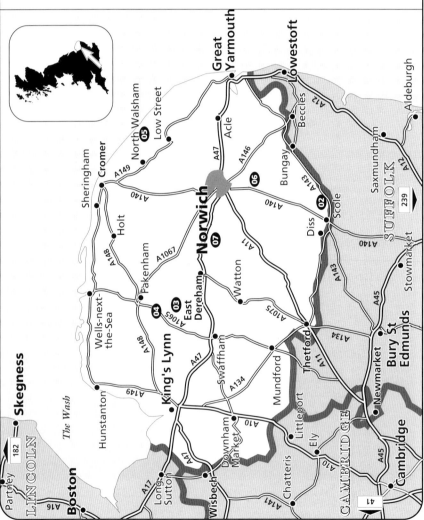

Column headers (rotated):
- rate £ from - to per double room
- children taken
- evening meals
- animals taken

£60.00 to £74.00	Y	Y	Y	**Grove Thorpe** Near Rd: A.143 Award-winning Grove Thorpe set in the Waveney Valley, a paradise for lovers of rural life. Grade II listed country house in 10 acres of secluded grounds with fishing lake. Inglenook fireplaces & a wealth of beams create a warm ambience, relax by a log fire in winter or watch the ducks from the gardens in summer. Bedrooms are en-suite with every luxury, antique furniture, 2 with super King-size beds, also a separate ground-floor suite. Dinner is available Nov-Mar by arrangement. Children 12+. E-mail: b-b@grovethorpe.co.uk www.grovethorpe.co.uk
(no smoking)				*Angela & John Morrish* **Grove Thorpe** *Grove Road* *Brockdish* *Diss IP21 4JR* *Norfolk* *Tel: (01379) 668305* *Open: ALL YEAR (Excl. Xmas & New Year)* *Map Ref No. 02*
£60.00 to £70.00	Y	Y	Y	**Litcham Hall** Near Rd: A.47 This Grade II listed house was built in 1781 & has been owned by only 3 families during its history. The house is beautifully furnished with a sitting room available to guests. The bedrooms, all 16ft sq., with large windows overlooking the garden, have private bathrooms, 2 en-suite. John & Hermione came to Litcham in 1967 & have much enjoyed restoring the house & garden. Now our guests can take advantage of our efforts. Single supplement. Use of pool, by arrangement. Evening meals are available, min. 4 persons. E-mail: h.birkbeck67@amserve.com
(no smoking)				*Hermione Birkbeck* **Litcham Hall** *Litcham* *Kings Lynn PE32 2QQ* *Norfolk* *Tel: (01328) 701389* *Fax 01328 701164* *Open: ALL YEAR* *Map Ref No. 03*
£70.00 to £80.00	Y	N	Y	**Manor House Farm** Near Rd: A.1065 Tucked away in the heart of rural Norfolk surrounded by lovely gardens next to the tiny 13th-century church. Conservation - award-winning farm. Beautifully converted old stables. 2 en-suite double/twin bedrooms with extra large beds & pure cotton bedlinen. A sitting room with woodburner & small kitchen. The emphasis here is on charm & comfort. Stripped pine, lovely rugs, artefacts, complete the restful ambience. A delicious breakfast using home produced fruit, eggs & bacon etc. 20 mins' North Norfolk Coast & close to Sandringham. Wheelchair friendly. Children 10+.
(no smoking)				*Elisabeth Ellis* *Manor House Farm* *Wellingham* *Nr. Fakenham* *Kings Lynn PE32 2TH* *Norfolk* *Tel: (01328) 838227* *Fax 01328 838348* *Open: ALL YEAR* *Map Ref No. 04*
£54.00 to £72.00	Y	Y	Y	**Mill Common House** Near Rd: A.149 Mill Common House is an elegant Georgian farmhouse set in a quiet rural location, close to the market town of North Walsham & only 1 mile from sandy beaches. Standing in its own mature grounds, beside the original brick & flint buildings dating back more than 200 years. 2 attractive bedrooms, with all amenities, a large conservatory & open log fires on cooler days all add to the relaxed atmosphere & surroundings, typical of comfortable stylish living. Children over 12. E-mail: johnpugh@millcommon.freeserve.co.uk www.millcommonhouse.co.uk
(no smoking)				*Mrs Wendy Pugh* *Mill Common House* *Mill Common Road* *Ridlington* *North Walsham NR28 9TY* *Tel: (01692) 650792* *Fax 01692 651480* *Open: ALL YEAR (Excl. Xmas)* *Map Ref No. 05*

Norfolk

Greenacres Farmhouse

Near Rd: A.140

A period 17th-century farmhouse on a 30-acre common with ponds & wildlife, only 10 miles from Norwich. All of the en-suite/private bedrooms (2 double/1 twin) are tastefully furnished to complement the oak beams & period furniture, with tea/coffee facilities & T.V.. Relax in the beamed sitting room with inglenook fireplace & enjoy a leisurely breakfast in the sunny dining room. Snooker table & tennis court. Therapeutic massage, aromatherapy & reflexology service available.

E-mail: greenacresfarm@tinyworld.co.uk
www.abreakwithtradition.co.uk

| £50.00 to £60.00 | N | N | N |

Joanna Douglas   Greenacres Farmhouse   Woodgreen   Long Stratton   Norwich   NR15 2RR   Norfolk
Tel: (01508) 530261   Fax 01508 530261   Open: ALL YEAR   Map Ref No. 06

The Buttery

Near Rd: A.47

Originally the dairy for Berry Hall, the Buttery is a unique thatched building, beautifully converted into a self-contained tranquil place to stay. The accommodation consists of a mezzanine bedroom (up a steep wooden staircase), a sitting room with a large comfortable sofabed (as an alternative), bathroom with Jacuzzi & a small country kitchen filled with all the ingredients for you to make a full English breakfast. Walk in the woods and meadows, or use this as a convenient base to explore Norfolk.

E-mail: thebuttery@paston.co.uk
www.bestbandb.co.uk

| £70.00 to £80.00 | N | N | N |

Mrs Deborah Meynell   The Buttery   Berry Hall   Honingham   Norwich   NR9 5AX   Norfolk
Tel: (01603) 880541   Open: ALL YEAR   Map Ref No. 07

All the establishments mentioned in this guide are members of
The Worldwide Bed & Breakfast Association

When booking your accommodation please mention
The Best Bed & Breakfast

Northumbria

Northumbria

Mountains & moors, hills & fells, coast & country are all to be found in this Northern region which embraces four counties - Northumberland, Durham, Cleveland & Tyne & Wear.

Saxons, Celts, Vikings, Romans & Scots all fought to control what was then a great wasteland between the Humber & Scotland.

Northumberland

Northumberland is England's Border country, a land of history, heritage & breathtaking countryside. Hadrian's Wall, stretching across the county from the mouth of the Tyne in the west to the Solway Firth, was built as the Northern frontier of the Roman Empire in 122 AD. Excavations along the Wall have brought many archaeological treasures to light. To walk along the wall is to discover the genius of Roman building & engineering skill. They left a network of roads, used to transport men & equipment in their attempts to maintain discipline among the wild tribes.

Through the following centuries the Border wars with the Scots led to famous battles such as Otterburn in 1388 & Flodden in 1513, & the construction of great castles including Bamburgh & Lindisfarne. Berwick-on-Tweed, the most northerly town, changed hands between England & Scotland 13 times.

Northumberland's superb countryside includes the Cheviot Hills in the Northumberland National Park, the unforgettable heather moorlands of the Northern Pennines to the west, Kielder Water (Western Europe's largest man-made lake), & 40 miles of glorious coastline.

Holy Island, or Lindisfarne, is reached by a narrow causeway that is covered at every incoming tide. Here St. Aidan of Iona founded a monastery in the 7th century, & with St. Cuthbert set out to Christianise the pagan tribes. The site was destroyed by the Danes, but Lindisfarne Priory was built by the monks of Durham in the 11th century to house a Benedictine community. The ruins are hauntingly beautiful.

Durham

County Durham is the land of the Prince Bishops, who with their armies, nobility, courts & coinage controlled the area for centuries. They ruled as a virtually independent State, holding the first line of defence against the Scots.

In Durham City, the impressive Norman Castle standing proudly over the narrow mediaeval streets was the home of the Prince Bishops for 800 years.

Durham Cathedral, on a wooded peninsula high above the River Wear, was built in the early 12th century & is undoubtably one of the world's finest buildings, long a place of Christian pilgrimage.

The region's turbulent history led to the building of forts & castles. Some like Bowes & Barnard Castle are picturesque ruins whilst others, including Raby, Durham & Lumley still stand complete.

The Durham Dales of Weardale, Teesdale & the Derwent Valley cover about one third of the county & are endowed with some of the highest & wildest scenery. Here are High Force, England's highest waterfall, & the Upper Teesdale National Nature Reserve.

The Bowes Museum at Barnard Castle is a magnificent French-style chateau & houses an important art collection.

In contrast is the award-winning museum at Beamish which imaginatively recreates Northern life at the turn of the century.

Northumbria

Cleveland

Cleveland, the smallest 'shire' in England, has long been famous for its steel, chemical & shipbuilding industries but it is also an area of great beauty. The North Yorkshire National Park lies in the south, & includes the cone-shaped summit of Roseberry Topping, "Cleveland's Matterhorn".

Cleveland means 'land of cliffs', & in places along the magnificent coastline, cliffs tower more than 600 feet above the sea, providing important habitat for wild plants & sea-birds.

Pretty villages such as Hart, Elwick & Staithes are full of steep, narrow alleys. Marton was the birthplace of Captain James Cook & the museum there traces the explorer's early life & forms the start of the 'Cook Heritage Trail'.

The Tees estuary is a paradise for birdwatchers, whilst walkers can follow the Cleveland Way or the 38 miles of the Langbaurgh Loop. There is surfing, windsurfing & sailing at Saltburn, & for the less energetic, the scenic Esk Valley Railway runs from Middlesbrough to Whitby.

Tyne & Wear

Tyne & Wear takes its name from the two rivers running through the area, & includes the large & lively city of Newcastle-on-Tyne.

Weardale lies in a beautiful valley surrounded by wild & bleak fells. Peaceful now, it was the setting for a thriving industry mining coal & silver, zinc & lead. Nature trails & recreation areas have been created among the old village & market towns.

The county was the birthplace of George Stephenson, railway engineer, who pioneered the world's first passenger railway on the Stockton to Darlington Line in 1825.

Durham Cathedral.

Northumbria

Northumbria Gazeeter

Areas of Outstanding Natural Beauty
The Heritage Coast, the Cheviot Hills, the North Pennine chain.

Historic Houses & Castles

Alnwick Castle - Alnwick
A superb mediaeval castle of the 12th century.
Bamburgh Castle-Bamburgh
A restored 12th century castle with Norman keep.
Callaly Castle - Whittingham
A 13th century Pele tower with 17th century mansion. Georgian additions.
Durham Castle - Durham
Part of the University of Durham - a Norman castle.
Lindisfarne Castle - Holy Island
An interesting 14th century castle.
Ormesby Hall - Nr. Middlesbrough
A mid 18th century house.
Raby Castle - Staindrop, Darlington
14th century with some later alteration .
Fine art & furniture. Large gardens.
Wallington Hall -Combo
A 17th century house with much alteration & addition.
Washington Old Hall-Washington
Jacobean manor house, parts of which date back to 12th century.

Cathedrals & Churches

Brancepeth (St. Brandon)
12th century with superb 17th century woodwork. Part of 2 mediaeval screens.
Flemish carved chest.
Durham Cathedral
A superb Norman cathedral. A unique Galilee chapel & early 12th century vaults.
Escombe
An interesting Saxon Church with sundial.
Hartlepool (St. Hilda)
Early English with fine tower & buttresses.
Hexham (St. Andrews)
Remains of a 17th century church with Roman dressing. A unique night staircase & very early stool. Painted screens.
Jarrow (St. Pauls)
Bede worshipped here. Strange in that it was originally 2 churches until 11th century. Mediaeval chair.

Newcastle (St. Nicholas)
14th century with an interesting lantern tower.
Heraldic font. Roundel of 14th century glass.
Morpeth (St. Mary the Virgin)
Fine mediaeval glass in east window - 14th century.
Pittington (St. Lawrence)
Late Norman nave with wall paintings.
Carved tombstone - 13th century.
Skelton (St. Giles)
Early 13th century with notable font, gable crosses, bell-cote & buttresses.
Staindrop (St. Mary)
A fine Saxon window.
Priests dwelling.
Neville tombs & effigies.

Museums & Galleries

Aribea Roman Fort Museum - South Shields
Interesting objects found on site.
Berwick-on-Tweed Museum - Berwick
Special exhibition of interesting local finds.
Bowes Museum - Bernard Castle
European art from mediaeval to 19th century.
Captain Cook Birthplace Museum - Middlesbrough
Cook's life & natural history relating to his travels.
Clayton Collection - Chollerford
A collection of Roman sculpture, weapons & tools from forts.
Corbridge Roman Station - Corbridge
Roman pottery & sculpture.
Dormitory Musuem - Durham Cathedral
Relics of St. Cuthbert.
Mediaeval seats & manuscripts.
Gray Art Gallery - Hartlepool
19th-20th century art & oriental antiquities.
Gulbenkian Museum of Oriental Art - University of Durham
Chinese pottery & porcelain, Chinese jade & stone carvings, Chinese ivories, Chinese textiles, Japenese & Tibetan art.
Egyptian & Mesopotamian antiquities.
Jarrow Hall - Jarrow
Excavation finds of Saxon & mediaeval monastery.
Fascinating information room dealing with early Christian sites in England.

Northumbria

Keep Museum - Newcastle-upon-Tyne
Mediaeval collection.
Laing Art Gallery - Newcastle-upon-Tyne
17th-19th century British arts, porcelain,
glass & silver.
National Music Hall Museum -
Sunderland
19th-20th century costume & artefacts
associated with the halls.
Preston Hall Museum - Stockton-on-Tees
Armour & arms, toys, ivory period room
University - New Castle -Upon -Tyne
The Hatton Gallery - housing a fine
collection of Italian paintings.
Museum of Antiquities
Prehistoric, Roman & Saxon collection
with an interesting reconstruction of a
temple.
**Beamish North of England Open Air
Museum** - European Museum of the Year
Chantry Bagpipe Museum - Morpeth
Darlington Museum & Railway Centre.

Historic Monuments

Ariiea Roman Fort - South Shields
Remains which include the gateways &
headquarters.
Barnard Castle - Barnard Castle
17th century ruin with interesting keep.
Bowes Castle - Bowes
Roman Fort with Norman keep.
The Castle & Town Walls - Berwick-on-
Tweed
12th century remains, reconstructed later.
Dunstanburgh Castle - Alnwick
14th century remains.
Egglestone Abbey - Barnard Castle
Remains of a Poor House.
Finchdale Priory - Durham
13 th century church with much
remaining.
Hadrian's Wall - Housesteads
Several miles of the wall including castles
& site museum.
Mithramic Temple - Carrawbrough
Mithraic temple dating back to the 3rd
century.
Norham Castle - Norham
The partial remains of a 12th century
castle.
Prudhoe Castle - Prudhoe
Dating from the 12th century with
additions. Bailey & gatehouse well
preserved.

The Roman Fort - Chesters
Extensive remains of a Roman bath
house.
Tynemouth Priory & Castle - Tynemouth
11th century priory - ruin - with 16th
century towers & keep.
Vindolanda - Barton Mill
Roman fort dating from 3rd century.
Warkworth Castle - Warkworth
Dating from the 11th century with
additions.
A great keep & gatehouse.
Warkworth Hermitage - Warkworth
An interesting 14th century Hermitage.
Lindisfarne Priory - Holy Island
(Lindisfarne)
11th century monastery. Island accessible
only at low tide.

Other things to see & do

Botanical Gardens - Durham University
Bird & Seal Colonies - Farne Islands
Conducted tours by boat
Marine Life Centre & Fishing Museum -
Seahouses
Museum of sealife, & boat trips to the
Farne Islands.
Tower Knowe Visitor Centre - Keilder
Water

Saltburn Victorian Festival.

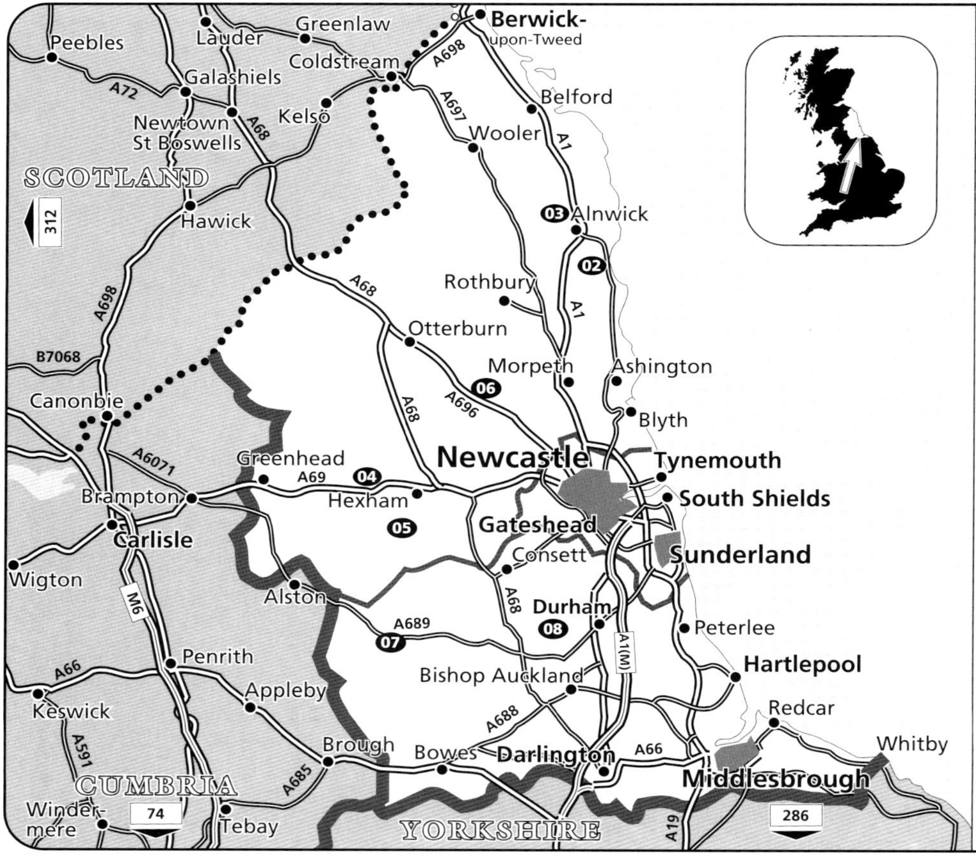

NORTHUMBERLAND, DURHAM & TYNE & WEAR

Map reference

- 02 Jackson
- 03 Armstrong
- 04 Clyde
- 05 Courage
- 06 Gay
- 07 Reed
- 08 Booth

NORTHUMBERLAND

TYNE & WEAR

DURHAM

Northumberland

Bilton Barns Farmhouse

Near Rd: A.1

Dating back to 1715, Bilton Barns has fantastic views over Alnmouth & Warkworth Bay, only 1 1/2 miles away. The spacious & beautifully furnished rooms are all en-suite with T.V. & tea/coffee-making facilities; or stay in one of the lovely suites, 1 has a 4-poster bed, all have beamed lounges. Choose Craster kippers from the extensive breakfast menu. Alnwick Gardens & Castle are easily accessible being only 5 miles from Bilton Barns.
E-mail: dorothy@biltonbarns.com
www.biltonbarns.com

£60.00 to £70.00 · Y · N · N

see PHOTO over p. 197

Dorothy Jackson   Bilton Barns Farmhouse   Alnmouth   Alnwick NE66 2TB   Northumberland
Tel: (01665) 830427   Fax 01665 833909   Open: ALL YEAR (Excl. Xmas)   Map Ref No. 02

North Charlton Farm

Near Rd: A.1

Afternoon tea with home-baking is served on arrival in the visitors lounge at North Charlton Farm. The house has just been completely restored & is beautifully furnished with antiques, yet offers every modern comfort in elegant surroundings. Enjoy breakfast in the dining room with views out to the sea (Full English, Craster kippers, home-made preserves & more). The Armstrongs also have a Household & Farming Museum at North Charlton, which is a real 'treasure trove'. Children over 10.
E-mail: stay@northcharltonfarm.co.uk
www.northcharltonfarm.co.uk

£60.00 to £70.00 · Y · N · N

Mr & Mrs C Armstrong   North Charlton Farm   North Charlton   Alnwick NE67 5HP   Northumberland
Tel: (01665) 579443   Fax 01665 579407   Open: APR - OCT   Map Ref No. 03

Allerwash Farmhouse

Near Rd: A.69

Allerwash is an elegant Regency farm house which is full of character & has secluded gardens surrounded by rolling countryside. Bedrooms are stylishly decorated & include private facilities. Open fires in the 2 drawing rooms add to the warmth of the house, & elegant furnishings plus antiques & paintings make this a real house of distinction. Meals are delicious & Angela has many cookery awards to her credit. The Roman Wall, the Lake District, the Northumberland coast & many castles, country houses & gardens are within easy reach. Children over 8. Animals by arrangement.

£95.00 to £95.00 · Y · Y · Y

Ian & Angela Clyde   Allerwash Farmhouse   Newbrough   Hexham NE47 5AB   Northumberland
Tel: (01434) 674574   Fax 01434 674574   Open: ALL YEAR   Map Ref No. 04

Rye Hill Farm

Near Rd: A.68, A.69

Rye Hill Farm dates back some 300 years & is a traditional livestock unit in beautiful countryside just 5 miles south of Hexham. Recently, some of the stone barns adjoining the farmhouse have been converted into superb modern guest accommodation. There are 3 bedrooms, all with private facilities, & all have radio, T.V. & tea/coffee-making facilities. Delicious home-cooked meals. Perfect for a get-away-from-it-all holiday. Single occupancy from £30 per night.
E-mail: info@ryehillfarm.co.uk
www.ryehillfarm.co.uk

£50.00 to £75.00 · Y · Y · Y

VISA: M'CARD:

Elizabeth Courage   Rye Hill Farm   Slaley   Nr. Hexham NE47 0AH   Northumberland
Tel: (01434) 673259   Open: ALL YEAR   Map Ref No. 05

Bilton Barns Farmhouse.   Alnmouth.

Northumberland & Durham

Table column headers (rotated): rate £ from - to per double room | children taken | evening meals | animals taken

Shieldhall

Near Rd: A.696

Within acres of well-kept gardens, offering unimpeded views & overlooking the National Trust's Wallington estate, this meticulously restored 18th-century farmhouse is built around a pretty courtyard. All of the 3 en-suite bedrooms are beautifully furnished & have T.V.. Comfortable lounges & an extremely charming inglenooked dining room where home produce is often used for delicious meals which are specially prepared when booked in advance. Children over 10 & animals by arrangement.
E-mail: Robinson.Gay@btinternet.com
www.shieldhallguesthouse.co.uk

£60.00 to £76.00 — Y Y Y

Celia & Stephen Gay   Shieldhall   Wallington   Morpeth NE61 4AQ   Northumberland
Tel: (01830) 540387   Fax 01830 540490   Open: MAR - NOV   Map Ref No. 06

Lands Farm

Near Rd: A.689

You will be warmly welcomed to Lands Farm, an old stone-built farmhouse within walking distance of Westgate village. A walled garden with stream meandering by. Accommodation is in centrally heated double & family rooms with luxury en-suite facilities, T.V., tea/coffee-making facilities. Full English breakfast or Continental alternative served in an attractive dining room. This is an ideal base for touring (Durham, Hadrian's Wall, Beamish Museum, etc.) & for walking.
E-mail: barbara@landsfarm.fsnet.co.uk
www.bestbandb.co.uk

£48.00 to £52.00 — Y N N

Mrs Barbara Reed   Lands Farm   Westgate-in-Weardale   Bishop Auckland DL13 1SN   Durham
Tel: (01388) 517210   Fax 01388 517210   Open: ALL YEAR   Map Ref No. 07

Ivesley

Near Rd: A.68

Ivesley is an elegantly furnished country house set in the middle of 220 acres approached by England's oldest beech avenue which is over 650 years old. 3 en-suite bedrooms & 2 sharing a bathroom. An ideal centre for walking, sightseeing & mountain biking. Durham 7 miles. Wine cellar. Excellent cuisine. Adjacent equestrian centre with comprehensive facilities. Children over 8, dogs & horses welcome. Rate incl. Continental breakfast. Handy for Durham University & the Beamish Museum.
E-mail: ivesley@msn.com
www.ridingholidays.co.uk

£51.00 to £62.00 — Y Y Y

VISA: M'CARD: AMEX:

Roger & Pauline Booth   Ivesley   Waterhouses   Durham DH7 9HB   Durham
Tel: (0191) 3734324 Fax 0191 3734757 Open: ALL YEAR (Excl. Xmas & New Year) Map Ref No. 08

Visit our website at:
http://www.bestbandb.co.uk

Oxfordshire

Oxfordshire
(Thames & Chilterns)

Oxfordshire is a county rich in history & delightful countryside. It has prehistoric sites, early Norman churches, 15th century coaching inns, Regency residences, distinctive cottages of black & white chalk flints & lovely Oxford, the city of dreaming spires.

The countryside ranges from lush meadows with willow-edged river banks scattered with small villages of thatched cottages, to the hills of the Oxfordshire Cotswolds in the west, the wooded Chilterns in the east & the distinctive ridge of the Berkshire Downs in the south. "Old Father Thames" meanders gently across the county to Henley, home of the famous regatta.

The ancient track known as the Great Ridgeway runs across the shire, & a walk along its length reveals barrows, hill forts & stone circles. The 2,000 year old Uffington Horse cut into the chalk of the hillside below an ancient hill fort site, is some 360 feet in length & 160 feet high.

The Romans built villas in the county & the remains of one, including a magnificent mosaic can be seen at North Leigh. In later centuries lovely houses were built. Minster Lovell stands beside the Windrush; Rousham house with its William Kent gardens is situated near Steeple Aston & beside the Thames lies Elizabethan Mapledurham House with its working watermill.

At Woodstock is Blenheim Palace, the largest private house in Britain & birthplace of Sir Winston Churchill. King Alfred's statue stands at Wantage, commemorating his birth there, & Banbury has its cross, made famous in the old nursery rhyme.

Oxford is a town of immense atmosphere with fine college buildings around quiet cloisters, & narrow cobbled lanes. It was during the 12th century that Oxford became a meeting place for scholars & grew into the first established centre of learning, outside the monasteries, in England.

The earliest colleges to be founded were University College, Balliol & Merton. Further colleges were added during the reign of the Tudors, as Oxford became a power in the kingdom. There are now 35 university colleges & many other outstanding historic buildings in the city . Christ Church Chapel is now the Cathedral of Oxford, a magnificent building with a deservedly famous choir.

St. Mary's Church.

Oxfordshire

Oxfordshire Gazeteer

Areas of Ounstanding Natural Beauty
The North Wessex Downs. The Chiltern Hills. The Cotswolds.

Historic Houses & Castles

Ashdown House - Nr. Lambourn
17th century, built for Elizabeth of Bohemia, now contains portraits associated with her. Mansard roof has cupola with golden ball.

Blenheim Palace - Woodstock
Sir John Vanbrugh's classical masterpiece. Garden designed by Vanbrugh & Henry Wise. Further work done by Capability Brown who created the lake. Collection of pictures & tapestries.

Broughton Castle- Banbury.
14th century mansion with moat - interesting plaster work fine panelling & fire places

Chaselton House-Morton in Marsh
17th century,fine examples of plaster work & panelling.Still has original furniture & tapestries. topiary garden from1700.

Grey Court - Henly-on-Thames
16th century house containing 18th century plasterwork & furniture. Mediaeval ruins. Tudor donkey-wheel for raising water from well.

Mapledurham House - Mapledurham
16th century Elizabethan house. Oak staircase, private chapel, paintings, original moulded ceilings. Watermill nearby.

Milton Manor House - Nr. Abingdon
17th century house designed by Inigo Jones - Georgian wings, walled garden, pleasure grounds.

Rousham House - Steeple Ashton
17th century - contains portraits & miniatures.

University of Oxford Colleges

University college ------------------1249
Balliol---------------------------------1263
Merton--------------------------------1264
Hertford------------------------------1284
Oriel-----------------------------------1326
New-----------------------------------1379
All Souls------------------------------1438
Brasenose----------------------------1509
Christ Church----------------------1546
St. John's--------------------------1555
Pembroke-------------------------1624
Worcester--------------------------1714
Nuffield ----------------------------1937
St. Edmund Hall------------------1270
Exeter-----------------------------1314
The Queen's----------------------1340
Lincoln---------------------------1427
Magdalen ------------------------1458
Corpus Christi -------------------1516
Trinity-----------------------------1554
Jesus-----------------------------1571
Wadham--------------------------1610
Keble------------------------------1868

Cathedrals & Churches

Abingdon (St. Helen)
14th-16th century perpendicular. Painted roof. Georgian stained & enamelled glass.

Burford (St. John the Baptist)
15th century. Sculptured table tombs in churchyard.

Chislehampton (St. Katherine)
18th century. Unspoilt interior of Georgian period. Bellcote.

Dorchester (St. Peter & St. Paul)
13th century knight in stone effigy. Jesse window.

East Hagbourne (St. Andrew)
14th -15th century. Early glass, wooden roofs, 18th century tombs.

North Moreton (All Saints)
13th century with splendid 14th century chantry chapel - tracery.

Oxford Cathedral
Smallest of our English cathedrals. Stone spire form 1230. Norman arcade has double arches, choir vault.

Ryecote (St. Michael & All Angels)
14th century benches & screen base. 17th century altar-piece & communion rails, old clear glass, good ceiling.

Stanton Harcourt (St. Michael)
Early English - old stone & marble floor. Early screen with painting, monuments of 17th -19th century.

Yarnton (St. Bartholomew)
13th century - late perpendicular additions. Jacobean screen. 15th century alabaster reredos.

Oxfordshire

Museums & Galleries

The Ashmolean Museum of Art & Archaeology - Oxford
British ,European ,Mediterranean, Egyptian & Near Eastern archaeology. Oil paintings of Italian, Dutch, Flemish, French & English schools. Old Master watercolours, prints, drawings, ceramics, silver, bronzes & sculptures. Chinese & Japanese porcelain, lacquer & painting, Tibetan, Islamic & Indian art.
Christ Church Picture Gallery - Oxford
Old Master drawings & paintings.
Museum of Modern Art - Oxford
Exhibitiors of contemporary art.
Museum of Oxford
Many exhibits depicting the history of Oxford & its University.
The Rotunda - Oxford
Privately owned collection of dolls' houses 1700-1900, with contents such as furniture, china, silver, dolls, etc.
Oxford University Museum
Entomological, zoological, geological & mineralogical collections.
Pendon Museum of Miniature Landscape & Transport - Abingdon.
Showing in miniature the countryside & its means of transport in the thirties, with trains & thatched village. Railway relics.

Town Museum - Abingdon
17th century building exhibiting fossil, archaeological items & collection of charters & documents.
Tolsey Museum - Burford
Seals, maces, charters & bygones - replica of Regency room with period furnishings & clothing.

Historic Monuments

Uffington Castle & White Horse - Uffington
White horse cut into the chalk - iron age hill fort.
Rollright Stones - Nr. Chipping Norton
77 stones placed in circle - an isolated King's stone & nearby an ancient burial chamber.
Minster Lovell House - Minster Lovell
15th century mediaeval house - ruins.
Deddington Castle - Deddington

Other things to see & do

Didcot railway centre -a large collection of locomotives etc., from Brunel's Great Western Railway.
Filkins -a working wool mill where rugs & garments are woven in traditional way.

Blenheim Palace. Woodstock.

OXFORDSHIRE
Map reference

02 Connolly
03 Dunipace
04 Wadsworth
05 Talfourd-Cook
07 Crofts
08 Hill
09 Alexander
10 Watsham
11 Simpson
12 Geddes
13 Hamilton

The Craven. Uffington.

Oxfordshire

The Mill House

Near Rd: A.361

£75.00 to £99.00

Y | N | N

Referred to in Shakespeare's Henry VI, this peaceful, rurally situated 17th century former mill house, is where husband & wife, Andrew & Sharon, offer a warm welcome to their guests. 3 en-suite bedrooms & 4 superbly renovated courtyard cottages available on a B & B or self-catering basis. Ideal for the Cotswolds, Stratford-upon-Avon, Oxford & Blenheim Palace. Good local pubs & restaurants offering evening meals. Attractive lounge & beautiful gardens for guests use. Licensed honesty bar.
E-mail: lamadonett@aol.com
www.themillhousebanbury.co.uk

VISA: M'CARD:

Andy Marshall & Sharon Connolly The Mill House North Newington Banbury OX15 6AA Oxfordshire
Tel: (01295) 730212   Fax 01295 730363   Open: ALL YEAR (Excl. Xmas)   Map Ref No. 02

The Glebe House

Near Rd: A.40

£70.00 to £90.00

Y | Y | N

The Glebe House is a pretty 18th-century Cotswold farmhouse on the edge of the beautiful quiet village of Westwell, 2 miles from historic Burford, with views over open countryside. Offering 1 double & 1 twin bedroom, each with a private bathroom. Also, an elegantly furnished sitting room & a terrace in the secluded garden. Ideal for Oxford, Blenheim Palace, Bath, Cheltenham & Stratford. Enjoy a warm welcome, relaxed comfort & delicious food. French spoken. Self-catering option.
E-mail: clare.dunipace@amserve.net
www.oxford-cotswold-holidays.com

Robin & Clare Dunipace   The Glebe House   Westwell   Burford OX18 4JT   Oxfordshire
Tel: (01993) 822171   Fax 01993 824125   Open: ALL YEAR   Map Ref No. 03

The Craven

Near Rd: A.420

£70.00 to £95.00

Y | Y | N

Roses & clematis cover this pretty 17th-century thatched cottage where breakfast is served around the huge pine table in the farmhouse kitchen. The beamed bedrooms have lovely views. One has a 17th-century 4-poster bed with cabbage rose chintz drapes &, as with all bedrooms, hand-embroidered sheets & pillow slips. Daughter, Katie, produces excellent meals using as much local produce as possible. Glorious walks from the doorstep & a shaggy Old English sheepdog.
E-mail: carol@thecraven.co.uk
www.thecraven.co.uk

see PHOTO over
p. 203

VISA: M'CARD:

Mrs Carol Wadsworth   The Craven   Fernham Road   Uffington   Faringdon SN7 7RD   Oxfordshire
Tel: (01367) 820449   Fax 01367 820351   Open: ALL YEAR   Map Ref No. 04

Holmwood

Near Rd: A.4155

£50.00 to £70.00

Y | N | N

Holmwood is a large elegant Georgian country house, Grade II listed, furnished with antique, period furniture. There is a galleried hall, carved mahogany doors & marble fireplaces (wood fires in winter). All bedrooms are spacious & have en-suite facilities. The beautiful gardens extend to 3 1/2 acres & have extensive views over the Thames Valley. A good base for London & the South East. Heathrow Airport 30 mins', Reading 4 miles, Henley 2 1/2 miles. Children over 12 years.
E-mail: wendy.cook@freenet.co.uk
www.bestbandb.co.uk

see PHOTO over
p. 205

VISA: M'CARD:

Mr & Mrs Brian Talfourd-Cook   Holmwood   Shiplake Row   Binfield Heath   Henley RG9 4DP
Tel: (0118) 9478747   Fax 0118 9478637   Open: ALL YEAR (Excl. Xmas)   Map Ref No. 05

Holmwood. Binfield Heath.

Oxfordshire

Crofters Guest House

Near Rd: A.40

Situated in a lively market town, 10 miles from Oxford, on the edge of the Cotswolds, Blenheim Palace & Burford, & within easy reach of Stratford. Guests are accommodated in comfortable family, double & twin rooms, all with excellent facilities. En-suite & luxury ground-floor garden rooms are available. Your hosts Jean & Peter will make your stay a memorable experience. Arrive as a guest, leave as a friend.
E-mail: crofters.ghouse@virgin.net
www.SmoothHound.co.uk

£50.00 to £65.00 — Y | N | N

Jean A. Crofts   Crofters Guest House   29 Oxford Hill   Witney   Oxford OX28 3JU   Oxfordshire
Tel: (01993) 778165   Fax 01993 778165   Open: ALL YEAR   Map Ref No. 07

Shipton Grange House

Near Rd: A.361

A unique conversion of a Georgian coach house & stabling situated in the former grounds of Shipton Court. Secluded in its own walled garden, & approached by a gated archway. 3 elegantly furnished bedrooms, with an en-suite/private bathroom, T.V. & beverage facilities. Delicious breakfasts served in the attractive dining room. The friendly hosts are animal lovers & have a number of pet dogs. A delightful house, & ideal for visiting Oxford, Blenheim, etc. Children over 12.
E-mail: veronica@shiptongrangehouse.com
www.shiptongrangehouse.com

£65.00 to £75.00 — Y | N | N

see PHOTO over
p. 207

Veronica Hill   Shipton Grange House   Shipton-under-Wychwood OX7 6DG   Oxfordshire
Tel: (01993) 831298   Fax 01993 832082   Open: ALL YEAR (Excl. Xmas)   Map Ref No. 08

The Well Cottage

Near Rd: A.329

The Well Cottage is situated in a pretty garden, close to the River Thames, the historic town of Wallingford, the Berkshire Downs & the Ridgway. The cottage has been extended & now offers a secluded garden flat with 2 twin-bedded rooms, each with a private bathroom, T.V. & tea/coffee-making facilities. Each room has its own private entrance. A charming home for a relaxing break. Within easy reach of Oxford & Henley-on-Thames. Single supplement.
E-mail: joanna@thewellcottage.com
www.thewellcottage.com

£40.00 to £70.00 — Y | N | Y

Mrs Joanna Alexander   The Well Cottage   Caps Lane   Cholsey   Wallingford OX10 9HQ   Oxfordshire
Tel: (01491) 651959   Mobile 07887 958920   Fax 01491 651675   Open: ALL YEAR   Map Ref No. 09

White House

Near Rd: A.329

White House is an attractive, detached family home in the picturesque Thameside village of Moulsford on the edge of the Berkshire Downs, close to the Ridgeway & Thames Paths. The accommodation is at ground-floor level with its own separate front door, making access easy for disabled guests. Each room is very comfortable. There is a large garden with croquet lawn, which guests are welcome to enjoy. A delightful home.
E-mail: mwatsham@tiscali.co.uk
www.stayatwhitehouse.co.uk

£60.00 to £60.00 — Y | N | N

Mrs Maria Watsham   White House   Moulsford   Wallingford OX10 9JD   Oxfordshire
Tel: (01491) 651397   Fax 01491 652560   Open: ALL YEAR (Excl. Xmas & New Year)   Map Ref No. 10

Shipton Grange House. Shipton-under-Wychwood.

Oxfordshire

Field View

Near Rd: A.40

An attractive Cotswold stone house set in 2 acres, situated on picturesque Wood Green, mid-way between Oxford University & the Cotswolds. It is an ideal base for touring & yet is only 8 minutes' walk from the centre of the lively market town of Witney. A peaceful setting & a warm, friendly atmosphere await you. There are 3 comfortable en-suite rooms with all modern amenities, including tea/coffee, T.V. & hairdryer. Capture the quiet of the country-side, within walking distance of the town centre.
E-mail: bandb@fieldview-witney.co.uk
www.fieldview-witney.co.uk

£56.00 to £60.00 — N | N | N

Liz & John Simpson   Field View   Wood Green   Witney OX28 1DE   Oxfordshire
Tel: (01993) 705485   Mobile 07768 614347   Open: ALL YEAR (Excl. Xmas & NY)   Map Ref No. 11

The Garden House of The Old Vicarage

Near Rd: A.40

Built in the 19th century, the River Windrush trick-les through the garden & the church & ruins of Minster Lovell Hall stand close by. The Garden House is ideal for a self-catering arrangement, it is a self-contained cottage on one level with French windows looking on to the orchard, the use of which goes with the cottage. Breakfast fixings are provided for you to take at your leisure. The village pub is within walking distance. An easy drive from Stratford, Buford, Cirencester & Oxford. A wonder-ful location for Cotswold exploring.
E-mail: ageddes@lix.compulink.co.uk

£75.00 to £75.00 — Y | N | Y

Bridget Geddes   The Garden House of The Old Vicarage   Minster Lovell   Witney OX29 0RR
Tel: (01993) 775630   Fax 01993 772534   Open: ALL YEAR   Map Ref No. 12

Gorselands Hall

Near Rd: A.4095

Gorselands Hall is a lovely old Cotswold stone country house with oak beams & flagstone floors in a delightful rural setting, convenient for Oxford (8 miles), Blenheim Palace (4 miles), the Roman Villa at East End & many Cotswold villages. There are 6 attractively furnished en-suite bedrooms, a guest sitting room & a large secluded garden with a grass tennis court. This is good walking country & there is a wide choice of excellent eating places within easy reach. Dogs by arrangement.
E-mail: hamilton@gorselandshall.com
www.gorselandshall.com

£50.00 to £60.00 — Y | N | Y

VISA: M'CARD:

Mr & Mrs N. Hamilton   Gorselands Hall   Boddington Lane   North Leigh   Witney OX29 6PU
Tel: (01993) 882292   Fax 01993 883629   Open: ALL YEAR   Map Ref No. 13

Visit our website at:
http://www.bestbandb.co.uk

Shropshire

Shropshire
(Heart of England)

Shropshire is a borderland with a very turbulent history. Physically it straddles highlands & lowlands with border mountains to the west, glacial plains, upland, moorlands & fertile valleys & the River Severn cutting through. It has been quarrelled & fought over by rulers & kings from earliest times. The English, the Romans & the Welsh all wanted to hold Shropshire because of its unique situation. The ruined castles & fortifications dotted across the county are all reminders of its troubled life. The most impressive of these defences is Offa's Dyke, an enormous undertaking intended to be a permanent frontier between England & Wales.

Shropshire has great natural beauty, countryside where little has changed with the years. Wenlock Edge & Clun Forest, Carding Mill Valley, the Long Mynd, Caer Caradoc, Stiperstones & the trail along Offa's Dyke itself, are lovely walking areas with magnificent scenery.

Shrewsbury was & is a virtual island, almost completely encircled by the Severn River. The castle was built at the only gap, sealing off the town. In this way all comings & goings were strictly controlled. In the 18th century two bridges, the English bridge & the Welsh bridge, were built to carry the increasing traffic to the town but Shrewsbury still remains England's finest Tudor city.

Massive Ludlow Castle was a Royal residence, home of Kings & Queens through the ages, whilst the town is also noted for its Georgian houses.

As order came out of chaos, the county settled to improving itself & became the cradle of the Industrial Revolution. Here Abraham Darby discovered how to use coke (from the locally mined coal) to smelt iron. There was more iron produced here in the 18th century than in any other county. A variety of great industries sprang up as the county's wealth & ingenuity increased. In 1781 the world's first iron bridge opened to traffic.

There are many fine gardens in the county. At Hodnet Hall near Market Drayton, the grounds cover 60 acres & the landscaping includes lakes & pools, trees, shrubs & flowers in profusion. Weston Park has 1,000 acres of parkland, woodland gardens & lakes landscaped by Capability Brown.

The house is Restoration period & has a splendid collection of pictures, furniture, china & tapestries.

Shrewsbury hosts an annual poetry festival & one of England's best flower shows whilst a Festival of Art, Music & Drama is held each year in Ludlow with Shakespeare performed against the castle ruins.

Coalbrookedale Museum.

Shropshire

Shropshire Gazeteer

Areas of Outstanding Natural Beauty
The Shropshire Hills.

Historic Houses & Castles

Stokesay Castle - Craven Arms
13th century fortified manor house. Still occupied - wonderful setting - extremely well preserved. Fine timbered gatehouse.
Weston Park - Nr. Shifnal
17th century - fine example of Restoration period - landscaping by Capability Brown. Superb collection of pictures.
Shrewsbury Castle - Shrewsbury
Built in Norman era - interior decorations - painted boudoir.
Benthall Hall - Much Wenlock
16th century. Stone House - mullioned windows. Fine wooden staircase - splendid plaster ceilings.
Shipton Hall - Much Wenlock
Elizabethan. Manor House - walled garden - mediaeval dovecote.
Upton Cressett Hall - Bridgnorth
Elizabethan. Manor House & Gatehouse. Excellent plaster work. . 14th century great hall.

Cathedrals & Churches

Ludlow (St. Lawrence)
14th century nave & transepts. 15th century pinnacled tower. Restored extensively in 19th century. Carved choir stalls, perpendicular chancel - original glass. Monuments.
Shrewsbury (St. Mary)
14th, 15th, 16th century glass. Norman origins.
Stottesdon (St. Mary)
12th century carvings.Norman font. Fine decorations with columns & tracery.
Lydbury North (St. Michael)
14th century transept, 15th century nave roof, 17th century box pews and altar rails. Norman font.
Longor (St. Mary the Virgin)
13th century having an outer staircase to West gallery.
Cheswardine (St. Swithun)
13th century chapel - largely early English. 19th century glass and old brasses. Fine sculpture.

Tong (St. Mary the Virgin with St. Bartholomew)
15th century. Golden chapel of 1515, stencilled walls, remains of paintings on screens, gilt fan vaulted ceiling. Effigies, fine monuments

Museums & Galleries

Clive House - Shrewsbury
Fine Georgian House - collection of Shropshire ceramics. Regimental museum of 1st Queen's Dragoon Guards.
Rowley's House Museum - Shrewsbury
Roman material from Viroconium and prehistoric collection.
Coleham Pumping Station - Old Coleham
Preserved beam engines
Acton Scott Working Farm Museum - Nr. Church Stretton
Site showing agricultural practice before the advent of mechanization.
Ironbridge Gorge Museum - Telford
Series of industrial sites in the Severn Gorge.
CoalBrookdale Museum & Furnace Site
Showing Abraham Darby's blast furnace history. Ironbridge information centre is next to the world's first iron bridge.
Mortimer Forest Museum - Nr. Ludlow
Forest industries of today and yesterday. Ecology of the forest.
Whitehouse Museum of Buildings & Country life - Aston Munslow
4 houses together in one, drawing from every century 13th to 18th, together with utensils and implements of the time.
The Buttercross Museum - Ludlow
Geology, natural & local history of area.
Reader`s House-Ludlow
Splendid example of a 16th century town house. 3 storied porch.
Much Wenlock Museum.-Much Wenlock
Geology, natural & local history.
Clun Town Museum - Clun
Pre-history earthworks, rights of way, commons & photographs.

Historic Monuments

Acton Burnell Castle - Shrewsbury
13th century fortified manor house - ruins only.

Shropshire

Boscobel House - Shifnal
17th century house.
Bear Steps - Shrewsbury
Half timbered buildings. Mediaeval.
Abbot's House - Shrewsbury
15th century half-timbered.
Buildwas Abbey - Nr. Telford
12th century - Savignac Abbey - ruins.
The church is nearly complete with 14
Norman arches.
Haughmond Abbey - Shrewsbury
12th century - remains of house of
Augustinian canons.
Wenlock Priory - Much Wenlock
13th century abbey - ruins.
Roman Town - Wroxeter
2nd century - remains of town of
Viroconium including public baths and
colonnade.
Moreton Corbet Castle - Moreton Corbet
13th century keep, Elizabethan features -
gatehouse altered 1519.
Lilleshall Abbey
12th century - completed 13th century,
West front has notable doorway.
Bridgnorth Castle - Bridgnorth
Ruins of Norman castle whose angle of
incline is greater than Pisa.
Whiteladies Priory - Boscobel
12th century cruciform church - ruins.
Old Oswestry - Oswestry
Iron age hill fort covering 68 acres; five
ramparts and having an elaborate western
portal.

Other things to see & do

Ludlow Festival of Art and Drama -
annual event
Shrewsbury Flower Show - every August
Severn Valley Railway - the longest full
guage steam railway in the country

Kings Head Inn. Shrewsbury.

SHROPSHIRE
Map reference

01 Sanders
02 Hunter
03 Mitchell
04 Dawson

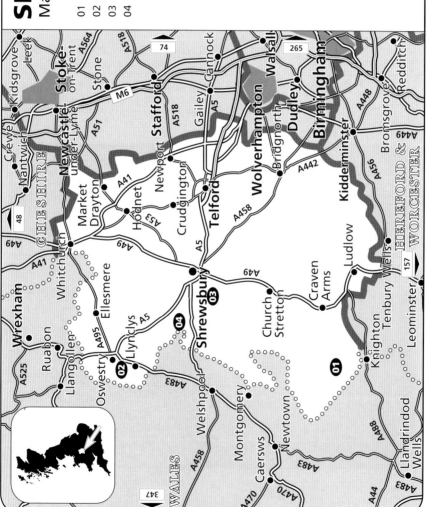

Pen-Y-Dyffryn Country Hotel . Rhydycroesau.

Shropshire

Cottage Farm

Near Rd: A.49

Clunton is a small village on the B.4368 between Ludlow & Clun in the beautiful Clun Valley, with superb landscapes & numerous public footpaths. Cottage Farm, which dates back 400 years, has many exposed timbers & stonewalls, which, along with roaring log fires in winter, help to create a wonderful ambience. Evening meals by arrangement. 3 bedrooms (each with tea/coffee-making facilities) decorated in true country style - 2 doubles (1 en-suite). Plus, a single @ £24.50. A charming home within easy reach of Ludlow & Clun & Stokesay Castles. Children over 12.

| £47.00 to £51.00 | Y | Y | N |

Mrs Maureen Sanders   Cottage Farm   Clunton   Nr. Craven Arms SY7 0HZ   Shropshire
Tel: (01588) 660555   Open: ALL YEAR (Excl. Xmas)   Map Ref No. 01

Pen-Y-Dyffryn Hotel

Near Rd: A.5

Set almost a thousand feet up in the peaceful Shropshire/Wales border hills, this silver-stone Georgian rectory has a real 'away from it all' atmosphere. But the medieval towns of Chester & Shrewsbury are only a short drive, so civilisation is close by. High-quality local food is served in the restaurant, complete with its own log fire. All bedrooms are en-suite, with T.V., telephone, etc. & some have their own private patios & spa baths. Licensed. Excellent walking country. Children over 3.
E-mail: stay@peny.co.uk
www.peny.co.uk

| £49.00 to £67.00 | Y | Y | Y |

see PHOTO over p. 213

VISA: M'CARD: AMEX:

Miles Hunter   Pen-Y-Dyffryn Hotel   Rhydycroesau   Oswestry SY10 7JD   Shropshire
Tel: (01691) 653700   Fax 01691 650066   Open: ALL YEAR (Excl. 1-24 Jan)   Map Ref No. 02

The White House

Near Rd: A.488

A lovely, 16th-century, black-and-white, half-timbered home with nearly 2 acres of gardens & river, 3 miles south-west of medieval Shrewsbury. Ironbridge, Mid-Wales & the Long Mynd within a half-hour drive. 6 guest rooms, some en-suite, each with tea/coffee-making facilities. 2 sitting rooms, residents' bar & log fires. Car parking. Your hosts menagerie at the time of going to print consists of chickens, doves, alpacas, bees & one mad duck called Mrs Vlad. Children over 12.
E-mail: mgm@whitehousehanwood.freeserve.co.uk
www.whitehousehanwood.freeserve.co.uk

| £65.00 to £75.00 | Y | N | N |

Mike & Gill Mitchell   The White House   Hanwood   Shrewsbury SY5 8LP   Shropshire
Tel: (01743) 860414   Open: ALL YEAR   Map Ref No. 03

Brimford House

Near Rd: A.458

Relax & unwind in this elegant Grade II listed Georgian farmhouse, set in tranquil, scenic countryside with breathtaking views of the Shropshire/ Welsh border. Wonderful walks & wildlife; log fires & stylish spacious en-suite bedrooms. Farmhouse breakfast served with free range eggs & homemade preserves. Country pub 3 mins' walk or many excellent pubs & restaurants in the area. Private fishing along the River Severn. Shrewsbury & Welshpool 15 mins' drive. Dogs by arrangement.
E-mail: info@brimford.co.uk
www.brimford.co.uk

| £50.00 to £60.00 | Y | N | Y |

Mrs Elizabeth Dawson   Brimford House   Criggion   Shrewsbury SY5 9AU   Shropshire
Tel: (01938) 570235   Open: ALL YEAR   Map Ref No. 04

Somerset, Bath & Bristol

Somerset
(West Country)

Fabulous legends, ancient customs, charming villages, beautiful churches, breathtaking scenery & a glorious cathedral, Somerset has them all, along with a distinctively rich local dialect. The essence of Somerset lies in its history & myth & particularly in the unfolding of the Arthurian tale.

Legend grows from the bringing of the Holy Grail to Glastonbury by Joseph of Arimathea, to King Arthur's castle at Camelot, held by many to be sited at Cadbury, to the image of the dead King's barge moving silently through the mists over the lake to the Isle of Avalon. Archaeological fact lends support to the conjecture that Glastonbury, with its famous Tor, was an island in an ancient lake. Another island story surrounds King Alfred, reputedly sheltering from the Danes on the Isle of Athelney & there burning his cakes.

Historically, Somerset saw the last battle fought on English soil, at Sedgemoor in 1685. The defeat of the Monmouth rebellion resulted in the wrath of James II falling on the West Country in the form of Judge Jeffreys & his "Bloody Assize".

To the west of the county lies part of the Exmoor National Park, with high moorland where deer roam & buzzards soar & a wonderful stretch of cliffs from Minehead to Devon. Dunster is a popular village with its octagonal Yarn market, & its old world cottages, dominated at one end by the castle & at the other by the tower on Conygar Hill.

To the east the woods & moors of the Quantocks are protected as an area of outstanding natural beauty. The Vale of Taunton is famous for its apple orchards & for the golden cider produced from them.

The south of the county is a land of rolling countryside & charming little towns, Chard, Crewkerne, Ilchester & Ilminster amongst others.

To the north the limestone hills of Mendip are honeycombed with spectacular caves & gorges, some with neolithic remains, as at Wookey Hole & Cheddar Gorge.

Wells is nearby, so named because of the multitude of natural springs. Hardly a city, Wells boasts a magnificent cathedral set amongst spacious lawns & trees. The west front is one of the glories of English architecture with its sculptured figures & soaring arches. A spectacular feature is the astronomical clock, the work of 14th century monk Peter Lightfoot. The intricate face tells the hours, minutes, days & phases of the moon. On the hour, four mounted knights charge forth & knock one another from their horses.

Wells Cathedral Choir.

215

Somerset, Bath & Bristol

Bath is one of the most loved historic cities in England. It owes its existence to the hot springs which bubble up five hundred thousand gallons of water a day at a temperature of some 120' F. According to legend, King Bladud appreciated the healing qualities of the waters & established his capital here, calling it Aquae Sulis. He built an elaborate healing & entertainment centre around the springs including reservoirs, baths & hypercaust rooms.

The Roman Baths, not uncovered until modern times, are on the lowest of three levels. Above them came the mediaeval city & on the top layer at modern street level is the elegant Georgian Pump Room.

Edward was crowned the first King of all England in 973, in the Saxon Abbey which stood on the site of the present fifteenth century abbey. This building, in the graceful perpendicular style with elegant fan vaulting, is sometimes called the "lantern of the West", on account of its vast clerestories & large areas of glass.

During the Middle Ages the town prospered through Royal patronage & the development of the wool industry. Bath became a city of weavers, the leading industrial town in the West of England.

The 18th century gave us the superb Georgian architecture which is the city's glory. John Wood, an ambitious young architect laid out Queen Anne's Square in the grand Palladian style, & went on to produce his masterpiece, the Royal Crescent. His scheme for the city was continued by his son & a number of other fine architects, using the beautiful Bath stone. Bath was a centre of fashion, with Beau Nash the leader of a glittering society.

In 1497 John & Sebastian Cabot sailed from the Bristol quayside to the land they called Ameryke, in honour of the King's agent in Bristol, Richard Ameryke. Bristol's involvement in the colonisation of the New World & the trade in sugar, tobacco & slaves that followed, made her the second city in the kingdom in the 18th century. John Cabot is commemorated by the Cabot Tower on grassy Brandon Hill - a fine vantage point from which to view the city. On the old docks below are the Bristol Industrial Museum & the SS Great Britain, Brunel's famous iron ship. Another achievement of this master engineer, the Clifton Suspension Bridge, spans Bristol's renowned beauty spot, the Clifton Gorge. For a glimpse of Bristol's elegant past, stroll through Clifton with its stately terraces & spacious Downs.

A short walk from the busy city centre & modern shopping area, the visitor in search of history will find cobbled King Street with its merchant seamen's almhouses & The Theatre Royal, the oldest theatre in continuous use in England, & also Llandoger Trow, an ancient inn associated with Treasure Island & Robinson Crusoe.

Bath Abbey.

Somerset, Bath & Bristol

Somerset, Bath & Bristol Gazeteer

Areas of Outstanding Natural Beauty
Mendip Hills. Quantock Hills. National Park - Exmoor. The Cotswolds.

Historic Houses & Castles

Abbot's Fish House - Meare
14th century house.
Barrington Court - Ilminster
16th century house & gardens.
Blaise Castle House - Henbury Nr. Bristol
18th century house - now folk museum, extensive woodlands.
Brympton D'Evercy - Nr. Yeovil
Mansion with 17th century front & Tudor west front. Adjacent is 13th century priest's house & church. Formal gardens & vineyard.
Claverton Manor - Nr. Bath
Greek revival house - furnished with 17th, 18th, 19th century American originals.
Clevedon Court - Clevedon
14th century manor house, 13th century hall, 12th century tower. Lovely garden with rare trees & shrubs. This is where Thackerey wrote much of 'Vanity Fair'.
Dyrham Park - Between Bristol & Bath
17th century house - fine panelled rooms, Dutch paintings, furniture.
Dunster Castle - Dunster
13th century castle with fine 17th century staircase & ceilings.
East Lambrook Manor - South Petherton
15th century house with good panelling.
Gaulden Manor - Tolland
12th century manor. Great Hall having unique plaster ceiling & oak screen. Antique furniture.
Halsway Manor - Crowcombe
14th century house with fine panelling.
Hatch Court - Hatch Beauchamp
Georgian house in the Palladian style with China room.
King John's Hunting Lodge - Axbridge
Early Tudor merchant's house.
Lytes Carry - Somerton
14th & 15th century manor house with a chapel & formal garden.
Montacute House - Yeovil
Elizabethan house with fine examples of Heraldic Glass, tapestries, panelling & furniture. Portrait gallery of Elizabethan & Jacobean paintings.
Tintinhull House - Yeovil
17th century house with beautiful gardens.
Priory Park College - Bath
18th century Georgian mansion, now Roman Catholic school.
No. 1 Royal Crescent - Bath
An unaltered Georgian house built 1767.
Red Lodge - Bristol
16th century house - period furniture & panelling.
St. Vincent's Priory - Bristol
Gothic revival house, built over caves which were sanctuary for Christians.
St Catherine's Court - Nr. Bath
Small Tudor house - associations with Henry VIII & Elizabeth I.

Cathedrals & Churches

Axbridge (St. John)
1636 plaster ceiling & panelled roofs.
Backwell (St. Andrew)
12th to 17th century, 15th century tower, repaired 17th century. 15th century tomb & chancel, 16th century screen, 18th century brass chandelier.
Bath Abbey
Perpendicular - monastic church, 15th century foundation. Nave finished 17th century, restorations in 1674.
Bishop's Lydeard (St. Mary)
15th century. Notable tower, rood screen & glass.
Bristol Cathedral
Mediaeval. Eastern halfnave Victorian. Chapterhouse richly ornamented. Iron screen, 3 fonts, "fairest parish church in all England".
Bristol (St. Mary Radcliffe)
Bristol (St. Stephens')
Perpendicular - monuments, magnificent tower.
Bruton (St. Mary)
Fine 2 towered 15th century church. Georgian chancel, tie beam roof, Georgian reredos. Jacobean screen. 15th century embroidery.
Chewton Mendip (St. Mary Magdalene)
12th century with later additions. 12th century doorway, 15th century bench ends, magnificent 16th century tower & 17th century lecturn.

Somerset, Bath & Bristol

Crewkerne (St. Bartholomew)
Magnificent west front & roofs, 15th & 16th century. South doorway dating from 13th century, wonderful 15th century painted glass & 18th century chandeliers.

East Brent (St. Mary)
Mainly 15th century. Plaster ceiling, painted glass & carved bench ends.

Glastonbury (St. John)
One of the finest examples of perpendicular towers. Tie beam roof, late mediaeval painted glass, mediaeval vestment & early 16th century altar tomb.

High Ham (St. Andrew)
Sumptuous roofs & vaulted rood screen. Carved bench ends. Jacobean lecturn, mediaeval painted glass. Norman font.

Kingsbury Episcopi (St. Martin)
14th-15th century. Good tower with fan vaulting. Late mediaeval painted glass.

Long Sutton (Holy Trinity)
15th century with noble tower & magnificent tie beam roof. 15th century pulpit & rood screen, tower vaulting.

Martock (All Saints)
13th century chancel. Nave with tie beam roof, outstanding of its kind. 17th century paintings of Apostles.

North Cadbury (St. Michael)
painted glass.

Pilton (St. John)
12th century with arcades. 15th century roofs.

Taunton (St. Mary Magdalene)
Highest towers in the county. Five nave roof, fragments of mediaeval painted glass.

Trull (All Saints)
15th century with many mediaeval art treasures & 15th century glass.

Wells Cathedral-Wells
Magnificent west front with carved figures. Splendid tower. Early English arcade of nave & transepts. 60 fine misericords c.1330. Lady chapel with glass & star vault. Chapter House & Bishop's Palace.

Weston Zoyland (St. Mary)
15th century bench ends. 16th century heraldic glass. Jacobean pulpit.

Wrington (All Souls)
15th century aisles & nave; font, stone pulpit, notable screens.

Museums & Galleries

Admiral Blake Museum - Bridgewater
Exhibits relating to Battle of Sedgemoor, archaeology.

American Museum in Britain - Claverton Nr. Bath
American decorative arts 17th to 19th century displayed in series of furnished rooms & galleries of special exhibits. Paintings, furniture, glass wood & metal work, textiles, folk sculpture, etc.

Borough Museum - Hendford Manor Hall, Yeovil
Archaeology, firearms collections & Bailward Costume Collection.

Bristol Industrial Museum - Bristol
Collections of transport items of land, sea & air. Many unique items.

Burdon Manor - Washford
14th century manor house with Saxon fireplace & cockpit.

City of Bristol Art Gallery - Bristol
Permanent & loan collections of paintings, English & Oriental ceramics.

Glastonbury Lake Village Museum - Glastonbury
Late prehistoric antiquities.

Gough's Cave Museum - Cheddar
Upper Paleolithic remains, skeleton, flints, amber & engraved stones.

Holburne of Menstrie Museum - Bath
Old Master paintings, silver, glass, porcelain, furniture & miniatures in 18th century building. Work of 20th century craftworkers.

Hinton Priory - Hinton Charterhouse
13th century - ruins of Carthusian priory.

Kings Weston Roman Villa - Lawrence Weston
3rd & 4th centuries - mosaics of villa - some walls.

Museum of Costume - Bath
Collection of fashion from 17th century to present day.

Roman Baths - Bath

Roman Museum - Bath
Material from remains of extensive Roman baths & other Roman sites.

Stoney Littleton Barrow - Nr. Bath
Neolithic burial chamber - restoration work 1858.

St. Nicholas Church & City Museum - Bristol
Mediaeval antiquities relating to local

Somerset, Bath & Bristol

history, Church plate & vestments. Altarpiece by Hogarth.

Temple Church - Bristol
14th & 15th century ruins.

Victoria Art Gallery - Bath
Paintings, prints, drawings, glass, ceramics, watches, coins, etc. Bygones - permanent & temporary exhibitions. Geology collections.

Wookey Hole Cave Museum - Wookey Hole
Remains from Pliocene period. Relics of Celtic & Roman civilization. Exhibition of handmade paper-making.

Historic Monuments

Cleeve Abbey - Cleeve
Ruined 13th century house, with timber roof & wall paintings.

Farleigh Castle - Farleigh Hungerford
14th century remains - museums in chapel.

Glastonbury Abbey - Glastonbury
12th & 13th century ruins of St. Joseph's chapel & Abbot's kitchen.

Muchelney Abbey - Muchelney
15th century ruins of Benedictine abbey.

Other things to see & do

Black Rock Nature Reserve - Cheddar
Circular walk through plantation woodland, downland grazing.

Cheddar Caves
Show caves at the foot of beautiful Cheddar Gorge.

Clifton Zoological Gardens - Bristol
Flourishing zoo with many exhibits - beautiful gardens.

Clifton Suspension Bridge - Bristol
Designed by Isambard Kingdom Brunel, opened in 1864. Viewpoint & picnic spot Camera Obscura.

Cricket St. Thomas Wildlife Park - Nr. Chard
Wildlife park, heavy horse centre, countryside museum, etc.

The Pump Room - Bath
18th century neo-classical interior. Spa.

Clifton Suspension Bridge. Bristol.

SOMERSET, BATH & BRISTOL

Map reference

01	Dodd	06	Riley
01	Greenwood	07	Hill
01	Besley	08	Deacon
01	Potter	09	Nurcombe
01	Close	10	Bale
01	Beckett	11	Mott
01	Huxley	13	Redmond
01	Lanz	14	Knight
01	Metcalf	15	Copeland
01	Bryan	16	Orr
01	Selby	17	Mitchem
02	Tiley	18	Mogford
03	Westlake	20	Green
04	Priddle	21	Frost
04	Rhys-Roberts	22	Nowell
05	Jones	23	Read

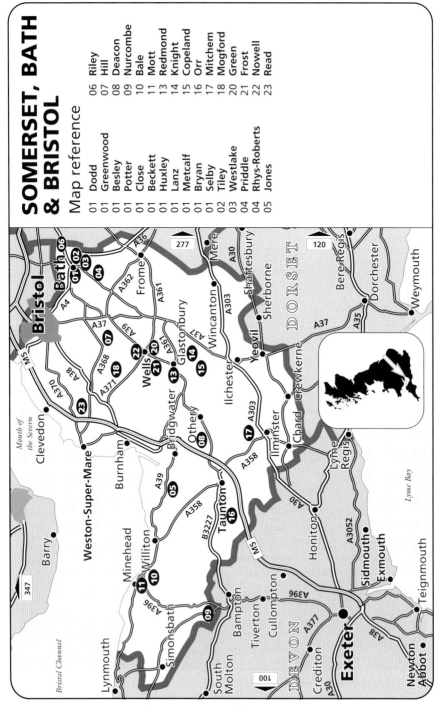

rate £ from - to per double room	children taken	evening meals	animals taken		

£72.00 to £90.00

Y | N | N

VISA: M'CARD:

Brocks

Near Rd: A.4

Brocks is a beautiful Georgian town house built in 1765 by John Wood, situated between the Circus and Royal Crescent. Very close to the Roman Baths, Assembly Rooms, etc. This really is a wonderful part of Bath. This historic house has all modern conveniences, & all of the comfortable bedrooms have en-suite facilities. The aim here is to offer guests the highest standards, and personal attention. A delightful base for exploring Bath.
E-mail: marion@brocksguesthouse.co.uk
www.brocksguesthouse.co.uk

Marion Dodd   *Brocks*   *32 Brock Street*   *Bath BA1 2LN*   *Somerset*
Tel: (01225) 338374 Fax (01225) 334245 Open: ALL YEAR (Excl. Xmas & New Year) Map Ref No. 01

£55.00 to £105.00

Y | N | N

VISA: M'CARD:

Number 30

Near Rd: A.4

Number Thirty is a Victorian house situated within 5 mins' level walk of the city centre & Roman Baths, the Pump Room, Circus & Royal Crescent. Number Thirty has been completely refurbished & all rooms are light & airy. The bedrooms all have en-suite bathrooms & are decorated mainly in blue & white. Each one is named after a famous person who has influenced the building or character of this wonderful city. Private parking. Children over 12.
E-mail: david.greenwood12@btinternet.com
www.numberthirty.com

David & Caroline Greenwood   *Number 30*   *Crescent Gardens*   *Bath BA1 2NB*   *Somerset*
Tel: (01225) 337393   *Fax 01225 337393*   *Open: ALL YEAR*   *Map Ref No. 01*

£55.00 to £75.00

Y | N | N

VISA: M'CARD:

The Old Red House

Near Rd: A.4

This charming Victorian Gingerbread House is colourful, comfortable & warm; full of unexpected touches & intriguing little curiosities. Its leaded & stained glass windows are now double-glazed to ensure a peaceful stay. The extensive breakfast menu, a delight in itself, is served around a large family dining table. Parking. Special rates for 3 or more nights. Dinner available at a local riverside pub. A non-smoking home. Children over 5.
E-mail: orh@amserve.net
www.oldredhouse.co.uk

Chrissie Besley   *The Old Red House*   *37 Newbridge Road*   *Bath BA1 3HE*   *Somerset*
Tel: (01225) 330464   *Fax 01225 331661*   *Open: FEB - DEC*   *Map Ref No. 01*

£40.00 to £80.00

Y | N | N

VISA: M'CARD:

Weston Lawn

Near Rd: A.4

Welcome to this Georgian family house set in its own grounds complete with fossils & Roman remains. Approx. 1 mile from the centre of Bath & only yards from the Cotswold Way, this is a premium base for city visits, leaving your car on the drive & exploring the surrounding country. The 3 bedrooms, all en-suite or with private bathroom, have colour T.V, & beverages, . Take your breakfast in the conservatory overlooking the lawn. Evening meals are available at the local pub.
E-mail: reservations@westonlawn.co.uk
www.westonlawn.co.uk

William & Fiona Close   *Weston Lawn*   *Lucklands Road*   *Weston*   *Bath BA1 4AY*   *Somerset*
Tel: (01225) 421362   *Fax 01225 319106*   *Open: ALL YEAR*   *Map Ref No. 01*

Somerset

rate £ from - to per double room | children taken | evening meals | animals taken

Cranleigh

Near Rd: A.431

Cranleigh has 9 delightfully appointed rooms, all decorated & furnished in their own individual style with every comfort imaginable to ensure the enjoyment of your stay. The regal decor of the 4-poster room offers the perfect choice for a special occasion. Many of the rooms have views over the garden & Avon Valley & all have en-suite/private facilities, T.V., phone, etc. After a hard day in the city why not come & relax in the secluded garden with hot tub. Parking. Licensed. Children over 4.

E-mail: cranleigh@btinternet.com
www.cranleighguesthouse.com

| | £60.00 to £95.00 | Y | N | N |

see PHOTO over p. 223

VISA: M'CARD: AMEX:

Denise & Colin Potter   Cranleigh   159 Newbridge Hill   Bath BA1 3PX   Somerset
Tel: (01225) 310197   Fax 01225 423143   Open: ALL YEAR (Excl. Xmas)   Map Ref No. 01

Cedar Lodge

Near Rd: A.4, A.46

Within easy level walk to the historic city centre, this beautiful, detached Georgian house offers period elegance with modern amenities. 3 lovely bedrooms (1 with 4-poster, 1 half-tester, 1 twin), all with en-suite/private bathrooms. Delightful gardens & comfortable drawing room, with fire, to relax in. Ideally situated for excursions to Avebury, Stonehenge, Salisbury, Longleat, Wells, Cotswolds, Wales & many other attractions. Secure private parking. Children over 10.

www.bestbandb.co.uk

| | £65.00 to £75.00 | Y | N | N |

Derek & Maria Beckett   Cedar Lodge   13 Lambridge   London Road   Bath BA1 6BJ   Somerset
Tel: (01225) 423468   Open: ALL YEAR   Map Ref No. 01

Dolphin House

Near Rd: A.4

Dolphin House is a detached Georgian Grade II listed house with a mature terraced walled garden. Centrally heated & with period furnishings. There is a private suite consisting of a twin-bedded room, lounge & large bathroom. Also, a large double bedroom with private bathroom. T.V. & tea/coffee-making facilities in each room. All meals are served in the privacy of your own room or on the terrace. The historic city of Bath is only 2 1/2 miles away. Children over 12 years welcome.

E-mail: georgeandjane@hotmail.com
www.batheaston.net/dolphinhouse/

| | £55.00 to £75.00 | Y | N | N |

George & Jane Riley   Dolphin House   8 Northend   Batheaston   Bath BA1 7EN   Somerset
Tel/Fax: (01225) 858915   Mobile 07801 444521   Open: ALL YEAR (Excl. Xmas & NY) Map Ref No. 06

Paradise House Hotel

Near Rd: A.367

Paradise House was built in the 1720s, on the ancient Roman Fosse Way. The Fosse Way, now a cul-de-sac, is one of the quietest streets in Bath & provides easy access to the city centre. (The Roman Baths are only 7 mins' walk away.) 11 attractively furnished & well-appointed en-suite bedrooms, & delightful 4-poster garden rooms with en-suite jacuzzi. Paradise House enjoys fine views over the Georgian city & has over 1/2 an acre of splendid walled gardens.

E-mail: info@paradise-house.co.uk
www.paradise-house.co.uk

| | £65.00 to £160.00 | Y | N | N |

VISA: M'CARD: AMEX:

David & Annie Lanz   Paradise House Hotel   88 Holloway   Bath BA2 4PX   Somerset
Tel: (01225) 317723   Fax 01225 482005   Open: ALL YEAR (Excl. Xmas)   Map Ref No. 01

Cranleigh.   Bath.

Somerset

Lavender House

Near Rd: A.367

Set in a quiet conservation area, within easy reach of Bath city centre. Lavender House is an Edwardian house which offers 5 lovely guest rooms. Each is individually designed & has a large, luxurious bathroom, T.V. & hospitality tray. In addition to serving a traditional English breakfast, using free-range & fresh local produce, there are special vegetarian Cordon Vert options. Lavender House is a special place to unwind, relax & be spoiled. Parking. Children over 8.
E-mail: lavenderhouse@btinternet.com
www.lavenderhouse-bath.com

£80.00 to £95.00 — Y N N

see PHOTO over
p. 225

VISA: M'CARD:

| Carol & Bill Huxley | Lavender House | 17 Bloomfield Park | Bath BA2 2BY | Somerset |
| Tel: (01225) 314500 | Fax 01225 448564 | | Open: ALL YEAR | Map Ref No. 01 |

Northwick House

Near Rd: A.36

With outstanding views over Bath & the surrounding countryside, this comfortable & unusual Grade II listed Georgian house was built in 1821 on the upper slopes of Bathwick Hill, renowned for its Italianate villas. 5 mins' to city centre, near a regular bus route & also near the university. Wonderful walks in National Trust woodland & the popular Sham Castle Golf Course. 3 attractively furnished bedrooms, each with T.V., radio/alarm, etc. Children over 12. Dogs by arrangement.
E-mail: info@northwickhousebath.co.uk
www.northwickhousebath.co.uk

£60.00 to £80.00 — Y N Y

| Veronica Metcalfe | Northwick House | North Road | Bath BA2 6HD | Somerset |
| Tel: (01225) 420963 | Mobile 0771 4246929 | | Open: ALL YEAR | Map Ref No. 01 |

Ravenscroft

Near Rd: A.36

Built in 1876, Ravenscroft is an elegant Victorian residence with a wealth of period features. Its elevated position provides spectacular views over the city of Bath & countryside beyond. Only a few minutes from the city centre, it is surrounded by an acre of secluded, mature gardens which offer guests peace & tranquillity. There are 3 lovely bedrooms with colour T.V., tea/coffee & hairdrying facilities. Private parking. Children over 12.
E-mail: patrick@ravenscroftbandb.co.uk
www.ravenscroftbandb.co.uk

£70.00 to £80.00 — Y N N

| Patrick & Hilary Bryan | Ravenscroft | North Road | Bathwick | Bath BA2 6HZ | Somerset |
| Tel: (01225) 461919 | Fax 01225 461919 | | Open: ALL YEAR (Excl. Xmas) | | Map Ref No. 01 |

Lindisfarne Guest House

Near Rd: A.36

Your welcoming & knowledgeable hosts, Ian & Carolyn, invite you to enjoy their spacious & comfortable en-suite rooms, some overlooking the pretty garden. There are 1 twin, 2 doubles & 1 triple room, all with T.V./DVD, refreshment trays & complimentary toiletries. Lindisfarne is easily accessible to Bath but away from the hustle & bustle of the city centre in the semi-rural environment of Bathampton. Good local eating places, & pleasant walks along the Kennet & Avon canal. Children 8+.
E-mail: lindisfarne-bath@talk21.com
www.bath.org/hotel/lindisfarne.htm

£55.00 to £65.00 — Y N N

VISA: M'CARD: AMEX:

| Ian & Carolyn Tiley | Lindisfarne Guest House | 41a Warminster Road | Bath BA2 6XJ | Somerset |
| Tel: (01225) 466342 | | Open: ALL YEAR (Excl. Xmas) | | Map Ref No. 02 |

Lavender House. Bath.

Monkshill. Monkton Combe.

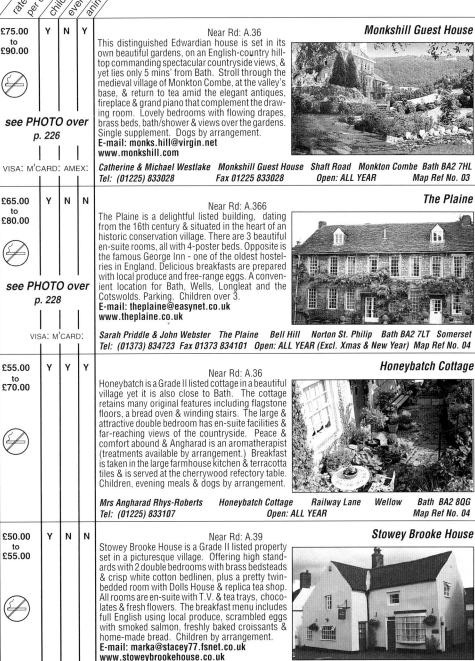

rate £ from - to per double room	children taken	evening meals	animals taken		

£75.00 to £90.00 — Y N Y

🚭 (no smoking)

see PHOTO over p. 226

VISA: M'CARD: AMEX:

Monkshill Guest House

Near Rd: A.36

This distinguished Edwardian house is set in its own beautiful gardens, on an English-country hill-top commanding spectacular countryside views, & yet lies only 5 mins' from Bath. Stroll through the medieval village of Monkton Combe, at the valley's base, & return to tea amid the elegant antiques, fireplace & grand piano that complement the drawing room. Lovely bedrooms with flowing drapes, brass beds, bath/shower & views over the gardens. Single supplement. Dogs by arrangement.
E-mail: monks.hill@virgin.net
www.monkshill.com

Catherine & Michael Westlake   Monkshill Guest House   Shaft Road   Monkton Combe   Bath BA2 7HL
Tel: (01225) 833028   Fax 01225 833028   Open: ALL YEAR   Map Ref No. 03

£65.00 to £80.00 — Y N N

🚭 (no smoking)

see PHOTO over p. 228

VISA: M'CARD:

The Plaine

Near Rd: A.366

The Plaine is a delightful listed building, dating from the 16th century & situated in the heart of an historic conservation village. There are 3 beautiful en-suite rooms, all with 4-poster beds. Opposite is the famous George Inn - one of the oldest hostelries in England. Delicious breakfasts are prepared with local produce and free-range eggs. A convenient location for Bath, Wells, Longleat and the Cotswolds. Parking. Children over 3.
E-mail: theplaine@easynet.co.uk
www.theplaine.co.uk

Sarah Priddle & John Webster   The Plaine   Bell Hill   Norton St. Philip   Bath BA2 7LT   Somerset
Tel: (01373) 834723 Fax 01373 834101 Open: ALL YEAR (Excl. Xmas & New Year) Map Ref No. 04

£55.00 to £70.00 — Y Y Y

🚭 (no smoking)

Honeybatch Cottage

Near Rd: A.36

Honeybatch is a Grade II listed cottage in a beautiful village yet it is also close to Bath. The cottage retains many original features including flagstone floors, a bread oven & winding stairs. The large & attractive double bedroom has en-suite facilities & far-reaching views of the countryside. Peace & comfort abound & Angharad is an aromatherapist (treatments available by arrangement.) Breakfast is taken in the large farmhouse kitchen & terracotta tiles & is served at the cherrywood refectory table. Children, evening meals & dogs by arrangement.

Mrs Angharad Rhys-Roberts   Honeybatch Cottage   Railway Lane   Wellow   Bath BA2 8QG
Tel: (01225) 833107   Open: ALL YEAR   Map Ref No. 04

£50.00 to £55.00 — Y N N

🚭 (no smoking)

Stowey Brooke House

Near Rd: A.39

Stowey Brooke House is a Grade II listed property set in a picturesque village. Offering high standards with 2 double bedrooms with brass bedsteads & crisp white cotton bedlinen, plus a pretty twin-bedded room with Dolls House & replica tea shop. All rooms are en-suite with T.V. & tea trays, chocolates & fresh flowers. The breakfast menu includes full English using local produce, scrambled eggs with smoked salmon, freshly baked croissants & home-made bread. Children by arrangement.
E-mail: marka@stacey77.fsnet.co.uk
www.stoweybrookehouse.co.uk

Mr Stacey & Ms Jones   Stowey Brooke House   18 Castle Street   Nether Stowey   Bridgwater TA5 1LN
Tel: (01278) 733356   Open: ALL YEAR   Map Ref No. 05

The Plaine. Norton St. Philip.

Somerset

£80.00 to £80.00	Y	Y	N	

Near Rd: A.368 **Harptree Court**

A delightful, Grade II listed Georgian country house set in its own extensive parkland extending over 17 acres. Ideally situated for exploring Bath, Wells, Bristol & the Mendip Hills. The elegant bedrooms are furnished with antiques & all have views of the gardens. All rooms have a TV with either a video or dvd player. A guest sitting room, where a complimentary cream tea can be taken in front of a roaring fire in winter. Linda's delicious meals are served in the candlelit dining room. Children over 12.
E-mail: location.harptree@tiscali.co.uk
www.harptreecourt.co.uk

Linda Hill   *Harptree Court*   *East Harptree*   *Nr. Bristol BS40 6AA*   *Somerset*
Tel: (01761) 221729   *Open: ALL YEAR (Excl. Xmas)*   *Map Ref No. 07*

£50.00 to £50.00	N	Y	N	

Near Rd: A.361 **Saltmoor House**

Saltmoor House, a Grade II listed building, is an elegant country home overlooking the River Parrett. The property has a delightful walled garden set in 15 acres of pasture. Flagstone floors, log fires & classical wall paintings characterize the stylish interior. 2 double bedrooms with private bathrooms, 1 double/twin en-suite. A wide choice is offered for breakfast with home-produced eggs & a superb dinner is always available. The area is wonderfully placed for walking & touring.
E-mail: saltmoorhouse@aol.com
www.saltmoorhouse.co.uk

Crispin & Elizabeth Deacon   *Saltmoor House*   *Burrowbridge TA7 0RL*   *Somerset*
Tel: (01823) 698092   *Open: ALL YEAR*   *Map Ref No. 08*

£48.00 to £60.00	Y	Y	Y	

Near Rd: A.396 **Marsh Bridge Cottage**

Marsh Bridge Cottage is peacefully & idyllically situated alongside the sparkling River Barle on the edge of a woodland walkway to Tarr Steps (one of Exmoor's most popular walks & beauty spots.) Built in the 1860s as a gamekeeper's cottage it has gradually been attractively extended by Carole & John Nurcombe. Bedrooms are fresh & prettily decorated with luxury bathrooms & lovely river views. Enjoy delicious traditional home-cooking using fresh vegetables from the garden, when in season, & other locally sourced produce.
E-mail: carolenurcombe@yahoo.co.uk

John & Carole Nurcombe   *Marsh Bridge Cottage*   *Dulverton TA22 9QG*   *Somerset*
Tel: (01398) 323197   *Open: ALL YEAR*   *Map Ref No. 09*

£54.00 to £60.00	N	N	N	

Near Rd: A.39 **Conygar House**

Conygar House is situated in a quiet road just off the main street of medieval Dunster village. Restaurants, bars & shops are all within 1 mins' walking distance. Wonderful views of castle & moors. Delightful sunny garden & patio for guests' use. Ideal for exploring Exmoor & coast. All of the rooms are decorated & furnished to a high standard. Personal service & your comfort is guaranteed. Dunster Beach is 1 1/2 miles away, Minehead 2 1/2 miles & Porlock 8 miles.
E-mail: bale.dunster@virgin.net
www.conygarhouse.co.uk

Mrs B. Bale   *Conygar House*   *2A The Ball*   *Dunster TA24 6SD*   *Somerset*
Tel: (01643) 821872   *Fax 01643 821872*   *Open: FEB - NOV*   *Map Ref No. 10*

Number Three Hotel.   Glastonbury.

Somerset

rate £ from - to per double room	children taken	evening meals	animals taken		

Dollons House

£55.00 to £55.00 — N N N

Near Rd: A.358, A.39

17th-century Grade II listed Dollons House nestles beneath the castle in this delightful medieval village in the Exmoor National Park. 3 attractive & very comfortable en-suite rooms, each with its own character & special decor. 100 years ago, the local pharmacist had his shop in Dollons, & in the back he made marmalade for the Houses of Parliament. Dunster is ideal for touring. Pull up outside the front door to unload & get instructions for parking.
E-mail: jmott@onetel.com
www.SmoothHound.co.uk/hotels/dollons.html

VISA: M'CARD:

Mrs Janet Mott   Dollons House   10-12 Church Street   Dunster TA24 6SH   Somerset
Tel: (01643) 821880   Open: ALL YEAR (Excl. Xmas)   Map Ref No. 11

Number Three Hotel

£100.00 to £110.00 — Y N N

Near Rd: M.5 Ex. 23

Number Three is a beautiful Georgian town house; once the home of Winston Churchill's mother & also Frederick Bligh Bond. 5 individually designed rooms, all with en-suite bathrooms, T.V., telephone & tea/coffee-making facilities. 2 rooms are in the main house & 3 are in the Garden House, set within the large walled garden; with wonderful mature trees, floodlit at night. Cars are parked here behind security gates. Number Three stands beside Glastonbury Abbey & is a place of peace & tranquillity.
E-mail: info@numberthree.co.uk
www.numberthree.co.uk

*see PHOTO over
p. 230*

VISA: M'CARD: AMEX:

Patricia Redmond   Number Three Hotel   3 Magdalene Street   Glastonbury BA6 9EW   Somerset
Tel: (01458) 832129   Fax 01458 834227   Open: ALL YEAR (Excl. Xmas)   Map Ref No. 13

Mill House

£56.00 to £72.00 — Y N N

Near Rd: A.37, A.303

Ideally situated & beautifully restored, listed Georgian mill house in peaceful garden with mill stream. Close to Glastonbury & Wells with many National Trust properties & classical gardens nearby. Fish without leaving the garden, walk or cycle for miles & enjoy birdwatching on the panoramic Somerset Levels. Beautifully decorated, luxury en-suite bedrooms with wonderful views, an elegant Georgian dining room & delicious Aga breakfasts await you. Children over 10 years welcome.
E-mail: BandB@millhousebarton.co.uk
www.millhousebarton.co.uk

VISA: M'CARD:

Rita & Michael Knight   Mill House   Mill Road   Barton St. David   Somerton TA11 6DF   Somerset
Tel: (01458) 851215   Fax 01458 851372   Mobile 07780 961912   Open: FEB - DEC Map Ref No. 14

The Lynch Country House

£60.00 to £95.00 — Y N Y

Near Rd: A.372

The Lynch is a charming small hotel, standing in acres of carefully tended, wonderfully mature grounds. Beautifully refurbished & decorated to retain all its Georgian style & elegance, it now offers 8 attractively presented rooms, some with 4-posters, others with Victorian bedsteads, all with thoughtful extras including bathrobes & magazines. Each room has en-suite/private facilities, T.V. & tea/coffee etc. The elegant dining room overlooks the lawns & lake. Single-supplement.
E-mail: the_lynch@talk21.com
www.thelynchcountryhouse.co.uk

*see PHOTO over
p. 232*

VISA: M'CARD: AMEX:

Roy Copeland   The Lynch Country House   4 Behind Berry   Somerton TA11 7PD   Somerset
Tel: (01458) 272316 Fax 01458 272590   Open: ALL YEAR (Excl. Xmas & New Year) Map Ref No. 15

The Lynch Country House Hotel.   Somerton.

rate £ from - to per double room	children taken	evening meals taken	animals taken		

£60.00 to £60.00 — Y Y N

🚭

Near Rd: A.38, M.5

Causeway Cottage

Privately tucked away within easy reach of J.26 M.5. A 200-year-old stone cottage standing in a lovely garden with apple orchard & views up to the church. The interior is simple with antique pine & beams. All 3 bedrooms have en-suite facilities & there is a spacious restful sitting room for guests. Lesley is renowned for her cooking. Home-baked bread, free range eggs & farm sausages for breakfast. An informal, relaxed & comfortable family home. Children over 10. Dinner by arrangement.
E-mail: orrs@westbuckland.freeserve.co.uk
www.causewaycottage.co.uk

Lesley Orr   Causeway Cottage   West Buckland   Taunton TA21 9JZ   Somerset
Tel: (01823) 663458   Fax 01823 663458   Open: ALL YEAR   Map Ref No. 16

£56.00 to £62.00 — Y N N

🚭

Near Rd: A.358

Whittles Farm

Guests at Whittles Farm can be sure of a high standard of accommodation & service. A superior 16th-century farmhouse set in 200 acres of pastureland, it is luxuriously carpeted & furnished in traditional style. Inglenook fireplaces & log-burners. 2 en-suite bedrooms, individually furnished, with T.V. & tea/coffee-making facilities. Super farmhouse food, using own meat, eggs & vegetables, & local Cheddar cheese & butter. Table licence. Children over 12 yrs.
E-mail: dj.CM.MITCHEM@themail.co.uk
www.whittlesfarm.co.uk

Mrs Claire Mitchem   Whittles Farm   Beercrocombe   Taunton TA3 6AH   Somerset
Tel: (01823) 480301   Fax 01823 480301   Open: FEB - NOV   Map Ref No. 17

£50.00 to £52.00 — Y N Y

🚭

VISA: M'CARD: AMEX:

Near Rd: A.371

The Old Stores

This charming conversion of The Old Stores is between the church & the pub in the heart of this Mendip village. The en-suite bedrooms, music, open fires & a library provide a high standard of cosy comfort. You will be welcomed with home-made cakes & the use of local organic produce & home-made bread - we cater for all tastes. Malcolm can provide maps & books for visits & walks, including his own book on local footpaths. Animals by arrangement.
E-mail: moglin980@aol.com
www.s-h-sytems.co.uk/hotels/oldstore.html

Malcolm & Linda Mogford   The Old Stores   Westbury-sub-Mendip   Wells BA5 1HA   Somerset
Tel: (01749) 870817 Fax 01749 870980   Mobile 07771 905262 Open: MAR - NOV Map Ref No. 18

£50.00 to £60.00 — Y Y N

🚭

Near Rd: A.39

Tynings House

A former farmhouse, parts of which date back to the 1680s, Tynings is set in its own grounds of 4 acres & offers relaxed & comfortable surroundings. Tynings offers 2 double rooms, & 1 twin-bedded room, all en-suite. Ideally located for many places of interest including the historic & picturesque city of Wells 2 miles away, the mystical Isle of Avalon & Glastonbury 3 miles, & the Mendips & Somerset Levels with its multitude of wildlife. Children over 12. Evening meals by arrangement.
E-mail: info@tynings.co.uk
www.tynings.co.uk

Tish Hopkins & Mike Green Tynings House Harters Hill Lane Coxley Wells BA5 1RF Somerset
Tel: (01749) 675368   Fax 01749 674217   Open: ALL YEAR (Excl. Xmas)   Map Ref No. 20

Somerset

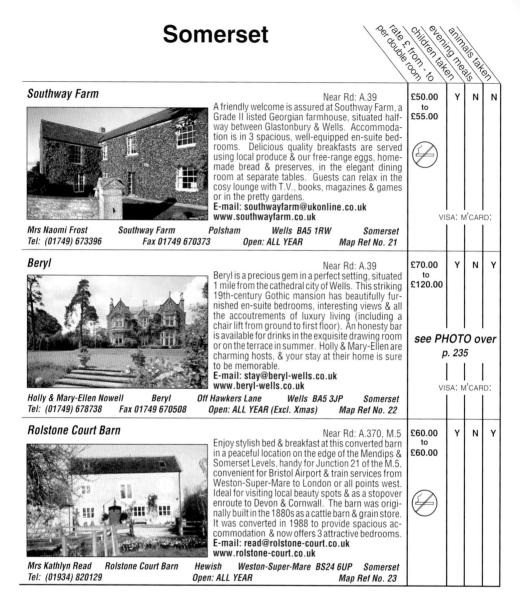

Southway Farm

Near Rd: A.39

A friendly welcome is assured at Southway Farm, a Grade II listed Georgian farmhouse, situated half-way between Glastonbury & Wells. Accommodation is in 3 spacious, well-equipped en-suite bedrooms. Delicious quality breakfasts are served using local produce & our free-range eggs, home-made bread & preserves, in the elegant dining room at separate tables. Guests can relax in the cosy lounge with T.V., books, magazines & games or in the pretty gardens.
E-mail: southwayfarm@ukonline.co.uk
www.southwayfarm.co.uk

£50.00 to £55.00 — Y N N

VISA: M'CARD:

Mrs Naomi Frost Southway Farm Polsham Wells BA5 1RW Somerset
Tel: (01749) 673396 Fax 01749 670373 Open: ALL YEAR Map Ref No. 21

Beryl

Near Rd: A.39

Beryl is a precious gem in a perfect setting, situated 1 mile from the cathedral city of Wells. This striking 19th-century Gothic mansion has beautifully furnished en-suite bedrooms, interesting views & all the accoutrements of luxury living (including a chair lift from ground to first floor). An honesty bar is available for drinks in the exquisite drawing room or on the terrace in summer. Holly & Mary-Ellen are charming hosts, & your stay at their home is sure to be memorable.
E-mail: stay@beryl-wells.co.uk
www.beryl-wells.co.uk

£70.00 to £120.00 — Y N Y

see PHOTO over p. 235

VISA: M'CARD:

Holly & Mary-Ellen Nowell Beryl Off Hawkers Lane Wells BA5 3JP Somerset
Tel: (01749) 678738 Fax 01749 670508 Open: ALL YEAR (Excl. Xmas) Map Ref No. 22

Rolstone Court Barn

Near Rd: A.370, M.5

Enjoy stylish bed & breakfast at this converted barn in a peaceful location on the edge of the Mendips & Somerset Levels, handy for Junction 21 of the M.5, convenient for Bristol Airport & train services from Weston-Super-Mare to London or all points west. Ideal for visiting local beauty spots & as a stopover enroute to Devon & Cornwall. The barn was originally built in the 1880s as a cattle barn & grain store. It was converted in 1988 to provide spacious accommodation & now offers 3 attractive bedrooms.
E-mail: read@rolstone-court.co.uk
www.rolstone-court.co.uk

£60.00 to £60.00 — Y N Y

Mrs Kathlyn Read Rolstone Court Barn Hewish Weston-Super-Mare BS24 6UP Somerset
Tel: (01934) 820129 Open: ALL YEAR Map Ref No. 23

Visit our website at:
http://www.bestbandb.co.uk

Beryl.   Wells.

Suffolk

Suffolk
(East Anglia)

In July, the lower reaches of the River Orwell hold the essence of Suffolk. Broad fields of green and gold with wooded horizons sweep down to the quiet water. Orwell Bridge spans the wide river where yachts and tan-sailed barges share the water with ocean-going container ships out of Ipswich. Downstream the saltmarshes echo to the cry of the Curlew. The small towns and villages of Suffolk are typical of an area with long seafairing traditions. This is the county of men of vision; like Constable and Gainsborough, Admiral Lord Nelson and Benjamin Britten.

The land is green and fertile and highly productive. The hedgerows shelter some of our prettiest wild flowers, & the narrow country lanes are a pure delight. Most memorable is the ever-changing sky, appearing higher and wider here than elsewhere in England. There is a great deal of heathland, probably the best known being Newmarket where horses have been trained and raced for some hundreds of years. Gorse-covered heath meets sandy cliffs on Suffolks Heritage Coast. Here are bird reserves and the remains of the great mediaeval city of Dunwich, sliding into the sea.

West Suffolk was famous for its wool trade in the Middle Ages, & the merchants gave thanks for their good fortune by building magnificent "Wool Churches". Much-photographed Lavenham has the most perfect black & white timbered houses in Britain, built by the merchants of Tudor times. Ipswich was granted the first charter by King John in 1200, but had long been a trading community of seafarers. Its history can be read from the names of the streets - Buttermarket, Friars Street, Cornhill, Dial Lane & Tavern Street. The latter holds the Great White Horse Hotel mentioned by Charles Dickens in Pickwick Papers. Sadly not many ancient buildings remain, but the mediaeval street pattern and the churches make an interesting trail to follow. The Market town of Bury St. Edmunds is charming, with much of its architectural heritage still surviving, from the Norman Cornhill to a fine Queen Anne House. The great Abbey, now in ruins, was the meeting place of the Barons of England for the creation of the Magna Carta, enshrining the principals of individual freedom, parliamentary democracy and the supremacy of the law. Suffolk has some very fine churches, notably at Mildenhall, Lakenheath, Framlingham, Lavenham & Stoke-by-Nayland, & also a large number of wonderful houses & great halls, evidence of the county's prosperity.

Lavenham.

Suffolk

Suffolk Gazeteer

Areas of Outstanding Natural Beauty
Suffolk Coast. Heathlands. Dedham Vale.

Historic Houses & Castles

Euston Hall - Thetford
18th century house with fine collection of pictures. Gardens & 17th century Parish Church nearby.

Christchurch Mansion - Ipswich
16th century mansion built on site of 12th century Augustinian Priory. Gables & dormers added in 17th century & other alteration & additions made in 17th & 18th centuries.

Gainsborough's House - Sudbury
Birthplace of Gainsborough, well furnished, collection of paintings.

The Guildhall - Hadleigh
15th century.

Glemham Hall - Nr Woodbridge
Elizabethan house of red brick - 18th century alterations. Fine stair, panelled rooms with Queen Anne furniture.

Haughley Park - Nr. Stowmarket
Jacobean manor house.

Heveningham Hall - Nr. Halesworth
Georgian mansion - English Palladian - Interior in Neo-Classical style. Garden by Capability Brown.

Ickworth - Nr. Bury St. Edmunds
Mixed architectural styles - late Regency & 18th century. French furniture, pictures & superb silver. Gardens with orangery.

Kentwell Hall - Long Melford
Elizabethan mansion in red brick, built in E plan, surrounded by moat.

Little Hall - Lavenham
15th century hall house, collection of furniture, pictures, china, etc.

Melford Hall - Nr. Sudbury
16th century - fine pictures, Chinese porcelain, furniture. Garden with gazebo.

Somerleyton Hall - Nr. Lowestoft
Dating from 16th century - additional work in 19th century. Carving by Grinling Gibbons. Tapestries, library, pictures.

Cathedrals & Churches

Bury St. Edmunds (St. Mary)
15th century. Hammer Beam roof in nave, wagon roof in chancel. Boret monument 1467.

Bramfield (St. Andrew)
Early circular tower. Fine screen & vaulting. Renaissance effigy.

Bacton (St. Mary)
15th century timbered roof. East Anglian stone & flintwork.

Dennington (St. Mary)
15th century alabaster monuments & bench ends. Aisle & Parclose screens with lofts & parapets.

Earl Stonhay (St. Mary)
14th century - rebuilt with fine hammer roof & 17th century pulpit with four hour-glasses.

Euston (St. Genevieve)
17th century. Fine panelling, reredos may be Grinling Gibbons.

Framlingham (St. Michael)
15th century nave & west tower, hammer beam roof in false vaulting. Chancel was rebuilt in 16th century for the tombs of the Howard family, monumental art treasures. Thamar organ. 1674.

Fressingfield (St. Peter & St. Paul)
15th century woodwork - very fine.

Lavenham (St. Peter & St. Paul)
15th century. Perpendicular. Fine towers. 14th century chancel screen. 17th century monument in alabaster.

Long Melford (Holy Trinity)
15th century Lady Chapel, splendid brasses. 15th century glass of note. Chantry chapel with fine roof. Like cathedral in proportions.

Stoke-by-Nayland (St. Mary)
16th-17th century library, great tower. Fine nave & arcades. Good brasses & monuments.

Ufford (St. Mary)
Mediaeval font cover - glorious.

Museums & Galleries

Christchurch Mansion - Ipswich
Country house, collection of furniture, pictures, bygones, ceramics of 18th century. Paintings by Gainsborough, Constable & modern artists.

Ipswich Museum - Ipswich
Natural History; prehistory, geology & archaeology to mediaeval period.

Suffolk

Moyse's Hall Musuem - Bury St. Edmunds
12th century dwelling house with local antiquities & natural history.

Abbot's Hall Museum of Rural Life - Stowmarket
Collections describing agriculture, crafts & domestic utensils.

Gershom-Parkington Collection - Bury St. Edmunds
Queen Anne House containing collection of watches & clocks.

Dunwich Musuem - Dunwich
Flora & fauna; local history.

Historic Monuments

The Abbey - Bury St. Edmunds
Only west end now standing.

Framlingham Castle
12th & 13th centuries - Tudor almshouses.

Bungay Castle - Bungay
12th century. Restored 13th century drawbridge & gatehouse.

Burgh Castle Roman Fort - Burgh
Coastal defences - 3rd century.

Herringfleet Priory - Herringfleet
13th century - remains of small Augustinian priory.

Leiston Abbey - Leiston
14th century - remains of cloisters, choir & trancepts.

Orford Castle - Orford
12th century - 18-sided keep - three towers.

The House in the Clouds. Thorpeness.

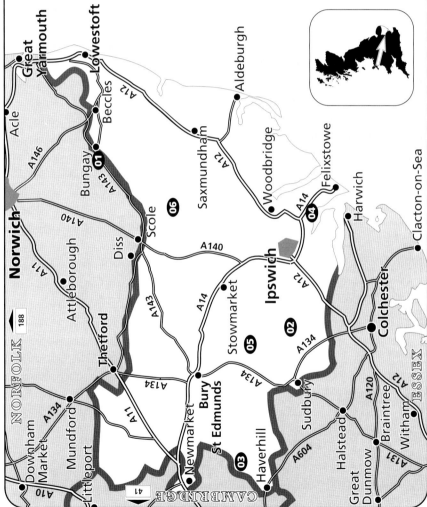

SUFFOLK
Map reference

01 Watchorn
02 Rolfe
03 Sheppard
04 Elliot
05 Pitt
06 Bagnall

Suffolk

Earsham Park Farm

Near Rd: A.143

Set on a hill with stunning views over the garden, lake & countryside, the farmhouse is a haven of peace & quietness. Wake up to birdsong & delicious award-winning breakfasts featuring home-made bread & preserves, the farms own outdoor reared bacon & sausages & local free-range eggs. Your comfort is a priority in the beautifully furnished en-suite rooms, which are spacious & light, with T.V.s, tea trays, embroidered linen & thick fluffy towels. Dogs & horses by arrangement.
E-mail: Bestb@earsham-parkfarm.co.uk
www.earsham-parkfarm.co.uk

| £40.00 to £70.00 | Y | N | Y |

VISA: M'CARD:

Mrs Bobbie Watchorn   Earsham Park Farm   Old Railway Road   Earsham Bungay NR35 2AQ Suffolk
Tel: (01986) 892180   Fax 01986 894796   Open: ALL YEAR   Map Ref No. 01

Edge Hall

Near Rd: A.1071

Edge Hall is a family-run Georgian house in central Hadleigh. Beautifully restored & tastefully modernised, it offers the ultimate luxury en-suite bedrooms, ranging from an antique 4-poster to pretty attic family rooms. Situated in the most picturesque part of Suffolk, it is an ideal base from which to explore the surrounding towns & unspoilt villages. Your hosts pride themselves on making your stay at Edge Hall a memorable experience.
E-mail: r.rolfe@edgehall-hotel.co.uk
www.egdehall-hotel.co.uk

| £75.00 to £95.00 | Y | N | Y |

Angela Rolfe   Edge Hall   2 High Street   Hadleigh IP7 5AP   Suffolk
Tel: (01473) 822458   Fax 01473 827751   Open: ALL YEAR   Map Ref No. 02

The Old Vicarage

Near Rd: A.1307

Set in mature grounds & woodlands, this delightful Old Vicarage has a friendly family atmosphere. Complete peace & comfort are assured with wonderful views of the Suffolk countryside. Guests are welcome to use the large garden. Open log fires welcome you in winter. The attractively furnished bedrooms have en-suite or private facilities & tea/coffee trays. Evening meals are available with prior notice & there are excellent pubs nearby. Perfectly situated for Newmarket, Cambridge, Long Melford, Lavenham & Constable country. Children over 7.

| £64.00 to £68.00 | Y | Y | N |

Mrs Jane Sheppard   The Old Vicarage   Great Thurlow   Haverhill CB9 7LE   Suffolk
Tel: (01440) 783209   Fax 01638 667270   Open: ALL YEAR   Map Ref No. 03

Buttermans

Near Rd: A.14

Buttermans is set in the grounds of Broke Hall (the 18th-century home of Admiral Broke). Originally the blacksmiths' forge, this delightful home is just 150 metres from the River Orwell & offers spectacular views across unspoilt countryside designated as an Area of Outstanding Natural Beauty. Bedrooms are beautifully appointed with en-suite bath/shower room, T.V. & tea/coffee facilities. Home-made bread & local produce are served with a full English breakfast. Dinner can be arranged.
E-mail: tim_elliot@compuserve.com
www.buttermans.com

| £60.00 to £90.00 | N | Y | N |

see PHOTO over
p. 241

Tim & Janet Elliot   Buttermans   Broke Hall Park   Nacton   Ipswich IP10 0ET   Suffolk
Tel: (01473) 655133   Open: MAR - OCT   Map Ref No. 04

Buttermans. Nacton.

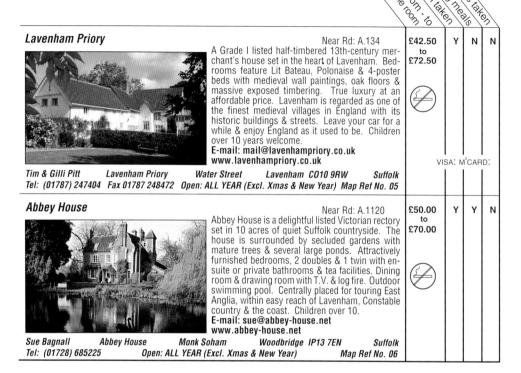

	rate £ from - to per double room	evening meals children taken	animals taken

Lavenham Priory

Near Rd: A.134

A Grade I listed half-timbered 13th-century merchant's house set in the heart of Lavenham. Bedrooms feature Lit Bateau, Polonaise & 4-poster beds with medieval wall paintings, oak floors & massive exposed timbering. True luxury at an affordable price. Lavenham is regarded as one of the finest medieval villages in England with its historic buildings & streets. Leave your car for a while & enjoy England as it used to be. Children over 10 years welcome.
E-mail: mail@lavenhampriory.co.uk
www.lavenhampriory.co.uk

£42.50 to £72.50 Y N N

VISA: M'CARD:

Tim & Gilli Pitt   Lavenham Priory   Water Street   Lavenham CO10 9RW   Suffolk
Tel: (01787) 247404   Fax 01787 248472   Open: ALL YEAR (Excl. Xmas & New Year) Map Ref No. 05

Abbey House

Near Rd: A.1120

Abbey House is a delightful listed Victorian rectory set in 10 acres of quiet Suffolk countryside. The house is surrounded by secluded gardens with mature trees & several large ponds. Attractively furnished bedrooms, 2 doubles & 1 twin with en-suite or private bathrooms & tea facilities. Dining room & drawing room with T.V. & log fire. Outdoor swimming pool. Centrally placed for touring East Anglia, within easy reach of Constable country & the coast. Children over 10.
E-mail: sue@abbey-house.net
www.abbey-house.net

£50.00 to £70.00 Y Y N

Sue Bagnall   Abbey House   Monk Soham   Woodbridge IP13 7EN   Suffolk
Tel: (01728) 685225   Open: ALL YEAR (Excl. Xmas & New Year)   Map Ref No. 06

Surrey

Surrey
(South East)

One of the Home Counties, Surrey includes a large area of London, south of the Thames. Communications are good in all directions so it is easy to stay in Surrey & travel either into central London or out to enjoy the lovely countryside which, despite urban development, survives thanks to the 'Green Belt' policy. The county is also very accessible from Gatwick Airport.

The land geographically, is chalk sandwiched in clay, & probably the lack of handy building material was responsible for the area remaining largely uninhabited for centuries. The North Downs were a considerable barrier to cross, but gradually settlements grew along the rivers which were the main

Polesden Lacey.

routes through. The Romans used the gap created by the River Mole to build Stane Street between London & Chichester, this encouraged the development of small towns. The gap cut by the passage of the River Wey allows the Pilgrims Way to cross the foot of the Downs. Dorking, Reigate & Farnham are small towns along this route, all with attracitve main streets & interesting shops & buildings.

Surrey has very little mention in the Domesday Book, &, although the patronage of the church & of wealthy families established manors which developed over the years, little happened to disturb the rural tranquility of the region. As a county it made little history but rather reflected passing times, although Magna Carta was signed at Egham in 1215.

The heathlands of Surrey were a Royal playground for centuries. The Norman Kings hunted here & horses became part of the landscape & life of the people, as they are today on Epsom Downs.

Nearness to London & Royal patronage began to influence the area, & the buildings of the Tudor period reflect this. Royal palaces were built at Hampton Court & Richmond, & great houses such as Loseley near Guildford often using stone from the monasteries emptied during the Reformation. Huge deer parks were enclosed & stocked. Richmond, described as the "finest village in the British Dominions", is now beset by 20th century traffic but still has a wonderful park with deer, lakes & woodland that was enclosed by Charles I. The terraces & gardens of such buildings as Trumpeters House & Asgill House on the slopes of Richmond overlooking the Thames, have an air of spaciousness & elegance & there are lovely & interesting riverside walks at Richmond.

Surrey

Surrey Gazeteer

Historic Houses & Castles

Albury Park - Albury, Nr. Guildford
A delightful country mansion designed by Pugin.

Clandon Park - Guildford
A fine house in the Palladian style by Leoni. A good collection of furniture & pictures. The house boasts some fine plasterwork.

Claremont - Esher
A superb Palladian house with interesting interior.

Detillens - Limpsfield
A fine 15th century house with inglenook fireplaces & mediaeval furniture. A large, pleasant garden.

Greathed Manor- Lingfield
An imposing Victorian manor house.

Hatchlands - East Clandon
A National Trust property of the 18th century with a fine Adam interior

Loseley House - Guildford
A very fine Elizabethan mansion with superb panelling, furniture & paintings.

Polesden Lacy - Dorking
A Regency villa housing the Grevill collection of tapestries, pictures & furnishings. Extensive gardens.

Cathedrals & Churches

Compton (St. Nicholas)
The only surviving 2-storey sanctuary in the country. A fine 17th century pulpit.

Esher (St. George)
A fine altar-piece & marble monument.

Hascombe (St. Peter)
A rich interior with much gilding & painted reredos & roofs.

Lingfield (St. Peter & St. Paul)
15th century. Holding a chained bible.

Ockham (St. Mary & All Saints)
Early church with 13th century east window.

Stoke D'Abernon (St. Mary)
Dating back to Pre-conquest time with additions from the 12th-15th centuries. A fine 13th century painting. Early brasses.

Museums & Galleries

Charterhouse School Museum - Godalming
Peruvian pottery, Greek pottery, archaeology & natural history.

Chertsey Museum - Chertsey
18th-19th century costume & furnishing displayed & local history.

Guildford House - Guildford
The house is 17th century & of architectural interest housing monthly exhibitions.

Guildford Museum - Guildford
A fine needlework collection & plenty on local history.

Old Kiln Agricultural - Tilford
A very interesting collection of old farm implements.

Watermill Museum - Haxted
A restored 17th century mill with working water wheels & machinery.

Weybridge Museum - Weybridge
Good archaeological exhibition plus costume & local history.

The Gardens. Wisley

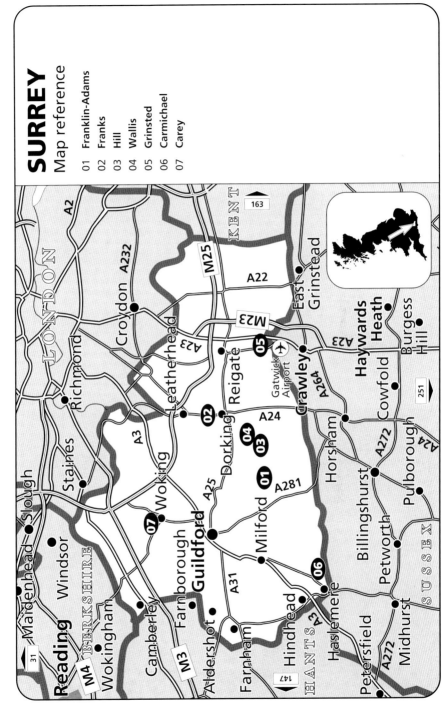

SURREY
Map reference

01 Franklin-Adams
02 Franks
03 Hill
04 Wallis
05 Grinsted
06 Carmichael
07 Carey

Surrey

High Edser

Near Rd: A.25

A large, handsome Grade II listed home, the earliest part built in the 16th century, situated in an Area of Outstanding Natural Beauty. There are three attractively furnished rooms available: two doubles and one twin. Residents' lounge and T.V.. Tennis court in grounds, and golf nearby. 35 minutes to Gatwick and London Airports. Approximately an hour's drive to London. High Edser is a delightful home, ideal for a relaxing break.
E-mail: beds@highedser.co.uk
www.highedser.co.uk

| £60.00 to £65.00 | Y | N | N |

Carol Franklin-Adams   High Edser   Shere Road   Ewhurst   Cranleigh GU6 7PQ   Surrey
Tel: (01483) 278214   Fax 01483 278200   Open: ALL YEAR   Map Ref No. 01

Denbies Wine Estate

Near Rd: A.24

Denbies is Britain's largest vineyard standing in 265 acres. The B & B is beautifully positioned within the vineyard & it is close to the Visitor Centre, where you can enjoy superb wine tours & lunches. 7 very comfortable double bedrooms with en-suite facilities, beverage tray & T.V. etc. (Single supplement.) The historic market town of Dorking is just a short drive or walk away & there is a vineyard train, which (weather-permitting) can take you up the North Downs Way.
E-mail: info@denbiesvineyard.co.uk
www.denbiesvineyard.co.uk

| £40.00 to £42.50 | Y | N | N |

VISA: M'CARD: AMEX:

Mike & Lynda Franks   Denbies Wine Estate   London Road   Dorking RH5 6AA   Surrey
Tel: (01306) 876777   Fax 01306 888930   Open: ALL YEAR   Map Ref No. 02

Bulmer Farm

Near Rd: A.25

Enjoy a warm welcome at this delightful 17th-century farmhouse, complete with many beams & an inglenook fireplace. Adjoining the house around a courtyard are 5 attractive barn-conversion en-suite bedrooms for non-smokers. Farm produce & home-made preserves are provided. Situated in a picturesque village, it is convenient for London airports. Children over 12 years welcome. Self-catering is also available. Brochure available on request. Dogs by arrangement.
www.bestbandb.co.uk

| £58.00 to £60.00 | Y | N | Y |

Gill Hill   Bulmer Farm   Pasturewood Road   Holmbury St. Mary   Dorking RH5 6LG   Surrey
Tel: (01306) 730210   Open: ALL YEAR   Map Ref No. 03

Park House Farm

Near Rd: A.25

A delightful large family home, tastefully furnished with many antiques. Accommodation is very comfortable with en-suite/private facilities, satellite T.V., tea/coffee-making facilities etc. It is set in 25 acres in an Area of Outstanding Natural Beauty within easy reach of Heathrow & Gatwick Airports, many gardens & National Trust properties. Good train service to London. Ideal walking country, with many village pubs for food. Children over 12.
E-mail: Peterwallis@msn.com
www.smoothhound.co.uk/hotels/parkhous

| £50.00 to £70.00 | Y | N | N |

VISA: M'CARD:

Ann & Peter Wallis   Park House Farm   Hollow Lane   Abinger Common   Dorking RH5 6LW   Surrey
Tel: (01306) 730101   Fax 01306 730643   Open: ALL YEAR   Map Ref No. 04

rate £ from - to per double room	children taken	evening meals	animals taken		

					The Lawn Guest House
£58.00 to £80.00	Y	N	Y	**Near Rd: A.23** A well-appointed Victorian house only 5 mins' from Gatwick Airport & 25 miles to London or Brighton. Very useful as a base for travelling, it is close to the rail station & town centre. There are 12 bedrooms, all with en-suite facilities & all very comfortable & well decorated, with T.V., hairdryer, 'phone & tea/coffee facilities, etc. A full English breakfast, or a healthy alternative including fruit, yoghurt & muesli, is served in the pleasant dining room. A garden for guests' use. Single supplement. Parking. **E-mail: info@lawnguesthouse.co.uk** **www.lawnguesthouse.co.uk**	

VISA: M'CARD: AMEX:

Carole & Adrian Grinsted   The Lawn Guest House   *30 Massetts Road   Horley   Gatwick RH6 7DF*
Tel: (01293) 775751   Fax 01293 821803   *Open: ALL YEAR   Map Ref No. 05*

					Deerfell
£50.00 to £55.00	Y	Y	Y	**Near Rd: A.286** A warm welcome at a spacious & comfortable stone-built home set in downland countryside, with breathtaking views to the hills & valleys of Surrey/Sussex. 3 pretty rooms with en-suite/private bathrooms, tea/coffee facilities & T.V.. Wonderful walks right on doorstep. Light suppers available on request. Close by - Lurgashall village, Haslemere (4 miles), London (45 mins'), Guildford/Chichester (20 miles), Heathrow/Gatwick Airports 1 hr. Children over 6. Dogs by arrangement. **E-mail: deerfell@tesco.net** **www.deerfell.co.uk**	

Elizabeth Carmichael   Deerfell   Blackdown Park   *Fernden Lane   Haslemere GU27 3BU   Surrey*
Tel: (01428) 653409   Fax 01428 656106   *Open: Mid Jan- Mid Dec   Map Ref No. 06*

					Swallow Barn
£45.00 to £90.00	Y	N	N	**Near Rd: A.3046** Situated in quiet, secluded surroundings on the edge of Chobham, attractively converted outbuildings & stables with outdoor swimming pool. 3 bedrooms with en-suite/private bathrooms, T.V. & tea/coffee. Ideal for Sunningdale, Wentworth & Foxhills golf courses. Also, Wisley & Savill Gardens within easy reach. Convenient for M.3, M.25, Heathrow Airport, Windsor, Ascot & Hampton Court. Woking station 2 miles - London 25 mins' by train. Single supplement. Children over 8. **E-mail: swallowbarn@web-hq.com** **www.swallow-barn.co.uk**	

Joan & David Carey   Swallow Barn   Milford Green   *Chobham   Woking GU24 8AU   Surrey*
Tel: (01276) 856030   Fax 01276 856030   *Open: ALL YEAR   Map Ref No. 07*

Visit our website at:
http://www.bestbandb.co.uk

Sussex

Sussex
(South East)

The South Downs of Sussex stretch along the coast, reflecting the expanse of the North Downs of Kent, over the vast stretches of the Weald.

The South Downs extend from dramatic Beachy Head along the coast to Chichester & like the North Downs, they are crossed by an ancient track-way. There is much evidence of pre-historic settlement on the Downs. Mount Caburn, near Lewes, is crowned by an iron age fort, & Cissbury Ring is one of the most important archaeological sites in England. This large earthwork covers 80 acres & must have held a strategic defensive position. Hollingbury Fort carved into the hillside above Brighton, & the Trundle (meaning circle) date from 300-250 B.C., & were constructed on an existing neolithic settlement. The Long Man of Wilmington stands 226 feet high & is believed to be Nordic, possibly representing Woden, the God of War.

Only two towns are located on the Downs but both are of considerable interest. Lewes retains much of its mediaeval past & there is a folk museum in Ann of Cleves' house, which itself is partly 16th century. Arundel has a fascinating mixture of architectural styles, a castle & a superb park with a lake, magnificent beech trees & an unrivalled view of the Arun valley.

The landscape of the inland Weald ranges from bracken-covered heathlands where deer roam, to the deep woodland stretches of the Ashdown Forest, eventually giving way to soft undulating hills & valleys, patterned with hop-fields, meadows, oast houses, windmills & fruit orchards. Originally the whole Weald was dense with forest. Villages like Midhurst & Wadhurst hold the Saxon suffix "hurst" which means wood. As the forests were cleared for agriculture the names of the villages changed & we find Bosham & Stedham whose suffix "ham" means homestead or farm.

Battle, above Hastings, is the site of the famous Norman victory & 16th century Bodiam Castle, built as defence against the French in later times, has a beautiful setting encircled by a lily-covered moat.

Sussex has an extensive coastline, with cliffs near Eastbourne at Beachy Head, & at Hastings. Further east, the great flat Romney Marshes stretch out to sea, & there is considerable variety in the coastal towns.

Chichester has a magnificent cathedral & a harbour reaching deep into the coastal plain that is rich in archaeological remains. The creeks & mudflats make it an excellent place for bird watching.

Brighton is the most famous of the Sussex resorts with its Pier, the Promenade above the beaches, the oriental folly of George IV's Royal Pavilion & its Regency architecture. "The Lanes" are a maze of alleys & small squares full of fascinating shops, a thriving antique trade, & many good pubs & eating places. Hastings to the east preserves its "Old Town" where timbered houses nestle beneath the cliffs & the fishing boats are drawn up on the shingle whilst the nets are hung up to dry in curious tall, thin net stores. Winchelsea stands on a hill where it was rebuilt in the 13th century by Edward I when the original town was engulfed by the sea. It is a beautiful town with a fine Norman church, an excellent museum in the Town Hall, & many pretty houses. Across the Romney Marshes on the next hill stands Rye, its profile dominated by its church. It is a fascinating town with timbered houses & cobbled streets.

Sussex

Sussex Gazeteer

Areas of Outstanding Natural Beauty
The Sussex Downs. Chichester Harbour.

Historic Houses & Castles

Arundel Castle - Arundel
18th century rebuilding of ancient castle, fine portraits, 15th century furniture.
Cuckfield Park - Cuckfield
Elizabethan manor house, gatehouse. Very fine panelling & ceilings.
Danny - Hurstpierpoint
16th century - Elizabethan .
Goodwood House - Chichester
18th century - Jacobean house - Fine Sussex flintwork, paintings by Van Dyck, Canaletto & Stubbs, English & French furniture, tapestries & porcelain.
Newtimber Place - Newtimber
Moated house - Etruscan style wall paintings.
Purham - Pulborough
Elizabethan house containing important collection of Elizabethan, Jacobean & Georgian portraits, also fine furniture.
Petworth House - Petworth
17th century - landscaped by Capability Brown - important paintings - 14th century chapel.
St. Mary's - Bramber
15th century timber framed house - rare panelling.
Tanyard - Sharpthorne
Mediaeval tannery - 16th & 17th century additions.
The Thatched Cottage - Lindfield
Close-studded weald house - reputedly Henry VII hunting lodge.
Uppark - Petersfield
17th century - 18th century interior decorations remain unaltered.
Alfriston Clergy House - Nr. Seaford
14th century parish priest's house - pre-reformation.
Battle Abbey - Battle
Founded by William the Conqueror.
Charleston Manor - Westdean
Norman, Tudor & Georgian architectural styles - Romanesque window in the Norman wing.
Bull House - Lewes
15th century half-timbered house - was home of Tom Paine.

Bateman's - Burwash
17th century - watermill - home of Rudyard Kipling.
Bodiam Castle - Nr. Hawkshurst
14th century - noted example of mediaeval moated military architecture.
Great Dixter - Northiam
15th century half-timbered manor house - great hall - Lutyens gardens
Glynde Place - Nr. Lewes
16th century flint & brick - built around courtyard-collection of paintings by Rubens, Hoppner, Kneller, Lely, Zoffany.
Michelham Priory - Upper Dicker, Nr. Hailsham
13th century Augustinian Priory - became Tudor farmhouse - working watermill, ancient stained glass, etc., enclosed by moat.
Royal Pavilion - Brighton
Built for Prince Regent by Nash upon classical villa by Holland. Exotic Building - has superb original works of art lent by H.M. The Queen. Collections of Regency furniture also Art Nouveau & Art Deco in the Art Gallery & Museum.
Sheffield Park - Nr. Uckfield
Beautiful Tudor House - 18th century alterations - splendid staircase.

Cathedrals & Churches

Alfriston (St. Andrew)
14th century - transition from decorated style to perpendicular, Easter sepulchre.
Boxgrove (St. Mary & St. Blaise)
13th century choir with 16th century painted decoration on vaulting. Relic of Benedictine priory. 16th century chantry. Much decoration.
Chichester Cathedral
Norman & earliest Gothic. Large Romanesque relief sculptures in south choir aisle.
Etchingham (St. Mary & St. Nicholas)
14th century. Old glass, brasses, screen, carved stalls.
Hardham (St. Botolph)
11th century - 12th century wall paintings.
Rotherfield (St. Denys)
16th century font cover, 17th century canopied pulpit, glass by Burne-Jones, wall paintings, Georgian Royal Arms.

Sussex

Sompting (St. Mary)
11th century Saxon tower - Rhenish Helm Spire - quite unique.
Worth (St. Nicholas)
10th century - chancel arch is the largest Saxon arch in England. German carved pulpit c.1500 together with altar rails.
Winchelsea (St. Thomas the Apostle)
14th century - choir & aisles only. Canopied sedilia & piscina.

Museums & Galleries

Barbican House Museum - Lewes
Collection relating to pre-historic, Romano-British & , mediaeval antiquities of the area. Prints & water colours of the area.
Battle Museum-Battle
Remains from archeological sites in area. Diorama of Battle of Hastings.
Bignor Roman Villa Collection - Bignor
4th century mosaics, Samian pottery, hypocaust, etc.
Brighton Museum & Art Gallery - Brighton
Old Master Paintings, watercolours, ceramics, furniture. Surrealist paintings, Art Nouveau & Art Deco applied art, musical instruments & many other exhibits.

Marlipins Museum - Shoreham
12th century building housing collections of ship models, photographs, old maps, geological specimens, etc.
Royal National Lifeboat Institution Museum - Eastbourne
Lifeboats of all types used from earliest times to present.
Tower 73 - Eastbourne
Martello tower restored to display the history of these forts. Exhibition of equipment, uniforms & weapons of the times.
The Toy Museum - Rottingdean, Brighton
Toys & playthings from many countries - children's delight.

Other things to see & do

Bewl Water - Nr. Wadhurst
Boat trips, walks, adventure playground
Chichester Festival Theatre - Chichester
Summer season of plays from May to September.
Goodwood Racecourse

The Royal Pavilion. Brighton.

SUSSEX

Map reference

01	Breeze	08	Kent
01	Fuente	09	Cox
02	Hansell	10	Skinner
03	Birchell	11	Walters
04	Waller	12	Costaras
04	Reeves	13	Brinkhurst
05	Gittoes	13	Hadfield
06	Johns	13	Kingsland
07	Hobcraft	14	Ramus

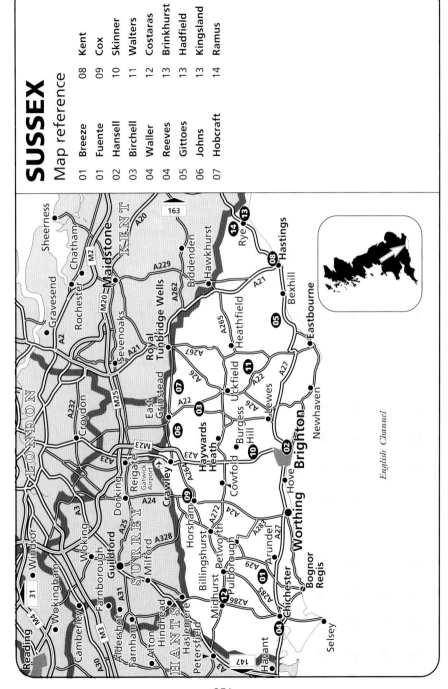

English Channel

251

Sussex

Avisford Cottage

Near Rd: A.27

Avisford Cottage is set in 1 acre of secluded wooded gardens just off the main A.27 coastal road, within 1 mile of historic Arundel, Chichester 5 miles. Goodwood & Fontwell racecourses are a few mins' away. Restaurants & country pubs within walking distance. The cottage backs onto Slindon Woods & in the morning the deer often graze on the lawn. Bedrooms are spacious, en-suite & well-appointed. Breakfast can be served (weather permitting) on the verandah overlooking the garden.
E-mail: breeze@avisfordcottage.fsnet.co.uk
http://avisfordbb.mysite.freeserve.com

£60.00 to £70.00	Y	N	Y

VISASHING M'CARDSHING AMEXSHING

Mrs Alexa Breeze   Avisford Cottage   Shellbridge Road   Slindon Common   Arundel   BN18 0LT   Sussex
Tel: (01243) 814429   Open: ALL YEAR   Map Ref No. 01

Mill Lane House

Near Rd: A.29

Partly 17th-century house in beautiful National Trust village of Slindon, backing onto South Downs, with large gardens & views from the 1st floor down to the coast (approx. 5 miles away.) All rooms en-suite, with tea-making, hairdryer, colour T.V./video & full English breakfasts served all year round. Excellent walking on the doorstep, with pubs & restaurants within short driving distance & many tourist attractions in the surrounding areas of Chichester, Goodwood, Bignor & Arundel.
E-mail: Jan.Fuente@btopenworld.com
www.Mill-Lane-House.co.uk

£60.00 to £75.00	Y	N	Y

Jan Fuente   Mill Lane House   Slindon   Arundel BN18 0RP   Sussex
Tel: (01243) 814440   Mobile 07909 923206   Open: ALL YEAR   Map Ref No. 01

Trouville Hotel

Near Rd: A.23

The Trouville is a Regency, Grade II listed townhouse, tastefully restored & furnished. Accommodation is in 8 attractive bedrooms, 6 are en-suite & each room has a colour T.V. & tea/coffee-making facilities. 4-poster rooms available. Situated in a charming sea-front square, the Trouville is convenient for shopping, the Pavilion, the Lanes, Marina & Conference Centre & the many restaurants which are all within walking distance.
www.bestbandb.co.uk

£65.00 to £85.00	Y	N	N

VISASHING M'CARDSHING AMEXSHING

John & Daphne Hansell   Trouville Hotel   11 New Steine   Brighton BN2 1PB   Sussex
Tel: (01273) 697384   Open: FEB - DEC   Map Ref No. 02

Holly House

Near Rd: A.275

Holly House, an early-Victorian forest farmhouse with character, offers a warm, friendly welcome to visitors. A 1-acre garden with long views. Situated in an Ashdown Forest village & ideal for touring Sussex, with many National Trust properties nearby. A comfortable lounge is available, & breakfast is taken in the conservatory overlooking the garden. The 5 pleasant rooms, 3 en-suite, have tea-making facilities & T.V.. A small swimming pool heated during the summer. Children over 12.
E-mail:db@hollyhousebnb.demon.co.uk
www.hollyhousebnb.demon.co.uk

£60.00 to £60.00	Y	Y	Y

Mrs D. Birchell   Holly House   Beaconsfield Road   Chelwood Gate RH17 7LF   Sussex
Tel: (01825) 740484   Fax 01825 740172   Open: ALL YEAR   Map Ref No. 03

Hatpins. Old Bosham.

	rate £ from - to per double room	children taken	evening meals	animals taken

Hatpins

Near Rd: A.259

Situated in the charming, picturesque harbour village of Old Bosham, 3 miles west of Chichester, & near to Goodwood House, H.M.S. Victory & the Mary Rose, this elegant property offers luxurious & inviting interior-designed decor & antiques, including a half-tester & Victorian brass beds. Suitable, & welcoming, for honeymoon couples. All rooms have private/en-suite bathrooms. Hatpins is a charming home.

E-mail: mary@hatpins.co.uk
www.hatpins.co.uk

£70.00 to £100.00 — N N N

see PHOTO over p. 253

Mrs Mary Waller   Hatpins   Bosham Lane   Old Bosham   Chichester   PO18 8HG   Sussex
Tel: (01243) 572644   Fax 01243 572644   Open: ALL YEAR   Map Ref No. 04

White Barn

Near Rd: A.259

White Barn is a unique open-plan, single-storey house on different levels in the beautiful Saxon harbour village of Bosham. 3 privately located en-suite rooms, each furnished with home-from-home comforts, including T.V. & tea/coffee facilities. Dinner, which is available from Oct to March, & breakfast is served in the dining area overlooking the garden. Ideal for visiting Chichester, the South Downs, beaches & marinas, Portsmouth & Goodwood. Gatwick Airport 1 hr. Children over 12.

E-mail: chrissie@whitebarn.biz
www.whitebarn.biz

£60.00 to £90.00 — Y Y N

VISA: M'CARD:

Christine Reeves   White Barn   Crede Lane   Bosham   Chichester   PO18 8NX   Sussex
Tel: (01243) 573113   Fax 01243 573113   Open: ALL YEAR   Map Ref No. 04

Wartling Place

Near Rd: A.27, A.271

Award-winning Georgian country house - Wartling exudes classic elegance with antique furniture & rich fabrics. Each bedroom proudly displays an identity all of its own, some on a grand scale, with magnificent 4-posters, others with a more intimate atmosphere. All are exceptionally comfortable with large en-suite bathrooms. Close to National Trust castles & gardens of Sussex & Kent. Private parking. Self-catering lodge cottage available. Evening meals by prior arrangement.

E-mail: accom@wartlingplace.prestel.co.uk
www.countryhouseaccommodation.co.uk

£95.00 to £135.00 — Y Y N

see PHOTO over p. 255

VISA: M'CARD: AMEX:

Barry & Rowena Gittoes   Wartling Place   Wartling   Herstmonceux   Eastbourne BN27 1RY
Tel: (01323) 832590   Fax 01323 831558   Open: ALL YEAR   Map Ref No. 05

Tiltwood House

Near Rd: A.264

The centre part of an elegant Victorian country house set in tranquil, semi-landscaped gardens. Luxurious, en-suite bedrooms, high ceilings with beautiful mouldings & cornices, king-size beds, T.V./videos etc. Full English breakfast, fresh fruits & more offer hearty sustenance for visiting N.T. gardens, Hickstead, South Downs, Glynbourne, Lingfield Racecourse, Brighton & London. Gatwick 7 miles, Heathrow 35 miles. Evening meals by arrangement. Children over 12.

E-mail: vjohnstiltwood@aol.com
www.tiltwood-bedandbreakfast.co.uk

£55.00 to £87.00 — Y Y N

Mrs Valerie Johns   Tiltwood House   Hophurst Lane   Crawley Down   Nr. Gatwick RH10 4LL
Tel: (01342) 712942   Open: ALL YEAR (Excl. Xmas)   Map Ref No. 06

Wartling Place. Wartling.

	rate £ from - to per double room	children taken	evening meals	animals taken

Bolebroke Watermill (Bolebroke Castle)

Near Rd: B.2026

A magical watermill, first recorded in 1086 A.D., & an Elizabethan miller's barn offer 5 en-suite rooms of genuine, unspoilt rustic charm, set amid woodland, water & pasture, & used as the idyllic setting for the film 'Carrington'. The mill is complete with machinery, trap doors & very steep stairs. The barn has low doors & beamed ceilings, & includes the honeymooners' hayloft with a 4-poster bed. Light supper trays are available, & award-winning breakfasts are served in the mill-house. Children over 8.
E-mail: bolebrokemill@btinternet.com
www.bolebrokemillhotel.co.uk

£79.00 to £99.00 — Y Y Y

see PHOTO over
p. 257

VISA: M'CARD: AMEX:

Peter Hobcraft   Bolebroke Watermill   (Bolebroke Castle)   Edenbridge Road   Hartfield TN7 4JJ
Tel: (01892) 770061   Fax 01892 771041   Open: ALL YEAR   Map Ref No. 07

Parkside House

Near Rd: A.21

Located in a quiet residential conservation area, & set in an elevated position opposite a beautiful park. This elegant Victorian house retains all its original features, but with every modern facility. High standards of hospitality, comfort & good home-cooking are provided, creating an informal, friendly & welcoming atmosphere. Bedrooms are en-suite & offer every luxury. The 'Apricot' room has an antique French bed. A quiet location only 15 mins' walk from the town centre & sea front.
E-mail: bkent.parksidehouse@talk21.com
www.bestbandb.co.uk

£50.00 to £65.00 — Y N N

VISA: M'CARD: AMEX:

Brian W. Kent   Parkside House   59 Lower Park Road   Hastings TN34 2LD   Sussex
Tel: (01424) 433096   Fax 01424 421431   Open: ALL YEAR   Map Ref No. 08

Glebe End

Near Rd: A.24

A fascinating medieval house, with a secluded, sunny, walled garden, set in the heart of Warnham. Retaining many original features, including heavy flagstones, curving ships' timbers & an inglenook fireplace. En-suite single, twin & double rooms are charmingly furnished with antiques & paintings. 1, with its own staircase, has an adjoining bedroom making it an ideal family suite. All rooms with T.V. Breakfasts are delicious. 2 Inns within 5 mins' walk. 5 well-known National Trust houses & famous gardens 30 mins' drive. Gatwick 20 mins .
E-mail: coxeswarnham@aol.com

£50.00 to £54.00 — Y N Y

Liz & Chris Cox   Glebe End   Church Street   Warnham   Nr. Horsham RH12 3QW   Sussex
Tel: (01403) 261711   Fax 01403 257572   Open: ALL YEAR   Map Ref No. 09

Clayton Wickham Farmhouse

Near Rd: A.23

A delightful, secluded 14th-century farmhouse with lovely views, set amidst the beautiful Sussex countryside. The friendly hosts have refurbished their home to a high standard, yet have retained many original features, hence there are a wealth of beams & a huge inglenook fireplace in the drawing room. A variety of tastefully furnished & well-appointed bedrooms, including a super 4-poster en-suite. 4-course candlelit dinner by arrangement. Tennis court. Animals by arrangement.
E-mail: susie@cwfbandb.co.uk
www.cwfbandb.co.uk

£75.00 to £90.00 — Y Y Y

Mike & Susie Skinner   Clayton Wickham Farmhouse   Belmont Lane   Hurstpierpoint BN6 9EP
Tel: (01273) 845698   Fax 01273 841970   Open: ALL YEAR   Map Ref No. 10

Bolebroke Watermill.   Hartfield.

Jeake's House.   Rye.

Sussex

| £65.00 to £80.00 | Y | N | N | **Shortgate Manor Farm** |

Near Rd: A.22

Shortgate Manor Farm is an enchanting 18th-century farmhouse set in 8 acres approached by an avenue of poplars festooned with rambling roses. The 3 charming bedrooms all offer en-suite/private facilities, T.V.'s, courtesy trays, with bathrobes provided for your comfort. The house is surrounded by 2 acres of landscaped gardens which are open under the National Gardens Scheme every June. Glyndebourne 4 miles. A charming home from which to explore Sussex. Children over 10.
E-mail: david@shortgate.co.uk
www.shortgate.co.uk

see PHOTO over
p. 260

| *David & Ethel Walters* | *Shortgate Manor Farm* | *Halland* | *Lewes BN8 6PJ* | *Sussex* |
| Tel: *(01825) 840320* | Fax *01825 840320* | *Open: ALL YEAR* | *Map Ref No. 11* |

| £65.00 to £80.00 | N | N | N | **Amberfold** |

Near Rd: A.286

Amberfold is a charming 17th-century listed cottage, situated in quiet, idyllic countryside yet only 5 mins' drive from Midhurst. 2 private self-contained annexes with access all day. 1 is situated on the ground floor. Each annex is comfortably furnished & has private facilities, T.V., clock/radio, etc. To allow you complete freedom & privacy, a large Continental breakfast is self-service & is taken in your room. An ideal base for exploring Goodwood, Singleton, Chichester & the coast.
E-mail: a.costaras@yahoo.com
www.amberfold.com

| *Annabelle & Alex Costaras* | *Amberfold* | *Heyshott* | *Midhurst GU29 0DA* | *Sussex* |
| Tel: *(01730) 812385* | Fax *01730 812842* | *Open: ALL YEAR* | *Map Ref No. 12* |

| £80.00 to £100.00 | N | N | N | **Little Orchard House** |

Near Rd: A.259

This charming Georgian townhouse, with traditional walled garden & Smuggler's Watchtower, is at the heart of ancient Rye. A perfect touring base, it retains many original features. Open fires, antique furnishings & books ensure a peaceful, relaxed atmosphere. Generous country breakfasts feature organic & free-range local products. The 2 lovely en-suite bedrooms have 4-poster beds & include T.V., VCR, fridge & hot-drinks tray.
E-mail: info@littleorchardhouse.com
www.littleorchardhouse.com

VISA: M'CARD:

| *Sara Brinkhurst* | *Little Orchard House* | *3 West Street* | *Rye TN31 7ES* | *Sussex* |
| Tel/Fax: *(01797) 223831* | Mobile *07790 363950* | *Open: ALL YEAR* | *Map Ref No. 13* |

| £39.00 to £120.00 | Y | N | Y | **Jeake's House Hotel** |

Near Rd: A.259

Jeakes House is an outstanding 17th-century Grade II listed building. Retaining original features, including oak beams & wood panelling, & decorated throughout with antiques. 11 bedrooms overlook the gardens, with en-suite/private facilities, T.V. etc. 4-poster available. Dine in the galleried former Baptist chapel, where a choice of full English, wholefood vegetarian or Continental breakfast is served. Located in one of Britain's most picturesque medieval streets. Parking. Children over 12.
E-mail: stay@jeakeshouse.com
www.jeakeshouse.com

see PHOTO over
p. 258

VISA: M'CARD:

| *Mrs Jennifer Hadfield* | *Jeake's House Hotel* | *Mermaid Street* | *Rye TN31 7ET* | *Sussex* |
| Tel: *(01797) 222828* | Fax *01797 222623* | *Open: ALL YEAR* | *Map Ref No. 13* |

Shortgate Manor Farm.   Halland.

Sussex

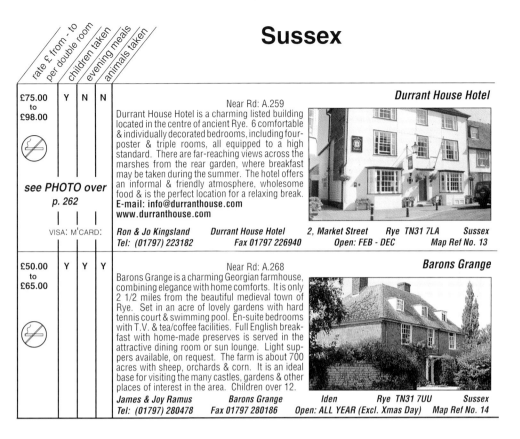

rate £ - from - to per double room	children taken	evening meals	animals taken		
£75.00 to £98.00	Y	N	N	Near Rd: A.259 Durrant House Hotel is a charming listed building located in the centre of ancient Rye. 6 comfortable & individually decorated bedrooms, including four-poster & triple rooms, all equipped to a high standard. There are far-reaching views across the marshes from the rear garden, where breakfast may be taken during the summer. The hotel offers an informal & friendly atmosphere, wholesome food & is the perfect location for a relaxing break. E-mail: info@durranthouse.com www.durranthouse.com	**Durrant House Hotel**

see PHOTO over p. 262

VISA: M'CARD:

Ron & Jo Kingsland	Durrant House Hotel	2, Market Street	Rye TN31 7LA	Sussex
Tel: (01797) 223182	Fax 01797 226940	Open: FEB - DEC		Map Ref No. 13

| £50.00 to £65.00 | Y | Y | Y | Near Rd: A.268 Barons Grange is a charming Georgian farmhouse, combining elegance with home comforts. It is only 2 1/2 miles from the beautiful medieval town of Rye. Set in an acre of lovely gardens with hard tennis court & swimming pool. En-suite bedrooms with T.V. & tea/coffee facilities. Full English breakfast with home-made preserves is served in the attractive dining room or sun lounge. Light suppers available, on request. The farm is about 700 acres with sheep, orchards & corn. It is an ideal base for visiting the many castles, gardens & other places of interest in the area. Children over 12. | **Barons Grange** |

James & Joy Ramus	Barons Grange	Iden	Rye TN31 7UU	Sussex
Tel: (01797) 280478	Fax 01797 280186	Open: ALL YEAR (Excl. Xmas Day)		Map Ref No. 14

All the establishments mentioned in this guide are members of
The Worldwide Bed & Breakfast Association

When booking your accommodation please mention
The Best Bed & Breakfast

Durrant House Hotel.   Rye.

Warwickshire

Warwickshire
(Heart of England)

Warwickshire contains much that is thought of as traditional rural England, but it is a county of contradictions. Rural tranquillity surrounds industrial towns, working canals run along with meandering rivers, the mediaeval splendour of Warwick Castle vies with the handsome Regency grace of Leamington Spa.

Of course, Warwickshire is Shakespeare's county, with his birthplace, Stratford-upon-Avon standing at the northern edge of the Cotswolds. You can visit any of half a dozen houses with Shakespearian associations, see his tomb in the lovely Parish church or enjoy a performance by the world famous Royal Shakespeare Company in their theatre on the banks of the River Avon.

Warwickshire was created as the Kingdom of Mercia after the departure of the Romans. King Offa of Mercia left us his own particular mark - a coin which bore the imprint of his likeness known as his "pen" & this became our penny. Lady Godiva was the wife of an Earl of Mercia who pleaded with her husband to lessen the taxation burden on his people. He challenged her to ride naked through the streets of Coventry as the price of her request. She did this knowing that her long hair would cover her nakedness, & the people, who loved her, stayed indoors out of respect. Only Peeping Tom found the temptation irresistible.

The 15th, 16th, & 17th centuries were the heyday of fine building in the county, when many gracious homes were built. Exceptional Compton Wynyates has rosy pink bricks, twisted chimney stacks, battlements & moats & presents an unforgettably romantic picture of a perfect Tudor House.

Coventry has long enjoyed the reputation of a thriving city, noted for its weaving of silks and ribbons, learned from the refugee Huguenots. When progress brought industry, watches, bicycles & cars became the mainstay of the city. Coventry suffered grievously from aerial bombardment in the war & innumerable ancient & treasured buildings were lost.

A magnificent new Cathedral stands besides the shell of the old. Mystery plays enacting the life of Christ are performed in the haunting ruin.

Warwick Castle.

Warwickshire

Warwickshire

Gazeteer

Areas of Outstanding Natural Beauty
The Edge Hills

Historic Houses & Castles

Arbury Hall - Nuneaton
18th century Gothic mansion - made famous by George Elliot as Cheverel Manor - paintings, period furnishings, etc.

Compton Wynyates
15th century - famous Tudor house - pink brick, twisted chimneys, battlemented walls. Interior almost untouched - period furnishing.

Coughton Court - Alcester
15th century - Elizabethan half-timbered wings. Holds Jacobite relics.

Harvard House - Stratford-upon-Avon
16th century - home of mother of John Harvard, University founder.

Homington Hall - Shipston-on-Stour
17th century with fine 18th century plasterwork.

Packwood House - Hockley Heath
Tudor timber framed house - with 17th century additions. Famous yew garden.

Ragley Hall - Alcester
17th century Palladian - magnificent house with fine collection of porcelain, paintings, furniture, etc. & a valuable library.

Shakespeare's Birthplace Trust Properties - Stratford-upon-Avon

Anne Hathaway's Cottage - Shottery
The thatched cottage home of Anne Hathaway.

Hall's Croft - Old Town
Tudor house where Shakespeare's daughter Susanna lived.

Mary Arden's House - Wilmcote
Tudor farmhouse with dovecote. Home of Shakespeare's mother.

New Place - Chapel Street
Shakespeare's last home - the foundations of his house are preserved in Elizabethan garden.

Birthplace of Shakespeare - Henley Street
Many rare Shakespeare relics exhibited in this half-timbered house.

Lord Leycester Hospital - Warwick
16th century timber framed group around courtyard - hospital for poor persons in the mediaeval guilds.

Upton House - Edge Hill
Dating from James II reign - contains Brussels tapestries, Sevres porcelain, Chelsea figurines, 18th century furniture & other works of art, including Old Masters.

Warwick Castle - Warwick
Splendid mediaeval castle - site was originally fortified more than a thousand years ago. Present castle 14th century. Armoury.

Cathedrals & Churches

Astley (St. Mary the Virgin)
17th century - has remains of 14th century collegiate church. 15th century painted stalls.

Beaudesert (St. Nicholas)
Norman with fine arches in chancel.

Brailes (St. George)
15th century - decorated nave & aisles - 14th century carved oak chest.

Crompton Wynyates
Church of Restoration period having painted ceiling.

Lapworth (St. Mary)
13th & 14th century - steeple & north aisle connected by passage.

Preston-on-Stour (The Blessed Virgin Mary)
18th century. Gilded ceiling, 17th century glass

Tredington (St. Gregory)
Saxon walls in nave - largely14th century, 17th century pulpit. Fine spire.

Warwick (St. Mary)
15th century Beauchamp Chapel, vaulted choir, some 17th century Gothic.

Wooten Wawen (St. Peter)
Saxon, with remnants of mediaeval wall painting, 15th century screens & pulpit: small 17th century chained library.

Museums & Galleries

The Royal Shakespeare Theatre Picture Gallery - Stratford-upon-Avon
Original designs & paintings, portraits of famous actors, etc.

Motor Museum - Stratford-upon-Avon
Collection of cars, racing, vintage, exotic, replica of 1930 garage. Fashions, etc. of 1920's era.

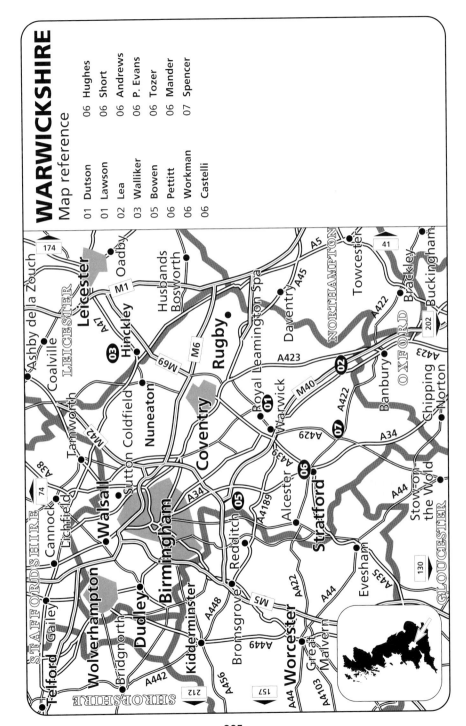

WARWICKSHIRE
Map reference

01	Dutson	06	Hughes
01	Lawson	06	Short
02	Lea	06	Andrews
03	Walliker	06	P. Evans
05	Bowen	06	Tozer
06	Pettitt	06	Mander
06	Workman	07	Spencer
06	Castelli		

	rate £ from – to per double room	children taken	evening meals	animals taken

8 Clarendon Crescent

Near Rd: A.452

A Grade II listed Regency house overlooking a private dell. Situated in a quiet backwater of Leamington. Elegantly furnished with antiques, & offering accommodation in 5 tastefully furnished bedrooms, 4 en-suite. A delicious full English breakfast is served. Only 5 mins' walk from the town centre. Very convenient for Warwick, Stratford, Stoneleigh Agricultural Centre, Warwick University & the N.E.C.. Children over 4 years welcome. Animals by arrangement.
E-mail: lawson@lawson71.fsnet.co.uk

£70.00 to £70.00 — Y — N — N

🚭 🐾

see PHOTO over p. 267

Christine Lawson   8 Clarendon Crescent   Leamington Spa CV32 5NR   Warwickshire
Tel: (01926) 429840   Fax 01926 424641   Open: ALL YEAR   Map Ref No. 01

Crandon House

Near Rd: B.4100

This lovely farmhouse is set in 20 acres of unspoilt countryside. Your hosts offer a warm welcome & an exceptionally high standard of comfort & service. 5 bedrooms (1 ground-floor) all with en-suite/private bathroom & much more. Freshly prepared breakfasts from an extensive menu. A tranquil retreat, within easy reach of Warwick, Stratford, Oxford & the Cotswolds. Good places to eat just 5 mins drive. Located between the M.40 Jts 11 & 12. Children over 8. Single rate from £40.00.
E-mail: crandonhouse@talk21.com
www.crandonhouse.co.uk

£48.00 to £64.00 — Y — N — N

🚭

VISA: M'CARD:

Deborah Lea   Crandon House   Dassett Road   Avon Dassett   Nr. Leamington Spa CV47 2AA
Tel: (01295) 770652   Fax 01295 770632   Open: ALL YEAR (Excl. Xmas)   Map Ref No. 02

Ambion Court Hotel

Near Rd: A.5

Charming, modernised Victorian farmhouse overlooking Dadlington's village green in rolling countryside near Ashby Canal. Rustic character, warm hospitality & exceptional tranquillity abound. All 7 rooms have bathroom, T.V., phone etc; the king-sized Pine Room is particularly imposing. Relax in the comfortable lounge & cocktail bar, savour the excellent cuisine, or amble to good pubs nearby. Well-placed for Coventry, Warwick, Stratford, motorways & airports. Restricted smoking areas.
E-mail: stay@ambionhotel.co.uk
www.ambionhotel.co.uk

£65.00 to £75.00 — Y — Y — N

VISA: M'CARD:

John & Wendy Walliker   Ambion Court Hotel   The Green   Dadlington   Nuneaton CV13 5JB
Tel: (01455) 212292   Fax 01455 213141   Open: ALL YEAR   Map Ref No. 03

Grange Farm B & B

Near Rd: A.435

A warm welcome awaits you at this peaceful 17th-century farmhouse, set in 200 acres of beautiful countryside with footpaths & wildlife pools. Grange Farm has sloping floors, oak beams & log fires. There are 3 very attractive en-suite bedrooms with colour T.V., tea/coffee-making facilities, clock/radio alarms & hairdryers. The house is centrally located for easy access to the NEC, NAC, Stratford-upon-Avon, the Cotswolds, Warwick & Worcester. Children over 4. Evening meals by arrangement.
www.grange-farm.com

£60.00 to £70.00 — Y — Y — N

🚭

Christine Bowen   Grange Farm B & B   Forde Hall Lane   Tanworth-in-Arden   Solihull B94 5AX
Tel: (01564) 742911   Open: ALL YEAR   Map Ref No. 05

8 Clarendon Crescent. Leamington Spa.

Sequoia House. Stratford-upon-Avon.

rate £ from - to per double room | children taken | evening meals | animals taken

---

| £55.00 to £55.00 | Y | N | Y |

(no smoking)

VISA: M'CARD:

Parkfield

Near Rd: B.435

A delightful Victorian house, in a quiet location in Old Town just 5 mins' walk to the town centre & the Royal Shakespeare Theatre. Ideally situated for touring the Cotswolds, Warwick Castle, etc.. 7 spacious & comfortable rooms, all en-suite with colour T.V. & tea/coffee-making facilities. Excellent breakfasts. Private parking. Lots of tourist information available. Guests can be collected from the station. Children over 12 yrs.
E-mail: Parkfield@btinternet.com
www.ParkfieldBandB.co.uk

Roger & Joanna Pettitt Parkfield 3 Broad Walk Stratford-upon-Avon CV37 6HS Warwickshire
Tel: (01789) 293313 Fax 01789 293313 Open: ALL YEAR Map Ref No. 06

| £48.00 to £54.00 | Y | N | N |

(no smoking)

VISA: M'CARD:

Ravenhurst

Near Rd: A.4390

A Victorian town house with a warm & friendly atmosphere. Ideally situated on the edge of the old town & only a few mins' walk from the Shakespeare Theatre, town centre & places of historical interest. Enjoy the comfort & quiet of this family-run guest house, where all bedrooms have colour T.V. & tea/coffee-making facilities. Special double en-suite rooms available with 4-poster beds. The Workmans are Stratfordians, therefore local knowledge is a speciality. Children over 5.
E-mail: ravaccom@waverider.co.uk
www.stratford-ravenhurst.co.uk

Richard Workman Ravenhurst 2 Broad Walk Stratford-upon-Avon CV37 6HS Warwickshire
Tel: (01789) 292515 Fax 01789 292515 Open: ALL YEAR Map Ref No. 06

| £60.00 to £89.00 | Y | N | Y |

(no smoking)

see PHOTO over p. 270

VISA: M'CARD: AMEX:

Melita Private Hotel

Near Rd: A.3400

An extremely friendly family-run hotel. Offering pleasant service, good food & accommodation in 12 excellent bedrooms, with en-suite/private facilities, T.V., tea/coffee & 'phones. A comfortable lounge/bar & a beautiful garden for guests to relax in. A pleasant 5-min. walk to Shakespearian properties/theatres, shopping centre & riverside gardens. Superbly situated for Warwick Castle, Coventry & the Cotswolds. On-site private car park.
E-mail: info@melitahotel.co.uk
www.melitahotel.co.uk

Patricia Andrews Melita Private Hotel 37 Shipston Road Stratford-upon-Avon CV37 7LN
Tel: (01789) 292432 Fax 01789 204867 Open: ALL YEAR (Excl. Xmas & New Year) Map Ref No. 06

| £69.00 to £89.00 | Y | N | N |

(no smoking)

see PHOTO over p. 268

VISA: M'CARD:

Sequoia House Hotel

Near Rd: A.3400

A beautifully appointed private hotel situated across the River Avon from the Royal Shakespeare Theatre. 23 bedrooms (all en-suite), a cocktail bar, a cottage annex & a fully air-conditioned dining room. The hotel is comfortably furnished, & decorated in a warm & restful style, with many extra thoughtful touches. The garden overlooks the town cricket ground & the old tramway. Pleasant walks along the banks of the River Avon opposite the Theatre & Holy Trinity Church. Children over 5.
E-mail: info@sequoiahotel.co.uk
www.sequoiahotel.co.uk

Philip & Jean Evans Sequoia House Hotel 51 Shipston Road Stratford-upon-Avon CV37 7LN
Tel: (01789) 268852 Fax 01789 414559 Open: ALL YEAR Map Ref No. 06

Melita Hotel. Stratford-upon-Avon.

Victoria Spa Lodge. Stratford-upon-Avon.

	rate £ from - to per double room	evening meals children taken	animals taken

Minola House

Near Rd: A.439

A comfortable house with a relaxed atmosphere, offering good accommodation in 5 pleasantly furnished bedrooms, 1 with private shower, 3 ensuite; all have T.V. & tea/coffee-making facilities. Stratford offers a myriad of delights for the visitor, including the Royal Shakespeare Theatre. Set by the River Avon, this makes a lovely place for a picnic lunch or early evening meal before the performance. Children over 10. Italian & French spoken.
www.bestbandb.co.uk

£54.00 to £60.00 — Y | N | N

Danielle Castelli   Minola House   25 Evesham Place   Stratford-upon-Avon CV37 6HT   Warwickshire
Tel: (01789) 293573   Fax 01789 551525   Open: ALL YEAR (Excl. Xmas)   Map Ref No. 06

Stretton House

Near Rd: A.4390

Stretton House is a 'home from home' where a warm & friendly welcome awaits you. Very comfortable accommodation at reasonable prices. Pretty, full en-suite bedrooms & standard rooms, all having T.V. & tea/coffee-making facilities. Excellent full English breakfast, vegetarians catered for. Limited car parking. Situated opposite lovely Fir Park, within easy reach of the country, yet only 3 mins' walk from the town centre. Children over 5.
E-mail: shortpbshort@aol.com
www.strettonhouse.co.uk

£60.00 to £60.00 — Y | N | N

Paul & Beverley Short   Stretton House   38 Grove Road   Stratford-upon-Avon CV37 6PB
Tel: (01789) 268647   Fax 01789 268647   Open: ALL YEAR   Map Ref No. 06

Fulready Manor

Near Rd: A.422

Michael & Mauveen Spencer invite you to experience their unique home, Fulready Manor, set in 120 acres overlooking its own lake, in the beautiful south Warwickshire countryside. It is on the doorstep of the Cotswolds. Stratford-upon-Avon is only 7 miles. Fulready Manor boasts sumptuously furnished, individually designed 4-poster bedrooms, all with dramatic views & en-suite bathrooms. All of the rooms have been skilfully created by an interior designer. Children over 12.
E-mail: stay@fulreadymanor.co.uk
www.fulreadymanor.co.uk

£95.00 to £140.00 — Y | N | N

see PHOTO over p. 273

Michael & Mauveen Spencer   Fulready Manor   Ettington   Stratford-upon-Avon CV37 7PE
Tel: (01789) 740152   Fax 01789 740247   Open: ALL YEAR   Map Ref No. 07

Victoria Spa Lodge

Near Rd: A.3400

Large 19th-century house overlooking Stratford canal, with ample parking. A royal coat of arms was built into the gables (with the permission of Queen Victoria) of this Grade II listed building. 7 attractive & comfortable en-suite bedrooms, each having a hostess tray, T.V., radio/alarm & hairdryer. 1 mile from the centre of town. Victoria Spa Lodge is an excellent base for the Cotswolds & Shakespearian properties. Pleasant walks along the tow path to Stratford & Wilmcote. Single supplement.
E-mail: ptozer@victoriaspalodge.demon.co.uk
www.stratford-upon-avon.co.uk/victoriaspa.htm

£65.00 to £65.00 — Y | N | N

see PHOTO over p. 271

VISA: M'CARD:

Paul & Dreen Tozer   Victoria Spa Lodge   Bishopton Lane   Bishopton   Stratford-upon-Avon CV37 9QY
Tel: (01789) 267985   Fax 01789 204728   Open: ALL YEAR   Map Ref No. 06

Fulready Manor. Ettington.

Wiltshire

Wiltshire
(West Country)

Wiltshire is a county of rolling chalk downs, small towns, delightful villages, fine churches & great country houses. The expanse of Salisbury Plain is divided by the beautiful valleys of Nadder, Wylye, Ebble & Avon. In a county of open landscapes, Savernake Forest, with its stately avenues of trees strikes a note of contrast. In the north west the Cotswolds spill over into Wiltshire from neighbouring Gloucestershire.

No other county is so rich in archaeological sites. Long barrows and ancient hill forts stand on the skylines as evidence of the early habitation of the chalk uplands. Many of these prehistoric sites are at once magnificent and mysterious. The massive stone arches and monoliths of Stonehenge were built over a period of 500 years with stones transported over great distances. At Avebury the small village is completely encircled by standing stones and a massive bank and ditch earthwork. Silbury Hill is a huge, enigmatic man-made mound. England's largest chambered tomb is West Kennet Long Barrow and at Bush Barrow, finds have included fine bronze and gold daggers and a stone sceptre-head similar to one found at Mycenae in Greece.

Some of England's greatest historic houses are in Wiltshire. Longleat is an Elizabethan mansion with priceless collections of paintings, books & furniture. The surrounding park was landscaped by Capability Brown and its great fame in recent years has been its Safari Park, particularly the lions which roam freely around the visiting cars. Stourhead has celebrated 18th century landscaped gardens which are exceptional in spring when rhododendrons bloom.

Two delightful villages are Castle Combe, nestling in a Cotswold valley, & Lacock where the twisting streets hold examples of buildings ranging from mediaeval half-timbered, to Tudor & Georgian. 13th century Lacock Abbey, converted to a house in the 16th century, was the home of Fox Talbot, pioneer of photography.

There are many notable churches in Wiltshire. In Bradford-on-Avon, a fascinating old town, is the church of St. Lawrence, a rare example of an almost perfect Saxon church from around 900. Farley has an unusual brick church thought to have been designed by Sir Christopher Wren, & there is stained glass by William Morris in the church at Rodbourne.

Devizes Castle

Salisbury stands where three rivers join, on a plain of luxuriant water-meadows, where the focal point of the landscape is the soaring spire of the Cathedral; at 404 feet, it is the tallest in England. The 13th century cathedral has a marvellous & rare visual unity. The body of the building was completed in just 38 years, although the spire was added in the next century. Salisbury, or "New Sarum" was founded in 1220 when the Bishop abandoned the original cathedral at Old Sarum, to start the present edifice two miles to the south. At Old Sarum you can see the foundation of the old city including the outline of the first cathedral.

Wiltshire

Wiltshire Gazeteer

Area of Outstanding Natural Beauty
The Costwolds & the North Wessex Downs.

Historic Houses & Castles

Corsham Court - Chippenham
16th & 17th centuries from Elizabethan & Georgian periods. 18th century furniture, British, Flemish & Italian Old Masters. Gardens by Capability Brown.

Great Chalfield Manor - Melksham
15th century manor house - moated.

Church House - Salisbury
15th century house.

Chalcot House - Westbury
17th century small house in Palladian manner.

Lacock Abbey - Nr. Chippenham
13th century abbey. In 1540 converted into house - 18th century alterations. Mediaeval cloisters & brewery.

Longleat House - Warminster
16th century - early Renaissance, alterations in early 1800's. Italian Renaissance decorations. Splendid state rooms, pictures, books, furniture. Victorian kitchens. Game reserve.

Littlecote - Nr. Hungerford
15th century Tudor manor. Panelled rooms, moulded plaster ceilings.

Luckington Court - Luckington
Queen Anne for the most part - fine ancient buildings.

Malmesbury House - Salisbury
Queen Anne house - part 14th century. Rococo plasterwork.

Newhouse - Redlynch
17th century brick Jacobean trinity house - two Georgian wings,

Philips House - Dinton
1816 Classical house.

Sheldon Manor - Chippenham
13th century porch & 15th century chapel in this Plantagenet manor.

Stourhead - Stourton
18th century Palladian house with framed landscape gardens.

Westwood Manor - Bradford-on-Avon
15th century manor house - alterations in 16th & 17th centuries.

Wardour Castle - Tisbury
18th century house in Palladian manner.

Wilton House - Salisbury
17th century - work of Inigo Jones & later of James Wyatt in 1810. Paintings, Kent & Chippendale furniture.

Avebury Manor - Nr Malborough
Elizabethan manor house - beautiful plasterwork, panelling & furniture. Gardens with topiary.

Bowood - Calne
18th century - work of several famous architects. Gardens by Capability Brown - famous beechwoods.

Mompesson House - Salisbury
Queen Anne town house - Georgian plasterwork.

Cathedrals & Churches

Salisbury Cathedral
13th century - decorated tower with stone spire. Part of original stone pulpitum is preserved. Beautiful large decorated cloister. Exterior mostly early English.

Salisbury (St. Thomas of Canterbury)
15th century rebuilding - 12th century font, 14th & 15th century glass, 17th century monuments. 'Doom' painting over chancel & murals in south chapel

Amesbury (St. Mary & St. Melor)
13th century - refashioned 15th & restored in 19th century. Splendid timber roofs, stone vaulting over chapel of north transept, mediaeval painted glass, 15th century screen, Norman font.

Bishops Cannings (St. Mary the Virgin)
13th-15th centuries. Fine arcading in transept - fine porch doorway. 17th century almsbox, Jacobean Holy table.

Bradford-on-Avon (St. Lawrence)
Best known of all Saxon churches in England.

Cricklade (St. Sampson)
12th -16th century. Tudor central tower vault, 15th century chapel.

Inglesham (St. John the Baptist)
Mediaeval wall paintings, high pews, clear glass, remains of painted screens.

Malmesbury (St. Mary)
Norman - 12th century arcades, refashioning in 14th century with clerestory, 15th century stone pulpitum added. Fine sculpture.

Wiltshire

Tisbury (St. John the Baptist)
14th-15th centuries. 15th-17th century roofing to nave & aisles. Two storeyed porch & chancel.
Potterne (St. Mary)
13th,14th,15th centuries. Inscribed Norman tub font. Wooden pulpit.

Museums & Galleries

Salisbury & South Wiltshire Museum - Salisbury
Collections showing history of the area in all periods. Models of Stonehenge & Old Sarum - archaeologically important collection.
Devizes Museum - Devizes
Unique archaeological & geological collections, including Sir Richard Colt-Hoare's Stourhead collection of prehistoric material.
Alexander Keiller Museum - Avebury
Collection of items from the Neolithic & Bronze ages & from excavations in district.
Athelstan Museum - Malmesbury
Collection of articles referring to the town - household, coin, etc.
Bedwyn Stone Museum - Great Bedwyn
Open-air museum showing where Stonehenge was carved.
Lydiard Park - Lydiard Tregoze
Parish church of St. Mary & a splendid Georgian mansion standing in park & also permanent & travelling exhibitions.

Borough of Thamesdown Museum & Art Gallery - Swindon
Natural History & Geology of Wiltshire, Bygones, coins, etc. 20th century British art & ceramic collection.
Great Western Railway Museum - Swindon
Historic locomotives.

Historic Monuments

Stonehenge - Nr. Amesbury
Prehistoric monument - encircling bank & ditch & Augrey holes are Neolithic. Stone circles possibly early Bronze age.
Avebury
Relics of enormous circular gathering place B.C. 2700-1700.
Old Sarum - Nr. Salisbury
Possibly first Iron Age camp, later Roman area, then Norman castle.
Silbury Hill - Nr. Avebury
Mound - conical in shape - probably a memorial c.3000-2000 B.C.
Windmill Hill - Nr. Avebury
Causewayed camp c.3000-2300 B.C.
Bratton Camp & White Horse - Bratton
Hill fort standing above White Horse.
West Kennet Long Barrow
Burial place c.4000-2500 B.C.
Ludgershall Castle - Lugershall
Motte & bailey of Norman castle, earthworks, also flint walling from later castle.

Castle Combe.

WILTSHIRE
Map reference

01	Roberts	10	Green
02	Denning	12	Robathan
03	Sexton	13	Sykes
05	Stafford	14	Mertens
06	Daniel	15	Fergie-Woods
07	Read	16	Hocken
08	Eavis		

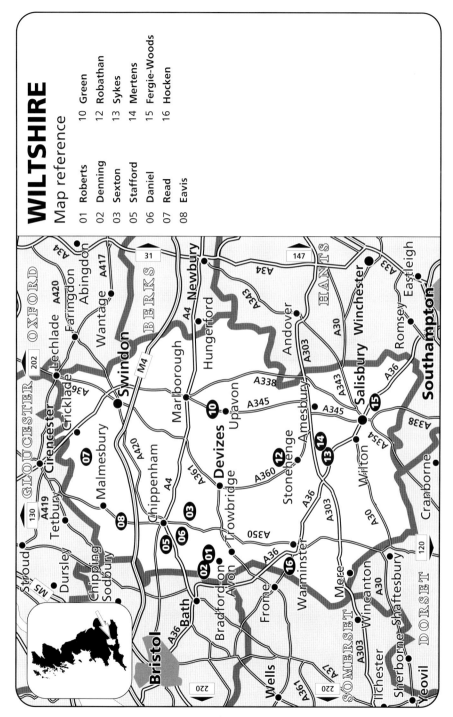

	rate £ from - to per double room	children taken	evening meals	animals taken

Bradford Old Windmill

Near Rd: A.363

£65.00 to £109.00 — Y Y N

A cosy, relaxed atmosphere greets you at this converted windmill high on the hill above the town. The old stone tower overflows with character, & with the many finds picked up by Peter & Priscilla on their backpacking trips around the world. All of the unusually shaped bedrooms have en-suite bathrooms. Imaginative healthy & unhealthy breakfasts are served beneath the massive grain weighing scales. Evening meals by arrangement. 5 mins' walk from the town centre. Children over 6 years.
E-mail: bbbw@bradfordoldwindmill.co.uk
www.bradfordoldwindmill.co.uk

VISA: M'CARD:

Peter & Priscilla Roberts Bradford Old Windmill 4 Masons Lane Bradford-on-Avon Bath BA15 1QN
Tel: (01225) 866842   Fax 01225 866648   Open: MAR - OCT   Map Ref No. 01

Burghope Manor

Near Rd: A.36

£95.00 to £100.00 — Y N N

This lovely old home has stood here for 7 centuries overlooking the wonderful valley below - 5 miles from Bath & 1 1/2 miles from Bradford-on-Avon. Although steeped in history, Burghope Manor is first & foremost a living family home, which has been carefully modernised so that the wealth of historical features may complement the present-day comforts. A village pub & restaurant nearby. Evening meals for groups only. Children over 10. Single supplement.
E-mail: info@burghope.co.uk
www.burghope.co.uk

VISA: M'CARD: AMEX:

Elizabeth & John Denning   Burghope Manor   Winsley   Bradford-on-Avon BA15 2LA   Wiltshire
Tel: (01225) 723557 Fax 01225 723113 Open: ALL YEAR (Excl. Xmas & New Year) Map Ref No. 02

The Old Rectory

Near Rd: A.350

£60.00 to £75.00 — Y N Y

Situated in the medieval village of Lacock, The Old Rectory, built in 1866, is a fine example of Victorian Gothic architecture, with creeper-clad walls & mullioned windows. It stands in 12 acres of its own carefully tended grounds, which include a tennis court & croquet lawn. The Old Rectory offers 6 very attractive bedrooms (1 on the ground floor), all with en-suite/private facilities. An excellent base from which to explore the glorious West Country.
E-mail: sexton@oldrectorylacock.co.uk
www.oldrectorylacock.co.uk

Elaine Sexton   The Old Rectory   Cantax Hill   Lacock   Chippenham SN15 2JZ   Wiltshire
Tel: (01249) 730335   Fax 01249 730166   Open: ALL YEAR (Excl. Xmas)   Map Ref No. 03

Pickwick Lodge Farm

Near Rd: A.4

£55.00 to £65.00 — Y N N

A delightful 17th-century Cotswold stone farmhouse, set in peaceful surroundings. 3 well-appointed & tastefully furnished bedrooms, each with an en-suite/private bathroom, radio, T.V. & tea/coffee-making facilities. Hearty & delicious breakfasts are served. Ideally situated for visiting many sites of historical interest, such as the Wiltshire White Horses, Avebury & Stonehenge; many stately homes & National Trust properties within easy reach. Ample car parking. Children over 12 years.
E-mail: b&b@pickwickfarm.freeserve.co.uk
www.pickwickfarm.co.uk

Gill Stafford   Pickwick Lodge Farm   Guyers Lane   Corsham SN13 0PS   Wiltshire
Tel: (01249) 712207   Fax 01249 701904   Open: ALL YEAR   Map Ref No. 05

Wiltshire

£58.00 to £64.00	Y	N	N

🚭

Heatherly Cottage

Near Rd: A.4

17th-century Heatherly Cottage is situated in a quiet lane approx. 9 miles from Bath. Close to the National Trust village of Lacock where several films have been made. The guests' accommodation is a separate wing of the house with its own entrance. There is one ground-floor twin & 2 first-floor double rooms (1 with queen-size bed), all en-suite & with T.V. etc. A full English breakfast is served with free-range eggs from the Daniels' own hens, or Continental with croissants. Children over 9.
E-mail: ladbrook1@aol.com
www.SmoothHound.co.uk/hotels/heather3.html

Jenny & Peter Daniel   Heatherly Cottage   Ladbrook Lane   Gastard   Corsham   SN13 9PE   Wiltshire
Tel: (01249) 701402   Fax 01249 701412   Open: FEB - DEC   Map Ref No. 06

£60.00 to £60.00	N	Y	N

🚭

Leighfield Lodge Farm

Near Rd: A.419

Leighfield Lodge is a lovely old farmhouse in a secluded & rural setting. It is built on the site of a former Royal hunting lodge. Discover en-suite rooms with comfortable beds, crisp cotton bedlinen, power showers, T.V. & tea/coffee facilities. Experience traditional cooking using locally sourced food where possible. Evening meals by prior arrangement. Guests' sitting room available. Well situated for Oxford, Bath, Stonehenge, Avebury, Thames Path & the Cotswolds. Brochure available.
E-mail: claireread@leighfieldlodge.fsnet.co.uk
www.leighfieldlodge.com

Mrs Claire Read   Leighfield Lodge Farm   Malmesbury Road   Leigh   Cricklade   SN6 6RH   Wiltshire
Tel: (01666) 860241   Fax 01666 860241   Open: ALL YEAR   Map Ref No. 07

£50.00 to £50.00	Y	N	N

🚭

Manor Farm

Near Rd: A.429

Relax & unwind in this charming award-winning 17th-century farmhouse, situated on a mixed working farm. 5 bedrooms, all with T.V. & hospitality trays. Eat your hearty breakfast in a dining room with a large inglenook fireplace. Ideal base for 1 night or longer stays for exploring the Cotswolds, Bath, Stonehenge, Lacock & many stately homes. Or just while away the time relaxing in the walled garden. Meals are available at the local pub within walking distance. Children over 12.
E-mail: ross@manorfarmbandb.fsnet.co.uk
www.manorfarmbandb.co.uk

VISA: M'CARD: AMEX:

Mrs Ross Eavis   Manor Farm   Corston   Malmesbury SN16 0HF   Wiltshire
Tel: (01666) 822148   Fax 01666 826565   Open: ALL YEAR (Excl. Xmas & New Year)   Map Ref No. 08

£70.00 to £80.00	Y	Y	Y

🚭

The Manor

Near Rd: A.342

The Manor is a charming, spacious 17th-century house, nestling in a quiet location in the village & is surrounded by 8 acres leading to the River Avon. The interior has been renovated to a high standard. The en-suite bedrooms & beds are extremely comfortable & many guests have commented on the wonderfully relaxed atmosphere. Upavon is well situated for many historical interests, including Salisbury, Stonehenge, Avebury & Marlborough etc. Evening meals & animals by arrangement.
E-mail: isabelbgreen@hotmail.com
www.themanorupavon.co.uk

Isabel Green   The Manor   Upavon   Pewsey SN9 6EB   Wiltshire
Tel: (01980) 635115   Open: ALL YEAR   Map Ref No. 10

Wiltshire

Maddington House

Near Rd: A.360

Maddington House is the family home of Dick & Joan Robathan. An elegant 17th-century Grade II listed house in the centre of the pretty village of Shrewton - about 2 1/2 miles from Stonehenge & 11 miles from Salisbury. 3 attractive guest rooms, 2 with en-suite facilities. The village has 3 pubs, all within easy walking distance. A delightful home, & the perfect base for a relaxing break. Children over 7. Self-catering cottages available.
E-mail: rsrobathan@freenet.co.uk
www.maddingtonhouse.co.uk

| £60.00 to £65.00 | Y | N | N |

Dick & Joan Robathan   Maddington House   Maddington Street   Shrewton   Salisbury SP3 4JD
Tel: (01980) 620406   Open: ALL YEAR   Map Ref No. 12

Elm Tree Cottage

Near Rd: A.36

Elm Tree Cottage is a 17th-century character cottage with inglenook & beams & a flower garden to relax in. The bedrooms, each with an en-suite/private bathroom, are light & airy, attractively decorated & have T.V. & tea/coffee. The atmosphere is relaxed & warm, & breakfast is served as required. Situated in a picturesque village, with valley views, & it is a good centre for Salisbury, Wilton, Longleat, Stonehenge, Avebury, etc. Animals by arrangement. Excellent pubs nearby.
E-mail: jaw.sykes@virgin.net

| £55.00 to £57.00 | Y | N | Y |

Mrs Christine Sykes   Elm Tree Cottage   Chain Hill   Stapleford   Salisbury SP3 4LH   Wiltshire
Tel: (01722) 790507   Mobile 07786 880275   Open: APR - NOV   Map Ref No. 13

Mill House

Near Rd: A.36, A.303

Stonehenge is only 3 miles away. Diana welcomes you to The Mill House set in acres of nature reserve abounding in wild flowers & infinite peace. An island paradise with the River Till running through the working mill & gardens. Diana's old fashioned roses long to see you as do the lovely walks, antiquities & houses. Built by the miller in 1785, the bedrooms all have tea/coffee & T.V.. Fishing in the mill pool & close to golf course & riding. Attention to healthy & organic food. Sample fine cuisine at the Boot Inn. Children over 5. Restricted smoking.
www.millhouse.org.uk

| £70.00 to £70.00 | Y | N | N |

see PHOTO over
p. 281

Michael Mertens (son) & Diana Gifford Mead   Mill House   Berwick St. James   Salisbury SP3 4TS
Tel/Fax: (01722) 790331   Fax 01722 790753   Open: ALL YEAR   Map Ref No. 14

Witherington Farm

Near Rd: A.36

Ian & Annette offer you bed & breakfast in their oak-beamed Grade II listed 17th-century farmhouse. 2 bedrooms have stunning views to the Wiltshire Downs, the 3rd room is in the very oldest part of the house, overlooking the old farmyard. A beautiful 2-acre garden surrounds the house. The farm extends to 600 acres. If you are looking for peace & quiet this is the place for you & only 15 mins' drive from Salisbury. Children over 12.
E-mail: bandb@witheringtonfarm.co.uk
www.witheringtonfarm.co.uk

| £60.00 to £75.00 | Y | N | N |

VISA: M'CARD: AMEX:

Ian & Annette Fergie-Woods   Witherington Farm   Nr. Downton   Salisbury SP5 3QT   Wiltshire
Tel: (01722) 710222   Open: ALL YEAR (Excl. Xmas)   Map Ref No. 15

The Mill House. Berwick St. James

		rate £ from - to per double room	evening meals children taken	animals taken
Bugley Barton  *Mrs J. Hocken* *Tel/Fax: (01985) 213389*	Near Rd: A.362 Ideally placed for trips to Bath, Salisbury, Longleat, Stonehenge & Stourhead; Bugley provides the perfect opportunity to stay in a truly elegant & comfortable Grade II listed Georgian house. Julie & Brian are easy-going & friendly. Home-made cake, delicious breakfasts served in the farmhouse kitchen overlooking the fountain. The spacious & well-equipped en-suite bedrooms overlook the beautiful garden & have many thoughtful added touches. Good local pubs, parking, train station within easy reach. Single supplement. Children over 12. **E-mail: bugleybarton@aol.com**	£70.00 to £75.00	Y N	N

Bugley Barton *Warminster BA12 8HD* *Wiltshire*
Open: ALL YEAR (Excl. Xmas & New Year) *Map Ref No. 16*

All the establishments mentioned in this guide are members of
The Worldwide Bed & Breakfast Association

When booking your accommodation please mention
The Best Bed & Breakfast

Yorkshire

Yorkshire & Humberside

England's largest county is a region of beautiful landscapes, of hills, peaks, fells, dales & forests with many square miles of National Park. It is a vast area taking in big industrial cities, interesting towns & delightful villages. Yorkshire's broad rivers sweep through the countryside & are an angler's paradise. Cascading waterfalls pour down from hillside & moorland.

The North sea coast can be thrilling, with wild seas & cliff-top walks, or just fun, as at the many resorts where the waves break on long beaches & trickle into green rock-pools. Staithes & Robin Hoods Bay are fascinating old fishing villages. Whitby is an attractive port where, Abbey, the small town tumbles in red-roofed tiers down to the busy harbour from which Captain Cook sailed.

The Yorkshire Dales form one of the finest landscapes in England. From windswept moors to wide green valleys the scenery is incomparable. James Herriot tells of of the effect that the broad vista of Swaledale had on him. "I was captivated", he wrote, "completely spell-bound....". A network of dry stone walls covers the land; some are as old as the stone-built villages but those which climb the valley sides to the high moors are the product of the 18th century enclosures, when a good wall builder would cover seven meters a day.

Each of the Dales has a distinctive character; from the remote upper reaches of Swaledale & Wensleydale, where the air sings with the sound of wind, sheep, & curlew, over to Airedale & the spectacular limestone gorges of Malham Cove & Gordale Scar, & down to the soft meadows & woods of Wharfedale where the ruins of Bolton Priory stand beside the river.

To the east towards Hull with its mighty River Humber crossed by the worlds largest single-span suspension bridge, lie the Yorkshire Wolds. This is lovely countryside where villages have unusual names like Fridaythorpe & Wetwang. Beverley is a picture-postcard town with a fine 13th century Minster.

The North Yorks National Park, where the moors are ablaze with purple fire of heather in the late summer, is exhilarating country. There is moorland to the east also, on the Pennine chain; famous Ilkley Moor with its stone circle known as the twelve apostles, & the Haworth Moors around the plain Yorkshire village where the Bronte sisters lived; "the distant dreamy, dim blue chain of mountains circling every side", which Emily Bronte describes in Wuthering Heights.

The Yorkshire Pennines industrial heritage is being celebrated in fascinating museums, often based in the original Woolen Mills & warehouses, which also provide workshop space for skilled craftspeople.

Yorkshires Monastic past is revealed in the ruins of its once great Abbeys. Rievaulx, Jervaux & Fountains, retain their tranquil beauty in their pastoral settings. The wealth of the county is displayed in many historic houses with glorious gardens, from stately 18th Century Castle Howard of 'Brideshead Revisited' fame to Tudor Shibden Hall, portrayed in Wuthering Heights.

York is the finest mediaeval city in England. It is encircled by its limestone city walls with four Great Gates. Within the walls are the jumbled roof line, dog-leg streets & sudden courtyards of a mediaeval town. Half timbered buildings with over-sailing upper storeys jostle with Georgian brick houses along the network of narrow streets around The Shambles & King Edward Square.

Yorkshire

Yorkshire Gazeteer

Areas of Outstanding Natural Beauty.
The North Yorkshire Moors & The Yorkshire Dales.

Historic Houses & Castles.

Carlton Towers
17th century, remodelled in later centuries. paintings, silver, furniture, pictures. Carved woodwork, painted decorations, examples of Victorian craftmanship.

Castle Howard - Nr. York
18th century - celebrated architect, Sir John Vanbrugh - paintings, costumes, furniture by Chippendale, Sheraton, Adam. Not to be missed.

East Riddlesden Hall - Keighley
17th century manor house with fishponds & historic barns, one of which is regarded as very fine example of mediaeval tithe barn.

Newby Hall - Ripon
17th century Wren style extended by Robert Adam. Gobelins tapestry, Chippendale furniture, sculpture galleries with Roman rotunda, statuary. Award-winning gardens.

Nostell Priory - Wakefield
18th century, Georgian mansion, Chippendale furniture, paintings.

Burton Constable Hall - Hull
16th century, Elizabethan, remodelled in Georgian period. Stained glass, Hepplewhite furniture, gardens by Capability Brown.

Ripley Castle - Harrogate
14th century, parts dating during 16th & 18th centuries. Priest hole, armour & weapons, beautiful ceilings.

The Treasurer's House - York
17th & 18th centuries, splendid interiors, furniture, pictures.

Harewood House - Leeds
18th century - Robert Adam design, Chippendale furniture, Italian & English paintings. Sevres & Chinese porcelain.

Benningbrough Hall - York
18th century. Highly decorative woodwork, oak staircase, friezes etc. Splendid hall.

Markenfield Hall - Ripon
14th to 16th century - fine Manor house surrounded by moat.

Heath Hall - Wakefield

18th century, palladian. Fine woodwork & plasterwork, rococo ceilings, excellent furniture, paintings & porcelain

Bishops House - Sheffield
16th century. Only complete timber framed yeoman farmhouse surviving. Vernacular architecture. Superb

Skipton Castle- Skipton
One of the most complete & well preserved mediaeval castles in England.

Cathedral & Churches

York Minster
13th century. Greatest Gothic Cathedral north of the Alps. Imposing grandeur - superb Chapter house, contains half of the mediaeval stained glass of England. Outstandingly beautiful.

York (All Saints, North Street)
15th century roofing in parts - 18th century pulpit wonderful mediaeval glass.

Ripon Cathedral
12th century - though in some parts Saxon in origin. Decorated choir stalls - gables buttresses. Church of 672 preserved in crypt, , Caxton Book, ecclesiastic treasures.

Bolton Percy (All Saints)
15th century.
Maintains original glass in east window. Jacobean font cover. Georgian pulpit. Interesting monuments.

Rievaulx Abbey
12th century, masterpiece of Early English architecture.
One of three great Cistercian Abbeys built in Yorkshire.
Impressive ruins.

Campsall (St. Mary Magdalene)
Fine Norman tower - 15th century rood screen, carved & painted stone altar.

Fountains Abbey - Ripon
Ruins of England's greatest mediaeval abbey - surrounded by wonderful landscaped gardens. Enormous tower, vaulted cellar 300 feet long.

Whitby (St. Mary)
12th century tower & doorway, 18th century remodelling - box pews much interior woodwork painted - galleries. High pulpit. Table tombs.

Yorkshire

Whitby Abbey - Whitby (St. Hilda)
7th century superb ruin - venue of Synod
of 664. Destroyed by Vikings, restored
1078 - magnificent north transept.
Halifax (St. John the Baptist)
12th century origins, showing work from
each succeeding century - heraldic
ceilings. Cromwell glass.
Beverley Minster - Beverley
14th century. Fine Gothic Minster -
remarkable mediaeval effigies of
musicians playing instruments. Founded
as monastery in 700.
Bolton Priory - Nr. Skipton
Nave of Augustinian Priory, now Bolton's
Parish Church, amidst ruins of choir &
transepts, in beautiful riverside setting.
Selby Abbey - Selby
11th century Benedictine abbey of which
the huge church remains. Roof &
furnishings are modern after a fire of 1906,
but the stonework is intact.

Museums & Galleries

Aldborough Roman Museum -
Boroughbridge
Remnants of Roman period of the town -
coins, glass, pottery, etc.
Great Ayton
Home of Captain Cook, explorer &
seaman. Exhibits of maps, etc.
Art Gallery - City of York
Modern paintings, Old Masters,
watercolours, prints, ceramics.
Lotherton Hall - Nr. Leeds
Museum with furniture, paintings, silver,
works of art from the Leeds collection &
oriental art gallery.
National Railway Museum - York
Devoted to railway engineering & its
development.
York Castle Museum
The Kirk Collection of bygones including
cobbled streets, shops, costumes, toys,
household & farm equipment - fascinating
collection.
Cannon Hall Art Gallery - Barnsley
18th century house with fine furniture &
glass, etc. Flemish & Dutch paintings.
Also houses museum of the 13/18 Royal
Hussars.
Mappin Art Gallery - Sheffield
Works from 18th,19th & 20th century.

Graves Art gallery-Sheffield.
British portraiture. European works, &
examples of Asian & African art. Loan
exhibitions are held there.
Royal Pump Room Museum - Harrogate
Original sulphur well used in the Victorian
Spa. Local history costume & pottery.
Bolling Hall - Bradford
A period house with mixture of styles -
collections of 17th century oak furniture,
domestic utensils, toys & bygones.
Georgian Theatre - Richmond
Oldest theatre in the country - interesting
theatrical memorabilia.
Jorvik Viking Centre - York
Recently excavated site in the centre of
York showing hundreds of artifacts dating
from the Viking period. One of the most
important archaeological discoveries this
century.
Abbey House Museum - Kirkstall, Leeds
Illustrated past 300 years of Yorkshire life.
Shows 3 full streets from 19th century with
houses, shops & workplaces.
Piece Hall - Halifax
Remarkable building - constructed around
huge quadrangle - now Textile Industrial
Museum, Art Gallery & has craft & antique
shops.
**National Museum of Photography, Film
& Television** - Bradford
Displays look at art & science of
photography, film & T.V. Britain's only
IMAX arena.
The Colour Museum - Bradford
Award-winning interactive museum,which
allows visitors to explore the world of
colour & discover the story of dyeing &
textile printing.
Calderdale Industrial Museum - Halifax
Social & industrial Museum of the year
1987
Shibden Hall & Folk Museum of Halifax
Half-timbered house with folk museum,
farmland, miniature train & boating lake.
**Leeds City Art Gallery & Henry Moore
Sculpture Gallery**
Yorkshire Sculpture Park - Wakefield
Yorkshire Museum of Farming - Murton
Award-winning museum of farming & the
countryside.

YORKSHIRE & HUMBERSIDE

Map reference

01	Williams		13	Wood
01	Gill		14	Sugars
02	Knox		15	Johnson
03	Canning		16	Howard-Barker
04	Greenwood		17	Goodall
05	Berry		18	Steele
06	Bendtson		19	Clough
06	Evans		20	Watts
06	Thomson		21	Goodrum
07	King		22	Bradley
08	Banks		22	Knibbs
09	Braithwaite		22	W.Wood
10	Murray		22	Sluter-Robbins
11	Schofield		22	Smith
12	Layfield		22	J. Wood

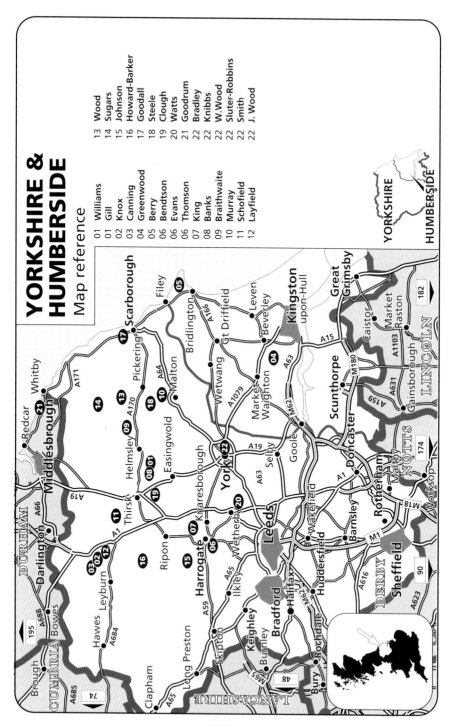

rate £ from - to per double room	children taken	evening meals	animals taken		

Daleside

£60.00 to £70.00 — Y N N

Near Rd: A.170

Daleside is listed the oldest house in this charming stone village, with 400-year-old cruck beams & oak panelling. The house has been sympathetically restored, with the 2 en-suite guests' rooms (1 twin, 1 double with half-tester bed) overlooking the garden. There are 2 inns in the village & other good restaurants nearby. Ampleforth is on the edge of the North York Moors National Park, with excellent walks all around. Children from 11.
E-mail: dalesidepaul@hotmail.com
www.bestbandb.co.uk

Paul & Pat Williams   Daleside   East End   Ampleforth YO62 4DA   Yorkshire
Tel: (01439) 788266   Open: ALL YEAR (Excl. Xmas & New Year)   Map Ref No. 01

Shallowdale House

£82.00 to £99.00 — Y Y N

Near Rd: A.170

An outstanding modern country house, with 2 acres of hillside garden, on the edge of the North York Moors National Park, 20 miles north of York. Each of the 3 spacious guest rooms, furnished with style & attention to detail, enjoys stunning views of the unspoilt countryside. Imaginative meals are prepared from fresh seasonal ingredients. Drinks licence. Award-winning Shallowdale House is a perfect place to unwind when exploring Herriot country & York. Children over 12.
E-mail: stay@shallowdalehouse.co.uk
www.shallowdalehouse.co.uk

VISA: M'CARD:

Phillip Gill & Anton Van Der Horst   Shallowdale House   West End   Ampleforth YO62 4DY
Tel: (01439) 788325 Fax 01439 788885   Open: ALL YEAR (Excl. Xmas & New Year) Map Ref No. 01

Mill Close Farm

£55.00 to £80.00 — N N N

Near Rd: A.684

Award-winning farmhouse surrounded by beautiful rolling countryside at the foothills of the Yorkshire Dales. Luxurious en-suite bedrooms, 2 with spa baths, 1 4-poster suite. Rooms have super king-size beds, guest fridges with complimentary fruit, handmade chocolates & spring water. Very tranquil with exceptional views. Walled garden with pond & waterfall. Traditional & speciality breakfasts prepared with local produce. Brochure.
E-mail: pat@millclose.co.uk
www.millclose.co.uk

see PHOTO over p. 288

VISA: M'CARD: AMEX:

Mrs Patricia Knox   Mill Close Farm   Patrick Brompton   Bedale DL8 1JY   Yorkshire
Tel: (01677) 450257   Fax 01748 813612   Open: All Year (Excl. Xmas & New Year)   Map Ref No. 02

Elmfield Country House

£60.00 to £80.00 — Y Y N

Near Rd: A.684

Located in its own grounds in the country. Enjoy a relaxed, friendly atmosphere in spacious surroundings, with a high standard of furnishings. 9 en-suite bedrooms comprising twin-bedded, double & family rooms. 2 rooms have been adapted for disabled guests & another has a 4-poster bed. All rooms have satellite colour T.V., 'phone, radio/alarm & tea/coffee makers. A games room & solarium are also available. Excellent farmhouse cooking. Residential licence. Single supplement.
E-mail: stay@elmfieldhouse.freeserve.co.uk
www.elmfieldhouse.co.uk

VISA: M'CARD:

Mrs Canning   Elmfield Country House   Arrathorne   Bedale DL8 1NE   Yorkshire
Tel: (01677) 450558   Fax 01677 450557   Open: ALL YEAR   Map Ref No. 03

Mill Close Farm.   Patrick Brompton.

Yorkshire

Rudstone Walk Country Accommodation

rate £ from - to per double room	children taken	evening meals	animals taken
£65.00 to £65.00	Y	Y	Y

Near Rd: A.1034

Rudstone Walk is renowned for its hospitality & good food. Accommodation is in the very tastefully converted farm buildings, adjacent to the main farmhouse where meals are served. Each of the attractive bedrooms has excellent en-suite facilities, T.V., 'phone & internet access. Rudstone provides a peaceful retreat after a tiring day. Ideal for a relaxing break, & within easy reach of York & many other attractions. Dogs by arrangement. Special offer Nov - May, 3 nights for the price of 2.
E-mail: admin@rudstone-walk.co.uk
www.rudstone-walk.co.uk

VISA: M'CARD: AMEX:

Laura & Charlie Greenwood   Rudstone Walk   South Cave   Nr. Beverley HU15 2AH   Yorkshire
Tel: (01430) 422230   Fax 01430 424552   Open: ALL YEAR   Map Ref No. 04

The Manor House

£74.00 to £84.00	Y	N	Y

Near Rd: B.1255

Flamborough Manor, dating from c.1770, offers spacious, comfortable accommodation. Pefectly situated to explore the Flamborough Heritage Coast & the gannet colony & puffins (early summer) at Bempton RSPB Sanctuary. Burton Agnes Hall, Sledmere House, Castle Howard, the North York Moors, Robin Hood's Bay & York are nearby. The larger en-suite room features an imposing 17th century Portuguese bed; the 2nd has a Victorian brass bed & private bathroom. Children over 8.
E-mail: gm@flamboroughmanor.co.uk
www.flamboroughmanor.co.uk

VISA: M'CARD:

Lesley Berry & Geoffrey Miller The Manor House Flamborough   Bridlington YO15 1PD Yorkshire
Tel/Fax: (01262) 850943   Mobile 07718 415234   Open: ALL YEAR (Excl. Xmas)   Map Ref No. 05

Ashwood House

£60.00 to £65.00	Y	N	N

Near Rd: A.61

A charming 5-bedroomed Edwardian house retaining many of its original features. Situated in a quiet, residential cul-de-sac mins' from the town centre. The attractive en-suite bedrooms are spacious, some with 4-poster beds, all with hospitality tray, T.V., hairdryer & complimentary toiletries. A delicious breakfast is served from lovely Royal Copenhagen china in the elegant dining room. A high standard of service & a warm welcome is assured. Scandinavian languages spoken. Children over 7.
E-mail: ashwoodhouse@aol.com
www.ashwoodhouse.co.uk

VISA: M'CARD:

Gill & Kristian Bendtson   Ashwood House   7 Spring Grove   Harrogate HG1 2HS   Yorkshire
Tel: (01423) 560081 Fax 01423 527928 Open: ALL YEAR (Excl. Xmas & New Year) Map Ref No. 06

Shannon Court

£64.00 to £70.00	Y	N	N

Near Rd: A.59

A charming Victorian house, overlooking the 'Stray' in High Harrogate. Enjoy real home cooking in this charming home. Accommodation is in 8 delightful bedrooms, all of which are en-suite & have every modern comfort including radio/alarm, colour T.V. & tea/coffee-making facilities. Licensed for residents & their guests. Close to town centre, railway station & conference centre, with easy parking & direct main routes for moors & dales. Evening meals by prior arrangement.   **E-mail: shannon@courthotel.freeserve.co.uk**
www.shannon-court.com

VISA: M'CARD: AMEX:

Kath & Bob Evans Shannon Court   65 Dragon Avenue   Harrogate HG1 5DS   Yorkshire
Tel: (01423) 509858   Fax 01423 530606   Open: ALL YEAR (Excl. New Year)   Map Ref No. 06

Yorkshire

Fountains House

| | £55.00 to £65.00 | N | Y | N |

Near Rd: A.61

A charming 18th-century limestone cottage with lovely south-facing garden; situated in the pretty village of Burton Leonard halfway between Harrogate & Ripon, ideally placed for both town & country. 2 twin/double rooms with en-suite facilities, T.V. & hospitality tray, delightfully furnished & decorated to a high standard. Delicious breakfasts are cooked to order & include home-made preserves & freshly baked bread from the Aga. Evening meals available by prior arrangement. Parking.

E-mail: gillandclive@btinternet.com
www.fountainshouse.co.uk

Clive & Gill King   Fountains House   Burton Leonard   Nr. Harrogate HG3 3RU   Yorkshire
Tel: (01765) 677537   Open: ALL YEAR   Map Ref No. 07

Oldstead Grange

| | £64.00 to £84.00 | Y | N | Y |

Near Rd: A.19

A 17th-century historic farmhouse set amidst superb National Park countryside. A relaxed, uncomplicated friendly atmosphere uniquely combined with exceptionally high quality accommodation. 3 spacious en-suite bedrooms, including a special 4-poster suite, each with comfortable king-size beds, T.V., robes, & home-made chocolates. Breakfasts feature freshly prepared traditional & speciality dishes. Renowned eating places in the local picturesque villages. Children 9+. Dogs by arrangement.

E-mail: anne@yorkshireuk.com
www.yorkshireuk.com

see PHOTO over
p. 291

VISA: M'CARD:

Mrs Anne Banks   Oldstead Grange   Oldstead   Coxwold   Helmsley YO61 4BJ   Yorkshire
Tel: (01347) 868634   Open: ALL YEAR   Map Ref No. 08

Plumpton Court

| | £52.00 to £62.00 | Y | N | N |

Near Rd: A.170

A family-run 17th-century guest house set in the foothills of the North York Moors. Ideally situated for York & exploring the east coast. Offering 9 en-suite, comfortable & well-appointed bedrooms including 2 luxury king-size bedrooms, all with tea/coffee facilities & T.V.. A comfortable lounge in which guests may relax, with real fire & a small bar. Delicious breakfasts are served in the comfortable dining room. Chris's scrambled eggs are a treat. Gated car park & garden. Children over 12 years.

E-mail: mail@plumptoncourt.com
www.plumptoncourt.com

VISA: M'CARD: AMEX:

Chris & Sarah Braithwaite   Plumpton Court   High Street   Nawton   Helmsley YO62 7TT Yorkshire
Tel: (01439) 771223   Open: ALL YEAR (Excl. Xmas & New Year)   Map Ref No. 09

Manor Farm

| | £60.00 to £70.00 | Y | Y | Y |

Near Rd: A.169

A charming Georgian manor house set in spacious grounds with hard tennis court, croquet lawn & views to the Howardian Hills. Accommodation is in 3 attractive bedrooms, with either an en-suite or a private bathroom. Excellent cooking caters for all tastes. Manor Farm is within easy reach of York, Scarborough, the Moors, Castle Howard & Flamingoland. Dogs, & children over 5, are most welcome. Minimum 2 nights stay.

E-mail: cphmurray@compuserve.com
www.bestbandb.co.uk

Mrs Judith Murray   Manor Farm   Little Barugh   Malton YO17 6UY   Yorkshire
Tel: (01653) 668262   Open: ALL YEAR   Map Ref No. 10

Oldstead Grange. Helmsley.

Rose Cottage Farm. Cropton.

Column headers (rotated):
- rate £ from - to per double room
- children taken
- evening meals taken
- animals taken

| £56.00 to £56.00 | Y | N | N |

🚭 (no smoking)

Near Rd: A.684

Elmscott

Elmscott is a charming property which is set in a delightful landscaped garden. It is situated close to the centre of Northallerton, a thriving market town. Your hosts offer 2 attractively furnished bedrooms, each with an en-suite bathroom, tea/coffee-making facilities & T.V.. A delicious breakfast is served. Elmscott is located mid-way between the North York Moors & the beautiful Yorkshire Dales National Parks, with their famous 'Herriott' connections. A lovely home, perfect for a relaxing break.
E-mail: elmscott@freenet.co.uk
www.elmscottbedandbreakfast.co.uk

Mike & Pauline Schofield   *Elmscott*   *Hatfield Road*   *Northallerton DL7 8QX*   *Yorkshire*
Tel: (01609) 760575   *Open: ALL YEAR*   *Map Ref No. 11*

| £55.00 to £60.00 | Y | Y | Y |

🚭 (no smoking)

Near Rd: A.1

Little Holtby

With one foot in the past, but with present day comforts, Little Holtby is the 'somewhere special' in which to relax & unwind. Antiques, beams, polished wood floors & cosy log fires all add to the ambience of a period farmhouse. The 3 guest rooms have wonderful views over rolling countryside to the Dales. En-suite or private facilities. Golf, tennis, riding, fishing & walking close by. Children over 12. Dinner & animals by arrangement. Come & spoil yourself - other guests do again & again.
E-mail: littleholtby@yahoo.co.uk
www.littleholtby.co.uk

Dorothy Layfield   *Little Holtby*   *Leeming Bar*   *Northallerton DL7 9LH*   *Yorkshire*
Tel: (01609) 748762   *Fax 01609 748822*   *Open: ALL YEAR (Excl. Xmas)*   *Map Ref No. 12*

| £52.00 to £60.00 | N | Y | N |

🚭 (no smoking)

see PHOTO over p. 292

Near Rd: A.170

Rose Cottage Farm

A warm welcome awaits you at Rose Cottage Farm. Your hosts aim to provide good food using home produce & comfortable accommodation in a cosy informal atmosphere. The 3 spacious & attractively decorated en-suite rooms include colour T.V. & tea/coffee-making facilities. Guests may relax in the cosy lounge, which has cruck beams & many original features. Afternoon tea is served on arrival & evening meals can be taken in the attractive conservatory dining room. Easy access to the beautiful moors, coast & York.
www.smoothhound.co.uk

Mrs Joan Wood   *Rose Cottage Farm*   *Main Street*   *Cropton*   *Pickering YO18 8HL*   *Yorkshire*
Tel: (01751) 417302   *Open: ALL YEAR*   *Map Ref No. 13*

| £55.00 to £60.00 | Y | N | N |

🚭 (no smoking)

see PHOTO over p. 294

Near Rd: A.170

Sevenford House

Originally a vicarage, & built from the stones of Rosedale Abbey, Sevenford House stands in 4 acres of lovely gardens in the heart of the beautiful Yorkshire Moors National Park. 3 tastefully furnished, en-suite bedrooms, with T.V., radio & tea/coffee facilities, offering wonderful views overlooking valley & moorland. A relaxing guests' lounge/library with an open fire. Riding & golf locally. Also, ruined abbeys, Roman roads, steam railways, beautiful coastline & pretty fishing towns.
E-mail: sevenford@aol.com
www.sevenford.com

Linda Sugars   *Sevenford House*   *Rosedale Abbey*   *Pickering YO18 8SE*   *Yorkshire*
Tel: (01751) 417283   *Open: ALL YEAR*   *Map Ref No. 14*

Sevenford House. Rosedale Abbey.

rate £ from - to per double room	children taken	evening meals taken	animals taken		

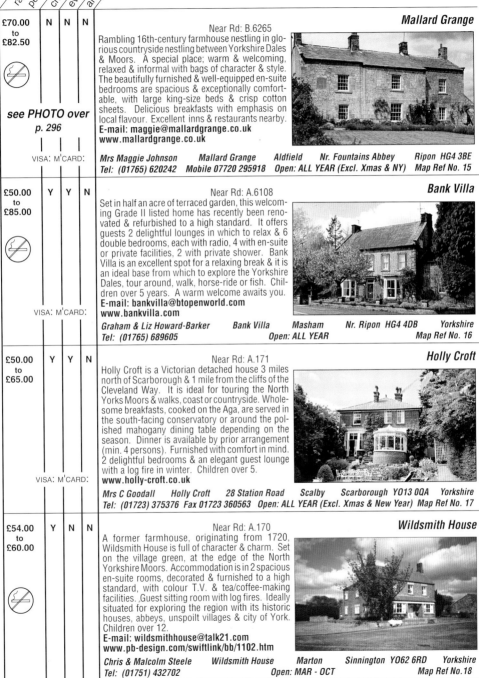

Mallard Grange

£70.00 to £82.50 — N N N

(no smoking)

see PHOTO over p. 296

VISA : M'CARD :

Near Rd: B.6265

Rambling 16th-century farmhouse nestling in glorious countryside nestling between Yorkshire Dales & Moors. A special place; warm & welcoming, relaxed & informal with bags of character & style. The beautifully furnished & well-equipped en-suite bedrooms are spacious & exceptionally comfortable, with large king-size beds & crisp cotton sheets. Delicious breakfasts with emphasis on local flavour. Excellent inns & restaurants nearby.
E-mail: maggie@mallardgrange.co.uk
www.mallardgrange.co.uk

Mrs Maggie Johnson   Mallard Grange   Aldfield   Nr. Fountains Abbey   Ripon HG4 3BE
Tel: (01765) 620242   Mobile 07720 295918   Open: ALL YEAR (Excl. Xmas & NY)   Map Ref No. 15

Bank Villa

£50.00 to £85.00 — Y Y N

(no smoking)

VISA : M'CARD :

Near Rd: A.6108

Set in half an acre of terraced garden, this welcoming Grade II listed home has recently been renovated & refurbished to a high standard. It offers guests 2 delightful lounges in which to relax & 6 double bedrooms, each with radio, 4 with en-suite or private facilities, 2 with private shower. Bank Villa is an excellent spot for a relaxing break & it is an ideal base from which to explore the Yorkshire Dales, tour around, walk, horse-ride or fish. Children over 5 years. A warm welcome awaits you.
E-mail: bankvilla@btopenworld.com
www.bankvilla.com

Graham & Liz Howard-Barker   Bank Villa   Masham   Nr. Ripon HG4 4DB   Yorkshire
Tel: (01765) 689605   Open: ALL YEAR   Map Ref No. 16

Holly Croft

£50.00 to £65.00 — Y Y N

VISA : M'CARD :

Near Rd: A.171

Holly Croft is a Victorian detached house 3 miles north of Scarborough & 1 mile from the cliffs of the Cleveland Way. It is ideal for touring the North Yorks Moors & walks, coast or countryside. Wholesome breakfasts, cooked on the Aga, are served in the south-facing conservatory or around the polished mahogany dining table depending on the season. Dinner is available by prior arrangement (min. 4 persons). Furnished with comfort in mind. 2 delightful bedrooms & an elegant guest lounge with a log fire in winter. Children over 5.
www.holly-croft.co.uk

Mrs C Goodall   Holly Croft   28 Station Road   Scalby   Scarborough YO13 0QA   Yorkshire
Tel: (01723) 375376   Fax 01723 360563   Open: ALL YEAR (Excl. Xmas & New Year)   Map Ref No. 17

Wildsmith House

£54.00 to £60.00 — Y N N

(no smoking)

Near Rd: A.170

A former farmhouse, originating from 1720, Wildsmith House is full of character & charm. Set on the village green, at the edge of the North Yorkshire Moors. Accommodation is in 2 spacious en-suite rooms, decorated & furnished to a high standard, with colour T.V. & tea/coffee-making facilities. Guest sitting room with log fires. Ideally situated for exploring the region with its historic houses, abbeys, unspoilt villages & city of York. Children over 12.
E-mail: wildsmithhouse@talk21.com
www.pb-design.com/swiftlink/bb/1102.htm

Chris & Malcolm Steele   Wildsmith House   Marton   Sinnington YO62 6RD   Yorkshire
Tel: (01751) 432702   Open: MAR - OCT   Map Ref No.18

Mallard Grange. Fountains Abbey.

Spital Hill. Thirsk.

Yorkshire

Spital Hill

Near Rd: A.19

This quiet, peaceful house with lovely furnishings & sparkling lamps is convenient for a stopover or for exploring the Dales, Moors, York & Harrogate. Set in 1 1/2 acres of garden & surrounded by parkland, the house is Georgian with Victorian additions. Bedrooms are comfortable, well-furnished with large bathrooms. Enjoy the warmth of the welcome & the delightful meals; everything is home-baked & always includes fresh produce from the garden when available. Children over 12.
E-mail: spitalhill@amserve.net
www.spitalhill.co.uk

£84.00 to £94.00 | Y | Y | N

see PHOTO over p. 297

VISA: M'CARD:

Ann & Robin Clough   Spital Hill   York Road   Thirsk YO7 3AE   Yorkshire
Tel: (01845) 522273   Fax 01845 524970   Open: ALL YEAR   Map Ref No. 19

Four Gables

Near Rd: A.659

This special art-and-craft movement house has a wealth of original features, stripped oak & terracotta floors, fireplaces & beautiful ceilings. A feature of the house is its 1/2 acre gardens which contain many interesting plants & a croquet lawn. A peaceful setting, down a private lane, yet only 3 mins' walk from the bustling Georgian stone village of Boston Spa with all its facilities, shops, restaurants, etc. 3 en-suite bedrooms, guests dining room & living room, log fires. Children over 3.
E-mail: info@fourgables.co.uk
www.fourgables.co.uk

£62.00 to £67.00 | Y | N | Y

David & Anne Watts   Four Gables   Oaks Lane   Boston Spa   Wetherby LS23 6DS   Yorkshire
Tel: (01937) 845592   Open: ALL YEAR (Excl. Xmas & New Year)   Map Ref No. 20

Cliffemount Hotel

Near Rd: A.174

As the name implies, this privately run hotel is situated on a clifftop with panoramic views over Runswick Bay. Built in the 1920s with later additions, the hotel is tastefully decorated throughout. There are 20 comfortably furnished bedrooms, all are en-suite, & the majority have spectacular sea views. Cliffemount, with its warm & friendly atmosphere, also enjoys a good reputation for its high standard of food. Fully licensed. Log fires in winter. Animals by arrangement.
E-mail: cliffemount@runswickbay.fsnet.co.uk
www.cliffemounthotel.co.uk

£68.00 to £110.00 | Y | Y | Y

VISA: M'CARD:

Mr & Mrs Rae   Cliffemount Hotel   Runswick Bay   Whitby TS13 5HU   Yorkshire
Tel: (01947) 840103   Fax 01947 841025   Open: ALL YEAR (Excl. Xmas)   Map Ref No. 21

Barbican House

Near Rd: A.19

A wonderful restored Victorian villa, overlooking the famous medieval city walls & York Minster. 7 bedrooms, each individually decorated to compliment the character of the period. All are en-suite & have T.V., 2 superior rooms with DVD players & king-size beds - 1 ground floor. 1 twin & 2 doubles with king-size beds & 2 doubles. A full English breakfast is served in the dining room, with a vegetarian alternative always available. Car park. Broadband WiFi internet access. Children over 9.
E-mail: info@barbicanhouse.com
www.barbicanhouse.com

£72.00 to £84.00 | Y | N | N

see PHOTO over p. 299

VISA: M'CARD:

Adrian & Ann Bradley   Barbican House   20 Barbican Road   York YO10 5AA   Yorkshire
Tel: (01904) 627617   Fax 01904 647140   Open: ALL YEAR (Excl. Xmas & New Year)   Map Ref No. 22

Barbican House.York.

Yorkshire

The Dairy Guesthouse

Near Rd: A.59, A.64

Dating from 1890 & tastefully renovated throughout, The Dairy retains many of its original features. Situated within walking distance of the centre & York Minster, it is just 200 yards from the medieval city walls. Offering 5 bedrooms, all with T.V., HiFi & hot drink facilities. A 4-poster room is available & most rooms are en-suite. A private & relaxing flower-filled courtyard is available for guests use. The breakfast menu ranges from traditional English to wholefood & vegetarian. Families are welcome.
E-mail: stay@dairyguesthouse.co.uk
www.dairyguesthouse.co.uk

| £56.00 to £75.00 | Y | N | N |

VISA: M'CARD: AMEX:

Ian Knibbs & Joanne Pease   The Dairy Guesthouse   3 Scarcroft Road   York YO23 1ND   Yorkshire
Tel: (01904) 639367   Open: ALL YEAR (Excl. Xmas & Jan.)   Map Ref No. 22

Curzon Lodge & Stable Cottages

Near Rd: A.1036

A charming 17th-century Grade II listed house & oak-beamed stables within city conservation area overlooking York racecourse. Once a home of the Terry 'chocolate' family, guests are now invited to share the unique atmosphere in 10 delightful & fully-equipped en-suite rooms, some with 4-poster & brass beds. Country antiques, prints, books, fresh flowers & complimentary sherry in the cosy sitting room lend traditional ambience. Delicious English breakfasts. Restaurants just 1-min walk. Parking in grounds. Warm & relaxed hospitality.
www.smoothhound.co.uk/hotels/curzon

| £65.00 to £80.00 | Y | N | N |

VISA: M'CARD:

Wendy Wood   Curzon Lodge & Stable Cottages   23 Tadcaster Road   York YO24 1QG   Yorkshire
Tel: (01904) 703157   Fax 01904 703157   Open: ALL YEAR (Excl. Xmas)   Map Ref No. 22

Arnot House

Near Rd: A.19

Overlooking Bootham Park, only 5 mins' walk from the York Minster & city centre. Award-winning Arnot House is a Victorian town house built for a wealthy merchant in 1865. The house is beautifully decorated, & there are fine antiques & paintings. Many of its original features have been retained, including marble fireplaces & ornate coving. The 4 attractive bedrooms have either Victorian brass or wooden beds & every facility. An excellent location.
E-mail: kim.robbins@virgin.net
www.arnothouseyork.co.uk

| £64.00 to £70.00 | N | N | N |

see PHOTO over
p. 301

VISA: M'CARD:

Mrs Ann & Miss Kim Sluter-Robbins   Arnot House   17 Grosvenor Terrace   Bootham   York YO30 7AG
Tel: (01904) 641966   Open: FEB - DEC   Map Ref No. 22

City Guest House

Near Rd: A.1036

A warm & friendly welcome is assured in this family-run Victorian guest house (built in 1840) & only a short distance from the ancient bar walls, Minster & many of York's historical landmarks. The tastefully furnished bedrooms boast a stylish interior & come with a host of thoughtful touches. 6 bedrooms are en-suite & 1 has private facilities. Choice of breakfasts including vegetarian, full English & Continental, served in the spacious dining room, & relax in the cosy lounge. Children over 12.
E-mail: info@cityguesthouse.co.uk
www.cityguesthouse.co.uk

| £64.00 to £72.00 | Y | N | N |

VISA: M'CARD: AMEX:

Allan & Julie Smith   City Guest House   68 Monkgate   York YO31 7PF   Yorkshire
Tel: (01904) 622483   Open: ALL YEAR (Excl. Xmas)   Map Ref No. 22

Arnot House.   Bootham.

Yorkshire

	rate £ from - to per double room	evening meals children taken	animals taken

Ascot House

Near Rd: A.1036

Ascot House is a family-run Victorian villa built in 1869. 15 en-suite rooms of character, many having four-poster or canopy beds. Each is well-equipped with T.V., tea/coffee-making facilities, etc. Delicious English or vegetarian breakfasts are served in the attractive dining room. Ascot House is only 15 mins' walk to the historic city centre with its ancient narrow streets, medieval churches, Roman, Viking & National Railway Museums & the York Minster. Residential licence. Sauna available. Car park.
E-mail: admin@ascothouseyork.com
www.ascothouseyork.com

£60.00 to £80.00   Y   N   Y

see PHOTO over p. 303

VISA: M'CARD:

June & Keith Wood   Ascot House   80 East Parade   York YO31 7YH   Yorkshire
Tel: (01904) 426826   Fax 01904 431077   Open: ALL YEAR (Excl. Xmas week)   Map Ref No. 22

All the establishments mentioned in this guide are members of
The Worldwide Bed & Breakfast Association

When booking your accommodation please mention
The Best Bed & Breakfast

Ascot House. York.

Scotland

Scotland

Scotland's culture & traditions, history & literature, languages & accents, its landscape & architecture, even its wildlife set it apart from the rest of Britain. Much of Scotland's history is concerned with the struggle to retain independence from England.

The Romans never conquered the Scottish tribes, but preferred to keep them at bay with Hadrian's Wall, stretching across the Border country from Tynemouth to the Solway Firth.

Time lends glamour to events, but from the massacre of Glencoe to the Highland Clearances, much of Scotland's fate has been a harsh one. Robert the Bruce did rout the English enemy at Bannockburn after scaling the heights of Edinburgh Castle to take the city, but in later years Mary, Queen of Scots was to spend much of her life imprisoned by her sister Elizabeth I of England. Bonnie Prince Charlie (Charles Edward Stuart) led the Jacobite rebellion which ended in defeat at Culloden.

These events are recorded in the folklore & songs of Scotland. The Border & Highland Gatherings & the Common Ridings are more than a chance to wear the Tartan, they are reminders of national pride.

Highland Games are held throughout the country where local & national champions compete in events like tossing the caber & in piping contests. There are sword dances & Highland flings, the speciality of young men & boys wearing the full dress tartan of their clan.

Scotland's landscape is rich in variety from the lush green lowlands to the handsome splendour of the mountainous Highlands, from the rounded hills of the Borders to the far-flung islands of the Hebrides, Orkney & Shetland where the sea is ever-present.

There are glens & beautiful lochs deep in the mountains, a spectacular coastline of high cliffs & white sandy beaches, expanses of purple heather moorland where the sparkling water in the burns runs brown with peat, & huge skies bright with cloud & gorgeous sunsets.

Argyll & The Islands

This area has ocean & sea lochs, forests & mountains, 3000 miles of coastline, about 30 inhabited islands, the warming influence of the Gulf Stream & the tallest tree in Britain (in Strone Gardens, near Loch Fyne).

Sites both historic & prehistoric are to be found in plenty. There is a hilltop fort at Dunadd, near Crinan with curious cup-&-ring carvings, & numerous ancient sites surround Kilmartin, from burial cairns to grave slabs.

Kilchurn Castle is a magnificent ruin in contrast to the opulence of Inveraray. Both are associated with the once-powerful Clan Campbell. There are remains of fortresses built by the Lords of the Isles, the proud chieftains who ruled the west after driving out the Norse invaders in the 12th century.

Oban is a small harbour town accessible by road & rail & the point of departure for many of the islands including Mull.

Tobermory. Isle of Mull.

Scotland

Mull is a peaceful island with rugged seascapes, lovely walks & villages, a miniature railway & the famous Mull Little Theatre. It is a short hop from here to the tiny island of Iona & St. Columba's Abbey, cradle of Christianity in Scotland.

Coll & Tiree have lovely beaches & fields of waving barley. The grain grown here was once supplied to the Lords of the Isles but today most goes to Islay & into the whisky. Tiree has superb windsurfing.

Jura is a wilder island famous for its red deer. The Isles of Colonsay & Oronsay are joined at low water.

Gigha, 'God's Isle', is a fertile area of gardens with rare & semitropical plants. The Island of Staffa has Fingal's Cave.

The Borders, Dumfries & Galloway

The borderland with England is a landscape of subtle colours & contours from the round foothills of the Cheviots, purple with heather, to the dark green valley of the Tweed.

The Lammermuir Hills sweep eastwards to a coastline of small harbours & the spectacular cliffs at St. Abbs Head where colonies of seabirds thrive.

The Border towns, set in fine countryside, have distinctive personalities. Hawick, Galashiels, Selkirk & Melrose all played their parts in the various Border skirmishes of this historically turbulent region & then prospered with a textile industry which survives today. They celebrate their traditions in the Common Riding ceremonies.

The years of destructive border warfare have left towers & castles throughout the country. Roxburgh was once a Royal castle & James II was killed here during a seige. Now there are only the shattered remains of the massive stone walls. Hermitage Castle is set amid wild scenery near Hawick & impressive Floors Castle stands above Kelso.

At Jedburgh the Augustine abbey is remarkably complete, & a visitors centre here tells the story of the four great Border Abbeys; Jedburgh itself, Kelso, Dryburgh & Melrose.

The lovely estate of Abbotsford where Sir Walter Scott lived & worked is near Melrose. A prolific poet & novelist, his most famous works are the Waverley novels written around 1800. His house holds many of his possessions, including a collection of armour. Scott's View is one of the best vantage points in the borderlands with a prospect of the silvery Tweed & the three distinctive summits of the Eildon Hills.

Eildon Hills.

There are many gracious stately homes. Manderston is a classical house of great luxury, & Mellerstain is the work of the Adam family. Traquair was originally a Royal hunting lodge. Its main gates were locked in 1745 after a visit from Bonnie Prince Charlie, never to be opened until a Stuart King takes the throne.

Dumfries & Galloway to the southwest is an area of rolling hills with a fine coastline.

Plants flourish in the mild air here & there are palm trees at Ardwell House & the Logan Botanic Garden.

Scotland

The gardens at Castle Kennedy have rhododendrons, azaleas & magnolias & Threave Gardens near Castle Douglas are the National Trust for Scotland's School of gardening.

The Galloway Forest Park covers a vast area of lochs & hills & has views across to offshore Ailsa Craig. At Caerlaveroch Castle, an early Renaissance building near the coast of Dumfries, there is a national nature reserve.

The first church in Scotland was built by St. Ninian at Whithorn in 400 on a site now occupied by the 13th century priory. The spread of Christianity is marked by early memorial stones like the Latinus stone at Whithorn, & the abbeys of Dundrennan, Crossraguel, Glenluce & Sweetheart, named after its founder who carried her husband's heart in a casket & is buried with it in the abbey.

At Dumfries is the poet Burns' house, his mausoleum & the Burns Heritage Centre overlooking the River Nith.

In Upper Nithsdale the Mennock Pass leads to Wanlockhead & Leadhills, once centres of the lead-mining industry. There is a fascinating museum here & the opportunity of an underground trip.

Lowland

The Frith of Clyde & Glascow in the west, & the Firth of Forth with Edinburgh in the east are both areas of rich history, tradition & culture.

Edinburgh is the capital of Scotland & amongst the most visually exciting cities in the world. The New Town is a treasure trove of inspired neo-classical architecture, & below Edinburgh Castle high on the Rock, is the Old Town, a network of courts, closes, wynds & gaunt tenements around the Royal Mile.

The Palace of Holyrood House, home of Mary, Queen of Scots for several years overlooks Holyrood Park & nearby Arthur's Seat, is a popular landmark.

The City's varied art galleries include The Royal Scottish Academy, The National Gallery, Portrait Gallery, Gallery of Modern Art & many other civic & private collections.

The Royal Museum of Scotland displays superb historical & scientific material. The Royal Botanic Gardens are world famous.

Cultural life in Edinburgh peaks at Festival time in August. The official Festival, the Fringe, the Book Festival, Jazz Festival & Film Festival bring together artistes of international reputation.

The gentle hills around the city offer many opportunities for walking. The Pentland Hills are easily reached,

Inverary Castle.

with the Lammermuir Hills a little further south. There are fine beaches at Gullane, Yellowcraigs, North Berwick & at Dunbar.

Tantallon Castle, a 14th century stronghold, stands on the rocky Firth of Forth, & 17th century Hopetoun House, on the outskirts of the city is only one of a number of great houses in the area.

North of Edinburgh across the Firth of Forth lies the ancient Kingdom of Fife. Here is St. Andrews, a pleasant town on the seafront, an old university

Scotland

town & Scotland's ecclesiastical capital, but famous primarily for golf.

Glasgow is the industrial & business capital of Scotland. John Betjeman called it the 'finest Victorian city in Britain' & many buildings are remarkable examples of Victorian splendour, notably the City Chambers.

Many buildings are associated with the architect Charles Rennie MacKintosh; the Glasgow School of Art is one of them. Glasgow Cathedral is a perfect example of pre-Reformation Gothic architecture.

Glasgow is Scotland's largest city with the greatest number of parks & fine Botanic Garden. It is home to both the Scottish Opera & the Scottish Ballet, & has a strong & diverse cultural tradition from theatre to jazz. Its museums include the matchless Burrell Collection, & the Kelvingrove Museum & Art Gallery, which houses one of the best civic collections of paintings in Britain, as well as reflecting the city's engineering & shipbuilding heritage.

The coastal waters of the Clyde are world famous for cruising & sailing, with many harbours & marinas. The long coastline offers many opportunities for sea-angling from Largs to Troon & Prestwick, & right around to Luce Bay on the Solway.

There are many places for birdwatching on the Estuary, whilst the Clyde Valley is famous for its garden centres & nurseries.

Paisley has a mediaeval abbey, an observatory & a museum with a fine display of the famous 'Paisley' pattern shawls.

Further south, Ayr is a large seaside resort with sandy beach, safe bathing & a racecourse. In the Ayrshire valleys there is traditional weaving & lace & bonnet making, & Sorn, in the rolling countryside boasts its 'Best Kept Village' award.

Culzean Castle is one of the finest Adam houses in Scotland & stands in spacious grounds on the Ayrshire cliffs.

Robert Burns is Scotland's best loved poet, & 'Burns night' is widely celebrated. The region of Strathclyde shares with Dumfries & Galloway the title of 'Burns Country' . The son of a peasant farmer, Burns lived in poverty for much of his life. The simple house where he was born is in the village of Alloway. In the town of Ayr is the Auld Kirk where he was baptised & the footbridge of 'The Brigs of Ayr' is still in use. The Tam O'Shanter Inn is now a Burns museum & retains its thatched roof & simple fittings. The Burns Trail leads on to Mauchline where Possie Nansie's Inn remains. At Tarbolton the National Trust now care for the old house where Burns founded the 'Batchelors Club' debating society.

Perthshire, Loch Lomond & The Trossachs

By a happy accident of geology, the Highland Boundary fault which separates the Highlands from the Lowlands runs through Loch Lomond, close to the Trossachs & on through Perthshire, giving rise to marvellous scenery.

In former times Highlanders & Lowlanders raided & fought here. Great castles like Stirling, Huntingtower & Doune were built to protect the routes between the two different cultures.

Stirling was once the seat of Scotland's monarchs & the great Royal castle is set high on a basalt rock. The Guildhall & the Kirk of the Holy Rude are also interesting buildings in the town, with Cambuskenneth Abbey & the Bannockburn Heritage Centre close by.

Perth 'fair city' on the River Tay,

Scotland

has excellent shops & its own repertory theatre. Close by are the Black Watch Museum at Balhousie Castle, & the Branklyn Gardens, which are superb in May & June.

Scone Palace, to the north of Perth was home to the Stone or Scone of Destiny for nearly 500 years until its removal to Westminster. 40 kings of Scotland were crowned here.

Pitlochry sits amid beautiful Highland scenery with forest & hill walks, two nearby distilleries, the famous Festival theatre, Loch Faskally & the Dam Visitor Centre & Fish Ladder.

In the Pass of Killiecrankie, a short drive away, a simple stone marks the spot where the Highlanders charged barefoot to overwhelm the redcoat soldiers of General MacKay.

Queens View.

Famous Queen's View overlooks Loch Tummel beyond Pitlochry with the graceful peak of Schiehallion completing a perfect picture.

Other lochs are picturesque too; Loch Earn, Loch Katrine & bonnie Loch Lomond itself, & they can be enjoyed from a boat on the water. Ospreys nest at the Loch of the Lowes near Dunkeld.

Mountain trails lead through Ben Lawers & the 'Arrocher Alps' beyond Loch Lomond. The Ochils & the Campsie Fells have grassy slopes for walking. Near Callander are the Bracklinn Falls, the Callander Crags & the Falls of Leny.

Wooded areas include the Queen Elizabeth Forest Park & the Black Wood of Rannoch which is a fragment of an ancient Caledonian forest. There are some very tall old trees around Killiecrankie, & the world's tallest beech hedge - 26 metres high - grows at Meikleour near Blairgowrie.

Creiff & Blairgowrie have excellent golf courses set in magnificent scenery.

The Grampians, Highlands & Islands

This is spacious countryside with glacier-scarred mountains & deep glens cut through by tumbling rivers. The Grampian Highlands make for fine mountaineering & walking.

There is excellent skiing at Glenshee, & a centre at the Lecht for the less experienced, whilst the broad tops of the giant mountains are ideal for cross-country skiing. The chair-lift at Glenshee is worth a visit at any season.

The Dee, The Spey & The Don flow down to the coastal plain from the heights. Some of the world's finest trout & salmon beats are on these rivers.

Speyside is dotted with famous distilleries from Grantown-on-Spey to Aberdeen, & the unique Malt Whisky Trail can be followed.

Royal Deeside & Donside hold a number of notable castles. Balmoral is the present Royal family's holiday home, & Kildrummy is a romantic ruin in a lovely garden. Fyvie Castle has five dramatic towers & stands in peaceful parkland. Nearby Haddo House, by contrast, is an elegant Georgian home.

There is a 17th century castle at Braemar, but more famous here is the Royal Highland Gathering. There are wonderful walks in the vicinity -

Scotland

Morrone Hill, Glen Quoich & the Linn O'Dee are just a few.

The city of Aberdeen is famed for its sparkling granite buildings, its university, its harbour & fish market & for North Sea Oil. It also has long sandy beaches & lovely year-round flower displays, of roses in particular.

Around the coast are fishing towns & villages. Crovie & Pennan sit below impressive cliffs. Buckie is a typical small port along the picturesque coastline of the Moray Firth.

The Auld Kirk at Cullen has fine architectural features & elegant Elgin has beautiful cathedral ruins. Pluscarden Abbey, Spynie Palace & Duffus Castle are all nearby.

Dunnottar Castle.

Nairn has a long stretch of sandy beach & a golf course with an international reputation. Inland are Cawdor Castle & Culloden Battlefield.

The Northern Highlands are divided from the rest of Scotland by the dramatic valley of the Great Glen. From Fort William to Inverness, sea lochs, canals & the depths of Loch Ness form a chain of waterways linking both coasts.

Here are some of the wildest & most beautiful landscapes in Britain. Far Western Knoydart, the Glens of Cannich & Affric, the mysterious lochs, including Loch Morar, deeper than the North Sea, & the marvellous coastline; all are exceptional.

The glens were once the home of crofting communities, & of the clansmen who supported the Jacobite cause. The wild scenery of Glencoe is a favourite with walkers & climbers, but it has a tragic history. Its name means 'the glen of weeping' & refers to the massacre of the MacDonald clan in 1692, when the Royal troops who had been received as guests treacherously attacked their hosts at dawn.

The valleys are empty today largely as a result of the infamous Highland Clearances in the 19th century when the landowners turned the tenant crofters off the land in order to introduce the more profitable Cheviot sheep. The emigration of many Scots to the U.S.A. & the British Colonies resulted from these events.

South of Inverness lie the majestic Cairngorms. The Aviemore centre provides both summer & winter sports facilities here.

To the north of Loch Ness are the remains of the ancient Caledonian forest where red deer & stags are a common sight on the hills. Rarer are sightings of the Peregrine Falcon, the osprey, the Golden Eagle & the Scottish wildcat. Kincraig has excellent wildlife parks.

Inverness is the last large town in the north, & a natural gateway to the Highlands & to Moray, the Black Isle & the north-east.

The east coast is characterised by the Firths of Moray, Cromarty & Dornoch & by its changing scenery from gentle pastureland, wooded hillsides to sweeping coastal cliffs.

On the Black Isle, which is not a true island but has a causeway & bridge links with the mainland, Fortrose & Rosemarkie in particular have lovely beaches, caves & coastal walks. There is golf on the headland at Rosemarkie & a 13th century cathedral of rosy pink sandstone stands in Fortrose.

Scotland

Scotland Gazeteer

Areas of outstanding natural beauty

It would be invidious, not to say almost impossible, to choose any particular area of Scotland as having a more beautiful aspect than another - the entire country is a joy to the traveller. The rugged Highlands, the great glens, tumbling waters, tranquil lochs - the deep countryside or the wild coastline - simply come & choose your own piece of paradise.

Historic Houses & Castles

Bowhill - Nr. Selkirk
18th-19th century - home of the Duke of Bucceleugh & Queensberry. Has an outstanding collection of pictures by Canaletto,Claude, Gainsborough, Reynolds & Leonardo da Vinci. Superb silver, porcelain & furniture.16th & 17th century miniatures.

Traquair House - Innerleithen
A unique & ancient house being the oldest inhabited home in Scotland. It is rich in associations with every form of political history & after Bonnie Prince Charlie passed through its main gates in 1745 no other visitor has been allowed to use them. There are treasures in the house dating from 12th century, & it has an 18th century library & a priest's room with secret stairs.

Linlithgow Palace - Linlithgow
The birthplace of Mary, Queen of Scots.

Stirling Castle - Stirling
Royal Castle.

Drumlanrigg Castle - Nr. Thornhill
17th century castle of pale pink stone - romantic & historic - wonderful art treasures including a magnificent Rembrandt & a huge silver chandelier. Beautiful garden setting.

Braemar Castle - Braemar
17th century castle of great historic interest. Has round central tower with spiral staircase giving it a fairy-tale appearance.

Drum Castle - Nr. Aberdeen
Dating in part from 13th century, it has a great square tower.

Cawdor Castle - Nairn
14th century fortress - like castle - has always been the home of the Thanes of Cawdor - background to Shakespeare's Macbeth.

Dunvegan Castle - Isle of Skye
13th century - has always been the home of the Chiefs of McLeod.

Hopetoun House - South Queensferry
Very fine example of Adam architecture & has a fine collection of pictures & furniture. Splendid landscaped grounds.

Inverary Castle - Argyll
Home of the Dukes of Argyll. 18th century - Headquarters of Clan Campbell.

Burn's Cottage - Alloway
Birthplace of Robert Burns - 1659 - thatched cottage - museum of Burns' relics.

Bachelors' Club - Tarbolton
17th century house - thatched - where Burns & friends formed their club - 1780.

Blair Castle - Blair Atholl
Home of the Duke of Atholl, 13th century Baronial mansion - collection of Jacobite relics, armour, paintings, china & many other items.

Glamis Castle - Angus
17th century remodelling in Chateau style - home of the Earl of Strathmore & Kinghorne. Very attractive castle - lovely grounds by Capability Brown.

Scone Palace - Perth
has always been associated with seat of Government of Scotland from earliest times. The Stone of Destiny was removed from the Palace in 1296 & taken to Westminster Abbey. Present palace rebuilt in early 1800's still incorporating parts of the old. Lovely gardens.

Edinburgh Castle
Fortress standing high over the town - famous for military tattoo.

Culzean Castle & Country Park - Maybole
Fine Adam house & spacious gardens perched on Ayrshire cliff.

Dunrobin Castle - Golspie
Ancient seat of the Earls & Dukes of Sutherland.

Eilean Donan Castle - Wester Ross
13th century castle, Jacobite relics.

Manderston - Duns
Great classical house with only silver staircase in the world. Stables, marble dairy, formal gardens.

Scotland

Cathedrals & Churches

Dunfermline Abbey - Dunfermline
Norman remains of beautiful church.
Modern east end & tower.

Edinburgh (Church of the Holy Rood)
15th century - was divided into two in 17th
century & re-united 1938. Here Mary,
Queen of Scots was crowned.

Glasgow (St. Mungo)
12th-15th century cathedral - 19th century
interior. Central tower with spire.

Kirkwall (St. Magnus)
12th century cathedral with very fine nave.

Falkirk Old Parish Church - Falkirk
The spotted appearance (faw) of the
church (kirk) gave the town its name. The
site of the church has been used since 7th
century, with succesive churches built
upon it. The present church was much
rebuilt in 19th century. Interesting
historically.

St Columba's Abbey - Iona

Museums & Galleries

Agnus Folk Museum - Glamis
17th century cottages with stone slab
roofs, restored by the National Trust for
Scotland & houses a fine folk collection.

Mary, Queen of Scots' House - Jedburgh
Life & times of the Queen along with
paintings, etc.

Andrew Carnegie Birthplace -
Dunfermline
The cottage where he was born is now
part of a museum showing his life's work.

Aberdeen Art Gallery & Museum -
Aberdeen
Sculpture, paintings, watercolours, prints
& drawings. Applied arts. Maritime
museum exhibits.

Provost Skene's House - Aberdeen
17th century house now exhibiting local
domestic life, etc.

Highland Folk Museum - Kingussie
Examples of craft work & tools - furnished
cottage with mill.

West Highland Museum - Fort William
Natural & local hsitory. Relics of Jacobites
& exhibition of the '45 Rising.

Clan Macpherson House - Newtonmore
Relics of the Clan.

Glasgow Art Gallery & Museum -
Glasgow
Archaeology, technology, local & natural
history. Old Masters, tapestries, porcelain,
glass & silver, etc. Sculpture.

Scottish National Gallery - Edinburgh
20th century collection - paintings &
sculpture - Arp, Leger, Giacometti,
Matisse, Picasso. Modern Scottish
painting.

**National Museum of Antiquities in
Scotland** - Edinburgh
Collection from Stone Age to modern
times - Relics of Celtic Church, Stuart
relics, Highland weapons, etc.

Gladstone Court - Biggar
Small indoor street of shops, a bank,
schoolroom, library, etc.

Burns' Cottage & Museum - Alloway
Relics of Robert Burns - National Poet.

Inverness Museum & Art Gallery -
Inverness
Social history, archaeology & cultural life
of the Highlands. Display of the Life of the
Clans - good Highland silver - crafts, etc.

Kirkintilloch - Nr. Glasgow
Auld Kirk Museum. Local history,
including archaeological specimens from
the Antonine Wall (Roman). Local
industries, exhibitions, etc

Pollock House & Park - Glasgow
18th century house with collection of
paintings, etc. The park is the home of the
award-winning Burrell Collection
The foregoing are but a few of the many
museums & galleries in Scotland - further
information is always freely available from
the Tourist Information.

Historic Monuments

Aberdour Castle - Aberdour
14th century fortification - part still roofed.

Balvenie Castle - Duffton
15th century castle ruins.

Cambuskenneth Abbey - Nr. Stirling
12th century abbey - seat of Bruce's
Parliament in 1326. Ruins.

Dryburgh Abbey - Dryburgh
Remains of monastery.

Loch Leven Castle - Port Glasgow
15th century ruined stronghold - once lived
in by Mary, Queen of Scots.

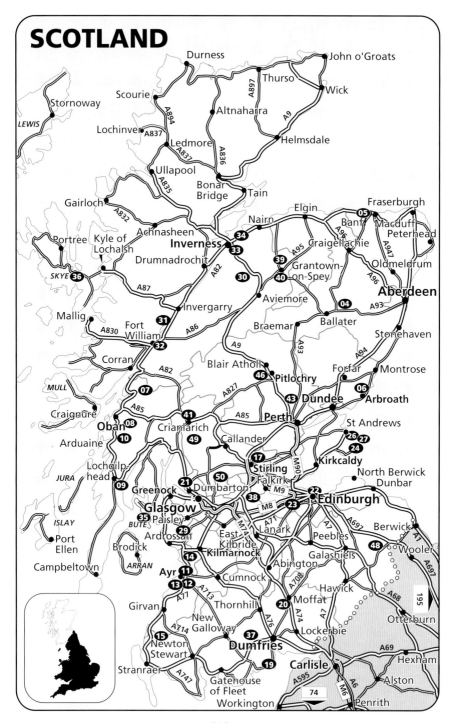

SCOTLAND

SCOTLAND
Map references

04	Chambers	22	Robins	38	Hunter
05	Watt	22	Drummond	39	Dickinson
06	De Morgan	22	A.Vidler	40	M. Stewart
07	Broadbent	23	D.Scott	41	Gaughan
08	Cugley	26	Fyfe	43	Andrew
09	Nicol	27	Erskine	46	Maxwell
10	Oatts	29	Anderson	46	Sanderson
11	C.McDonald	30	Gardner	46	Mathieson
12	Martin	31	Cairns	48	B.Smith
13	Gemmell	32	Campbell	49	Wilson
14	Payne	32	C.MacDonald	50	Haslam
15	Sweeney	33	Parsons		
17	O'Dell	34	Pottie		
19	Fordyce	35	Harrison		
20	Ash-Kuri	36	Wilcken		
21	S.Macdonald	36	Prall		
22	Sandeman	37	Dickson		
22	Stanley				
22	D.Vidler				
22	Urquhart				
22	Redmayne				
22	Gilbert				
22	Della-Porta				
22	Leishman				
22	Hill				
22	G. Stuart				
22	Virtue				
22	Welch				
22	Varma				

1 INVERCLYDE
2 DUNBARTON & CLYDEBANK
3 RENFREWSHIRE
4 EAST RENFREWSHIRE
5 GLASGOW
6 EAST DUNBARTONSHIRE
7 NORTH LANARKSHIRE
8 FALKIRK
9 CLACKMANNAN
10 WEST LOTHIAN
11 EDINBURGH
12 MID LOTHAIN

The Scottish Countryside.

rate £ from - to per double room	children taken	evening meals	animals taken

---

| £50.00 to £70.00 | Y | Y | Y |

Near Rd: A.93

Tigh na Geald

A beautifully restored Victorian house overlooking the village green in the centre of Aboyne on Royal Deeside. Aberdeen City & Balmoral Castle only 30 mins' drive away. Close to golf course, gliding strip & easy walking distance of shops, tennis courts & river bank. Near the hills & mountains & at the start point of the famous whisky trail. Shooting & fishing can be arranged. Offering 1 large double bedroom & 1 large twin-bedded room, both with spacious en-suite bathroom facilities.
E-mail: chambers@planet-talk.co.uk
www.bestbandb.co.uk

| Julia Chambers | Tigh na Geald | Ballater Road | Aboyne AB34 5HY | Aberdeenshire |
| Tel: (013398) 86668 | | Fax 013398 85606 | Open: ALL YEAR | Map Ref No. 04 |

| £56.00 to £56.00 | N | Y | N |

Near Rd: A.95

Balwarren B & B

A 30-acre croft in the heart of Aberdeenshire. It is teeming with wildlife; ducks, herons & buzzards inhabit the wood by the pond, along with badgers, roe deer & night owls. There are 2 lovely & immaculate twin-bedded rooms, each with en-suite facilities. Also, a sunny sitting room with a wood burning stove & a small garden in which to relax. Delicious breakfasts are served & include home-made jams & chutneys. An ideal touring base, situated close to 'castle & whisky country',
E-mail: balwarren@tiscali.co.uk
www.balwarrenbedandbreakfast.com

| Hazel Watt | Balwarren B & B | Ordiquhill | Cornhill | Banff AB45 7HR | Aberdeenshire |
| Tel: (01466) 751688 | | Fax 01466 751688 | | Open: MAR - NOV | Map Ref No. 05 |

| £75.00 to £75.00 | Y | Y | Y |

Near Rd: A.92

Ethie Castle

A warm welcome awaits you at the de Morgan family home. An ancient sandstone fortress dating from the 14th century, former home of Cardinal David Beaton Abbot of Arbroath & the Earls of Northesk. Ethie is reputed to be Scotland's second oldest inhabited castle. Immortalised by Sir Walter Scott as "Knockwhinnock" in his novel 'The Antiquary'. Ethie is now a haven of hospitality & peace with 3 elegant guest rooms. Who can resist the famous Arbroath smokie? Dogs by arrangement.
E-mail: kmydemorgan@aol.com
www.ethiecastle.com

| Kirstin de Morgan | Ethie Castle | By Arbroath DD11 5SP | Angus |
| Tel: (01241) 830434 | Fax 01241 830432 | Open: ALL YEAR | Map Ref No. 06 |

| £60.00 to £70.00 | Y | Y | Y |

Near Rd: A.828

Lochside Cottage

Total peace on the shore of Loch Baile Mhic Chailen, in an idyllic glen of outstanding beauty. There are many walks from the cottage garden; or visit Fort William, Glencoe & Oban, from where you can board a steamer to explore the Western Isles. At the end of the day, a warm welcome awaits you: delicious home-cooked dinner, a log fire & the certainty of a perfect night's sleep in one of 3 en-suite bedrooms. A charming home. Children & animals by prior arrangement.
E-mail: broadbent@lochsidecottage.fsnet.co.uk
www.lochsidecottage.fsnet.co.uk

| Earle & Stella Broadbent | Lochside Cottage | Fasnacloich | Appin PA38 4BJ | Argyll |
| Tel: (01631) 730216 | Fax 01631 730216 | Open: ALL YEAR | Map Ref No. 07 |

Scotland
Argyll & Ayrshire

Sithe Mor House

Near Rd: B.845

£70.00 to £110.00   Y   Y   N

Sithe Mor House is on the shores of Loch Awe & has its own bay, beach, jetty & private fishing rights on the loch. The 2 main en suite bedrooms have beautiful original frieze plasterwork, 20 feet domed ceilings, stunning views over the the loch & luxury en suite bathrooms. With its antlers, portraits & antiques this 1880's house oozes a Scots baronial feel. Fine local produce is a highlight at dinner. Kilts are encouraged & you can even borrow one for dinner. Enjoy Scottish hospitality at its best.
E-mail: patsy@sithemor.com
www.sithemor.com

VISA: M'CARD: AMEX:

Patsy & John Cugley   Sithe Mor House   Kilchrenan   Loch Awe PA35 1HF   Argyll
Tel: (01866) 833234   Open: ALL YEAR   Map Ref No. 08

Allt-na-Craig

Near Rd: A.83

£75.00 to £120.00   Y   Y   Y

Hamish & Charlotte warmly welcome all their guests to Allt-na-Craig, a lovely old Victorian mansion set in picturesque grounds overlooking Loch Fyne. Accommodation is in 5 comfortable en-suite bedrooms with tea/coffee makers, hairdryers & T.V. A guests' drawing room with open fire & dining room is also available. This is a perfect base for outdoor activities, like hill-walking, fishing, golf, riding & windsurfing, or for visiting the islands. Delicious evening meals by arrangement.
E-mail: information@allt-na-craig.co.uk
www.allt-na-craig.co.uk

VISA: M'CARD:

Hamish & Charlotte Nicol   Allt-na-Craig   Tarbert Road Ardrishaig   Lochgilphead PA30 8EP Argyll
Tel: (01546) 603245   Open: ALL YEAR (Excl. Xmas)   Map Ref No. 09

Glenmore

Near Rd: A.816

£60.00 to £86.00   Y   N   Y

Dating from the 1850s, Glenmore retains many original architectural features. This attractive family home is furnished throughout with antiques & interesting pictures. Superbly situated with spectacular views down Loch Melfort. Offering 1 double bedroom & 1 family suite, each with private facilities. Also, a drawing room with open fire in which to relax. An ideal location for exploring Argyll, with fishing, boat trips, horse riding & National Trust for Scotland gardens nearby. Dogs by arrangement.
E-mail: oatts@glenmore22.fsnet.co.uk
www.glenmorecountryhouse.co.uk

Alasdair & Melissa Oatts   Glenmore   Kilmelford   By Oban PA34 4XA   Argyll
Tel: (01852) 200314   Open: ALL YEAR (Excl. Xmas & New Year)   Map Ref No. 10

The Crescent

Near Rd: A.70

£60.00 to £70.00   Y   N   N

Built in 1898 at the height of Victorian splendour, No. 26 The Crescent lies amidst an impressive row of imposing terraced houses. Its location allows guests complete peace & quiet, yet enjoys close proximity & easy access to Ayr's busy shopping centre & seafront. The charming rooms have all been individually styled & decorated & include the Grand 4-poster bedroom, the ground floor Yellow room with French doors opening onto the garden & other equally delightful bedrooms. Children over 8.
E-mail: carrie@26crescent.freeserve.co.uk
www.26crescent.freeserve.co.uk

VISA: M'CARD:

Caroline McDonald   The Crescent   26 Bellevue Crescent   Ayr KA7 2DR   Ayrshire
Tel: (01292) 287329   Fax 01292 286779   Open: ALL YEAR (Excl. Xmas & New Year) Map Ref No. 11

rate £ from - to per double room	children taken	evening meals taken	animals taken

---

£60.00 to £60.00

N | N | N

🚭

Near Rd: A.719

Greenan Lodge

A warm welcome is assured at Greenan Lodge. Located on the coastal route yet only 2 miles from Ayr town centre, 1 1/2 miles from the A.77 & near Prestwick Airport. Set in the heart of Burns country, a perfect base for Turnberry, Troon & Prestwick golf courses & nearby Culzean Castle. All rooms are en-suite with T.V. & tea/coffee makers. Relax & unwind in the comfort of the lounge & enjoy breakfast in the conservatory style dining room. Ideal for a relaxing break. Single supplement.
E-mail: helen@greenanlodge.com
www.greenanlodge.com

| *Helen Martin* | *Greenan Lodge* | *39 Dunure Road* | *Ayr KA7 4HR* | *Ayrshire* |
| *Tel: (01292) 443939* | | *Open: ALL YEAR* | | *Map Ref No. 12* |

£55.00 to £65.00

N | N | N

🚭

VISA: M'CARD:

Near Rd: A.77

Dunduff House

A warm friendly welcome awaits you at Dunduff House. Situated just south of Ayr at the coastal village of Dunure, this 600 acre family-run beef & sheep unit is only 15 mins' from the shore. Excellent homely & comfortable accommodation. Bedrooms have panoramic coastal views over Arran, the Holy Isle, Mull of Kintyre & Ailsa Craig. Each is well-equipped & has beverage facilities, etc. & an en-suite/private bathroom. Ideal base for touring: Culzean Castle, Robert Burns' Cottage & more.
E-mail: gemmelldunduff@aol.com
www.gemmelldunduff.co.uk

| *Mrs Agnes Gemmell* | *Dunduff House* | *Dunure* | *Ayr KA7 4LH* | *Ayrshire* |
| *Tel: (01292) 500225* | *Fax 01292 500222* | *Open: FEB - NOV* | | *Map Ref No. 13* |

£80.00 to £80.00

Y | Y | N

🚭

Near Rd: A.77

Glenfoot House

Glenfoot is a former Georgian manse lying amidst beautiful Ayrshire countryside surrounding the 14th-century Dundonald Castle, which was built by Robert Stewart to mark his succession to the throne as Robert II in 1371. It is an ideal base for exploring Glasgow, the Isle of Arran & the Argyle Peninsula. For golfers the championship courses at Troon, Prestwick & Turnberry are within easy reach. The house is warm & comfortable & the upstairs drawing room has fine views.
E-mail: alan@onyxnet.co.uk
www.aboutscotland.com

| *Sheila Payne* | *Glenfoot House* | *Dundonald KA2 9HG* | *Ayrshire* |
| *Tel: (01563) 850311* | | *Open: ALL YEAR* | *Map Ref No. 14* |

£58.00 to £85.00

N | Y | N

🚭

VISA: M'CARD:

Near Rd: A.77

Balkissock Lodge

A warm welcome greets you at this comfortable Georgian house. Its secluded location amid stunning scenery offers the ideal spot for a peaceful break. Enjoy excellent meals in homely surroundings, relax in the spacious lounge by a crackling log fire, then retire to a delightful bedroom with full facilities. Near to Culzean Castle, Turnberry, Galloway Forest & ferries, ideal for walking, cycling, golf, fishing or touring the west of Scotland.
E-mail: frananden@aol.com
www.balkissocklodge.co.uk

| *Denis & Fran Sweeney* | *Balkissock Lodge* | *Ballantrae* | *Girvan KA26 0LP* | *Ayrshire* |
| *Tel/Fax: (01465) 831537* | *Mobile 07889 715899* | *Open: ALL YEAR* | | *Map Ref No. 15* |

Clackmannanshire
Dumfriesshire & Dunbartonshire

Westbourne House

Near Rd: A.91

A fascinating Victorian mill-owner's mansion set within wooded grounds beneath the Ochil Hills. The atmosphere is warm & friendly. All 3 bedrooms are comfortably furnished, 2 en-suite (1 ground floor) & 1 with private bathroom. All have T.V. etc. Enjoy Aga-cooked breakfasts including Jane's famous porridge & smoked salmon with scrambled eggs. Ideal for visiting Stirling (15 mins) & Edinburgh, Glasgow, St Andrews & the Trossachs (1hr.) Golf courses & an equestrian centre. Parking.
E-mail: info@westbournehouse.co.uk
www.westbournehouse.co.uk

£48.00 to £52.00 | Y | N | Y

VISA: M'CARD:

Adrian & Jane O'Dell   Westbourne House   10 Dollar Road   Tillicoultry   Stirling FK13 6PA
Clackmannanshire Tel: (01259) 750314 Open: ALL YEAR (Excl. Xmas & New Year) Map Ref No. 17

Cavens House

Near Rd: A.710

Formerly an old mansion with a strong American historical connection, Cavens, now a charming small country house hotel, offers 6 comfortable en-suite bedrooms. 2 lounges with open fires add to the ambience of the house. Standing in 11 acres of gardens & woodland, it is ideal for those wishing to explore the the Solway Coast. Sailing, walking, golfing, shooting, fishing & riding by arrangement. Award-winning cuisine; 3-course dinner £25.00. Children 12+. Dogs by arrangement.
E-mail: enquiries@cavens.com
www.cavens.com

£110.00 to £160.00 | Y | Y | Y

VISA: M'CARD: AMEX:

Angus Fordyce   Cavens House   Kirkbean   By Dumfries DG2 8AA   Dumfriesshire
Tel: (01387) 880234   Fax 01387 880467   Open: ALL YEAR   Map Ref No. 19

Hartfell House

Near Rd: A.701

Hartfell House is a splendid Victorian manor house located in a rural setting overlooking the hills, yet only a few mins' walk from the town. A listed building known locally for its fine interior woodwork. Accommodation is in 7 spacious & tastefully furnished bedrooms, each with en-suite facilities. Standing in gardens of lawns & trees, & providing an atmosphere of peaceful relaxation. A warm welcome awaits you. Animals by arrangement.
E-mail: enquiries@hartfellhouse.co.uk
www.hartfellhouse.co.uk

£55.00 to £55.00 | Y | N | Y

VISA: M'CARD:

Mr & Mrs Ash-Kuri   Hartfell House   Hartfell Crescent   Moffat DG10 9AL   Dumfriesshire
Tel: (01683) 220153   Open: ALL YEAR (Excl. Jan, Feb & Xmas)   Map Ref No. 20

Kirkton House

Near Rd: A.814

Experience a blend of "olde worlde" charm, modern amenities & superb views at this converted 18/19th-century farmstead, set in a tranquil countryside location yet handy for Glasgow City (34 mins by train/car), Glasgow Airport (25 mins by car), Loch Lomond, The Trossachs & the West Highland route. 6 en-suite bedrooms including 4 family rooms. Parking. Real fire on chilly evenings in lounge with 'Freeview' TV. Original stone walls & old "swee" for the cooking pots in the dining room.
E-mail: bbiw@kirktonhouse.co.uk
www.kirktonhouse.co.uk

£50.00 to £60.00 | Y | N | Y

see PHOTO over
p. 319

VISA: M'CARD: AMEX:

Stewart & Gillian Macdonald   Kirkton House   Darleith Road   Cardross   Dumbarton G82 5EZ
Dunbartonshire   Tel: (01389) 841951   Fax (01389) 841868   Open: FEB - NOV   Map Ref No. 21

Kirkton House. Cardross.

Scotland
Edinburgh

Sandeman House

Near Rd: A.702

Built in 1860, Sandeman House is a charming family home which has been sympathetically restored by Neil & Joyce Sandeman. The 3 bedrooms are individually furnished & are bright & tastefully decorated to a high standard. Each has an en-suite/private bathroom, T.V., tea/coffee, etc. A full traditional Scottish breakfast is served including homemade preserves. Shops, bars & restaurants close by. Within easy reach of most of the city's attractions. Children 12+. Dogs by arrangement.
E-mail: joycesandeman@freezone.co.uk
www.sandemanhouse.co.uk

£60.00 to £90.00   Y   N   Y

VISA: M'CARD:

Joyce Sandeman	Sandeman House	33 Colinton Road	Edinburgh EH10 5DR
Tel: (0131) 4478080	Fax 0131 4478080	Open: ALL YEAR	Map Ref No. 22

Joppa Turrets Guest House

Near Rd: A.1

This charming guest house is set in a peaceful location on a mile of sandy seaside, which will really add to your unmissable Edinburgh experience. The cosy pretty bedrooms all have sea views & private or shared facilities. Good restaurants are within a few mins' walk. There is an excellent & frequent bus service into the city centre for all that Edinburgh has to offer. A delightful home. Children over 3. (Please note: the guest house is located at the beach end of Morton Street).
E-mail: stanley@joppaturrets.com
www.joppaturrets.com

£58.00 to £82.00   Y   N   N

VISA: M'CARD:

Edward & Felicity Stanley	Joppa Turrets Guest House	1 Lower Joppa	Joppa	Edinburgh EH15 2ER
Tel: (0131) 6695806	Fax 0131 6695806	Open: ALL YEAR (Excl. Xmas)		Map Ref No. 22

Kenvie Guest House

Near Rd: A.1, A.7

Kenvie Guest House is charming, comfortable, warm, friendly & inviting. This small Victorian town house is situated in a quiet residential street, 1 small block from the main road, leading to the city centre (an excellent bus service) & the bypass to all routes. Offering, for your comfort, lots of caring touches, including complimentary tea/coffee, colour T.V. & no-smoking rooms. Private facilities available. You are guaranteed a warm welcome from Richard & Dorothy.
E-mail: dorothy@kenvie.co.uk
www.kenvie.co.uk

£52.00 to £70.00   Y   N   N

VISA: M'CARD:

Dorothy Vidler	Kenvie Guest House	16 Kilmaurs Road	Edinburgh EH16 5DA
Tel: (0131) 6681964	Fax 0131 6681926	Open: ALL YEAR	Map Ref No. 22

Kildonan Lodge Hotel

Near Rd: A.701

Ideally situated close to the city centre, Kildonan Lodge with its own private car park, is an outstanding example of Victorian elegance providing the perfect setting for your visit to Scotland's capital. Relax in the elegant lounge & enjoy a 'dram' from the Honesty Bar. Each of the individually designed en-suite bedrooms have T.V., free broadband wireless internet & complimentary sherry. In selected rooms there are 4-poster beds & spa baths.
E-mail: info@kildonanlodgehotel.co.uk
www.kildonanlodgehotel.co.uk

£89.00 to £149.00   Y   N   N

see PHOTO over
p. 321

VISA: M'CARD: AMEX:

Maggie Urquhart	Kildonan Lodge Hotel	27 Craigmillar Park	Edinburgh EH16 5PE
Tel: (0131) 6672793	Fax 0131 6679777	Open: ALL YEAR (Excl. Xmas)	Map Ref No. 22

Kildonan Lodge Hotel. Edinburgh.

Gerald's Place. Edinburgh.

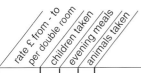

rate £ from - to per double room	children taken	evening meals	animals taken

Kingsley Guest House

£46.00 to £80.00 Y N N

Near Rd: A.701

A warm, friendly welcome awaits you at this Victorian terraced villa. Offering 5 comfortably furnished bedrooms, each with either en-suite or private facilities, T.V. & tea/coffee-making facilities. A full English or Continental breakfast is served. Kingsley Guest House is conveniently situated in the south of the city, with an excellent bus service at the door to & from the city centre which has many tourist attractions. Parking.
E-mail: lyn.kingsley@virgin.net
www.kingsleyguesthouse.co.uk

Mrs Lyn Redmayne	Kingsley Guest House	30 Craigmillar Park	Edinburgh EH16 5PS
Tel: (0131) 6673177	Fax 0131 6678439	Open: ALL YEAR	Map Ref No. 22

Frederick House Hotel

£50.00 to £130.00 Y N N

Near Rd: A.8

Frederick House Hotel is perfectly situated in the very heart of Edinburgh's city centre, a stones' throw from Princes Street. All of the 45 newly refurbished & tastefully decorated bedrooms feature en-suite bathrooms (with bath & shower); breakfast is served in your room. Your hosts' aim is to make your stay as comfortable & relaxing as possible, with all modern conveniences combined together with an 'olde worlde' atmosphere.
E-mail: frederickhouse@ednet.co.uk
www.townhousehotels.co.uk

VISA: M'CARD: AMEX:

Michael Gilbert	Frederick House Hotel	42 Frederick Street	Edinburgh EH2 1EX
Tel: (0131) 2261999	Fax 0131 6247064	Open: ALL YEAR	Map Ref No. 22

Gerald's Place

£63.00 to £119.00 N N N

Near Rd: A.1

Your host Gerald, welcomes you to his delightful home full of character, colour & comforts. The accommodation includes 2 double bedrooms (each with one king-size bed or 2 3ft beds of supreme comfort & quality) with 2 private bathrooms (each with power shower & bath tub). It is the ideal place for 2 couples travelling together. The full Scottish breakfast is a feast. Abercromby Place is at the very centre of the city, only 6 mins' walk from Waverley station. One of the finest streets in Edinburgh.
E-mail: gerald@geraldsplace.com
www.geraldsplace.com

see PHOTO over
p. 322

Gerald Della-Porta	Gerald's Place	21B Abercromby Place	Edinburgh EH3 6QE
Tel: (0131) 5587017	Mobile 077 6601 6840	Fax 0131 5587014	Open: ALL YEAR Map Ref No. 22

Elmview

£80.00 to £110.00 N N N

Near Rd: A.702

Robin & Nici Hill's luxurious bed & breakfast is situated in the heart of Edinburgh within easy walking distance of Edinburgh Castle & Princes Street (1 km). Elmview is a wonderful base from which to enjoy your stay in Edinburgh. Each bedroom has been elegantly furnished throughout & all have en-suite facilities. Direct-dial 'phones, fridges & fresh flowers are but a few of the thoughtful extras in each bedroom. A delightful home.
E-mail: nici@elmview.co.uk
www.elmview.co.uk

see PHOTO over
p. 324

VISA: M'CARD:

Robin & Nici Hill	Elmview	15 Glengyle Terrace	Edinburgh EH3 9LN
Tel: (0131) 228 1973		Open: 01 MAR - 01 DEC	Map Ref No. 22

Elmview. Edinburgh.

Ellesmere Guest House. Edinburgh.

	rate £ from - to per double room	children taken	evening meals	animals taken

Accommodation at The Stuarts

Near Rd: A.702

30 years talking with guests have enabled the Stuarts to give you all the facilities you want including a dedicated desk top computer in the hall for guests' exclusive use. Their central location & good-value rates do the rest. Your hosts have thought of everything. The spacious & luxurious bedrooms have comfortable twin beds or super king-size beds. A delightful home. Edinburgh has so much to offer that a 3 nights minimum stay is sincerely recommended.
E-mail: BBB@the-stuarts.com
www.the-stuarts.com

£85.00 to £110.00   Y   N   N

see PHOTO over
p. 327

Gloria Stuart   Accommodation at The Stuarts   17 Glengyle Terrace   Edinburgh EH3 9LN
Tel: (0131) 2299559   Open: ALL YEAR (Excl. Xmas)   Map Ref No. 22

VISA: M'CARD: AMEX:

Ellesmere Guest House

Near Rd: A.702

Guests are made welcome at this very elegant tastefully restored Victorian town house, quietly situated overlooking golf links in the centre of Edinburgh. Rooms are all en-suite, decorated to a very high standard & well-equipped with every comfort in mind. Delicious breakfasts are served. 'A home away from home.' Convenient for castle, Princes Street, Royal Mile, International Conference Centre, theatres & restaurants.
E-mail: celia@edinburghbandb.co.uk
www.edinburghbandb.co.uk

£70.00 to £90.00   N   N   N

see PHOTO over
p. 325

Cecilia & Tommy Leishman   Ellesmere Guest House   11 Glengyle Terrace   Edinburgh EH3 9LN
Tel: (0131) 229 4823   Open: ALL YEAR   Map Ref No. 22

The Town House

Near Rd: A.702

Attractive Victorian town house, located in the city centre. Theatres & restaurants are only minutes walk away. The Town House has been fully restored & tastefully decorated, retaining many original architectural features. The bedrooms are tastefully furnished & individually decorated, all have en-suite bath or shower & w.c., radio/alarm, colour T.V., hairdryer & tea/coffee tray. Parking is situated at the rear of the house. Self-catering apartment also available. Children over 9.
E-mail: susan@thetownhouse.com
www.thetownhouse.com

£76.00 to £100.00   Y   N   N

Susan Virtue   The Town House   65 Gilmore Place   Edinburgh EH3 9NU
Tel: (0131) 2291985   Open: ALL YEAR   Map Ref No. 22

Ravensdown Guest House

Near Rd: A.1

Built at the beginning of the 1900s, Ravensdown offers unsurpassed panoramic views of the Edinburgh skyline. 6 individually decorated rooms with T.V. & coffee/tea facilities & an en-suite or private bathroom. Guests may socialise in the lounge, with a bar service. Your friendly hosts are on hand to give advice about local attractions & tours. A delicious breakfast sets you up for a day. An excellent bus service means you can leave the car in the car park & commute the 2 miles to the centre.
E-mail: len@ravensdown.freeserve.co.uk
//members.edinburgh.org/ravensdown

£50.00 to £80.00   Y   N   N

Lisa Greenan   Ravensdown Guest House   248 Ferry Road   Edinburgh EH5 3AN
Tel: (0131) 5525438   Open: ALL YEAR   Map Ref No. 22

The Stuarts. Edinburgh.

Table legend (diagonal headers): rate £ from - to per double room / children taken / evening meals / animals taken

Ailsa Craig Hotel

Near Rd: A.1

Ailsa Craig Hotel is situated in the heart of Edinburgh near the city centre in one of the most prestigious terraces. This elegant Georgian town house hotel is situated only 10 mins' walk from Princes Street, Waverly Station & many attractions. 16 tastefully furnished & decorated bedrooms, all with en-suite facilities, 'phone, hairdryer, colour T.V. & tea/coffee-making facilities. A delicious breakfast & good evening meals are served. A perfect base for exploring Edinburgh.
E-mail: ailsacraighotel@ednet.co.uk
www.townhousehotels.co.uk

£50.00 to £100.00 — Y Y N

VISA: M'CARD: AMEX:

Navin Varma   Ailsa Craig Hotel   24 Royal Terrace   Edinburgh EH7 5AB
Tel: (0131) 5566055/5561022   Fax 0131 5566055   Open: ALL YEAR   Map Ref No. 22

Sonas Guest House

Near Rd: A.701, A.7

Sonas Guest House is a delightful Victorian villa, cira 1876, built for the directors of the railways & quietly situated 1 mile from the city centre. The well-appointed en-suite bedrooms have a colour T.V., welcome tray & hairdryer. Delicious Scottish breakfasts are served. Irene & Dennis wish to welcome you to an idyllic base for exploring the attractions of historic Edinburgh. Private parking. Many guests favour them with a return visit. 'Sonas' Gaelic for bliss.
E-mail: info@sonasguesthouse.com
www.sonasguesthouse.com

£50.00 to £90.00 — Y N N

VISA: M'CARD:

Irene Robins   Sonas Guest House   3 East Mayfield   Newington   Edinburgh EH9 1SD
Tel: (0131) 6672781   Open: ALL YEAR   Map Ref No. 22

Parklands Guest House

Near Rd: A.701

Parklands is an attractive Victorian terraced house conveniently located 1 1/2 miles from Princes Street & all the main tourist attractions. Accommodation is in 6 bedrooms, each is furnished to a high standard & is fully equipped with en-suite/private facilities, T.V. & tea/coffee makers. A full Scottish breakfast is served. Nearby are many excellent restaurants. Parklands is family-run with a friendly atmosphere. You are assured of a warm welcome.
E-mail: reservations@parklands-guesthouse.co.uk
www.bestbandb.co.uk

£45.00 to £70.00 — Y N N

Alan Drummond   Parklands Guest House   20 Mayfield Gardens   Edinburgh EH9 2BZ
Tel: (0131) 6677184   Fax 0131 6672011   Open: ALL YEAR   Map Ref No. 22

Ashcroft Farmhouse

Near Rd: A.71

New farmhouse set in beautifully landscaped gardens, enjoying lovely views of the surrounding farmland. Only 10 miles from Edinburgh, 5 miles from the airport, city bypass, M.8/M.9, Ingliston & Livingston. Bedrooms, including a 4-poster, are attractively furnished in pine with co-ordinating fabrics. Good bus/train service to city centre (20 mins). Choice of breakfasts with local produce. Children over 5. Parking. Elizabeth was runner-up in the UK Landlady of the Year awards 2005.
E-mail: scottashcroft7@aol.com
www.ashcroftfarmhouse.com

£64.00 to £70.00 — Y N N

see PHOTO over
p. 329

VISA: M'CARD:

Derek & Elizabeth Scott   Ashcroft Farmhouse   East Calder   Nr. Edinburgh EH53 0ET
Tel: (01506) 881810   Fax 01506 884327   Open: ALL YEAR   Map Ref No. 23

Ashcroft Farmhouse. East Calder.

Edinburgh
Fife & Glasgow

Rowan Guest House

Near Rd: A.701, A.7

Elegant Victorian home in one of the city's loveliest areas with free parking & only a 10 min. bus ride to the centre. The castle, Royal Mile, restaurants & other amenities easily reached. The charmingly decorated bedrooms are comfortably & tastefully furnished with complimentary tea/coffee & biscuits. Breakfast, including traditional porridge & freshly baked scones, will keep you going until dinner! Attentive friendly hosts.

E-mail: angela@rowan-house.co.uk
www.rowan-house.co.uk

| £50.00 to £78.00 | Y | N | N |

VISA: M'CARD:

Alan & Angela Vidler   Rowan Guest House   13 Glenorchy Terrace   Edinburgh EH9 2DQ
Tel: (0131) 6672463   Fax 0131 6672463   Open: ALL YEAR   Map Ref No. 22

Kinkell House

Near Rd: A.917

Kinkell is a family home near St. Andrews where Sandy & Frippy Fyfe offer a warm welcome, good food & informal hospitality, & are delighted for you to join them for dinner. They offer 3 very comfortable en-suite guest rooms. Kinkell runs down to the sea & has spectacular views of the coast & St. Andrews as well as access to walks on the coast. Attractions of the area include golf, historic buildings, scenic villages, the sea & wonderful beaches.

E-mail: info@kinkell.com
www.kinkell.com

| £80.00 to £80.00 | Y | Y | Y |

VISA: M'CARD: AMEX:

Sandy Fyfe   Kinkell House   St. Andrews KY16 8PN   Fife
Tel: (01334) 472003   Fax 01334 475248   Open: ALL YEAR   Map Ref No. 26

Cambo House

Near Rd: A. 917

This impressive Victorian house lies at the heart of the 1200 acre estate, which has been home to Peter's family since 1688 & is set among picturesque fishing villages, near St Andrews yet 1 1/2 hours from Edinburgh & the Highlands. 2 elegantly furnished bedrooms (1 with 4-poster) with en-suite/private facilities. Enjoy the restful atmosphere of the Victorian walled garden, woodland walks to sea or elegant sitting room overlooking the fountain. Evening meals & dogs by arrangement.

E-mail: cambo@camboestate.com
www.camboestate.com

| £84.00 to £104.00 | Y | Y | Y |

VISA: M'CARD: AMEX:

Peter & Catherine Erskine   Cambo House   Kingsbarns   St. Andrews KY16 8QD   Fife
Tel: (01333) 450313   Fax 01333 450987 Open: ALL YEAR (Excl. Xmas & New Year) Map Ref No. 27

East Lochhead Country House

Near Rd: A.760

A large 100-year-old Scottish farmhouse commanding beautiful views over Barr Loch & the Renfrewshire hills. Offering 3 beautifully furnished bedrooms with panoramic views, an en-suite/private bathroom, T.V. & tea/coffee-making facilities. Janet is an enthusiastic cook & meals are delicious. (Special diets catered for.) An ideal base for visiting Glasgow & touring Ayrshire, the Clyde coast, the Trossachs (Rob Roy country) & Loch Lomond. (Self-catering cottages also available.)

E-mail: admin@eastlochhead.co.uk
www.eastlochhead.co.uk

| £70.00 to £80.00 | Y | Y | Y |

VISA: M'CARD: AMEX:

Janet Anderson   East Lochhead Country House   Largs Road   Lochwinnoch PA12 4DX   Glasgow
Tel: (01505) 842610   Fax 01505 842610   Open: ALL YEAR   Map Ref No. 29

The Grange. Fort William.

Column headers (rotated): rate £ from - to per double room | children taken | evening meals | animals taken

Feith Mhor Lodge

Near Rd: A.9

Situated in a peaceful but accessible valley, 25 miles south of Inverness, Feith Mhor Lodge ('Fay Moor') offers bed & breakfast in an elegant Victorian country home with 6 charming en-suite bedrooms. Your hosts specialise in party bookings for groups enjoying the sporting activities of the area. Shooting, fishing, falconry & golf parties can be exclusively booked on a full-board basis. (Restricted smoking areas).
E-mail: feith.mhor@btinternet.com
www.feithmhor.co.uk

£20.00 to £56.00 — Y — N — Y

VISA: M'CARD:

John Gardner Feith Mhor Lodge Station Road Carrbridge Nr. Aviemore PH23 3AP Inverness-shire
Tel: (01479) 841621   Open: ALL YEAR   Map Ref No. 30

Invergloy House

Near Rd: A.82

A really interesting Scottish coach house, dating back 120 years, offering 2 charming & comfortable rooms (1 double & 1 twin-bedded room), each with modern facilities including an en-suite bath or shower room. 5 miles north of the village of Spean Bridge towards Inverness, it is signposted on the left, along a wooded drive. Guests have use of own sitting room, overlooking Loch Lochy in 50 acres of superb woodland filled with rhododendron & azaleas. Fishing from private beach. Children over 12.
E-mail: cairns@invergloy-house.co.uk
www.invergloy-house.co.uk

£60.00 to £60.00 — Y — N — N

Mrs Margaret Cairns   Invergloy House   Spean Bridge PH34 4DY   Inverness-shire
Tel: (01397) 712681 Fax 01397 712681 Open: ALL YEAR (Excl. Xmas & New Year) Map Ref No. 31

The Grange

Near Rd: A.82

Tucked away in its own grounds, The Grange sits quietly overlooking Loch Linnhe, yet it is only 10 mins' walk from the town centre & local restaurants. Log fires, crystal, fresh flowers, antiques, loch views, all add to the charm of this luxury B & B in the breathtaking scenery of the Scottish Highlands. One night is not enough to enjoy The Grange or the area surrounding, whether it be walking in famous Glen Nevis, sailing on Loch Linnhe or visiting the distillery.
E-mail: info@thegrange-scotland.co.uk
www.thegrange-scotland.co.uk

£98.00 to £110.00 — N — N — N

see PHOTO over
p. 331

M'CARD:

Mrs Joan Campbell   The Grange   Grange Road   Fort William PH33 6JF   Inverness-shire
Tel: (01397) 705516   Open: MAR - NOV   Map Ref No. 32

Ashburn House

Near Rd: A.82

Ashburn is a splendid Victorian house personally run by Highland hosts. Quietly situated by the shores of Loch Linnhe only 600 yards from the town centre & among others the renowned Crannog Seafood Restaurant. An excellent base for touring the Highlands. Sample an imaginative Highland breakfast, complemented with freshly baked scones from the Aga. 7 en-suite bedrooms, 4 with super-king-size beds & 3 single rooms. Parking. Weekly rates available. Single rooms from £40.
E-mail: christine@no-1.fsworld.co.uk
www.highland5star.co.uk

£80.00 to £100.00 — Y — N — N

see PHOTO over
p. 333

VISA: M'CARD:

Mrs Christine MacDonald Ashburn House Achintore Road Fort William PH33 6RQ Inverness-shire
Tel: (01397) 706000   Fax 01397 702024   Open: ALL YEAR   Map Ref No. 32

Ashburn House. Fort William.

Inverness-shire
Isle of Bute & Isle of Skye

Easter Dalziel Farmhouse

Near Rd: A.96

This Scottish farming family offer the visitor a friendly Highland welcome on their 200-acre stock/arable farm. 3 charming bedrooms are available in the delightful early-Victorian farmhouse. The lounge has log fire & T.V.. Delicious home cooking & baking served, including a choice of breakfasts. Evening meals available by arrangement. Ideal for exploring the scenic Highlands. Local attractions are Cawdor Castle, Culloden, Fort George, Loch Ness & Castle Stuart. Dogs by arrangement.
E-mail: BBB@easterdalzielfarm.co.uk
www.easterdalzielfarm.co.uk

| £42.00 to £50.00 | Y | N | Y |

VISA: M'CARD:

Mrs Margaret Pottie   Easter Dalziel Farmhouse   Dalcross   Inverness IV2 7JL   Inverness-shire
Tel: (01667) 462213   Fax 01667 462213   Open: ALL YEAR (Excl. Xmas & New Year)   Map Ref No. 34

Balmory Hall

Near Rd: A.844

Experience the delights of this beautifully restored Victorian mansion house, set within its own extensive natural grounds, located on the east coast of the Isle of Bute. Appointed with all modern comforts in mind & with that touch of elegance, which is synonymous with the Victorian age. Enjoy the peaceful serenity of the bright, exceptionally spacious public rooms & the warmth of the cosy bedrooms & bathrooms. Leave all stresses behind; relax & enjoy. A delightful home. Children over 12.
E-mail: enquiries@balmoryhall.com
www.balmoryhall.com

| £110.00 to £144.00 | Y | N | N |

VISA: M'CARD:

Tony & Beryl Harrison   Balmory Hall   Ascog PA20 9LL   Isle of Bute
Tel: (01700) 500669   Fax 01700 500669   Open: ALL YEAR   Map Ref No. 35

Corry Lodge

Near Rd: A.87

Corry Lodge, on the Isle of Skye, is a most attractive period house dating from the late 18th century. It has a fine open outlook over Broadford Bay, but with a sheltered location, & approximately 1,150 metres of unspoilt sea frontage. There are 4 comfortable & tastefully furnished bedrooms, each with en-suite bathroom, radio, T.V. & tea/coffee-making facilities. Corry Lodge forms an ideal base from which to tour the island either by car or bicycle, or on foot. Evening meals by arrangement.
E-mail: jane@corrylodge.freeserve.co.uk
www.corrylodge.co.uk

| £55.00 to £65.00 | Y | Y | Y |

VISA: M'CARD:

Anthony & Jane Wilcken   Corry Lodge   Liveras   Broadford IV49 9AA   Isle of Skye
Tel: (01471) 822235   Fax 01471 822318   Open: MAR - OCT   Map Ref No. 36

Shorefield House

Near Rd: A.850

Shorefield House nestles peacefully in the village of Edinbane with undisturbed views of Loch Greshornish & sunsets over the peninsula. A range of comfortable, high-quality en-suite accommodation & a warmth of hospitality adds a special touch to your stay. A la carte breakfasts make use of local produce & special diets are catered for where possible. Excellent (category 1) disabled facilities. Children's play area. Close to Dunvegan Castle & Talisker Distillery.
E-mail: shorefieldhouse@aol.com
www.shorefield.com

| £60.00 to £80.00 | Y | N | N |

VISA: M'CARD:

Mrs Hilary Prall   Shorefield House   Edinbane   Nr. Portree IV51 9PW   Isle of Skye
Tel: (01470) 582444   Fax 01470 582414   Open: Mid MAR - OCT   Map Ref No. 36

Chipperkyle. Castle Douglas.

Kirkcudbrightshire
Lanarkshire & Morayshire

Chipperkyle

Near Rd: A.75

Chipperkyle is a beautiful 18th-century Georgian family home, without a hint of formality. The Dicksons are both engaging & sociable & will endeavour to make you feel at ease in their elegant home. Bedrooms are light & charming, decorated with cast iron beds & excellent furniture. A drawing room with log fire. 200 acres of grazing land with a dog, cats, donkeys & free-ranging hens. Threave & Logan castles, Drumlanrig & Culzean castles are within an easy drive. Golf courses nearby.
E-mail: bestbandb@chipperkyle.co.uk
www.chipperkyle.co.uk

£80.00 to £80.00 — Y — N — N

see PHOTO over p. 335

Catriona & Willie Dickson Chipperkyle Kirkpatrick Durham Castle Douglas DG7 3EY
Kirkcudbrightshire Tel: (01556) 650223 Open: ALL YEAR Map Ref No. 37

Easter Glentore Farmhouse

Near Rd: A.73, B.803

Dating back to 1705 & providing quality ground-floor accommodation, with 3 delightful bedrooms with en-suite/private facilities & a tea/coffee tray. Great care is taken to ensure your comfort. Enjoy a homely atmosphere, home-made shortbread, scones & preserves. Choice of breakfasts. Guests' lounge with panoramic views. A working sheep farm with private woodlands, ideal for Stirling, Glasgow & Edinburgh, Falkirk Wheel. Easy access to M.8, M.74, M.9 & M.80. Children over 5.
E-mail: info@easterglentorefarm.com
www.easterglentorefarm.com

£54.00 to £56.00 — Y — N — N

VISA: M'CARD:

Elsie Hunter Easter Glentore Farmhouse Slamannan Road Greengairs Airdrie ML6 7TJ Lanarkshire
Tel: (01236) 830243 Fax 01236 830243 Open: ALL YEAR (Excl. Xmas) Map Ref No. 38

An Cala Guest House

Near Rd: A.95

An Cala is a large comfortable Victorian house retaining many of its original features. Set in 1/2 an acre & overlooked by woods yet within 10 minutes walking distance of the town centre. All rooms have en-suite facilities, doubles are king-size, including a magnificent mahogany 4-poster bed bought from Castle Grant. T.V., tea/coffee, hairdryers etc. are provided in all rooms. Your hosts aim to provide relaxing & comfortable accommodation with lovely gardens to enjoy. Parking. Children over 3.
E-mail: ancala@globalnet.co.uk
www.ancala.info

£52.00 to £60.00 — Y — Y — N

VISA: M'CARD:

Val Dickinson An Cala Guest House Woodlands Terrace Grantown on Spey PH26 3JU Morayshire
Tel: (01479) 873293 Fax 01479 873293 Open: ALL YEAR (Excl. Xmas) Map Ref No. 39

The Pines

Near Rd: A.95

A timeless atmosphere of peaceful tranquillity prevails at this spacious accommodation. Interesting objet d'art, a library, 2 dining rooms serving good country house food increase the sense of heritage in this fine 19th-century Scottish country house. All bedrooms have en-suite facilities & their own distinctive style & furnishings. The large maturing garden with its small woodland area provides pleasant private walks. Children over 12 years. Animals by arrangement.
E-mail: info@thepinesgrantown.co.uk
www.thepinesgrantown.co.uk

£100.00 to £140.00 — Y — Y — Y

VISA: M'CARD:

Gwen & Michael Stewart The Pines Woodside Avenue Grantown-on-Spey PH26 3JR Morayshire
Tel: (01479) 872092 Open: MAR - OCT (& by arrangement) Map Ref No. 40

Easter Dunfallandy Country House. Pitlochry.

rate £ from - to per double room | children taken | evening meals | animals taken

The Lodge House

Near Rd: A.82

Although just by the roadside, The Lodge is secluded & all rooms enjoy an excellent view of the surrounding hills & glens. With only 6 rooms, your hosts aim to provide a personal service & compliment this with good Scottish home-cooking. In the small, informal bar, there is an extensive selection of malts for guests to enjoy both before & after dinner. The Lodge House is the perfect location for a relaxing break.
E-mail: admin@lodgehouse.co.uk
www.lodgehouse.co.uk

| £55.00 to £60.00 | Y | Y | N |

VISA: M'CARD:

| Gordon Gaughan | The Lodge House | Crianlarich FK20 8RU | Perthshire |
| Tel: (01838) 300276 | Fax 01838 300276 | Open: ALL YEAR | Map Ref No. 41 |

Letter Farm

Near Rd: A.923

Situated next to Loch of Lowes Wildlife Reserve, home to nesting osprey, this family-run stock farm is a peaceful haven for guests seeking peace & tranquillity. There are 3 spacious en-suite bedrooms, 1 ground-floor with king-size bed. A large guest T.V. lounge with log fire. Full breakfast menu with local & homemade produce. Dinner by arrangement. Enjoy afternoon tea on the patio whilst watching the birdlife. Come & treat yourselves to an unforgettable stay. Children over 12.
E-mail: letterlowe@aol.com
www.letterfarm.co.uk

| £30.00 to £60.00 | Y | N | Y |

VISA: M'CARD:

| Mrs Jo Andrew | Letter Farm | Loch of Lowes | Dunkeld PH8 0HH | Perthshire |
| Tel: (01350) 724254 | Fax 01350 724341 | Open: MAY - OCT | Map Ref No. 43 |

Craigroyston House

Near Rd: A.9

Quietly situated in its own grounds, this fine Victorian villa has direct access from the grounds to the town centre. The spacious en-suite bedrooms, some with 4-poster beds & original antique pieces, are beautifully decorated in keeping with the period. So are the comfortable lounge with seasonal log fire & the dining room with views to the south, where guests can enjoy a traditional Scottish breakfast. Safe off-street parking.
E-mail: reservations@craigroyston.co.uk
www.craigroyston.co.uk

| £50.00 to £64.00 | Y | N | N |

| Gretta & Douglas Maxwell | Craigroyston House | 2 Lower Oakfield | Pitlochry | PH16 5HQ | Perthshire |
| Tel: (01796) 472053 | Fax 01796 472053 | Open: ALL YEAR | Map Ref No. 46 |

Easter Dunfallandy House

Near Rd: A.9, A.924

Perfectly situated in a quiet elevated rural position overlooking the tummel Valley, mountains & Pitlochry. The house is completely non-smoking & all attractive rooms are en-suite with every comfort. This is the perfect base for touring. Enjoy afternoon tea on arrival, relax in the gardens & prepare yourself for the best breakfast you may ever have eaten in the 19th century dining room, with local produce & Sue's home-made bread & preserves. Unwind & enjoy the Easter Dunfallandy experience.
E-mail: sue@dunfallandy.co.uk
www.dunfallandy.co.uk

| £60.00 to £70.00 | Y | N | Y |

see PHOTO over
p. 337

VISA: M'CARD:

| Sue Mathieson | Easter Dunfallandy House | Logierait Road | Pitlochry | PH16 5NA | Perthshire |
| Tel: (01796) 474128 | Fax 01796 474446 | Open: ALL YEAR | Map Ref No. 46 |

Culcreuch Castle.   Fintry.

rate £ from - to per double room · _children taken_ · _evening meals_ · _animals taken_

Tigh Dornie

Near Rd: A.9

Tigh Dornie is situated amid beautiful Perthshire scenery, approx. 5 miles north of Pitlochry. Offering attractive accommodation in 2 very comfortable & tastefully furnished guest bedrooms, each with an en-suite bathroom, T.V. & tea/coffee-making facilities. A warm & friendly welcome is assured from your hosts, who will ensure that your stay is a memorable one. An ideal spot for touring Scotland. Ample car parking. Children over 12.
E-mail: tigh_dornie@btinternet.com
www.btinternet.com/~tigh_dornie/

	rate £ from - to	children taken	evening meals	animals taken
	£50.00 to £54.00	Y	N	N

Elizabeth Sanderson Tigh Dornie Aldclune Killiecrankie Pitlochry PH16 5LR Perthshire
Tel: (01796) 473276 Fax 01796 473276 Open: EASTER - OCT Map Ref No. 46

Creag-Ard House

Near Rd: B.829

Nestling in 3 acres of beautiful gardens, this lovely Victorian home, enjoys some of the most magnificent scenery in Scotland; overlooking Loch Ard with superb views of Ben Lomond in a peaceful setting & yet only 1 mile from Aberfoyle. 6 delightful en-suite bedrooms. Enjoy the delicious Scottish breakfast looking out at the views. Private trout fishing & boat hire. Beautiful countryside for walking & cycling. Perfect spot for exploring the Trossachs. Children 12+. Dogs by arrangement.
E-mail: cara@creag-ardhouse.co.uk
www.creag-ardhouse.co.uk

	rate £ from - to	children taken	evening meals	animals taken
	£64.00 to £90.00	Y	N	Y

see PHOTO over p. 341

VISA: M'CARD:

Mrs Cara Wilson Creag-Ard House Lochard Road Aberfoyle FK8 3TQ Stirlingshire
Tel: (01877) 382297 Fax 01877 382297 Open: MAR - OCT Map Ref No. 49

Culcreuch Castle Hotel & Country Park

Near Rd: A.811, A.81

Retreat to 700 years of history at magical Culcreuch, the ancestral fortalice & clan castle of the Galbraiths, home of the Barons of Culcreuch, & now a country house hotel where the Laird and his family extend an hospitable welcome. Set in 1,600 spectacular acres, yet only 19 miles from central Glasgow & 17 miles from Stirling. 13 well-appointed bedrooms with en-suite or private facilities, 4-poster bedroom supplement. Elegant period-style decor, antiques & log fires. Animals by arrangement.
E-mail: info@culcreuch.com
www.culcreuch.com

	rate £ from - to	children taken	evening meals	animals taken
	£76.00 to £160.00	Y	Y	Y

see PHOTO over p. 339

VISA: M'CARD: AMEX:

Laird Andrew Haslam Culcreuch Castle Hotel & Country Park Fintry G63 0LW Stirlingshire
Tel: (01360) 860555 Fax 01360 860556 Open: ALL YEAR Map Ref No. 50

Visit our website at:
http://www.bestbandb.co.uk

Creag-Ard House. Aberfoyle.

Wales

Wales

Wales is a small country with landscapes of intense beauty. In the north are the massive mountains of the Snowdonia National Park, split by chasms & narrow passes, & bounded by quiet vales & moorland. The Lleyn peninsula & the Isle of Anglesey have lovely remote coastlines.

Forests, hills & lakeland form the scenery of Mid Wales, with the great arc of Cardigan Bay in the west.

To the south there is fertile farming land in the Vale of Glamorgan, mountains & high plateaux in the Brecon Beacons, & also the industrial valleys. The coastline forms two peninsulas, around Pembroke & the Gower.

Welsh, the oldest living language of Europe is spoken & used, most obviously in the north, & is enjoying a resurgence in the number of its speakers.

From Taliesin, the 6th century Celtic poet, to Dylan Thomas, Wales has inspired poetry & song. Every August, at the Royal National Eisteddfod, thousands gather to compete as singers, musicians & poets, or to listen & learn. In the small town of Llangollen, there is an International Music Eisteddfod for a week every July

North Wales.

North Wales is chiefly renowned for the 850 miles of the Snowdonia National Park. It is a land of mountains & lakes, rivers & waterfalls & deep glacier valleys. The scenery is justly popular with walkers & pony-trekkers, but the Snowdon Mountain Railway provides easy access to the summit of the highest mountain in the range with views over the "roof of Wales".

Within miles of this wild highland landscape is a coastline of smooth beaches & little fishing villages.

Barmouth has mountain scenery on its doorstep & miles of golden sands & estuary walks. Bangor & Llandudno are popular resort towns.

The Lleyn peninsula reaches west & is an area of great charm. Abersoch is a dinghy & windsurfing centre with safe sandy beaches. In the Middle Ages pilgrims would come to visit Bardsey, the Isle of 20,000 saints, just off Aberdaron, at the tip of the peninsula.

The Isle of Anglesey is linked to the mainland by the handsome Menai Straits Suspension Bridge. Beaumaris has a 13th century castle & many other fine buildings in its historic town centre.

Historically North Wales is a fiercely independent land where powerful local lords resisted first the Romans & later the armies of the English Kings.

The coastline is studded with 13th century castles. Dramatically sited Harlech Castle, famed in fable & song, commands the town, & wide sweep of the coastline.

The great citadel of Edward I at Caernarfon comprises the castle & the encircling town walls. In 1969 it was the scene of the investiture of His Royal Highness Prince Charles as Prince of Wales.

There are elegant stately homes like Plas Newydd in Anglesey & Eriddig House near Wrexham, but it is the variety of domestic architecture that is most charming. The timber-frame buildings of the Border country are seen at their best in historic Ruthin set in the

The Snowdon Mountain Railway.

Wales

beautiful Vale of Clwyd. Further west, the stone cottages of Snowdonia are built of large stones & roofed with the distinctive blue & green local slate. The low, snow-white cottages of Anglesey & the Lleyn Peninsula are typical of the "Atlantic Coast" architecture that can be found on all the western coasts of Europe. The houses are constructed of huge boulders with tiny windows & doors.

By contrast there is the marvellous fantasy of Portmeirion village. On a wooded peninsula between Harlech & Porthmadog, Sir Clough Williams Ellis created a perfect Italianate village with pastel coloured buildings, a town hall & luxury hotel.

Mid Wales

Mid Wales is farming country where people are outnumbered three to one by sheep. A flock of ewes, a lone shepherd & a Border Collie are a common sight on these green hills. Country towns like Old Radnor, Knighton & Montgomery with its castle ruin, have a timeless quality. The market towns of Rhyader, Lampeter & Dolgellau have their weekly livestock sales & annual agricultural festivals, the largest of which is the Royal Welsh Show at Builth Wells in July.

This is the background to the craft of weaving practised here for centuries. In the valley of the River Tefi & on an upper tributary of the Wye & the Irfon, there are tiny riverbank mills which produce the colourful Welsh plaid cloth.

Towards the Snowdonia National Park in the North, the land rises to the scale of true mountains. Mighty Cader Idris & the expanses of Plynlimon, once inaccessible to all but the shepherd & the mountaineer, are now popular centres for walking & pony trekking with well-signposted trails.

The line of the border with England is followed by a huge earth work of bank & ditch. This is Offa's Dyke, built by the King of Mercia around 750 A.D. to deter the Welsh from their incessant raids into his kingdom. Later the border was guarded by the castles at Hay-on-Wye, Builth Wells, Welshpool, & Chirk which date from mediaeval times.

North from Rhayader, lies the Dovey estuary & the historic town of Machynlleth. This is where Owain Glyndwr's parliament is thought to have met in 1404, & there is an exhibition about the Welsh leader in the building, believed to have been Parliament House.

Wales lost many fine religious houses during the Dissolution of the Monasteries under Henry VIII. The ruins at Cymer near Dolgellau & at Strata Florida were abbeys of the Cistercian order. However, many remote Parish Churches show evidence of the skills of mediaeval craftsmen with soaring columns & fine rood screens.

The Cambrian Coast (Cardigan Bay) has sand dunes to the north & cliffs to the south with sandy coves & miles of cliff walks.

Llangrannog Headland.

Aberystwyth is the main town of the region with two beaches & a yachting harbour, a Camera Obscura on the cliff top & some fine walks in the area.

Water-skiing, windsurfing &

Wales

sailing are popular at Aberdovey, Aberaeron, New Quay, Tywyn & Barmouth & there are delightful little beaches further south at Aberporth, Tresaith or Llangrannog.

South Wales

South Wales is a region of scenic variety. The Pembrokeshire coastline has sheer cliffs, little coves & lovely beaches. Most of the area is National Park with an 80 mile foot path running along its length, passing pretty harbour villages like Solva & Broad Haven.

A great circle of Norman Castles stands guard over South Pembrokeshire, Roch, Haverfordwest, Tenby, Carew, Pembroke & Manorbier.

The northern headland of Saint

Tenby.

Brides Bay is the most westerly point in the country & at the centre of a tiny village stands the Cathedral of Saint David, the Patron Saint of Wales. At Bosherton near Saint Govans Head, there is a tiny chapel hidden in a cleft in the massive limestone cliffs.

The Preseli Hills hold the vast prehistoric burial chambers of Pentre Ifan, & the same mountains provided the great blue stones used at faraway Stonehenge.

Laugharne is the village where Dylan Thomas lived & worked in what was a boat-house & is now a museum.

In the valleys, towns like Merthyr Tydfil, Ebbw Vale & Treorchy were in the forefront of the boom years of the Industrial Revolution. Now the heavy industries are fast declining & the ravages of the indiscriminate mining & belching smoke of the blast furnaces are disappearing. The famous Male Voice Choirs & the love of rugby football survives.

The Vale of Glamorgan is a rural area with pretty villages. Beyond here the land rises steeply to the high wild moorlands & hill farms of the Brecon Beacons National Park & the Black Mountains, lovely areas for walking & pony trekking.

The Wye Valley leads down to Chepstow & here set amidst the beautiful woodlands is the ruin of the Great Abbey of Tintern, founded in 1131 by the Cistercian Order.

Swansea has a strong sea-faring tradition maintained by its new Marine Quarter - marina, waterfront village, restaurants, art gallery & theatre.

Cardiff, the capital of Wales, is a pleasant city with acres of parkland, the lovely River Taff, & a great castle, as well as a new civic centre, two theatres & the ultra-modern St. David's Concert Hall. It is the home of the Welsh National Opera & here also is the National Stadium where the singing of the rugby crowd on a Saturday afternoon is a treat.

Pony Trekking

Wales

Wales
Gazeteer

Areas of Outstanding Natural Beauty
The Pembrokeshire Coast. The Brecon Beacons. Snowdonia. Gower.'

Historic Houses & Castles

Cardiff Castle - Cardiff
Built on a Roman site in the 11th century.
Caerphilly Castle - Caerphilly
13th century fortress.
Chirk Castle - Nr. Wrexham
14th century Border Castle. Lovely gardens.
Coity Castle - Coity
Mediaeval stronghold - three storied round tower.
Gwydir Castle - Nr. Lanrwst
Royal residence in past days - wonderful Tudor furnishings. Gardens with peacocks.
Penrhyn Castle - Bangor
Neo-Norman architecture 19th century - large grounds with museum & exhibitions. Victorian garden.
Picton Castle - Haverfordwest
12th century - lived in by the same family continuously. Fine gardens.
Caernarfon Castle - Caernarfon
13th century - castle of great importance to Edward I.
Conway Castle - Conwy
13th century - one of Edward I's chain of castles.
Powis Castle - Welshpool
14th century - reconstruction work in 17th century.
Murals, furnishings, tapestries & paintings, terraced gardens.
Pembroke Castle - Pembroke
12th century Norman castle with huge keep & immense walls.
Birthplace of Henry VII.
Plas Newydd - Isle of Anglesey
18th century Gothic style house.
Home of the Marquis of Anglesey.
Stands on the edge of the Menai Strait looking across to the Snowdonia Range.
Famous for the Rex Whistler murals.
The Tudor Merchant's House - Tenby
Built in 15th century.
Tretower Court & Castle - Crickhowell
Mediaeval - finest example in Wales.

Cathedrals & Churches

St. Asaph Cathedral
13th century - 19th century restoration.
Smallest of Cathedrals in England & Wales.
Holywell (St. Winifred)
15th century well chapel & chamber - fine example.
St. Davids (St. David)
12th century Cathedral - splendid tower - oak roof to nave.
Gwent (St. Woolos)
Norman Cathedral - Gothic additions - 19th century restoration.
Abergavenny (St. Mary)
14th century church of 12th century Benedictine priory.
Llanengan (St. Engan)
Mediaeval church - very large with original roof & stalls 16th century tower.
Esyronen
17th century chapel, much original interior remaining.
Llangdegley (St. Tegla)
18th century Quaker meeting house - thatched roof - simple structure divided into schoolroom & meeting room.
Llandaff Cathedral (St. Peter & St. Paul)
Founded in 6th century - present building began in 12th century. Great damage suffered in bombing during war, restored with Epstein's famous figure of Christ.

Museums & Galleries

National Museum of Wales - Cardiff (also Turner House)
Geology, archaeology, zoology, botany, industry, & art exhibitions.
Welsh Folk Museum - St. Fagans Castle - Cardiff
13th century walls curtaining a 16th century house - now a most interesting & comprehensive folk museum.
County Museum - Carmarthen
Roman jewellery, gold, etc. Romano-British & Stone Age relics.
National Library of Wales - Aberystwyth
Records of Wales & Celtic areas. Great historical interest.
University College of Wales Gallery - AberystwythTravelling exhibitions of painting & sculpture.

Wales

Museum & Art Gallery - Newport
Specialist collection of English
watercolours - natural history, Roman
remains, etc.
Legionary Museum - Caerleon
Roman relics found on the site of
legionary fortress at Risca.
Nelson Museum - Monmouth
Interesting relics of Admiral Lord Nelson &
Lady Hamilton.
Bangor Art Gallery - Bangor
Exhibitions of contemporary paintings &
sculpture.
Bangor Museum of Welsh Antiquities -
Bangor
History of North Wales is shown. Splendid
exhibits of furniture, clothing, domestic
objects, etc. Also Roman antiquities.
Narrow Gauge Railway Museum - Tywyn
Rolling stock & exhibitions of narrow
gauge railways of U.K.
Museum of Childhood - Menai Bridge
Charming museum of dolls & toys &
children's things.

Brecknock Museum - Brecon
Natural history, archaeology, agriculture,
local history, etc.
Glynn Vivian Art Gallery & Museum -
Swansea
Ceramics, old & contemporary, British
paintings & drawings, sculpture, loan
exhibitions.
Stone Museum - Margam
Carved stones & crosses from pre-
historic times.
Plas Mawr - Conwy
A beautiful Elizabethan town mansion
house in its original condition. Now holds
the Royal Cambrain Academy of Art.

Historic Monuments

Rhuddlan Castle - Rhuddlan
13th century castle - interesting diamond
plan.
Valle Crucis Abbey - Llangollen
13th century Cistercian Abbey Church.

Cader Idris.

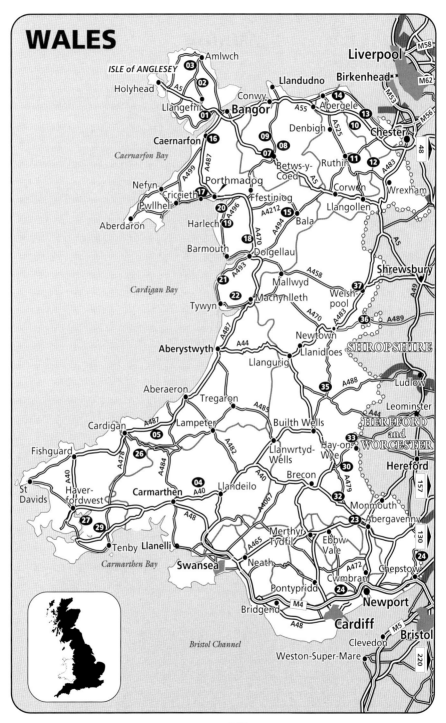

WALES

ISLE of ANGLESEY

Amlwch
Holyhead
Llangefni
Bangor
Conwy
Llandudno
Birkenhead
Liverpool
Abergele
Denbigh
Chester
Caernarfon
Caernarfon Bay
Betws-y-Coed
Ruthin
Corwen
Wrexham
Nefyn
Porthmadog
Ffestiniog
Llangollen
Criccieth
Pwllheli
Bala
Aberdaron
Harlech
Dolgellau
Barmouth
Shrewsbury
Tywyn
Mallwyd
Welsh-pool
Newtown
Cardigan Bay
Machynlleth
SHROPSHIRE
Aberystwyth
Llanidloes
Llangurig
Ludlow
Aberaeron
Tregaron
Leominster
Cardigan
Lampeter
Builth Wells
HEREFORD and WORCESTER
Fishguard
Hay-on-Wye
Hereford
St Davids
Haver-fordwest
Carmarthen
Llandeilo
Llanwrtyd-Wells
Brecon
Monmouth
Tenby
Llanelli
Abergavenny
Carmarthen Bay
Swansea
Neath
Merthyr Tydfil
Ebbw Vale
Chepstow
Cwmbran
Pontypridd
Newport
Bridgend
Cardiff
Bristol
Bristol Channel
Clevedon
Weston-Super-Mare

347

WALES
Map references

01 Roberts	18 Anderson-Kaye	32 C. Jackson
02 Bown	19 Stenberg	33 Newall
03 Hughes	20 Williams	35 Millan
04 Dent	21 Chadwick	36 Bright
05 Lewis	22 Howkins	37 S. Jones
07 Bidwell	23 Harris	
07 Howard	24 Stubbs	
08 Pitman	25 Price	
09 Nichols	26 Vickers	
10 C. Spencer	27 Lort-Phillips	
11 J. Spencer	29 Fielder	
12 Parry	30 Meredith	
13 M. Jones		
14 Steele-Mortimer		
15 Hind		
16 Bayles		
17 Williamson		

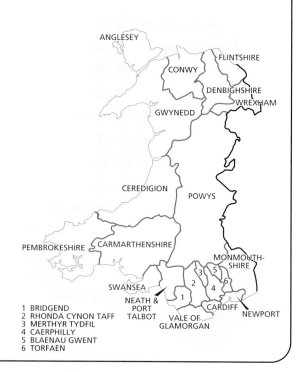

1 BRIDGEND
2 RHONDA CYNON TAFF
3 MERTHYR TYDFIL
4 CAERPHILLY
5 BLAENAU GWENT
6 TORFAEN

Beaumaris Castle. Isle of Anglesey. Wales.

Isle of Anglesey & Carmarthenshire

Bodlawen

Near Rd: A.480

A beautiful large house in a glorious location looking onto Snowdonia & Caernarfon Castle, a short walk to the shore of the tranquil Menai Strait. Ideally based for touring Anglesey & the mainland. Close to Plas Newydd (National Trust), the Sea Zoo & the Foel open farm. All bedrooms have en-suite facilities, T.V. & beverage tray. The lounge & dining room are exquisitely furnished & there is a grand piano. Your host, Marian, a well-known soprano soloist, is Welsh speaking & very welcoming.
E-mail: marion@bodlawen.com
www.bodlawen.com

| £55.00 to £58.00 | Y | N | N |

VISA: M'CARD:

Marian Roberts   Bodlawen   Brynsiencyn   Isle of Anglesey LL61 6TQ   Anglesey
Tel: (01248) 430379   Open: ALL YEAR (Excl. Xmas)   Map Ref No. 01

Drws-Y-Coed

Near Rd: A.5025

Enjoy wonderful panoramic views of Snowdonia & countryside at this beautifully appointed farmhouse on a 550-acre working beef, sheep & arable farm. It is centrally situated to explore the island. Tastefully decorated & furnished, superb en-suite bedrooms with all facilities. An inviting spacious lounge with antiques & log fire. The excellent breakfasts are served in the cosy dining room. Grade II listed farm buildings. Pleasant walks & private fishing. Only 25 mins to Holyhead Port.
E-mail: drwsycoed2@hotmail.com
www.smoothhound.co.uk/hotels/drwsycoed.html

| £60.00 to £60.00 | Y | N | N |

VISA: M'CARD:

Mrs Jane Bown   Drws-Y-Coed   Llannerch-Y-Medd   Isle of Anglesey LL71 8AD   Anglesey
Tel: (01248) 470473   Open: ALL YEAR   Map Ref No. 02

Llwydiarth Fawr Farm

Near Rd: A.55

Secluded Georgian mansion set in 800 acres of woodland & farmland, with lovely open views. Ideal touring base for the island's coastline, Snowdonia & North Wales coast. 3 delightfully furnished bedrooms with en-suite facilities & T.V.. Log fires. Enjoy a taste of Wales with delicious country cooking using farm & local produce. Personal attention & a warm Welsh welcome to guests, who will enjoy the scenic walks & private fishing. Convenient for Holyhead-to-Ireland crossings.
E-mail: llwydiarth@hotmail.com
www.angleseyfarms.com/llwydia.htm

| £60.00 to £70.00 | Y | N | N |

VISA: M'CARD:

Margaret Hughes   Llwydiarth Fawr Farm   Llanerchymedd   Isle of Anglesey LL71 8DF   Anglesey
Tel: (01248) 470321/470540   Open: ALL YEAR   Map Ref No. 03

Plas Alltyferin

Near Rd: A.40

A classic Georgian country house (Grade II listed), lying in the hills above the beautiful Towy Valley overlooking a Norman hill fort & down to the rushing salmon River Cothi. 2 spacious twin bedrooms, with en-suite/private bathroom & stunning views. Guests are encouraged to relax in the drawing room (log fires in winter) or to wander through 270 acres of woodland, fields & river valley. Good pubs & restaurants. Castles, beaches, the National Botanic Garden nearby. Children over 10.
E-mail: dent@alltyferin.fsnet.co.uk
www.alltyferin.co.uk

| £50.00 to £60.00 | Y | N | Y |

see PHOTO over p. 351

Mr & Mrs Dent Plas Alltyferin Pontargothi Nantgaredig Carmarthen SA32 7PF Carmarthenshire
Tel: (01267) 290662   Fax 01267 290662   Open: ALL YEAR (Excl. Xmas)   Map Ref No. 04

Plas Allt y Ferin. Nantgaredig.

Wervil Grange Farm. Pentregat.

rate £ from - to per double room	children taken	evening meals	animals taken

Wervil Grange Farm

£60.00 to £60.00

Y | N | Y

see PHOTO over p. 352

Near Rd: A.487

A warm welcome awaits you at this superb & luxurious Welsh Georgian farmhouse offering a very high standard of accommodation. The comfortable farmhouse is beautifully decorated & furnished, all bedrooms are en-suite. It is a traditional stock-rearing farm with a flock of breeding ewes & a herd of Pedigree Welsh Black cattle. Free fishing on the farm. Only 10 mins' from Llangranog beach in Cardigan Bay, home to the only resident population of bottle-nosed dolphins in Welsh waters. Your hosts aim is to provide you with an unforgettable holiday.

Mrs Ionwen Lewis   Wervil Grange Farm   Pentregat Llangranog   Llandysul SA44 6HW   Ceredigion
Tel: (01239) 654252   Open: ALL YEAR   Map Ref No. 05

The Courthouse (Henllys)

£54.00 to £78.00

Y | N | N

VISA: M'CARD:

Near Rd: A.5

Charming accommodation is provided in this Victorian property, a former police station & magistrate's court, set in a peaceful riverside garden within the village. Modern comforts include colour T.V.s, hospitality trays & en-suite facilities in every room except the former prison cell, which has its own private bathroom. Breakfast is served in the former court room. Bodnant Gardens, Port Meirion, Snowdon Mountain Railway & the castles of North Wales are nearby.
E-mail: gillian.bidwell@btconnect.com
www.guesthouse-snowdonia.co.uk

Mr & Mrs Bidwell   The Courthouse (Henllys)   Old Church Road   Betws-y-Coed LL24 0AL   Conwy
Tel: (01690) 710534   Fax 01690 710884   Open: ALL YEAR (Excl. Jan)   Map Ref No. 07

Tan Dinas Country House

£52.00 to £56.00

Y | N | Y

see PHOTO over p. 354

Near Rd: A.5

A Victorian country house, offering peace, seclusion & a wonderful view. Surrounded by woodland yet only 500 yds from the village.   Start your adventure with a delicious breakfast, coming home to relax in the comfortable lounge or retire with a video or book to an attractive, individually furnished bedroom which is appointed for your comfort.   Forest walks from house.   Ideal touring centre. Ample parking. A delightful home.
E-mail: anntandinas@hotmail.com
www.tandinas.4t.com

Ann Howard   Tan Dinas Country House   Coed Cyn Hellier Road   Betws-Y-Coed LL24 0BL   Conwy
Tel: (01690) 710635   Open: ALL YEAR   Map Ref No. 07

Tan-Y-Foel Country House

£145.00 to £160.00

Y | Y | N

see PHOTO over p. 355

VISA: M'CARD:

Near Rd: A.470, A.5

Personally run bijou house built of magnificent Welsh stone. Set away from traffic in secluded gardens with panoramic views of the rolling countryside to the majestic mountains of Snowdonia. Elegant & luxurious, with the ultimate in comfort. This contemporary country house offers every 5-star amenity & has been awarded top accolades for its cuisine. Ideal for relaxing or exploring the many famous castles within the National Park. Children over 7 years.
E-mail: enquiries@tyfhotel.co.uk
www.tyfhotel.co.uk

Mr & Mrs P.K. Pitman Tan-Y-Foel Country House   Capel Garmon   Betws-Y-Coed LL26 0RE   Conwy
Tel: (01690) 710507   Fax 01690 710681   Open: JAN - NOV   Map Ref No. 08

Tan Dinas. Betws–Y–Coed

Tan-y-Foel Country House. Capel Garmon

Pentre Cerrig Mawr. Maeshafn.

rate £ from - to per double room | children taken | evening meals | animals taken

---

£60.00 to £80.00

Y Y Y

(no smoking)

VISA: M'CARD: AMEX:

Hafod Country House

Near Rd: B.45106

Set in the lovely Conwy Valley, on the edge of Snowdonia, Yr Hafod (The Summer Dwelling) is a former 17th-century farmhouse, extensively furnished with antiques. The bedrooms each offer a highly individual sense of style. Warm hospitality at this award-winning hotel is complemented by outstanding food, while drinks can be enjoyed in the oak-panelled bar or in front of a log fire. Children over 12. Animals by arrangement.
E-mail: hafod@breathemail.net
www.hafodhouse.co.uk

Chris & Rosina Nichols   Hafod Country House   Trefriw   Llanrwst LL27 0RQ   Conwy
Tel: (01492) 640029   Fax 01492 641351   Open: Early Feb-Early Jan   Map Ref No. 09

£40.00 to £40.00

N N Y

(no smoking)

see PHOTO over p. 356

VISA: M'CARD:

Pentre Cerrig Mawr

Near Rd: A.494

Pheasants & badgers visit the gardens of this peaceful 17th-century country house. Convenient for Chester, Snowdonia, the coast, Holyhead & 50 mins' to Manchester or Liverpool. The principal rooms have beams & open fires. Bedrooms are en-suite with colour T.V., hospitality tray & magical views across the valley. Country pubs, walks, riding, golf & the theatre all nearby. The atmosphere is friendly & welcoming. Home-baking & local organic produce are on the breakfast menu.
E-mail: info@charmian.co.uk
www.pentrecerrigmawr.com

Charmian & Ted Spencer   Pentre Cerrig Mawr   Maeshafn   Nr. Mold CH7 5LU   Denbighshire
Tel: (01352) 810607   Fax 01352 810607   Open: ALL YEAR   Map Ref No. 10

£56.00 to £60.00

Y Y Y

see PHOTO over p. 358

VISA: M'CARD:

Eyarth Station

Near Rd: A.525

A warm & friendly reception awaits you at Eyarth Station. A super, converted, former railway station located in the beautiful countryside of the Vale of Clwyd. 6 en-suite bedrooms. T.V. lounge, & guests are welcome to use the garden, sun patio & outdoor heated pool. Conveniently located for the many historic towns in the region including Conwy, Caernarfon & Ruthin, with medieval banquet 2 mins' drive away. Chester is within driving distance. 1987 winner of Best Bed & Breakfast Award.
E-mail: stay@eyarthstation.com
www.eyarthstation.co.uk

Jen & Bert Spencer   Eyarth Station   Llanfair D. C.   Ruthin LL15 2EE   Denbighshire
Tel: (01824) 703643   Fax 01824 707464   Open: MAR - DEC   Map Ref No. 11

£40.00 to £44.00

Y N N

(no smoking)

Llainwen Ucha

Near Rd: A.525

A working farm set in 130 acres overlooking the very beautiful Vale of Clwyd. Offering 3 pleasantly decorated rooms with modern amenities, & accommodating up to 6 persons. All rooms are centrally heated. Delicious breakfasts made with fresh local produce; vegetarian options on request. Conveniently situated for visiting Chester, Llangollen, Snowdonia & the coast. Offa's Dyke & fishing nearby. Medieval banquets are held at Ruthin Castle throughout the year.
www.bestbandb.co.uk

Elizabeth A. Parry   Llainwen Ucha   Pentre Celyn   Ruthin LL15 2HL   Denbighshire
Tel: (01978) 790253   Open: ALL YEAR (Excl. Xmas)   Map Ref No. 12

Eyarth Station.   Llanfair D.C.

Abercelyn. Llanycil.

	rate £ from - to per double room	evening meals	children taken	animals taken

Greenhill Farm Guest House

Near Rd: A.55

A 16th-century working dairy farm, overlooking the Dee Estuary, which retains its old-world charm, with a beamed & panelled interior. Bedrooms are tastefully furnished, all have either en-suite or private bathrooms. Relax & enjoy typical farmhouse food in the attractive dining room. (Dinner by prior arrangement.) Children's play area & utility/games room also available. A lovely home, within easy reach of Chester, the coast & Snowdonia. No single supplement.
E-mail: mary@greenhillfarm.fsnet.co.uk
www.greenhillfarm.co.uk

£52.00 to £52.00 — Y Y N

VISA: M'CARD:

Mrs Mary Jones   Greenhill Farm Guest House   Bryn Celyn   Holywell CH8 7QF   Flintshire
Tel: (01352) 713270   Open: JAN - NOV   Map Ref No. 13

Golden Grove

Near Rd: A.5151

Beautiful Elizabethan manor house set in 1,000 acres, close to Chester, Bodnant Gardens & Snowdonia, & en route to Holyhead. The Steele-Mortimer brothers & wives, having returned to the family home from Canada & Ireland, provide a warm welcome for their guests. The menu features home produce, including lamb & game, together with interesting wines & home baking (advance notice required.) The atmosphere is friendly & informal. Children over 12. Licensed.
E-mail: golden.grove@lineone.net
www.bestbandb.co.uk

£55.00 to £90.00 — Y Y Y

see PHOTO over
p. 361

VISA: M'CARD:

N. & M. Steele-Mortimer   Golden Grove   Llanasa   Nr. Holywell CH8 9NA   Flintshire
Tel: (01745) 854452   Fax 01745 854547   Open: Mid FEB - Mid NOV   Map Ref No. 14

Abercelyn Country House

Near Rd: A.494

Set in landscaped gardens with its own mountain stream running alongside, this Grade II listed former rectory dates back to before 1729. Situated in the Snowdonia National Park, it is ideally located for walking or touring amongst the spectacular scenery. Bright & spacious en-suite bedrooms with views over Bala Lake, evenings relaxing before open log fires. Genuine home cooking a speciality. Evening meals by arrangement. Guided walking & outdoor activities available.
E-mail: info@abercelyn.co.uk
www.abercelyn.co.uk

£50.00 to £70.00 — Y Y N

see PHOTO over
p. 359

VISA: M'CARD:

Mrs Lindsay Hind   Abercelyn Country House   Llanycil   Bala LL23 7YF   Gwynedd
Tel: (01678) 521109   Fax 01678 520848   Open: ALL YEAR (Excl. Xmas)   Map Ref No. 15

The White House

Near Rd: A.487

The White House is a large detached house set in its own grounds, overlooking Foryd Bay, & with the Snowdonia mountains behind. There are 3 tastefully decorated bedrooms, all with bath or shower, tea/coffee-making facilities & colour T.V.. Guests are welcome to use the residents' lounge, outdoor pool & gardens. Ideally situated for birdwatching, walking, windsurfing, golf & visiting the historic Welsh castles. Animals by arrangement.
E-mail: RWBAYLES@SJMS.CO.UK
www.bestbandb.co.uk

£50.00 to £50.00 — Y N Y

Richard Bayles   The White House   Llanfaglan   Caernarfon LL54 5RA   Gwynedd
Tel: (01286) 673003   Open: MAR - NOV   Map Ref No. 16

Golden Grove. Llanasa.

	rate £ from - to per double room	children taken	evening meals	animals taken

Min-Y-Gaer Hotel

Near Rd: A.497

A pleasant, licensed house in a quiet residential area, offering very good accommodation in 10 comfortable rooms, all of which have a bathroom en-suite. All rooms have colour T.V. & tea/coffee-making facilities. The hotel enjoys commanding views of Criccieth Castle & the scenic Cardigan Bay coastline, & is only 2 mins' walk from the safe, sandy beach. Car parking on the premises. A completely no-smoking hotel. An ideal base for touring Snowdonia.
E-mail: info@minygaer.co.uk
www.minygaer.co.uk

£54.00 to £58.00 — Y — N — N

VISA: M'CARD:

Sue Williamson Min-Y-Gaer Hotel Porthmadog Road Criccieth LL52 OHP Gwynedd
Tel: (01766) 522151 Fax 01766 523540 Open: MAR - OCT Map Ref No. 17

Plas Dolmelyllyn Hall

Near Rd: A.470

Dolmelynllyn Hall is an ancient Welsh manor house standing in 3 1/2 acres of delightful gardens & superbly situated above the beautiful Mawddach Valley & Coed y Brenin forest. 9 unique bedrooms, including a 4-poster room, have lovely views & are equipped with every comfort. You will be offered warm & gracious hospitality in this immaculate home. Menus feature delicious local ingredients & vegetables from the kitchen garden.
E-mail: info@dolly-hotel.co.uk
www.dolly-hotel.co.uk

£90.00 to £180.00 — Y — Y — N

see PHOTO over
p. 363

VISA: M'CARD:

Janet Anderson-Kaye Plas Dolmelyllyn Hall Ganllwyd Dolgellau LL40 2HP Gwynedd
Tel: (01341) 440273 Fax 01341 440640 Open: FEB - DEC Map Ref No. 18

Maelgwyn House

Near Rd: A.496

Maelgwyn House, a former Edwardian manse built in 1907, is situated on a massive rock escarpment known as the 'Harlech Dome' 300ft above sea level. It enjoys magnificent views across Tremadog Bay to the Llyn peninsula & Mt Snowdon. The rooms have recently been refurbished to a very high standard & are all en-suite. Ideally situated for touring, Maelgwyn House is also only a few minutes walk from the castle & town centre.
E-mail: maelgwyn.harlech@virgin.net
www.maelgwynharlech.co.uk

£60.00 to £70.00 — N — N — N

Bridge & Derek Stenberg Maelgwyn House Ffordd Isaf Harlech LL46 2SW Gwynedd
Tel: (01766) 780087 Fax 01766 780835 Open: ALL YEAR Map Ref No. 19

Gwrach Ynys Country Guest House

Near Rd: A.496

A warm Welsh welcome awaits you at Gwrach Ynys, an Edwardian country house set in 1 acre of garden, nestled between the sea & the mountains in beautiful Snowdonia National Park. 5 en-suite bedrooms, individually decorated & furnished to a high standard. 2 guest lounges & a separate dining room. Superb area for ramblers, walkers, birdwatchers & golfers. Close to Harlech Castle, Portmeirion, Ffestiniog Railway, Snowdon, the Royal St. David's golf course & many sandy beaches.
E-mail: bestbandb@gwrachynys.co.uk
www.gwrachynys.co.uk

£54.00 to £64.00 — Y — N — N

Deborah Williams Gwrach Ynys Country Guest House Talsarnau Nr.Harlech LL47 6TS Gwynedd
Tel: (01766) 780742 Fax 01766 781199 Open: ALL YEAR (Excl. Xmas & New Year) Map Ref No. 20

Plas Dolmelynllyn Hall. Ganllwyd.

Parva Farmhouse and Restaurant. Tintern.

rate £ from - to / **per double room** / **children taken** / **evening meals taken** / **animals taken**

Cefn-Coch Country Guest House

£52.00 to £56.00	Y	Y	N

VISA: M'CARD:

Near Rd: A.493

Cefn Coch is an old coaching inn on the edge of Snowdonia National Park & is situated in over an acre of garden. It has been tastefully renovated throughout to provide quality accommodation. 3 attractively furnished en-suite bedrooms, with exceptional mountain views & a range of beverage facilities. Enjoy a formal dinner or lighter supper meal. A short distance from the beautiful mountains, beaches & coastline in mid/north Wales. Ideal for exploring the Snowdonia National Park.
E-mail: pat@cefn-coch.co.uk
www.cefn-coch.co.uk

Pat Chadwick   Cefn-Coch Country Guest House   Llanegryn   Tywyn LL36 9SD   Gwynedd
Tel: (01654) 712193   Open: ALL YEAR   Map Ref No. 21

Tan-Y-Coed Isaf

£50.00 to £60.00	Y	Y	N

Near Rd: A.493

A traditional Welsh farmhouse set amidst stunning scenery in a steep verdant valley between the mountains of Cader Idris & the sandy beaches of Cardigan Bay. Guest enjoy exclusive use of the beamed dining & sitting room with inglenook fireplace & log fires on cool nights. The en-suite bedrooms with mountain views overlook the garden. Excellent dinners by arrangement prepared by your host - a Cordon Bleu chef. Children 12+.
E-mail: tanhow@supanet.com
www.tanycoedisaf.co.uk

Mrs Jane Howkins   Tan-Y-Coed Isaf   Bryncrug   Tywyn LL36 9UP   Gwynedd
Tel: (01654) 782639   Fax 01654 782639   Open: ALL YEAR   Map Ref No. 22

The Wenallt

£48.00 to £56.00	Y	Y	Y

see PHOTO over p. 366

Near Rd: A.465

A 16th-century Welsh longhouse set in 50 acres of farmland in the Brecon Beacons National Park & commanding magnificent views over the Usk Valley. Retaining all its old charm, with oak beams & inglenook fireplace, yet offering a high standard of accommodation, with en-suite bedrooms, good food & a warm welcome. The Wenallt is an ideal base from which to see Wales & the surrounding areas. Animals by arrangement.
www.bestbandb.co.uk

B. L. Harris   The Wenallt   Gilwern   Abergavenny NP7 0HP   Monmouthshire
Tel: (01873) 830694   Open: ALL YEAR   Map Ref No. 23

Parva Farmhouse Hotel & Restaurant

£68.00 to £90.00	Y	Y	Y

see PHOTO over p. 364

VISA: M'CARD: AMEX:

Near Rd: A.466, M.48

A delightful 17th-century stone farmhouse situated 50 yards from the River Wye. The quaint en-suite bedrooms, with their designer fabrics, are gorgeous, & some offer breathtaking views over the River Wye & woodland. The beamed lounge, with log fire, leather Chesterfields & 'Honesty Bar', is a tranquil haven in which to unwind. Mouthwatering dishes, served in the intimate, candlelit Inglenook Restaurant, reflect the owner's love of cooking. Perfect for a relaxing break.
E-mail: parva_hoteltintern@hotmail.com
www.hoteltintern.co.uk

Dereck & Vickie Stubbs   Parva Farmhouse Hotel   Tintern   Nr. Chepstow NP16 6SQ   Monmouthshire
Tel: (01291) 689411   Fax 01291 689557   Open: ALL YEAR   Map Ref No. 24

The Wenallt. Gilwern.

rate £ from - to per double room	children taken	evening meals	animals taken

---

£65.00 to £70.00 · Y · N · N

🚭

Great House

Near Rd: A.48

A pretty 16th-century Grade II listed home on the banks of the River Usk, with clematis garden. Excellent night stopover for those travelling to Wales & Ireland. Retaining much of its original character (including beams & inglenook fireplaces), offering 3 bedrooms with T.V. & tea/coffee. A drawing room with T.V. & woodburner. Close to a superb golf course, fishing & forest trails. Caerleon is very near with its amphitheatre, museums & Roman Baths. Good pubs. Children over 6.
E-mail: dinah.price@amserve.net
www.visitgreathouse.co.uk

| Mrs Dinah Price | Great House | Isca Road | Old Village | Caerleon | Nr. Newport | NP18 1QG |
| Monmouthshire | Tel: (01633) 420216 | Fax 01633 423492 | | Open: ALL YEAR | Map Ref No. 25 |

£45.00 to £65.00 · Y · N · N

🚭

VISA: M'CARD:

Ailgynnau

Near Rd: B.4332

Ailgynnau, was built to take advantage of the fabulous views towards the Cych and Teifi valleys. Offering a warm welcome, scrummy traditional Welsh breakfast & other tasty treats. 3 bedrooms with T.V., tea/coffee facilities, an en-suite/private bathroom & little extras to make your stay memorable. Relax on the sun deck & enjoy afternoon tea or a drink in the evening & you may even catch a glimpse of a buzzard or red kite, which frequent the garden. Children over 12 years welcome.
E-mail: diana@ailgynnau.co.uk
www.ailgynnau.co.uk

| Diana Vickers | Ailgynnau | Abercych | Boncath SA37 0HD | Pembrokeshire |
| Tel: (01239) 842065 | Fax 01239 842066 | | Open: FEB - DEC | Map Ref No. 26 |

£54.00 to £65.00 · Y · Y · Y

🚭

Knowles Farm

Near Rd: A.4075

A lovely old farmhouse which faces south & overlooks organic farmland & ancient hanging woods. The boundary is the Cleddau Estuary & is a delight to discover. Your hosts can arrange river trips; leave the car & walk to castles, pubs, woodland or just enjoy the birds & wild flowers. Gardens, galleries, beaches, riding, fishing & ancient monuments nearby. Many pubs or restaurants,or enjoy a home-cooked organic meal in front of the fire or in the garden (by arrangement). Children over 12.
E-mail: ginilp@lawrenny.org.uk
www.lawrenny.org.uk

| Mrs Virginia Lort Phillips | Knowles Farm | Lawrenny SA68 0PX | Pembrokeshire |
| Tel: (01834) 891221 | | Open: MAR - OCT | Map Ref No. 27 |

£60.00 to £60.00 · Y · N · N

🚭

Old Stable Cottage

Near Rd: A.4075

The Cottage (Grade II listed), with inglenook fireplace & original bread oven, was once a stable & carthouse to 13th-century Carew Castle situated near the entrance & the creek of Carew River with its Tidal Mill. A spiral staircase leads to 2 charming, oak beamed en-suite bedrooms with colour T.V., home-baked Welsh cakes & tea/coffee. Delicious breakfasts are prepared in the farmhouse kitchen on the Aga. A conservatory overlooks the garden. Good local pub & restaurant offering evening meals, within walking distance. Children over 10.
www.bestbandb.co.uk

| Joyce Fielder | Old Stable Cottage | Picton Terrace | Carew | Tenby SA70 8SL | Pembrokeshire |
| Tel: (01646) 651889 | | Open: FEB - NOV | | Map Ref No. 29 |

Glangrwyney Court. Crickhowell.

rate £ from - to per double room	children taken	evening meals	animals taken

---

£52.00 to £56.00 Y Y Y

🚭

Near Rd: A.479

Lodge Farm

The Merediths welcome you to their 18th-century home, sharing its comfort, old family treasures & warm hospitality. Freshly prepared, interesting meals using home & local produce are a speciality & are served in the attractive dining room with original inglenook fireplace & flagstone floor. Cosy en-suite bedrooms. A lounge with T.V., literature & local maps etc to help you make the most of your stay. A large garden with mountain views; situated 1 1/2 miles from Talgarth within the Brecon Becons National Park. Animals by arrangement.
E-mail: marionlodgefarm@fwi.co.uk

| Marion Meredith | Lodge Farm | Talgarth | Brecon LD3 0DP | Powys |
| Tel: (01874) 711244 | Fax 01874 711244 | Open: ALL YEAR | | Map Ref No. 30 |

£55.00 to £80.00 Y Y Y

see PHOTO over p. 368

VISA: M'CARD:

Near Rd: A.40

Glangrwyney Court

Glangrwyney Court is a Georgian mansion set in 4 acres of established gardens & surrounded by parkland. All rooms are comfortably furnished with antiques, fine porcelain & paintings, & there is a welcoming & homely atmosphere. Accommodation is in 5 attractive & well-appointed bedrooms, each with a private or en-suite bathroom. During the winter, log fires burn in all the sitting rooms, & in the summer guests are able to relax with a drink in the gardens. Evening meals by arrangement.
E-mail: glangrwyne@aol.com
www.glancourt.co.uk

| Christina Jackson | Glangrwyney Court | Glangrwyney | Crickhowell NP8 1ES | Powys |
| Tel: (01873) 811288 | Fax 01873 810317 | Open: ALL YEAR | | Map Ref No. 32 |

£50.00 to £62.00 Y N N

🚭

VISA: M'CARD:

Near Rd: A.438

The Bear

The Bear is a 16th-century former coaching inn, in the centre of Hay, the famous book town. Attractive & comfortable bedrooms combine ancient beams & panelling with newly refurbished bathrooms. Ideal for book & antique browsers, Hay is also on Offa's Dyke footpath & the Wye Valley Walk; other outdoor activities are offered in this lovely area. Parking. Luggage transfers & packed lunches, if booked in advance. Good choice of restaurants nearby. Children over 9 by arrangement.
E-mail: jon@thebear-hay-on-wye.co.uk
www.thebear-hay-on-wye.co.uk

| Sue Newall & Jon Field | The Bear | 2 Bear Street | Hay-on-Wye HR3 5AN | Powys |
| Tel: (01497) 821302 | | Open: ALL YEAR | | Map Ref No. 33 |

£62.00 to £70.00 Y Y N

🚭

see PHOTO over p. 370

VISA: M'CARD:

Near Rd: A.483, A.44

Guidfa House

Licensed Georgian guest house, situated in an ideal location for touring lakes, mountains, national parks & the coast. The bedrooms are all comfortable, non-smoking & spacious, & all are en-suite with T.V. & tea/coffee-making facilities. A ground-floor room is also available. Meals are prepared by Anne, who is Cordon-Bleu trained. Dinner is a set menu, but special diets/requests can always be catered for with a little prior notice. Children over 10.
E-mail: guidfa@globalnet.co.uk
www.guidfa-house.co.uk

| Tony & Anne Millan | Guidfa House | Crossgates | Llandrindod Wells LD1 6RF | Powys |
| Tel: (01597) 851241 | Fax 01597 851875 | Open: ALL YEAR | | Map Ref No. 35 |

Guidfa House. Llandrindod Wells.

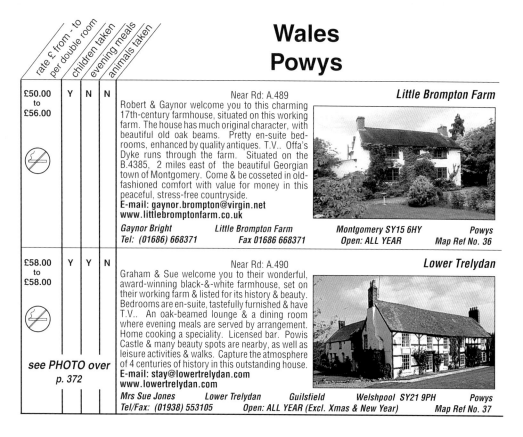

rate £ from - to per double room	children taken	evening meals	animals taken		
£50.00 to £56.00	Y	N	N		

Little Brompton Farm

Near Rd: A.489

Robert & Gaynor welcome you to this charming 17th-century farmhouse, situated on this working farm. The house has much original character, with beautiful old oak beams. Pretty en-suite bedrooms, enhanced by quality antiques. T.V.. Offa's Dyke runs through the farm. Situated on the B.4385, 2 miles east of the beautiful Georgian town of Montgomery. Come & be cosseted in old-fashioned comfort with value for money in this peaceful, stress-free countryside.
E-mail: gaynor.brompton@virgin.net
www.littlebromptonfarm.co.uk

Gaynor Bright   *Little Brompton Farm*   *Montgomery SY15 6HY*   *Powys*
Tel: (01686) 668371   Fax 01686 668371   Open: ALL YEAR   Map Ref No. 36

£58.00 to £58.00	Y	Y	N		

Lower Trelydan

Near Rd: A.490

Graham & Sue welcome you to their wonderful, award-winning black-&-white farmhouse, set on their working farm & listed for its history & beauty. Bedrooms are en-suite, tastefully furnished & have T.V.. An oak-beamed lounge & a dining room where evening meals are served by arrangement. Home cooking a speciality. Licensed bar. Powis Castle & many beauty spots are nearby, as well as leisure activities & walks. Capture the atmosphere of 4 centuries of history in this outstanding house.
E-mail: stay@lowertrelydan.com
www.lowertrelydan.com

see PHOTO over p. 372

Mrs Sue Jones   *Lower Trelydan*   *Guilsfield*   *Welshpool SY21 9PH*   *Powys*
Tel/Fax: (01938) 553105   Open: ALL YEAR (Excl. Xmas & New Year)   Map Ref No. 37

All the establishments mentioned in this guide
are members of
The Worldwide Bed & Breakfast Association

When booking your accommodation please mention
The Best Bed & Breakfast

Lower Trelydan Farm. Guilsfield.

Towns & Counties Index

Town	County	Country
Aberfoyle	Stirlingshire	Scotland
Abergavenny	Monmouthshire	Wales
Aboyne	Aberdeenshire	Scotland
Airdrie	Lanarkshire	Scotland
Alnwick	Northumberland	England
Ampleforth	Yorkshire	England
Andover	Hampshire	England
Appin	Argyll	Scotland
Arbroath	Angus	Scotland
Arundel	Sussex	England
Ascog	Isle of Bute	Scotland
Ashbourne	Derbyshire	England
Ashford	Kent	England
Axminster	Devon	England
Aylmerton	Norfolk	England
Ayr	Ayrshire	Scotland
Bala	Gwynedd	Wales
Banbury	Oxfordshire	England
Banff	Aberdeenshire	Scotland
Barnstaple	Devon	England
Bath	Somerset	England
Bath	Wiltshire	England
Bedale	Yorkshire	England
Bedford	Bedfordshire	England
Berkhamsted	Hertfordshire	England
Betws-y-Coed	Conwy	Wales
Beverley	Yorkshire	England
Bideford	Devon	England
Bishop Auckland	Durham	England
Bolney	Sussex	England
Boncath	Pembrokeshire	Wales
Boston	Lincolnshire	England
Bourne	Lincolnshire	England
Bourton-on-the-Water	Glos	England
Bowness-on-Windermere	Cumbria	England
Bradford-on-Avon	Wiltshire	England
Brampton	Cumbria	England
Brecon	Powys	Wales
Bridgwater	Somerset	England
Bridlington	Yorkshire	England
Bridport	Dorset	England
Brighton	Sussex	England
Bristol	Gloucestershire	England
Bristol	Somerset	England
Broadford	Isle of Skye	Scotland
Bude	Cornwall	England
Bungay	Suffolk	England
Buntingford	Hertfordshire	England
Burford	Oxfordshire	England
Burley	Hampshire	England
Burrowbridge	Somerset	England
Buttermere	Cumbria	England
Buxton	Derbyshire	England
Caerleon	Monmouthshire	Wales
Caernarfon	Gwynedd	Wales
Callington	Cornwall	England
Cambridge	Cambridgeshire	England
Canterbury	Kent	England
Carlisle	Cumbria	England
Carmarthen	Carmarthenshire	Wales
Carnforth	Lancashire	England
Carrbridge	Inverness-shire	Scotland
Castle Douglas	Dumfriesshire	Scotland
Chagford	Devon	England
Cheltenham	Gloucestershire	England
Chelwood Gate	Sussex	England
Chester	Cheshire	England
Chichester	Sussex	England
Chippenham	Wiltshire	England
Chipping Campden	Gloucestershire	England
Christchurch	Hampshire	England
Cirencester	Gloucestershire	England
Clitheroe	Lancashire	England
Coalville	Leicestershire	England
Cockermouth	Cumbria	England
Colyton	Devon	England
Corfe Castle	Dorset	England
Corsham	Wiltshire	England
Crackington Haven	Cornwall	England
Cranbrook	Kent	England
Cranleigh	Surrey	England
Craven Arms	Shropshire	England
Crediton	Devon	England
Crianlarich	Perthshire	Scotland
Criccieth	Gwynedd	Wales
Crickhowell	Powys	Wales

Towns & Counties Index

Town	County	Country	Town	County	Country
Cricklade	Wiltshire	England	Harrogate	Yorkshire	England
Dartmoor	Devon	England	Hartfield	Sussex	England
Dartmouth	Devon	England	Haslemere	Surrey	England
Daventry	Northamptonshire	England	Hastings	Sussex	England
Diss	Norfolk	England	Haverfordwest	Pembrokeshire	Wales
Dolgellau	Gwynedd	Wales	Haverhill	Suffolk	England
Dorchester	Dorset	England	Hawkhurst	Kent	England
Dorking	Surrey	England	Hawkshead	Cumbria	England
Dover	Kent	England	Hay-on-Wye	Powys	Wales
Dulverton	Somerset	England	Helmsley	Yorkshire	England
Dumbarton	Dunbartonshire	Scotland	Henley	Oxfordshire	England
Dumfries	Dumfriesshire	Scotland	Hereford	Herefordshire	England
Dundonald	Ayrshire	Scotland	Hexham	Northumberland	England
Dunkeld	Perthshire	Scotland	Hitchin	Hertfordshire	England
Dunster	Somerset	England	Holsworthy	Devon	England
Durham	Durham	England	Holywell	Flintshire	Wales
Dursley	Gloucestershire	England	Hope Valley	Derbyshire	England
Eastbourne	Sussex	England	Horsham	Sussex	England
Edinburgh	Edinburgh	Scotland	Hungerford	Berkshire	England
Ely	Cambridgeshire	England	Hurstpierpoint	Sussex	England
Exeter	Devon	England	Ilsington	Devon	England
Exmoor National Park	Somerset	England	Ingleby Greenhow	Yorkshire	England
Eyam	Derbyshire	England	Inverness	Inverness-shire	Scotland
Fairford	Gloucestershire	England	Ipswich	Suffolk	England
Falmouth	Cornwall	England	Isle of Anglesey	Anglesey	Wales
Faringdon	Oxfordshire	England	Isle of Wight	Hampshire	England
Faversham	Kent	England	Kelso	Roxburghshire	Scotland
Fintry	Stirlingshire	Scotland	Kendal	Cumbria	England
Folkestone	Kent	England	Kentallen of Appin	Argyll	Scotland
Fordham	Cambridgeshire	England	Keswick	Cumbria	England
Fordingbridge	Hampshire	England	Kettering	Northamptonshire	England
Fortwilliam	Inverness-shire	Scotland	Kings Lynn	Norfolk	England
Gatwick	Sussex	England	Kinross	Perthshire	Scotland
Gatwick	Surrey	England	Knutsford	Cheshire	England
Girvan	Ayrshire	Scotland	Launceston	Cornwall	England
Glastonbury	Somerset	England	Lavenham	Suffolk	England
Gloucester	Gloucestershire	England	Lawrenny	Pembrokeshire	Wales
Grantham	Lincolnshire	England	Leamington Spa	Warwickshire	England
Grantown on Spey	Morayshire	Scotland	Leek	Staffordshire	England
Grasmere	Cumbria	England	Leominster	Herefordshire	England
Grimsby	Lincolnshire	England	Lewes	Sussex	England
Hadleigh	Suffolk	England	Lincoln	Lincolnshire	England
Harlech	Gwynedd	Wales	Liskeard	Cornwall	England

Towns & Counties Index

Town	County	Country
Llandrindod Wells	Powys	Wales
Llandysul	Ceredigion	Wales
Llanrwst	Conwy	Wales
Loch Awe	Argyll	Scotland
Lochgilphead	Argyll	Scotland
Lochwinnoch	Glasgow	Scotland
London	London	England
Longhope	Gloucestershire	England
Looe	Cornwall	England
Lydney	Gloucestershire	England
Lyme Regis	Dorset	England
Lymington	Hampshire	England
Lyndhurst	Hampshire	England
Lynton	Devon	England
Maidenhead	Berkshire	England
Malmesbury	Wiltshire	England
Malton	Yorkshire	England
Malvern	Worcestershire	England
Mansfield	Nottinghamshire	England
Marlborough	Wiltshire	England
Mayfield	Sussex	England
Melton Mowbray	Leicestershire	England
Melton Mowbray	Nottinghamshire	England
Midhurst	Sussex	England
Mitcheldean	Gloucestershire	England
Moffat	Dumfriesshire	Scotland
Mold	Denbighshire	Wales
Montgomery	Powys	Wales
Moreton-in-Marsh	Gloucestershire	England
Moretonhampstead	Devon	England
Morpeth	Northumberland	England
Newark	Nottinghamshire	England
Newbury	Berkshire	England
Newquay	Cornwall	England
Newton Abbot	Devon	England
North Walsham	Norfolk	England
Northallerton	Yorkshire	England
Northleach	Gloucestershire	England
Norwich	Norfolk	England
Nottingham	Nottinghamshire	England
Nuneaton	Warwickshire	England
Oakham	Rutland	England
Oban	Argyll	Scotland
Okehampton	Devon	England
Oswestry	Shropshire	England
Oxford	Oxfordshire	England
Penrith	Cumbria	England
Penzance	Cornwall	England
Petersfield	Hampshire	England
Pewsey	Wiltshire	England
Pickering	Yorkshire	England
Pitlochry	Perthshire	Scotland
Plymouth	Devon	England
Polperro	Cornwall	England
Portree	Isle of Skye	Scotland
Reading	Berkshire	England
Redhill	Surrey	England
Redruth	Cornwall	England
Retford	Nottinghamshire	England
Ripon	Yorkshire	England
Romsey	Hampshire	England
Romsey	Hampshire	England
Ross-on-Wye	Herefordshire	England
Royal Forest of Dean	Glos	England
Royston	Cambridgeshire	England
Ruthin	Denbighshire	Wales
Rye	Sussex	England
Salisbury	Wiltshire	England
Sandy	Bedfordshire	England
Scarborough	Yorkshire	England
Sedbergh	Cumbria	England
Sevenoaks	Kent	England
Sherborne	Dorset	England
Shipton-under-Wychwood	Oxon	England
Shrewsbury	Shropshire	England
Sinnington	Yorkshire	England
Solihull	Warwickshire	England
Somerton	Somerset	England
South Brent	Devon	England
South Molton	Devon	England
St. Andrews	Fifeshire	Scotland
St. Austell	Cornwall	England
St. Briavels	Gloucestershire	England
St. Ives	Cornwall	England
Stevenage	Hertfordshire	England
Stirling	Clackmannanshire	Scotland

Towns & Counties Index

Town	County	Country	Town	County	Country
Stoke Lacy	Herefordshire	England	Uttoxeter	Staffordshire	England
Stoke-on-Trent	Staffordshire	England	Wadebridge	Cornwall	England
Stratford-upon-Avon	Warwickshire	England	Wallingford	Oxfordshire	England
Stroud	Gloucestershire	England	Wareham	Dorset	England
Sturminster Newton	Dorset	England	Warminster	Wiltshire	England
Tarporley	Cheshire	England	Wells	Somerset	England
Taunton	Somerset	England	Welshpool	Powys	Wales
Tavistock	Devon	England	Weston-Super-Mare	Somerset	England
Teignmouth	Devon	England	Wetherby	Yorkshire	England
Tenby	Pembrokeshire	Wales	Wheddon Cross	Somerset	England
Thirsk	Yorkshire	England	Whitby	Yorkshire	England
Thornton-le-Dale	Yorkshire	England	Whitehaven	Cumbria	England
Tintern	Monmouthshire	Wales	Wimborne	Dorset	England
Tiverton	Devon	England	Winchester	Hampshire	England
Tonbridge	Kent	England	Windermere	Cumbria	England
Torpoint	Cornwall	England	Witney	Oxfordshire	England
Torquay	Devon	England	Woking	Surrey	England
Totnes	Devon	England	Woodbridge	Suffolk	England
Truro	Cornwall	England	Wrexham	Cheshire	England
Tunbridge Wells	Kent	England	Yelverton	Devon	England
Tywyn	Gwynedd	Wales	York	Yorkshire	England

Recommendation 2006

Thank you for taking the trouble to supply this information .
We value your comments & will take appropriate action where necessary.
We regret that we are unable to reply to you individually.

Proprietors _____

House Name _____

Address _____

_____

Please give some general information about your stay, the house, rooms, food & hosts etc.

Date of stay _____

_____

_____

_____

_____

_____

_____

_____

Your Name _____

Address _____

_____

Reply to: W.W.B.B.A. P.O. Box 31655
London. W11 4WR

Recommendation 2006

Thank you for taking the trouble to supply this information .
We value your comments & will take appropriate action where necessary.
We regret that we are unable to reply to you individually.

Proprietors _____

House Name _____

Address _____

_____

Please give some general information about your stay, the house, rooms, food & hosts etc.

Date of stay _____

_____

_____

_____

_____

_____

_____

Your Name _____

Address _____

_____

Reply to: W.W.B.B.A. P.O. Box 31655
London. W11 4WR

Recommendation 2006

Thank you for taking the trouble to supply this information .
We value your comments & will take appropriate action where necessary.
We regret that we are unable to reply to you individually.

Proprietors —————————————————————————————

House Name —————————————————————————————

Address ————————————————————————————————

——

Please give some general information about your stay, the house, rooms, food & hosts etc.

Date of stay ————————————————————————————

——

——

——

——

——

——

——

Your Name —————————————————————————————

Address ————————————————————————————————

——

Reply to: W.W.B.B.A. P.O. Box 31655
London. W11 4WR

Recommendation 2006

Thank you for taking the trouble to supply this information .
We value your comments & will take appropriate action where necessary.
We regret that we are unable to reply to you individually.

Proprietors _____

House Name _____

Address _____

_____

Please give some general information about your stay, the house, rooms, food & hosts etc.

Date of stay _____

_____

_____

_____

_____

_____

_____

_____

Your Name _____

Address _____

_____

Reply to: W.W.B.B.A. P.O. Box 31655
London. W11 4WR

380

Complaint 2006

Thank you for taking the trouble to supply this information .
We value your comments & will take appropriate action where necessary.
We regret that we are unable to reply to you individually.

Proprietors _____

House Name _____

Address _____

_____

Please be specific about your complaint. State exactly what was wrong with your stay e.g. the room, food, house keeping etc.

Date of stay _____

_____

_____

_____

_____

_____

_____

Your Name _____

Address _____

_____

Reply to:W.W.B.B.A. P.O. Box 31655
London. W11 4WR

Complaint 2006

Thank you for taking the trouble to supply this information .
We value your comments & will take appropriate action where necessary.
We regret that we are unable to reply to you individually.

Proprietors_____

House Name_____

Address_____

_____

**Please be specific about your complaint. State exactly what was
wrong with your stay e.g. the room, food, house keeping etc.**

*Date of stay*_____

_____

_____

_____

_____

_____

_____

_____

Your Name_____

Address_____

_____

Reply to:W.W.B.B.A. P.O. Box 31655
London. W11 4WR

NOTES

NOTES